The Ends of Globalization

The Ends of Globalization

Bringing Society Back In

edited by
Don Kalb, Marco van der Land, Richard Staring,
Bart van Steenbergen, and Nico Wilterdink

ROWMAN & LITTLEFIELD PUBLISHERS, INC.
Lanham • Boulder • New York • Oxford

ROWMAN & LITTLEFIELD PUBLISHERS, INC.

Published in the United States of America
by Rowman & Littlefield Publishers, Inc.
4720 Boston Way, Lanham, Maryland 20706
http://www.rowmanlittlefield.com

12 Hid's Copse Road, Cumnor Hill, Oxford OX2 9JJ, England

British Library Cataloguing in Publication Information Available

Library of Congress Cataloging-in-Publication Data

The ends of globalization : bringing society back in / edited by Don Kalb . . . [et al.].
    p. cm.
    Includes bibliographical references and index.
    ISBN 0-8476-9884-X (cloth : alk. paper)—ISBN 0-8476-9885-8 (paper : alk. paper)
        1. International cooperation.   2. International relations.   I. Kalb, Don, 1959–
    JZ1318   E53   2000
    327.1'7—dc21   99-049347

Printed in the United States of America

♾ ™ The paper used in this publication meets the minimum requirements of
American National Standard for Information Sciences—Permanence of Paper for
Printed Library Materials, ANSI/NISO Z39.48-1992.

Contents

1

Localizing Flows: Power, Paths, Institutions, and Networks

Don Kalb

This book does not need to open by claiming that globalization is the big current buzzword that is preoccupying the minds of managers, politicians, journalists, and academics in this last decade of the century. All other texts on the topic have already done so. And because they have recently formed into a real flood that cannot be followed by any single researcher, and because some of them are being sold by the hundreds of thousands, there is every reason to assume that this claim might be correct. Certainly so, when one realizes that only ten years ago it would have been hard to encounter the term anywhere.

Globalization is a complex and multilayered concept and social phenomenon. In principle, it does not claim more than a geographic fact: people and places in the world are becoming more extensively and densely connected to each other as a consequence of increasing transnational flows of capital/goods, information/ideas, and people. But any effort at specification arouses intense debate. What is the relation between the three genres of items on the move? Is it a new phenomenon or not? What are its causes? What does it imply for the national state that had presumably become the pinnacle of the organization of social life in the postwar period—a "cordon-sanitaire," according to Arjun Appadurai (1996)? What about the civic rights that were enshrined in the constitutions and modes of operation of these states? What does it bring to presumably homogeneous national cultures? How does it relate to older concerns, such as imperialism, cultural homogenization, and Americanization? And, will we all be better off? Or do some classes and nations profit more than others? Does it imply more equality between people in various parts of the world, within national states, or within the advanced world? Does it bring more freedom, more democracy?

This book singles out some of these questions. In particular it hopes to advance our understanding of globalization's consequences for human equality and inequality; of the question of the role of the state; of the nature, effects, and driving forces of migration; of the question of cultural homogenization and heterogenization; and of the historical trajectory of the process. It will do so with a certain bias toward the experiences of the Western world, but not exclusively so. Moreover, it will deal with such questions in piecemeal fashion. Instead of sweeping statements about the state of humanity in the global age, the contributors to this book were asked to start to entangle more historically and empirically tractable issues—issues that also have a longer pedigree of scientific attention but are nevertheless basic to any overall discussion or broad vision of the topic. This book thus attempts to bring a sobering social science perspective to a public issue on which economists, business gurus, and philosophers have freely unleashed their abstract models and jumbo schemes.

The diverse empirical issues related to globalization discussed here have generally been dealt with in separate volumes. This book distinguishes itself by bringing them together in one interdisciplinary collection. It addresses elements of globalization that are studied by economists, historians, sociologists, anthropologists, political scientists, and philosophers. By doing so, we recognize the need to try to grasp the whole set of issues that globalization entails. This book therefore transcends the exclusive and disciplinarily enforced attention of most texts on the subject to either questions of cultural homogenization/pluralization/hybridization, the more quantitative issues of economics and finance, or the more historical questions about politics and international relations. We encourage researchers and students on the one side of such disciplinary divides to become informed on aspects studied by those on the other, simply because, in the ultimate outcome, such aspects happen to intertwine and together, in their mutual interrelationships, shape the actual ways in which societies change and respond to their changing environments.

The social sciences may have become too specialized to still adhere to such an integrative task. But we keep attaching importance to the basic methodological idea that what social scientists study is human relationships, in particular how configurations of human relationships change and what the vectors and direction of such changes are. Economics, politics, and culture (to use that trinity) are just different institutional windows to make such social processes visible. Reducing our attention to any one of them, as is generally done, would help sustain the simplifications that presently abound on the topic and see it as a far too simple, undifferentiated, and smooth process that lends itself well to the elegant description in single-stranded series of data, such as stock-market indices and capitalization ratios, or a clear-cut linear narrative, such as the end of the welfare state, the ends of history (Fukuyama 1992), or the McDonaldization of culture (Ritzer 1993). If social science wants to regain some of the terrain lost to quick neoclassical problem-solvers or guru-type make-believers, we are convinced that it tenaciously has to do just that: embrace conceptual and empirical complexity and historical contingency and show paradox, friction, and contradiction.

GLOBALIZATION AS GRAND NARRATIVE OF OUR TIME

This introduction is not intended to give a complete overview of the by now voluminous scientific literature on globalization. That would require too much space. Such an introduction must give serious attention to a highly varied body of work by authors such as Dani Rodrik (1997), Paul Hirst and Grahame Thompson (1996), David Harvey (1989), David Held (1995; 1999), John Gray (1998), Martin Albrow (1990), James Rosenau (1990), Saskia Sassen (1991; 1996), Zygmunt Bauman (1998), Arjun Appadurai (1996), Ulf Hannerz (1996), Roland Robertson (1992), or Ulrich Beck (1997), in addition to the earlier important work by Immanuel Wallerstein (1974; 1980), Eric Wolf (1982), William McNeill (1991; 1993), and Marshall McLuhan (1967; 1968).

Globalization is much more than a mere scientific topic or a systematically observable social phenomenon. Above all, it is an important, even dominant, political and economic discourse in the developed world, an ideology that shapes and permeates much of what is nowadays uttered in the media, in policy texts, and in business publications. For a decade it has informed the actions and fixed the attention of the major Western powers, the OECD (Organization for Economic Cooperation and Development), the IMF (International Monetary Fund), the World Trade Organization (WTO), and the World Bank. As a seminal tack on the issue, let us therefore first approach the globalization phenomenon as what it perhaps more than anything else is: a public discourse.

A future discourse analyst would probably conclude that the globalization discourse has been the dominant story in a small set of aspiring fin de siècle grand narratives that arose almost immediately after postmodernism claimed the end of all grand narratives, some decades ago (he or she will perhaps also judge that the period of its dominance lasted exactly ten years, from 1989 to 1999). The grand narratives of modernity, such as liberalism, socialism, and nationalism, had been closely associated with the formation of national states during the nineteenth and twentieth centuries and had found their great dynamic compromise in the welfare states of the postwar period, as well as their armed deadlock in the bipolar division of the world. Their dissolution, logically, was closely connected to the decline of these same national welfare states in the 1980s and to the implosion of the Soviet bloc. I claim that it is precisely the globalization narrative that has become their most influential and powerful successor in a period in which, as Mike Hanagan describes it, "states have collectively lost out against capital," and consequently lost out against the transnational flows of money, goods, information, and people that have strongly accelerated in its wake.

Indeed, the growing power of transnational enterprises, expanding world trade, exponentially increasing flows of capital through the quickly and globally diffused mechanism of stock markets and exchanges, the compression of space through new technologies, the concomitant deregulation of states and the increased commodification of social life, accelerating migrations, the end of the bipolar world, all of this, including the cultural flux that it has brought, has contributed to the widespread feeling that we are living in a new epoch in which the national state has been superseded as the pinnacle of social life by a more globally organized configuration of powers. Globalization, apart from being the empirical phenomenon of rapidly shrinking relative space, can be seen as a set of propositions, a meaningful framework of concepts and symbols, to interpret and give order to this new form of social organization. It claims that we are now living in one borderless world where the national and global divisions that once existed are progressively disappearing in favor of free exchange and cooperation to the common good of all humanity. It explains, like other grand narratives before, where this new form has come from, what its basic properties are, why it is good, and where it should lead us.

Some authors, like Ulrich Beck (1997), make a strict distinction between globalism and globalization. The first concept refers to the ideology of free-market neoliberalism that preaches the absolute truth and desirability of unregulated global capitalism, and the second to the real phenomenon of shrinking relative space and actual world-village formation. This distinction has the virtue of separating an imputed nasty norm from a supposed fine fact. But it is also a simplification.

The ideology of globalism, let us say the globalism of numbers, strongly associated as it is with the business world, cannot capture the hegemonic intricacies of various closely interwoven historical and sociopolitical visions and bits of visions that make up the current grand narrative of globalization. It is necessary to admit here that our imaginary future discourse analyst will not only or primarily deal with the utterances and actions of industrial managers and stock market dealers, although they will be taken into account. Nor does he or she mainly refer to great authors and leading intellectuals, though they must be considered too. The basic material for this discourse analysis, rather, just like the sources for Peter Burke's history of early modern popular culture (1983), comes from the circles of secondary authors, journalists, commentators, public relations officials, and party spokesmen, from those who, by their profession, are supposed to daily patch together comprehensive moral/factual visions from an immense wealth of disparate, contradictory, and highly specialist bits of available information and then turn them into headlines and sound bites. On this level of everyday ideology production, it is not simply a free-market globalism, such as discussed by Beck, that has emerged but a real grand narrative of globalization. This grand narrative connects history with current politics, facts with virtues, and class with justice and truth. In this text the terms "globalism" and "globalization as grand narrative" will therefore be used interchangeably, the former being only the ad hoc policy department of the latter.

Presently, this globalization narrative (which will be given more attention in a moment) is certainly the dominant narrative in the developed world, as well as in significant parts of the developing world. But it is not completely unchallenged. In reaction to it, and, as perceptive authors such as Anthony Smith (1995), Clifford Geertz (1998), Zygmunt Bauman (1998), and, in this volume, Peter Kloos, argue, in close association with it, there have emerged new counterideologies of territorialism.

These territorialisms are a varied brand, and not all of them should be seen as rivals of globalization. They can build on earlier nationalisms, regionalisms, and localisms and are often inspired by religion, language, and ethnicity. They can be hot: black, brown, or red, populist and sometimes extremist. But they can also be predominantly cool: technocratic and interest-based, such as Catalonese, Scottish, Lega Nord, and Flemish movements for more independence. These cooler movements for self-determination generally do not wish to disengage from global developments, indeed they use incorporation in more global networks as a resource against a dominant national state that is reputed to be ruled by different territorial and cultural interests. Some of these movements, however, are more virulent and violent, such as in the Sri Lankan case described by Kloos. But my point here is that this category of territorialisms does not tend to evolve into explicit rivalry with the politics of globalization. On the contrary, as Anthony Smith emphasizes, they call upon the globalized idea of national self-determination as proclaimed by the United Nations to legitimize their claims, itself a more or less subdued strand within globalization rhetoric.

In contrast, some of the hotter territorialisms derive their popular support from constituencies that feel alienated from the majority coalitions behind globalizing politics, or from technocratic or autocratic political leaderships that push such politics through. These territorialisms can develop into explicit antiglobalist grand narratives. They can command considerable support in countries where the politics of globalization have failed to bring the promised goods or have got stuck in corruption and autocratic regimes, enriching the few at the cost of the many, such as in Mexico, Russia, and Indonesia. In the advanced world, however, they mainly seem to attract protest votes and rarely attain prestige among the intellectual elite, though outcomes in countries such as France, Belgium, Denmark, Austria, and parts of Australia and the United States are still very much open. What is crucial to my discussion here, is that globalization discourse seems fully dominant while at the same time breeding opposite ideologies that emphasize the virtue and necessity of territorialism, which, as history shows, may crystallize into fully fledged alternatives for one-worldism (see Chirot 1993; Jowitt 1992). The basic political point that this book makes is that this particular choice between globalism in its pure "Washington Consensus" neoliberal form and the territorialist reactions against it, is, of course, a hopeless one. In a moment we will analyze the dominant version of the globalization grand narrative a bit further, but here it should be made clear that its critics are right to point out that there is a whole world of public problems and issues from which it stays immune, which it believes would be solved automatically if only people were honest enough to see their own failings, their historical errors, and patient enough to unlearn them. The critics are right that there are basic human issues that should be addressed by public policy and cannot be left to spontaneous resolution by markets at the "end of history" or better, outside it.

This exactly is the place where politics and the national state, in some form or another, come in again. The latter is not just a "competition-state" (Cerny 1990) that is focused on driving the politics of globalization forward and keeping ahead of others in basic economic performance, but also a community of fate that is expected to be sensitive to issues of equity, solidarity, democracy, and legitimacy. Between the really existing ideal-types of all-out globalizers on the one hand and pure territorialists on the other lies a whole world of really existing public problems to be analyzed and politically addressed.

The reason to bring in interdisciplinary social science is to reintroduce social complexity, contingency, and contradiction into the enveloping debate on globalization. This, indeed, is in stark contrast to the equilibrium assumptions and finalistic schemes that have so often been deployed in relation to current processes of globalization. One does not need a whole library to make that clear. It should be enough to point to the world-turbulence that has emerged in the wake of the Asian and Russian crises. The assumptions of the all-out globalizers simply do not provide for these situations, not for their possibility nor for any way out. President Clinton's pleas to the Russian government-in-decline to hold on to "reforms" and "freedom" are devoid of any meaning. The world clearly needs another language to talk about, and act within, the problems and dramas that erupt at the apparent end of this decade of globalism (1989–99). What an irony that ten years after the "end of history" we should start to learn the lessons of history anew.

The present book is not about globalization's impact on Asia or Russia. But these developments make clear, on a grandiose world-historic scale, that the grand narrative that has emerged in the wake of 1989 is not fool-proof. There has been too much dreaming about the purportedly liberating, wealth-creating, middle-class supporting, and Westernizing effects of pre-sumably footloose flows. The importance of bringing in grounded social science perspectives lies precisely in shifting the debate's center of gravity from the unleashed and de-territorialized flows themselves to the dynamic, territorial, human institutions and networks that produce them in the first place, and which, in the second place, serve to re-territorialize, translate, and resolidify them into concrete forms of social and spatial change.

The concern with institutions, networks, re-territorialization, and local-ization amounts to a plea for embracing social complexity, contingency, and contradiction. This will prevent us from telling straightforward stories and presenting self-conscious predictions. While asking attention for the contingent conjunction of the economic, political, and cultural dimensions of globalization, we cannot but refrain from any strong claim to the predic-tion of outcomes. Though there may be some valid building blocks for a general social theory of the causes and consequences of globalization at the end of this century, there cannot be any prediction about its precise empirical outcomes. This is so because such consequences, precisely and paradoxically in the globalizing epoch, are to a substantial extent deter-mined by location, that is, by a territory's relation to other locations, by its prior locational histories, and by its social properties, as well as by the hopes, needs, and actions of people, by its public policies, and actual or potential political mobilizations.

Empirical globalization outcomes will therefore depend on social power relationships, local development paths, territorially engraved social institu-tions, and the nature of and possible action within social networks, and cannot simply be derived from any general framework, let alone the reduc-tionistic and finalistic version that has become the world's dominant grand narrative in the past ten years. This is a more specific task that should be left to detailed, territorially delimited case studies and monographs (in the hope that academia will still allow the production of these in the future, which is far from certain). What this volume expressly intends to do, apart from offering a range of important social science insights into a basic pub-lic issue, is to contribute to a framework of thought, a vision and a method, that will help researchers and policymakers sharpen their questions and develop a more realistic, more socially and historically embedded ap-proach.

Essentially, by bringing networks of people, institutional histories, politics, and cultural process back into the perspective on transnational flows, we become capable of moving beyond three idols that have characterized the dominant discourse on globalization: beyond what Karl Polanyi (1944) once called "the economistic fallacy," beyond the bipolarity of local territorialism and universal globalism, and beyond cutting the present loose from the past. The political upshot of this endeavor is that we are making a case for the dramatically increased need for institution building at all levels as well as for the continued centrality of the national state precisely in this globalizing age.

Globalization is not only about financial flows that either wash away social settlements or liberate individual energies, depending on how you look at it. Nor is it just about accelerating cultural flux that makes existing forms of life, for the better or the worse, obsolete. We emphasize that it is just as much about the determinate social forms and territorial institutions in which the flow and the flux become at first socially produced, and then reappropriated, re-territorialized, localized, embodied, and reinstitutionalized. We recommend greater attention literally to the "ends of globalization": first, to the actual human purposes it should serve; second, to the social and territorial institutions that make the flows happen in the one place and then serve to localize them in the next; and third, to the possibility that the neoliberal regime of globalization that has reigned so far may have reached a turning point after which new institutional set-ups on various levels become necessary to secure its advantages and to redistribute its surpluses. In short: We want to bring society back in again.

FROM MONETARISM TO GLOBALIZATION: VIRTUOUS CIRCLE WITH A BIAS

The unprecedented speed with which the idea of globalization has nested itself so powerfully in our contemporary intellectual and political landscape rested precisely on a cognitive maneuver opposite in substance and style to the one advocated here. It was the neglect, denial, or even conscious repression, of institutional complexity, social relationships, contingency, and possible contradictions that made the concept into the ideological magnet it was soon to become. The future discourse analyst of the globalization grand narrative would probably judge that its public success had been based on two interrelated acts of reduction and simplification, one on the field of social theory, the other in its interpretation of recent history.

The historical simplification wrapped into the globalization concept brought together in one symbol, if only by association, the three recent epoch-making events that had determined the nature of the last quarter of the century: the neoliberal revolt against the welfare state initiated by Pinochet, Thatcher, and Reagan as a response to the economic crises of the 1970s; the revolution in information and telecommunications technology gathering pace in the 1980s; and the implosion of the Communist bloc after 1989. Though there can be no doubt that these events were somehow related (see for example Castells 1996, 1997, 1998; Berend 1996), the globalization concept was expressly not intended to encourage inquiry into the *specifica* of their sequential connection. Instead, the idea served to naturalize the underlying, contingent, and deeply political processes into an innocent geographic equation (shrinking space); it comfortably collapsed cause and consequence; it ironed out any possible tensions between its constituent elements; and it served to deny in retrospect that there could have been multiple ways out of the structural crises of these years. The concept came to express and celebrate the interests of the victorious geopolitical and capitalist agencies in the emerging global arena after 1989.

Indeed, after the fall of Communism, the idea of increasing interconnections between different parts of the now undivided world could easily be incorporated into the neoliberal myths elaborated during the preceding period: creating one borderless world of victorious market-driven democratic capitalism in which the role of the state would be fully reduced to serving the needs of the abstract self-governing market that acted on behalf of human freedom, world economic growth, individual independence, and opportunity.

The globalization concept was literally neoliberalism writ large. Since, with the victories of Reagan and Thatcher, neoliberalism had become the dominant ideology in the Anglo-Saxon countries, it had the opportunity to shape an interpretation of the fall of the Berlin Wall in its own image. Harking back on monetarism and the microeconomic innovations of Hayek and Friedman, it believed that collectivities and organizational hierarchies could not help but distort, and even kill, markets, simply because they killed the profit maximizing individual reasoning on which such markets, in this framework, were held to be based (for an overview see Skidelski 1995). The state was not only the protector of such collectivities, it was itself the prime example. After the onslaught on the welfare state and its social democratic supporters in the West, the breakdown of Communism was now interpreted as the ultimate verification that states had to be rolled back from economy and society, but now on a global scale. Monetarism turned out not to be just a medicine for stagflation in the West, it could now start to see itself as a universal historical truth for which the whole trajectory of the twentieth century provided proof.

Monetarism itself, however, did not really have a social vision of its own to accomplish this task. In fact it had only an antisocial vision on systematic individualism, markets, and inflation. In order for it to become a grand narrative it had to develop one. To that end it was now more firmly linked to a particular reading of the classic liberal social philosophy of Adam Smith, which expected universal human progress through free trade. This reading basically consisted of the axioma that (1) if commodities (capital, goods, information/ideas, people) were freely exchanged between places, (2) people everywhere would learn to prefer self-interest over collective passion and politics and (3) would consequently form into ideal-type modern independent middle classes/citizens, (4) who would demand civil rights and vote against costly policies and inefficiency, which (5) would further foster trade, prosperity, freedom, and growth (the well-known virtuous circle of liberalism). From being a technical vocabulary to turn inflation down, monetarism was now transformed into a genuine and totalizing social mythology in which questions of economy, history, politics, and morality were fully united. It became a powerful hegemonic instrument, an ideological watchdog that could bite in many directions at once.

This was encouraged by a clear bias in the contemporary interpretation of the classical liberal view. The bias concerned public policy and the state. Adam Smith was an optimist and assumed that redistributive policies would simply be unnecessary in a fully free world because of the high growth rates freedom would bring. But other enlightenment thinkers, such as Montesquieu or Rousseau, were less certain and saw social policy and redistribution as a necessary part of the new social contract without which a bourgeois order would fail to acquire popular legitimacy and could not survive. In contrast, neoliberalism, loyal to its roots in monetarism, saw redistributive public policy as universally inefficient, ineffective, and unwholesome. It was held to distort markets and turn healthy civic self-interest and self-help into dependency-syndromes among its recipients. States, it said, simply did not deliver. They were costly mechanisms, addicted to public debt and high taxes, serving unjust insider privileges and encouraging rent-seeking behavior by parasitic classes. The result was inflation and 1970s-type stagflation and finally the "crowding out" of any independent civic consciousness among citizens. Globalism perceived the crisis of the Western welfare state and the fall of Communism as caused essentially by the same perverse outcomes of state intervention. The future of mankind was seen to be dependent on a natural alliance of markets and citizens against the state everywhere in the world.

The rapid practical reception of the globalization concept in the early 1990s, finally, was probably supported by an unambiguous experiential fact. Every citizen could see that those transnational and (geo)political organizations that now boasted the virtues of globalization had successfully been involved in annihilating space and time with new information and telecommunications technology faster than in any prior era of industrial invention. Their globalization message could rapidly acquire a popular matter-of-factness that made it an ideal item for ideological fast-food consumption. Later discourse analysts should be aware that there had been a very material base to its success.

FROM FOOTLOOSE FLOWS TO EMBEDDED
INSTITUTIONS AND SOCIAL NETWORKS

It is not so much that liberalism's virtuous circle must be wrong in principle, although in its monetarist, anti-public policy update, it certainly is, as de Beus in his comprehensive chapter in this book underscores. More importantly, it has to be wrong in practice.

If we could assume the whole world to start anew, and could make sure that all individual human beings did so along Adam Smith's presumptions, and, in addition, it was possible to share all productive assets equally as well as to prevent the development of monopolies, then the deepening division of labor, spread of markets, growth of independent middle classes, freedom and prosperity for many could perhaps be realized. Perhaps; and de Beus's essay is exceptionally eloquent on identifying the preconditions under which this "'perhaps" could, to some degree, be the case. As he shows, this would result in a social democratic, pluralist, and multilateralist version of the globalization narrative, and not, to be sure, in its currently dominant version that finds it so hard to tune in to the wavelength of local and historical circumstances and steadily prefers to lecture on "structural adjustment" to a portable set of universal truths.

But the more basic point is this: we will never know. This is so simply because history is there, and its territorially engraved consequences for human institutions and social structures cannot be assumed away as in a laboratory experiment. Nor can the effects of what Leo Trotsky has called "combined and uneven development": the fact that some societies have advanced into more developed forms of capitalism, which in itself makes others already more backward and dependent on others, which again, in an open market environment, makes quite a difference for human prospects and possible local social developments. There simply is no level playing field; it only exists in the *ceteris paribus* formulae of the economic models.

The portable package of the globalizers, therefore, is principally unable to guarantee that outcomes in any place will confirm the predictions of liberalism's virtuous circle, just because of the prior, present, and interacting histories of uneven and dissimilar social development. Shock therapy in Colombia has evidently had different effects on local society than shock therapy in Russia. The recipes of what Robert Wade and Frank Veneroso

(1998) have called "The Washington–Wall Street–IMF Complex" work out differently in Argentina, Indonesia, or South Korea. If the outcome of globalization anno 1998 in Indonesia is massive impoverishment, xenophobia, and political stagnation; in Russia kleptocracy, mafia, popular dependence, and the death of internal markets; in South Korea unemployment, impoverishment of the middle class, and aggravating nationalism, then the portable package of the globalizers has turned out not to be so portable after all.

Moreover, no spontaneous trickle down of growing national incomes has occurred, causing a rise in inequality almost everywhere (as is discussed in relation to income inequality in Western nations in this book, in particular by Wilterdink, Schmitt, and Reijnders and van Zanden). For many, the instant recipes have failed to bring prosperity; democracy is in practice reduced to a formal property; the passions have not quite been separated from the interests; middle classes are everywhere under threat, also in the West, and remain fundamentally limited in their resources, their expected "independence," and their political capacities; citizenship in many places turns into xenophobia, nationalism, powerlessness, and dependency. "The more things come together, the more they remain apart. The uniform world is not much closer than the classless society," wrote the eminent anthropologist Clifford Geertz lately (Geertz 1998). And, from a different discipline, the international political economist Dani Rodrik concluded, "The tensions between globalization and social cohesion are real, and they are unlikely to disappear of their own accord. There is no formula that can be applied . . . some of the basic analytical and empirical work on the consequences of globalization remains to be done" (Rodrik 1997: 85).

If this basic analytical and empirical work is to succeed, it must reject the three idols that we have noted have characterized the grand narrative of globalization. First, it must learn to think with history, rather than giving in to the understandable *Sturm und Drang*–reflex to shock therapy it into oblivion, as argued above. Second, it should learn to see that local histories and territorial pathways of social development are not simply products of autonomous and parochial cultural development in isolation. Instead, all local outcomes nowadays (as they on closer scrutiny have always been, see the still pathbreaking work by Eric Wolf, 1982, as well as the oeuvre of William McNeill) are the creation of complex and patterned interactions between local social networks and institutions on the one hand, and the wider environment of world-system shaped, asymetric, economic, political, and cultural relationships on the other. "There is nothing mere to the local," emphasizes Arjun Appadurai (1996). And this point can not be stressed enough. Contemporary local developments everywhere, as cultural analysts have consistently stressed, can best be understood as forms of "glocalization" (Robertson 1992): local appropriations of global items and opportunities that either affiliate with dominant global trends or take some distance from them, mostly a combination of the two, the outcome being dependent on local social histories, the insertion in wider networks of exchange, and social relationships of power, advantage, and backwardness on various levels. This is not principally different for political economies as it is for cultural processes.

This is not only a criticism of the portable recipes of neoclassical global-izers. It is as much an argument against conservative accounts based on cultural essentialism and territorial isolationism. Russia is not in shambles because Russians are unable to become individualist profit-maximizers or decent citizens, nor does post–Communist Poland not look like Germany or Denmark because the Poles have the wrong dispositions. Russian and Polish developments should be understood as part and parcel of global processes that foster certain trends and inhibit others. It is this particular, and always particularistic, interaction that shapes possibilities and likely outcomes. Jumbo notions like the West versus the East, Eastern values versus Individualist Consumerism, Confucian versus Christian versus Islam: the culturalists' and territorialists' retreat into "a manichean struggle be-tween Abstract Principles," as Clifford Geertz (1998) has called it, must inevitably lead to fatefully mistaken conclusions. Particularism and uni-versalism, localism and globalism, are apparently not opposites, but just different standpoints from which to look at the real, networked spatial hy-brids and institutionalized syncretisms of which the real world consists. The either-or position on globalism and territorialism/culturalism is ana-lytically obsolete and politically insane.

And third, approaches to the outcomes of globalization should abandon the pervasive economism that has marked contemporary discourse, includ-ing the assumption that processes in the real world can be predicted as if the human community only existed as a random collection of individual profit-maximizers. Dominant globalization discourse is neoliberalism writ large, and as such it continuously reproduces the original problems to which it had been a response. It came into being in the 1970s to liberate markets from increasingly untenable societal regulations. It was there to disentangle markets from the specific grip that advanced societies had de-veloped in the afterwar period; it was there to disassemble them. But its birth-moment has been absolutized. The struggle against stagflation and inflation was won in the 1980s, but instead of acknowledging the limits of its program it went on, via the international organizations and supported by the increasingly powerful, now deregulated, financial communities, to subject the post-Wall world after 1989 to what Karl Polanyi (1944) has called the "stark utopia" of self-regulating markets. In so doing, globalism overlooked that world history had not just started in the stagflation years of 1970–80, but in fact somewhat earlier. It completely neglected what Polanyi had presented as "the lessons of history."

In his now increasingly important work *The Great Transformation*, Polanyi showed how the attempts to implement the "stark utopia" of self-regulating markets after the First World War had produced system collapse; broad popular suffering; and finally the emergence of Stalinism, fascism, and, on the bright sight of life, the New Deal and social democracy. Economies, his lessons of history taught, should not become disembedded from regulation by societies. They should be, and have practically always been, mediated by a combination of social policy in situ and institutional regulation on the international level. By pointing at the hard limits of commodification, Polanyi is really the bad and repressed conscience of the globalists.

By seeing global economism as what it is, a stark utopia that should better not be pushed through by global technocrats, room is also given to three interconnected and vitally important points. The first of these is what Karl Polanyi has called "the double movement." Polanyi emphasized that states that implemented the utopia of strong deregulation of markets had in history always encountered the growing opposition of popular movements demanding their reregulation. Globalists, instead of just fearing the interruption by popular opposition, could start to integrate the likelihood of protest into their predictive models. That would, second, give them more respect for the necessity and the legitimacy of public policy. Third, this would allow them to start to appreciate substantive citizenship, instead of the abbreviated neoliberal idea of citizenship inscribed into the current grand narrative. Indeed, globalism tends to condemn contemporary citizens to the nineteenth-century form of mere legal civic rights (voting rights and membership in the nation), including the attendant bourgeois moralism concerning the undeserving poor, paternalism, and patriarchy, as well as the prevalence of philanthropy plus minimal poverty alleviation over serious social policy.

Altogether, these three points could help global policymakers to have a deeper respect for the political space needed for public policy by national states and their political classes. This would help prevent popular disaffection from being channeled into cultural and territorial extremism by allowing respectable political networks to remain available for social problems and civic aspirations and remain or become accountable to citizens. The loosening of the control over populations by the stark utopia of unregulated global markets is a sine qua non.

If "some of the basic analytical and empirical work" (Rodrik 1997) finally starts to be done, the flaws in current assumptions and methods should be averted. The mass-mediated fascination with global flows, and the collective fantasy that they will find an equilibrium and by themselves improve the lives of people everywhere in the world along the prediction of the virtuous circle, has become a widely, solemnly, and repetitively performed cargo-cult in the West and elsewhere. Without membership in this contemporary civic congregation, one will nowadays be ruthlessly excluded from any official banquet. But it is time to open the windows. The authors in this book make a sobering plea for studying the institutions and social networks that make such flows happen; that give them meaning and direction; and that, in the next instance, serve to localize them, appropriate them, and help to solidify them into concrete patterns of social change. It is these institutions and networks, producing both de-territorialization and re-territorialization, which demand our attention now that the naïve phase of globalism as a grand narrative is running up against the rocky surfaces of the real world.

INSTITUTIONS OF GLOBALIZATION: STATES, CAPITAL, AND CITIZENSHIP

This book is divided into five parts, corresponding to the three forms of flow that can be distinguished: capital/goods, people, information/ideas. These sections concentrate on particular problems within each field of study and are preceded (with the exception of part I) by introductions of their own that place the individual contributions in a wider topical debate, thus making them better accessible for an interdisciplinary and nonspecialist public. These sections illustrate what we gain by approaching globalization as a socially instituted and institutionally mediated process and not just as a spontaneous cascade of natural market-flows aiming at an equilibrium.

Part II on capital flows and income distribution, for instance, shows that globalization has universally shifted the balance of power between labor and capital in Western societies in favor of the latter and has accordingly served to redistribute national income upwards. But the section also emphasizes that the particular territorial outcomes of such shifts are fundamentally structured by welfare state arrangements, systems of industrial relations, and other national public legacies. The outcome, therefore, is principally open to civic contestation and public choice.

Similarly, part III on migration underscores the fact that the origin, composition, and direction of flows of people, as well as their reception in host societies, cannot be explained by the assumption of migrants as profit-maximizing individuals responding to abstract market stimuli. Instead, migratory flows and migrants' behavior should be understood as complex forms of social network-building, in which past linkages between sets of regions and clusters of people structure motivations, chances, and options related to migration outcomes. Such outcomes, moreover, are firmly embedded in the public legacies of recipient countries.

Part IV on flows of ideas and images helps us understand why the increasingly mass-mediated flow of cultural items does not lead to any straightforward homogenization of cultural forms. This classical assumption of commodification theory is consistently falsified in recent cultural research, which emphasizes that the use, appropriation, and localization of flows of cultural items is strongly mediated by preexisting traditions, local social divisions, and the interests and needs of local social actors. It turns out that homogenization and heterogenization are not so much opposites as two strands within the same process. Moreover, the section shows that globalization of culture is not only about buying ideas and images on the global marketplace, but also about increasingly global political networks that promote universal projects such as the idea of nationalism and peoples' self-determination.

Part V on the world-institutional architecture of global governance acknowledges the importance and opportunities of increasing global interdependence vis-à-vis visions of national autarchy or autonomy. But it simultaneously denies the possibility of self-sustaining and self-regulating global markets by themselves producing desired or socially beneficial outcomes. The section underscores the idea that the national state in its capacity as the guarantor of a national culture, and the institutional embodiment of civic rights, popular democracy, and shared welfare, can become both endangered as well as revitalized within the process.

It is essential to see starting points and structures, as well as outcomes, of processes of globalization as the path-dependent result of social struggles over institutions, opportunities, and responsibilities. The question of social power relationships is crucial. It is precisely the historically grown and socially institutionalized balances of power both in national arenas as well as on more global and local scales that shape the varied menus of resources that labor, capital, citizens, and the state, as well as sexes, minorities, generations, urban regions, economic sectors, etc., can draw upon within a given context of globalization stimuli. As anticipated by Karl Polanyi, political institutions necessarily become both a focal point of, and a structuring influence on, the struggle that is unleashed by the differentiation of interests and the shifts in social power released by globalization. The outcomes of such struggles, as shown by recent events, are much more open than the grand narrative of globalism allows for. The chapters in part one help us to set the first general signs on the road toward such a more profound historical, institutional, and relational reading. The remainder of this introduction discusses some of the meanings of these signs.

Göran Therborn, in his contribution to this book, claims that "the capacity of states to do what their citizens or their leaders want in the face of increasing global interdependence is . . . the hottest issue of all in the globalization debates." He emphasizes that globalization is far from a recent phenomenon and insists on a long-term approach to the problem of national wealth, social opportunities, and growing international interdependence. Also, he emphasizes that globalization is far more than just an economic event. In talking about globalization, we must not overlook political and cultural globalizations, which, he contends, have clearly uplifting effects on less advanced countries. His long-run macro-social analysis of statistical evidence supports the view that while the spurts of economic globalization during this century have had "significant unequalizing effects," largely by permitting core countries to become ever more distant from the followers, "the divergent forces appear to derive more from the globally spiraling effects of unevenness in terms of . . . productivity and the use of the state, than from an inherent tendency of the global system." This is an important point also stressed by Jos de Beus in this book. Like many others, Therborn points to East Asian countries that over the last three decades have succeeded in narrowing the gap with the OECD elite significantly through state-coordinated export-led industrialization in unison with high public expenditures and policies underwriting relative class equality. "Economic globalization," he consequently argues, "provides no alibi for those who want to rob the welfare state."

However, those researchers, like Saskia Sassen, who emphasize the newness of current economic globalization, concentrate on financial globalization rather than on globalization through trade or foreign direct investment. National institutions, Sassen claims in her contribution, are losing substantial elements of their autonomy as the bulk of international transactions now consists of digitalized acts within a world-wide and interlinked network of deregulated stock markets. However, she warns against seeing such flows as anonymous. Some advanced capitalist states gain rather than lose power as a consequence, because they are host to the most important global financial corporations and keep privileged access to their services. Globalization, she warns, is therefore to a large extent Americanization. Certainly so, since the increase in global transactions is producing a web of private brokers and agencies in commercial law, arbitration, and debt-rating that increasingly operates along American or Anglo-Saxon lines, marginalizing even continental European institutions and modes of operation, let alone those of less powerful countries. She agrees with Susan Strange that globalization first of all implies the creation of common standards and procedures. But Sassen also shows which forces are at work behind any universalization of standards, in which direction they push, and who is gaining the most.

In addition, she points out the important phenomenon that American institutions, rules, and practices, through the influence of international lending by the IMF, tend to become virtually implanted into the constitutions of other nations, in fact transforming the modern idea of nationhood into a merely juridical event. This "constitutionalizing" of crucial features of the "Washington–Wall Street–IMF complex" has undergone a dramatic extension in the preceding years. IMF rescue operations in East Asia have served to forcefully introduce American rules concerning banking and capital accounts into economies with totally different traditions, even when such traditions have been uniquely successful in fostering GDP growth. These recent developments fall outside the scope of Sassen's chapter, but Robert Wade and Frank Veneroso (1998) have recently pointed out that this form of Americanization, if successful, might well be detrimental to the midterm recovery potentials of a country such as South Korea, which has been a prime example of tiger-type growth. If Therborn and many others point to the East Asian super-development state in order to illustrate the continued importance of national institutions and social equity in global competition, the increasingly dramatic effects of financial globalization, especially if based in massive short-term international lending combined with highly attentive currency trading, may well deprive them of their main historical examples.

Sassen's pessimism concerning the autonomy and integrity of all national states except the United States and its closest allies is deepened by Michael Hanagan, doubted by Erik Olin Wright, and strongly modified by Paul Hirst. Hanagan takes issue with those, like the anthropologist Jonathan Friedman, who argue that globalization is nothing new. The point is not that such authors are mistaken, says Hanagan, but rather that they thus overlook the particular historical context in which it happens, the exact processes at work within it, and therefore fail to see the directions and implications of social change. Hanagan contrasts the globalization cycle between 1850 and 1914 with the contemporary wave starting in 1950. Both waves, he claims, featured a phase of generalized growth and prosperity, after which a turning point was reached, markets became overcrowded, and inequality started to rise (see also Giovanni Arrighi 1994 and Arrighi's chapter in this book). The outcome, however, was different in each wave, Hanagan claims. He shows that in a context of increasingly massive fixed capital investments during the second industrial revolution, consolidated states acted to protect large capital outlays and were at the same time forced by enlightened reformers and organized industrial working classes to grant rights to worker-citizens. Thus, although threatened by de-skilling, dualization of the workforce, and immigration, and consciously mobilizing to limit the numbers of legitimate workers, wage labor "almost became a kind of fixed capital."

Hanagan subsequently points out that in the contemporary wave capital, sponsored by the core Western governments and by international institutions such as the IMF and the WTO, has responded to problems of overaccumulation by abandoning precisely these fixed outlays in circumscribed national territories while shifting its attention to increased circulation and flexibility on a global scale. This effectively left national policymakers and working classes locked into the nation-state and caused increasing inequality and a severe decline in citizenship rights. "As capital's relations to consolidated states have weakened, so have its concerns about maintaining the stability of national labor forces or of strong national polities," concludes Hanagan, suggesting that this is leading to a populist backlash in favor of protectionism.

Hanagan's argument closely resonates with the even more long-term analyses of cycles of globalization by Giovanni Arrighi (Arrighi 1994; and this book) and with the more specifically contemporary and nationally comparative analysis by Robert Brenner (1998). The latter's work, however, suggests that Hanagan's claim is more true for the United States than for Europe or Japan, where citizenship rights have been less negatively affected and wages have not stagnated, as is also stressed by Wilterdink and Schmitt in this book. Thus, while Michael Hanagan has captured a crucial contrast between the nineteenth and twentieth centuries and the specific processes at work within waves of globalization in these periods, his general characterization of change in capitalist relations and institutions seems to ask for more regional specification. His claim that transnationalized capital requires labor to organize itself on a comparable scale in order to call attention to "the differential impact of market expansions" is, however, universally valid. He might have added that this is true as well for the organizational scale of public policy in general, a point stressed by Paul Hirst in this book.

In the present context, however, given capital's apparent power to play communities and territories off against each other, the structural obstacles to a transnational organization of labor may be almost insurmountable. Erik Olin Wright, concentrating more on the technology-effects of globalization than on worldwide marketization, puts "scientific" hope in production-oriented meso-level corporatist arrangements between labor and capital. The requirements of technology, argues Wright, strengthen the functional need for capital to cooperate with labor above all in production. This is necessary, he says, in order to promote an atmosphere of trust, which in its turn is a precondition for people to make long-term investments in human capital. And though global capital's commitment to territorial social pacts on the domain of exchange (high wages) and politics (rights and redistribution) may have been diminished, as also described by Hanagan, Wright argues that in these fields too the functional requirements of technologically driven global competition put a real premium on cooperation.

Such cooperation, expects Wright, will only be accepted by capitalist agencies if the associational power of labor is potentially strong enough to enforce it, including the prevention of free-riding within the capitalist class itself. If organized labor is not strong enough to do so, it will eventually turn to adversarial practices, which are detrimental to high-technology production. Employers would then rather prefer an atomized working class, Wright contends. This is the moment where path-dependency, regional traditions and public institutions enter his equation. The "low road option" (low technology, atomized labor, low wages) must be closed off to employers. If public institutions and civic associations make it hard to take that road, for example as a consequence of universal coverage for collective contracts in European welfare states, capitalists will seek class cooperation. In the United States, Wright expects this to happen on the meso-level of regions rather than in the country at large and reports on some new initiatives in the Midwest.

Global competition, Wright reminds us, does not only or necessarily usher in the unchaining of circulating capital from fixed capital and in flexible modes of production as implied by Hanagan. It also leads to investment in technology-spurs. Social class relations and public institutions matter considerably in the regional class outcomes that such technology-spurs can have. They can either promote increased segmentation and segregation among workers and foster insider-privileges, or they can contribute to a general uplifting of social conditions and investments. In essence, Wright emphasizes, technology-based capital must be self-interested in the "high road." But it is up to civic associations and well-designed public institutions to help it do so. Globalization as a mantra of flows and footlooseness precisely operates to cow them away from such efforts.

Paul Hirst takes this line of reasoning a step further. He does not deny Sassen's and Hanagan's point that globalization is eroding national autonomy in favor of circulating capital and the institutions of the "Washington–Wall Street–IMF complex," but he wishes to shift the emphasis. Like Arrighi, he argues that whatever national autonomy existed in the past should not be exaggerated. Taking a long-term perspective similar to that of Mike Hanagan, he comes to different conclusions. Globalization itself being nothing new, the basic dichotomy is not the one between the global and the national, he suggests. The point is rather that while modes of international and transnational regulation have historically also served to enhance the internal policy capacities of national states (before 1914, between 1950 and 1973), the present global system singlemindedly sponsors short-term international dealing at the expense of long-term growth of territorial economies. Not internationalization and trade expansion itself are the problem, but the unregulated financial mode in which it proceeds. After 1980, Hirst points out, the orientation of international institutions and financial markets to trade and long-term investment was shifted toward short-term lending, currency speculation, and derivatives. This leads to a destabilizing excess of capital in the one place, such as recently in East Asia, and to paralyzing shortages in other places.

Against this state of affairs, he makes two basic claims. The first concerns the continued dependence of industrial as well as financial corporations on their "home" regional economies. Trade, even through portfolio investment and transnational enterprises, is predominantly based within one of the world-regions of the Triad (European Union, EU; North American Free Trade Agreement, NAFTA; Association of Southeast Asian Nations, ASEAN). This gives allegedly footloose capital a big stake in the real growth conditions of concrete territories. Provided that the finances of such territories are sound and the exposed sector is competitive, there is "considerable scope for public policy operating to localize trading by the major financial institutions," Hirst contends. The main precondition is that "electorates are willing to pay the price for infrastructure, training, and welfare." Like Wright, he warns that the globalization mantra works against this. Secondly, he contends that the international system needs "concerted public governance by the major powers" aimed at reversing the short-term orientation of the financial markets. This would help to force big capital to seek alliances with territorial states, public policy, and local societies, alliances that it needs in order to ensure long-term growth prospects in vital regions.[1]

Hirst makes an argument that is somehow analogous to Wright's, but lifts it up from regional production complexes to the world system at large. Crucial for both is the classic Marxist notion that unregulated capital, either in the form of international flows or as fixed investment, tends to choose the cheapest way to profits. And this cheap way is often exploitative of basic localized factors of production such as people, outlays, and infrastructure, and therefore not generally the most effective path toward creating optimal social and territorial preconditions for the next round. Self-regulating markets, as Polanyi insisted, are self-defeating. They need to be embedded in public institutions. Like Hanagan in relation to labor, Hirst concludes that public policymakers should not allow the international arena to become the exclusive playing field of short-term financial interests. The strength of his vantage point is that he, more emphatically than Sassen or Hanagan, urges us to see the current mode of globalization as just man-made and therefore changeable.

Giovanni Arrighi, working in a considerably longer time frame than Hanagan and Hirst, is both skeptical and hopeful about this. Skeptical, because his argument leads us to see current U.S. global deregulation policies not as an index of self-interested strength, but as a sign of increasing dependence on financial markets. Americanization as painted by Sassen, in Arrighi's vision, hides a drastic loss of hegemony over the world system. At the same time he is moderately hopeful, because, in contrast to earlier episodes when the power of a world-dominant nation-state leaked away to upcoming geopolitical rivals, the chance of a major war is negligible, the United States still effectively monopolizing the world means of coercion and protection.

Arrighi's key concept is not globalization but financial expansion. In his chapter, he argues that the modern world system has seen financial expansions at least three times before. They have always been "a sign of autumn" in a major cycle of growth in the capitalist world system, which was predicated on the hegemony of a territorial power (Spain/Genova, the Netherlands, the United Kingdom) that uniquely combined the military, social, and financial technologies to dominate the system and generate a new wave of capitalist expansion. While rival powers gradually copied these technologies, the growth-wave went over into a period of overaccumulation, producing increased competition, interstate contention, and general turbulence in the world system and the system of states. This always culminated in a financial expansion: the withdrawing of capital from productive activities into speculation, lending, *haute finance*. The turbulence only ended if and when a victorious territorial contender emerged with resources that allowed it to put the whole system on a new footing and lead it into a new period of continuous growth.

The present era is, according to Arrighi, just such a period of turbulence, rivalry, and haute finance. Since the late 1960s, Western Europe, and subsequently Japan and East Asia, both with the help of the U.S. system itself, have successfully competed with U.S. capitalism, leading to system-wide overaccumulation, a decline of profitability, and the emergence of rival centers of world power (see also Brenner 1998). Overaccumulation, according to Arrighi, both requires and invites capital to liberate itself from fixed territorial forms of material production and social regulation and seek self-multiplying forms of flexible investment. Historically, such a process of financial expansion has always been underwritten by the former leading country, whose capitalist institutions stand to gain the most. The late twentieth century, likewise, is characterized by "a declining hegemonic power (that) can neither afford to jump off the 'brakeless train' of unregulated financial speculation, nor reroute the train into a less self-destructive groove," Arrighi contends. The system may be man-made, as Hirst emphasizes, but nobody seems in control (see also Offe 1996). It needs "new tracklaying vehicles" (Michael Mann) that allow territorial organizations to reregulate social and economic life. The redistribution of wealth and incomes from all sorts of actors to finance-capitalist agencies that Arrighi finds is going on, will, if not reversed, relaxed, or rerouted, lead to increasing social and political turbulence that will threaten perhaps not the system itself anymore, given the United States' continued military superiority, but in any case many of its potential beneficiaries.

Arrighi's key notion of financial expansions being the result of system-wide overaccumulation leading to stepped-up competition, has recently acquired strong support in the work of Robert Brenner (1998). In his comprehensive analysis of the world economy since 1950, Brenner, although not directly addressing globalization, has offered a wealth of material to prove that stepped-up competition has indeed been at the roots of "post-1973" economic turbulence. Declining profitability in manufacturing and services was the system-wide consequence of global overproduction and underconsumption. According to Brenner's analysis, only the United States since the early 1990s escaped that pattern, as a consequence of a generation-long stagnation of incomes and a drastic decline of rights as described by Hanagan as well as by Schmitt in this book. German and Japanese private-sector profitability, in contrast, has continued to stagnate. This is the situation in which pension funds and other managers of capital stocks, after the deregulation of capital markets, have started to seek new profit opportunities elsewhere, as Hirst indicates. Developing countries such as Mexico, Brazil, South Korea, and Indonesia, which responded to the rapidly increasing supply of mobile global capital by creating a friendly regulatory environment did so in the hope of generating wealth and alleviating poverty in their countries, thus underwriting the globalists' program of promoting middle-class formation. But they also helped first to postpone, and then to aggravate and globalize, the overaccumulation problem. In the end this could not but lead to a wave of devaluations and massive destruction of capital, certainly in a context where huge speculative funds could legitimately be used to exploit and magnify temporary imbalances in national accounts. The newcomers were predictably the primary victims, including their nascent middle classes. This seems to be the Asian crisis in a nutshell.

There is therefore some firm historical evidence that the contemporary crisis of the world system is rooted in system-wide overproduction, partly expressing itself in powerful waves of short-term speculation. If globalization has failed to produce a virtuous circle of liberalism worldwide, as hoped for by the globalists, these are the fundamental forces that spoil the party. Everywhere, though in different (path-dependent) guises and combinations, these forces are exerting downward pressure on wages, living standards, workers' rights, civil rights, and employment. From the point of view of historical political economy, if not necessarily from a neoclassical angle, these are the fundamental obstacles preventing the spread or even the maintenance of citizenship, democracy, and prosperity.

Arrighi, like Hirst, Therborn, Falk, de Beus, and other authors in this collection, argues for more powerful efforts at international public gover-

stant high demand) and by accepting a long-term decline in the standards of living and citizenship for a growing part of the population.

In contrast to the United States, and in spite of twenty years of (sometimes halfhearted) neoliberal policies, European welfare states have by far not incurred the same degree of poverty and decline of basic civil rights as has the United States, and they have also maintained a much more responsible trade balance than the East Asian countries. On this level of world-regional comparison it really seems to be the case that traditions of citizenship within the European Union have prevented an onslaught on living standards and rights and have helped keep in place a commitment to redistribute GNP growth into more broadly based consumption, unlike either the East Asian economies or the United States.

Globalization as a shrinking of relative distances and a measure of increasing human interdependencies around the globe is an old and long-term process, disparate and uneven, that apparently comes in waves of acceleration and slow-down. The last quarter of the twentieth century has witnessed such a phase of acceleration. This phase has come under the sign of neoliberal policies that have successfully coined and disseminated an idea of globalization as a grand narrative of rootless flows in a borderless world, explaining and advocating the demise of state-based politics and social redistribution in favor of self-regulating global markets.

It increasingly looks, however, like the self-regulating global market is not going to deliver on its promises of sustained growth and middle-class formation the world over. Rather, it has led to dangerous instability in the world-system, as well as to stagnating incomes, widespread poverty, unemployment, and a decline of citizenship rights, threatening the less well-off, the precise outcome being dependent on place.

The broad sweep of this book is that globalization is a much more complicated process than just a natural history of increasing transnational flows. It is a social process based in and regulated by social and political institutions, as Therborn also emphasizes, even when these institutions are used for the purpose of deregulation. After twenty years of market-led growth, it seems that the process now requires new forms of public governance at all levels if it is not to destroy its own legitimacy. The emergence of such forms will depend on civic actionism and public legacies that can promote it. Creating an antithesis between global capital and culture on the one hand, and the national territory and heritage on the other, will not be of much help here, although it is clear that such oppositions have been nurtured by the neoliberal allegory of unregulated financial capitalism as the only imaginable face of the global. But as Hirst and others emphasize, contemporary capitalist society has become too complex and too large to be contained in any locale or country. Instead of opposing the local and the global, what are called for are innovative institutional practices on all levels that help capital to shift its orientation from unregulated financial speculation and short-term dealing toward more long-term investment in, and commitment to, regions anywhere in the world. This book stops short of advocating any particular policies. They can range from micro-level corporatism as advocated by Wright; to a more explicit national-civil-consumers' influence on pension funds as proposed by Robin Blackburn (Blackburn 1998) to initiatives at closer cooperation on world-region level, such as the European Union and finally to a revised architecture for the global financial arena as witnessed in the renewed interest in the Tobin tax and other tax-based ideas to regulate capital flows and redistribute surpluses worldwide. What seems clear is that such initiatives will hardly come about without concerted civic actionism. This book indicates that the whole array of citizenship rights on all levels will be needed to articulate needs and claims; to push policymakers to discuss, refine, and implement them; and to force transnational capital to adhere to the policies prescribed to them. The balance of power between citizens, states, and capital is shifting once again.

NOTES

This book comes out of a conference on "Globalization and the New Inequality" held in November 1996 at Utrecht University, the Netherlands. The conference was sponsored by grants from the Royal Netherlands Academy of Sciences, the Faculty of Social Sciences of Utrecht University, the Lustrum Committee of Utrecht University, the Urban Studies Program, the United States Information Service, and the Dutch Ministry for Social Affairs and Employment. For this introduction, I owe thanks to my coeditors, with whom it was more than just a pleasure to cooperate in this stimulating endeavor, as well as to August Carbonella, Zsusza Ferge, Michael Hanagan, Guenther Landsteiner, and Christopher Lloyd for comments on earlier drafts. I am also grateful to Ira Katnelson and Claus Offe for commenting on a few passages I was not certain about. Work on this book and this introduction has been facilitated by grants from the Niels Stensen Stichting, Amsterdam; the Dutch Organization for Scientific Research (NWO); and the Institute for Human Sciences, IWM, Vienna, where I have had the privilege to work during these years. Insights gained during the project have been put before audiences at the IWM during a Tuesday lecture in December 1997 and in two presentations at Janos Kovacs's globalization seminar in 1998 and 1999, as well as in a session at the European Sociological Association meeting in Essex, 1997, organized by Bart van Steenbergen. I am grateful for the opportunity and I am obliged to all active participants.

1. After the completion of this introduction these concerns have led to serious discussions about the global financial and institutional architecture at the highest levels of the United Nations and the IMF. See for example Kaul, Grunberg, and Stern 1999, as well as Soros 1998.

REFERENCES

Albrow, Martin, and E. King, eds. (1990). *Globalisation, Knowledge and Society.* London: Sage.

Amsden, Alice. (1992). *Asia's Next Giant: South Korea and Late Industrialization.* Oxford: Oxford University Press.

Appadurai, Arjun. (1996). *Modernity at Large: Cultural Dimensions of Globalization.* Minneapolis: University of Minnesota Press.

Arrighi, Giovanni. (1994). *The Long Twentieth Century: Money, Power and the Origins of Our Times.* London: Verso.

Bauman, Zygmunt. (1998). *Globalization: The Human Consequences.* Cambridge: Polity Press.

Beck, Ulrich. (1997). *Was ist Globalisierung?* Frankfurt: Suhrkamp.

Berend, Ivan. (1996). *Central and Eastern Europe, 1944–1993: Detour from Periphery to Periphery.* Cambridge: Cambridge University Press.

Blackburn, Robin. (1999). The New Collectivism: Pension Reform, Grey Capitalism, and Complex Socialism. *New Left Review* 233: 3–65.

Brenner, Robert. (1998). The Economics of Global Turbulence: A Special Report on the World Economy, 1950–98. *New Left Review* 229: 1–264.

Burke, Peter. (1983). *Popular Culture in Early Modern Europe.* Cambridge: Cambridge University Press.

Castells, Manuel. (1996). *The Rise of the Network Society.* Oxford: Basil Blackwell.

———. (1997). *The Power of Identity.* Oxford: Basil Blackwell.

———. (1998). *End of Millennium.* Oxford: Basil Blackwell.

Castoriadis, Cornelius. (1998). *La montee de l'insignificance.* Paris: Seuil.

Cerny, Philip. (1990). *The Changing Architecture of Politics.* London: Sage.

Chirot, Daniel. (1993). *Modern Tyrants: The Power and Prevalence of Evil in Our Age.* New York: The Free Press.

Fukuyama, F. (1992). *The End of History and the Last Man.* London: Hamish Hamilton.

Geertz, Clifford. (1998). The World in Pieces: Culture and Politics at the End of the Century. *Focaal. Tijdschrift voor antropologie* 32: 91–117.

Gray, John. (1998). *False Dawn: The Delusions of Global Capitalism.* London: Granta Books.

Hall, John A., ed. (1995). *Civil Society: Theory, History, Comparison.* Cambridge: Polity Press.

Hannerz, Ulf. (1996). *Transnational Connections: Culture, People, Places.* London and New York: Routledge.

Harvey, David. (1989). *The Condition of Postmodernity.* Oxford: Blackwell.

Held, David. (1995). *Democracy and the Global Order: From the Modern State to Cosmopolitan Governance.* Cambridge: Polity Press.

Held, David, et al. (1999). *Global Transformations: Politics, Economics, and Culture.* Cambridge: Polity Press.

Hirst, Paul, and Grahame Thompson. (1996). *Globalisation in Question.* Cambridge: Polity Press.

Jowitt, Ken. (1992). *New World Disorder: The Leninist Extinction.* Berkeley: University of California Press.

Kaul, Inge, Isabelle Grunberg, and Marc A. Stern. (1999). *Global Public Goods: International Cooperation in the Twenty-First Century.* Oxford: Oxford University Press.

McLuhan, Marshall, and Quentin Fiore. (1967). *The Medium Is the Massage.* London: Allan Lane.

———. (1968). *War and Peace in the Global Village.* New York: Bantam.

McNeill, William. (1991). *The Rise of the West.* Chicago: University of Chicago Press.

———. (1993). *The Global Condition.* Princeton, N.J.: Princeton University Press.

Offe, Claus. (1996). *Modernity and the State: East and West.* Cambridge: Polity Press.

Polanyi, Karl. (1944). *The Great Transformation.* Boston: Beacon Press.

Rieger, Elmar, and Stephan Leibfried. (1998). Welfare State Limits to Globalization. *Politics and Society* 26, no. 3: 363–90.

Ritzer, G. (1993). *The McDonaldization of Society.* Thousand Oaks, Calif.: Pine Forge.

Robertson, Roland. (1992). *Globalization.* London: Sage.

Rodrik, Dani. (1997). *Has Globalization Gone Too Far?* Washington, D.C.: Institute for International Economics.

Rosenau, James. (1990). *Turbulence in World Politics.* Princeton, N.J.: Princeton University Press.

Sassen, Saskia. (1991). *The Global City: New York, London, Tokyo.* Princeton, N.J.: Princeton University Press.

———. (1996). *Losing Control? Sovereignty in an Age of Globalization.* New York: Columbia University Press.

Skidelski, Robert. (1995). *The World after Communism: A Polemic for Our Times.* London: Macmillan.

Smith, Anthony. (1995). *Nations and Nationalism in a Global Era.* Cambridge: Polity Press.

Soros, George. (1998). *The Crisis of Global Capitalism: Open Society Endangered.* New York: Public Affairs.

Thurow, Lester. (1998). Asia: The Collapse and the Cure. *New York Review of Books*, February 5, 1998: 22–27.

Van Wolferen, Karel. (1990). *The Enigma of Japanese Power.* New York: Vintage.

Wade, Robert, and Frank Veneroso. (1998). The East Asian Crash and the Wall Street-IMF Complex. *New Left Review* 228: 3–24.

Wallerstein, Immanuel. (1974). *The Modern World-System.* New York: Academic Press.

———. (1980). *The Modern World-System II.* New York: Academic Press.

Wolf, Eric. (1982). *Europe and the People Without History.* Berkeley: California University Press.

Part I

Long-Term and Theoretical Perspectives

2

Dimensions of Globalization and the Dynamics of (In)Equalities

Göran Therborn

The theme of globalization and (in)equality may be approached from two sides, and I shall use the right-wing door, which is that of inequality. Our topic raises one-and-a-half basic questions. The first is whether globalization leads to equalization or polarization. The half question is a follow-up in case we should answer "equalization": Does globalization tend to level upward or downward?

Nineteenth-century social science left us two opposite diagnoses and prognoses with regard to (in)equality, both reflecting upon the experiences of the French Revolution and upon the new Anglo-Saxon world. Alexis de Tocqueville envisaged an age of equality and equalization, announced by the Revolution but most developed in *Democracy in America* (de Tocqueville 1970). Where de Tocqueville saw centuries of democracy succeeding centuries of aristocracy, Karl Marx saw the transition from feudalism to capitalism, with new and polarizing forms of economic inequality and a new round of class struggles. According to Marx, the legal equality of the bourgeois revolution laid bare even more starkly the accumulation of wealth on one side and of misery on the other.

I shall let these two eminent gentlemen of the previous century rest in peace, but their opposite conclusions should stimulate us to analytical specification, empirical scrupulousness, and concluding caution. One path of caution and circumspection is to try to disentangle the issues involved in the seemingly simple and straightforward question of globalization and inequality. There are at least four sets involved here: (1) What kind of globalization? (2) (In)Equality and globalization of what? (3) (In)Equality for whom? and (4) (In)Equality by what?

WHAT KIND OF GLOBALIZATION, AND EQUALITY FOR WHOM?

I will not enter into the usual discussions of globalization versus non-globalization, of the global versus the national, of "how much," "how fast," "how new," etcetera.[1] Let us simply assume, for the sake of the argument, that there are tendencies of globalization, of interconnecting all parts of our planet, and in particular all parts of humankind. More formally—and deliberately abstaining from the many baroque formulations—we may say that globalization refers to tendencies toward a worldwide reach or impact of social phenomena.

Globalization in this general sense may be of two different kinds. One is based on subglobal actors—generated and rooted outside globality, e.g., in national processes—and their interaction, including cases of dominant super-actors imposing their will on a number of less powerful actors. We may refer to this kind as global interaction. Another kind derives from the existence of a global system, which provides the actors with their scripts and locations on the stage. In the latter case there are common worldwide social processes, in which the actors take part, and in which states, corporations, other organizations, or individuals are involved. Hirst and Thompson (1996) make a similar distinction between an international and a globalized economy, although I do not quite agree with their bundled ideal-typical application of it. A pathbreaking theorization of the globality as a system was Wallerstein's (1974) concept of the modern world system.

However, both as interaction and as a system, globalization should be freed from any aprioristic economic reductionism, taking full account of the multidimensionality of social phenomena. In this context, we should discuss globalization in conjunction with (in)equality. To the extent that it is actually operating, globalization puts on the agenda equality or inequality for the whole of humankind. Indeed, we may even regard as aspects or moments of globalization all processes that raise issues about the equality or the inequality between people. But the question, Equality for whom? is, e.g., not asked in Amartya Sen's (1992) seminal book *Inequality Reexamined*.

Given that globalization may refer both to systemic global processes and to worldwide interaction among exogenous actors, we have two separate questions of (in)equality to answer. What is happening to (in)equality among humankind as a whole, or, alternatively put, among the clusters of actors? What is happening to the relations among members of the same cluster? In more concrete terms, global (in)equality is the sum of (in)equality within states and that between states, insofar as the latter have not become obliterated by global systemic processes.

Equality before God apart, human equality has de facto so far rarely been conceived and extended beyond the city, some rural peripheries, and the nation-state, beyond male citizens of the ancient Greek *polis*, the free men of the Icelandic sagas, the male burghers of the medieval city, and the denizens of the nation-state. There have been some functional circles of equality, among intellectuals—from the Confucian literati in classical China and the early modern European Republique des lettres—and among small closed religious communities. The antislavery campaigns from the late eighteenth century and afterward were probably the first manifestations of a universalistic, "this worldly" human egalitarianism. The current human rights activism is a contemporary heir of the latter.

INEQUALITY OF WHAT?

"The central question in the analysis and assessment of equality is . . . 'equality of what?' " the great Indian American economist Amartya Sen (1992) has argued. The importance of this question derives not only from the "basic heterogeneity of human beings," which makes some inequalities trivial, but also, as Sen points out, from the fact that people who argue against one kind of equality usually favor another. Sen also gives an interesting answer to his question. What matters above all is equality of capability, defined as the capability to achieve functionings, i.e., beings and doings, that a person has reason to value (Sen 1992: 4–5).

Sen's discussion is at a high level of abstraction, which may be empirically specified in various ways. But in contrast to much current social theorizing, Sen's can be well applied and measured. Thus, for instance, the United Nations Development Program (UNDP 1996: 109–12) has devised and put to use a "capability poverty measure" on the basis of Sen's theory.[2] To a sociologist, capability to achieve naturally relates to grounds for action. Sen's capability concept may then be specified as comprising almost all the elementary structural and cultural variables of sociology bearing upon social action. I have summarized these variables into a structural subset of tasks, rights, means, and risks and opportunities and into a cultural subset of identity, cognition, and values and norms. (Values and norms should in this context be taken as a social system, and not as the actor's own values and norms, since capability refers to achieving what one values.) A comprehensive empirical discussion about inequality should then involve the division of labor—hierarchical or egalitarian, the allocation of rights, the distribution of income and wealth, the structuring of health risks and of career opportunities; it should also pay attention to the patterning of self-images and self-confidence, the diffusion of knowledge, and to the openness or rigidity of value systems with regard to the range of individual options of life pursuits. All these aspects of inequality may be affected by a global system and/or by global interaction.

EQUALITY BY WHAT?

Equalization or leveling may operate upward, lifting those below, or downward, sinking those above, or as some mixture of the two. And unequalization may occur in the same three ways. The question is what mechanisms govern the outcomes. Social science has no corpus of specified answers and elaborate models pertaining to this question. Nevertheless, we may indicate where it seems most fruitful to search.

I suggest that we look for four major mechanisms of equalization and unequalization. Two we may call economic, both with regard to their location and effect, mainly on economic equality. One is productive effort and/or productivity, its patterns, and its developments, the expectation being that *ceteris paribus* more productive individuals, classes, and areas reap higher rewards than less productive ones. The other concerns opportunity structures, in particular market extensions. The wider the opportunities, be they product, financial, or labor markets, the more rewards there are for the successful. A third mechanism belongs more to what we usually regard as the realm of politics, i.e., measures and institutions backed up by power, in particular by state power. Power is a convertible currency. It can affect virtually all dimensions of equality, and in opposite directions. A fourth one, finally, is sociocultural, operating mainly through communication, of knowledge, persuasion and dissuasion, identities and values. It is important mainly for capabilities other than economic means.

Productivity and productive effort in the global context are always an attribute of actors, and as such they may be evenly or unevenly distributed. Communication and opportunity structures are systemic features and vary along the axis of inclusion and exclusion. Power may be looked at from both angles, at its even or uneven distribution and as an excluding/including aspect of the social system. The four mechanisms have very different relationships to globalization. Globalization involves widening opportunity structures and extending communications. Both are intrinsic to the definition of globalization. By contrast, globalization may have effects on productivity and effort, and on power.

Technological developments crucially affect all these mechanisms of (in)equality, especially those of productivity, opportunity structures, and communication. They are part of the generators of globalization. Technological changes have made productivity much less dependent on exogenously given factor endowments of energy and raw materials. Opportunity structures have widened because of decreasing transportation costs. Communication has become more inclusive with new world-encompassing communications technologies. Over the long run, say the last hundred years, the capacity of states has also increased due to technological advances bearing upon organizational management and upon the states' access to, monitoring of, and feedback from their populations.

GLOBALIZATION AND THE ECONOMIC
MECHANISMS OF (IN)EQUALITY

We may then open the door to the empirical world, by asking and at least hinting at answering the question of what globalization tendencies mean to these mechanisms.

Increasing structural interdependence and a wider diffusion of knowledge should tend to decrease productivity differences and therefore promote the process of "uplifting" equalization. This was the main route to intercountry and interregional equalization in Europe in the 1950s and 1960s, both in the West and in the East—where the enormous increase of investment effort was more important though—by means of industrialization, drastic agricultural rationalization, and urbanization (cf., Therborn 1995: ch. 10). In most countries, dire poverty is above all a rural phenomenon. Tendencies toward a globalization of agricultural productivity are likely to have an upwardly equalizing effect. They already have in East Asia.

There is no unambiguous conclusive evidence on the actual effects of market extensions. Sometimes the effect appears to have been small, as for instance the effect of the European Union (EU) on intercountry and interregional income differences. Polarizing effects arise from a differential capacity of populations to utilize a changed opportunity structure, be it of broadened access or lower transportation and other transaction costs. To those who succeed, by luck, skills, assets, or effort, a wider market means larger rewards. To those who do not, market extension means being left behind, marginalized, or impoverished by being outcompeted. The opening up of market structures in ex-Communist Eastern Europe, especially in Russia and China, has led to drastic increases of inequality, now reaching Latin American proportions (World Bank 1997a: Table 5). In the case of China, the World Bank (1997b) has even issued an explicit warning against the mounting inequality, accompanied with a series of recommendations for more equality, primarily between cities and the countryside and between coastal and peripheral inland regions.

Transnational migration, extending opportunity structures of labor beyond national boundaries, has had a significant uplifting effect in several sending countries, most notably in several Middle Eastern countries that are poor in oil, like Egypt, Jordan, Yemen, Lebanon, and Turkey, but also in countries like Portugal, Morocco, Greece, Pakistan, Bangladesh, the Philippines, and Mexico. Downward effects on the wages of (mainly) male unskilled labor in the receiving countries have nowhere been large, and small effects are estimated for the United States (The World Bank 1995: 53ff, 65ff; UNRISD 1995: 65ff).

The global sports, entertainment, and financial markets have so far clearly had such polarizing effects. It has even led to a niche industry of social interpretation, focusing on the alleged rise of a "winner-takes-all" society (Frank and Cook 1995). On the whole, the modern history of the world economy testifies to a diversity of trajectories and outcomes, including strong polarizing tendencies.

Africa and India have clearly fallen behind in the course of the twentieth century. China is now back at where it was around 1900 (relatively speaking), and so is, by and large, Latin America. Only Japan, Korea, and Taiwan have come close to the North Atlantic economies, excluding the oil deserts.

Over the last thirty years the distance between the least developed countries—most sub-Saharan Africa plus Haiti, Afghanistan, Bangladesh, Myanmar, and a few others—and the rest of the world has been widening. While the world per capita GDP has grown by more than 3 percent a year, the small product of the least developed countries has increased only by 0.4–0.5 percent a year. Sub-Saharan African GDP per capita actually declined between 1980 and 1993 (UNDP 1996: Table 25). An IMF (1997: 78) graph for economic regions of the world for the period from 1965 to 1995 shows a similar picture.

By the mid-1990s the difference in levels of prosperity between the rich world and Africa, Latin America, and the major oil exporters was much bigger than in 1965 (measured in GDP per capita, by purchasing power parities). This difference was somewhat smaller with regard to the Middle East (excluding the major oil exporters) and Asia as a whole (the East Asian industrializing economies excepted). Developing countries in gen-

Table 2.1   Gross Domestic Product (GDP) per Capita in Several Countries, 1900–92

	1900	1913	1950	1973	1992
W. Europe*	71	66	58	70	81
Brazil	17	16	17	24	22
Mexico	28	28	22	25	24
Egypt	12	10	5	6	9
Ghana	11	12	12	8	5
China	16	13	6	7	14
India	15	12	6	5	6

Source: Maddison 1995: 23–24.
Note: GDP is expressed as a percentage of the U.S. GDP and estimated in international dollars.
*Western Europe is the arithmetic average of eleven countries, from France and Austria to Norway.

eral, excluding the East Asian tigers, were about as far removed from the rich world as in 1965, maybe a little less. Spectacular gains have been made by Korea, Taiwan, Singapore, and Hong Kong, and substantial advances have also been made by China, Malaysia, Indonesia, Thailand, and Chile. The pickup of international trade and of capital flows since the mid-1980s, i.e., the most recent manifestations of economic globalization, has not spawned any change in the diversity of developments between countries.

These figures all refer to the inequality among humankind. We cannot tell properly to what extent the world market has contributed to this inequality. It may just as well derive from internal stagnation, destructive conflicts, or failures. In East Asia, investment and educational effort constituted the major forces of successful growth, but productivity increases have also been significant, especially in Japan, Korea, Taiwan, and China (World Bank 1993: 46ff). What is clear is that market globalization shows no tendency to bring economic equalization for humanity as a whole.

This implies, of course, that there is no downward pressure on the rich countries either. The rich Organization for Economic Cooperation and Development (OECD) countries accounted for three-fourths of world exports in 1965. The oil hitch of 1973–74 brought the share down to two-thirds, where it has stayed since then. In 1995, Western Europe, North America, Oceania, and Japan accounted for 65 percent of world exports (IMF 1988, 1996). The increasing market shares of the successful East Asian export economies have been borne completely by other developing countries, whose part of the pie has shrunk.

The effect of the recent advances of the new East Asian export economies—or their setback in 1997—on inequality in the rich countries is not very clear, and the empirical pattern is very uneven. However, it seems that eventual effects have been minor.

In the United States and Japan manufacturing imports from low-wage countries are much more important in terms of sectoral trade than in the EU. Relative prices in the import-competing sectors—such as textiles and apparel, rubber and plastics, and toys—declined in the 1980s, but relative wages declined only in the United States, not in Japan or in the EU. Sectoral productivity differences are much more important in explaining relative wages than differentials of trade price trends (OECD 1997: ch. 4; IMF 1997: 53ff.).

THE PERSISTENT POWER OF THE STATE

The diversity in patterns of development between countries—showing no uniform trend of either convergence or divergence—indicates that states and state-bounded societies still matter. The successive East Asian postwar success stories, of Japan, Korea, Taiwan, and China, have all been state-guided world-market-oriented economies, which is another hint at the importance of states.

Just how much states and state policies contribute to economic growth, or stagnation, is still a much contested issue. The evidence is less ambivalent with regard to a state's capacity to affect the level of inequality among its own inhabitants. Using World Bank and other data, Korzeniewicz and Moran (1997) have made a survey of the distribution of income in the world for the period from 1965 to 1992. The overall pattern is one of increased inequality. The ratio between the poorest and the richest fifth of the world population changed from 1:31 to 1:65. The steepest rise occurred during the acceleration of economic globalization in the second half of the 1980s, from 1:43 in 1985 to 1:65 five years later.

But the most interesting aspect of this study is that opposite tendencies were found in inequality between countries and within countries. Between countries overall inequality increased considerably, implying that the East Asian catch-up is so far a marginal phenomenon in the global totality. Within countries, on the other hand, inequality declined significantly. In 1965 within-country inequality accounted for a fourth of total income inequality in the world (24 percent); by 1992 this share had dropped to a fifth (19 percent).

States matter, and state capacity to ensure a measure of equality and social security is neither incompatible with, nor necessarily in a tradeoff with, a globalist world-market orientation of the economy. Societies that are wide open to the world market, as indicated by the proportion of foreign trade in GDP, are definitely not more unequal than societies with the same economic system but with less foreign trade. Rather, there is a tendency in the opposite direction. The small open economies in the OECD, the Nordic, and the Benelux countries, are more egalitarian than those of the United States or Australia, whose level of foreign trade is relatively low. Japan, on the other hand, is a relatively egalitarian country with a small foreign trade share (Atkinson et al. 1995). The East Asian export economies were and have remained more egalitarian than those of Third World countries (UNDP 1996: Tables 17 and 36; The World Bank 1993: 72ff).

Successful and very dependent world market competitors had relatively egalitarian distributions of factor incomes. This applies to Scandinavia, compared to the rest of Western Europe, and more recently to East Asian tiger economies—South Korea and Taiwan in particular—compared to Latin America. The world-market success of the Southeast Asian economies kept down their Gini coefficients of inequality in the 1970s and 1980s (World Bank 1993: 72ff). Given the absence of any comprehensive social

Table 2.2   Income Distribution (Degree of Inequality) and Trade Dependency in the OECD in the 1980s

	Inequality[a]	Trade Dependency[b]
Australia	29.5	17.9
Belgium	23.5	70.8
Canada	28.9	25.3
Finland	20.7	28.5
France	29.6	22.4
Germany	25.0	25.2
Ireland	33.0	55.2
Italy	31.0	21.9
The Netherlands	26.8	51.2
Norway	23.4	35.5
Sweden	22.0	31.6
Switzerland	32.3	37.0
United Kingdom	30.4	26.3
United States	34.1	10.6

Sources: Atkinson et al. 1995: 46; OECD 1996: 75.
Note: $r = -0.27$, that is, the less inequality, the more exports.
[a]Degree of inequality expressed as Gini coefficient of disposable income in mid-1980s.
[b]Trade dependency expressed as export share of GDP, 1980–89.

security institutions in these countries, the 1997 crisis is likely to produce more internal inequality.

In other words, state-bounded national settings still matter, even though a general tendency toward more inequality within countries can be observed for most of the OECD countries in the 1980s/early 1990s. Southern Europe (Italy, Portugal, and Spain) is an exception, as it has been quite unequal for a long time (Atkinson et al. 1995: 47ff, ch. 5).

State policies and institutions are intrinsically ambiguous in their effects on (in)equality, since they depend upon the configurations of power behind them. Some predatory and kleptocratic states among the poor countries clearly contribute significantly to economic inequality. Among developed or developing economies, on the other hand, there is a positive correlation between state interventionism and income equality.

Levels of productivity and the extension of markets obviously bear upon the capacity of states to pursue egalitarian or antiegalitarian policies. And the capacity of states to do what their citizens or their leaders want in the face of increasing global interdependence is perhaps the hottest issue of all in the globalization debates. This polemic will certainly continue, but an empirical social scientist might at least throw a bucket of cold facts upon it. Extensive and generous welfare states have historically in fact been built and today exist primarily in states whose economies are most dependent upon the world market (see table 2.3).

Put in nonstatistical terms, economic globalization provides no alibi for those who want to rob the welfare state. I agree with the American economist Paul Krugman (1994)—be it from another, social European angle—that the prevailing arguments about the threatened global competitiveness of nations amounts to a dangerous obsession.

In this context it is worth noting that world trade is not dramatically outgrowing national economies. In 1956, world exports constituted about a tenth of world GDP (9.4 percent according to the IMF). This figure remained almost unchanged until 1973–74, having been at 10.9 percent in 1972, just overtaking the share of 1913. The OPEC (Organization of Petroleum Exporting Countries) oil move raised the share to 16.1 percent in 1974. World exports then oscillated for two decades around that value, increasing to 17–18 percent around 1980–81, then slightly declining to approximately fifteen percent by the end of the 1980s (IMF 1988: 50–51), and finally rising again in the mid-1990s to 22 percent in 1996 (IMF 1996: 160).

Table 2.3   World Market Dependence and Welfare States among OECD Countries

	Export	Social Expenditure		Export	Social Expenditure
Low Dependence, Little Welfare			*Low Dependence, Much Welfare*		
United States	7	15	France	16	27
Japan	9	12	Greece	13	21
Australia	15	13	Italy	17	25
Portugal	18	15	Spain	16	20
High Dependence, Much Welfare			*High Dependence, Little Welfare*		
Austria	22	25	Canada	30	19
Belgium	53	25	New Zealand	24	19
Denmark	31	28	Switzerland	26	14*
Finland	32	27			
Germany	20	23			
Ireland	67	21			
Netherlands	45	29			
Norway	31	29			
Sweden	30	33			
United Kingdom	22	24			

Sources: UNDP 1996: 207; OECD 1994: 59ff.

Notes: Exports and public social expenditure as percentage of GDP, 1993 and 1990–91, respectively. The correlation between world-market dependence and welfare state size is significantly positive: 0.34.

*In 1980.

GLOBAL COMMUNICATION AND (IN)EQUALITY

Some suggest that sociocultural communication—compared to productivity patterns, market developments, and state policies—constitutes a marginal and mainly rhetorical contribution to the hard issues of equality and inequality in the world. In fact, it is and has been one of the most effective mechanisms.

First and foremost, the communication and practical diffusion of knowledge has had a tremendous effect upon life expectancy in the world. The capacity to survive is one of the few human capabilities that have increased almost universally between 1960 and 1990. State policies have played their part here, but the transnational diffusion of medical and hygienic knowledge has been crucial, largely through globalization by transnational action. The North–South gap in life expectancy narrowed significantly between 1960 and 1993, and as did that between Africa and the rich world. In 1960 sub-Saharan African life expectancy was 58 percent of that in the industrial world; in 1993 it was 68 percent. The literacy gap has also narrowed, the least developed countries moving up from a third to half of "industrial" literacy (UNDP 1996: Table 7).

The child mortality gap presents a somewhat different, more somber picture. Granted, in the least developed countries the under-five mortality rate, compared to that of industrial countries, declined from fifteen to twelve between 1960 and 1993. But infant mortality rates in India, Sri Lanka, Egypt, and Mexico have not declined as fast as they have in North America or Western Europe from 1900 or 1910. Only Chile has come relatively nearer to the United States and Western Europe. In absolute terms major advances have been made everywhere.

It is in the light of increasing chances of survival everywhere in the Third World—Uganda being the only exception for the 1960–93 period—that the gravity of the social disaster in the former Soviet Union stands out. Since 1991 life expectancy at birth has declined drastically there, in Russia by 4.7 years, in the Ukraine and in the Baltics by two years (UNICEF 1995: 111). (The figures refer to males in 1994. Female life expectancy has also declined, but less, about three years in Russia, two in the Ukraine, and one year or somewhat less in the Baltic republics.)

The spread of democracy in the world means equalization of rights. While this has mainly been the effect of political action in national settings, the current international opinion has and has had a strong impact. Global sociocultural communication has been even more important in enforcing equalization of gender rights. The global UN conferences, such as the Population Conference in Cairo, with its shift of perspective from family planning to reproductive health, and the two parallel women's conferences in China—one unofficial, the other official—have been significant

Table 2.4 Infant Mortality Rates, 1900–95

	1900	1910	1940	1995
W. Europe[a]	179	130	72	6
United States[b]	—	99[b]	43[b]	8
Argentina	—	148	90	22
Chile	340	333	217	12
Mexico	287	323	126	33
Egypt	—	137[c]	162	56
India	—	205	160	68
Sri Lanka	—	176	149	16

Sources: 1900, 1910 and 1940: Mitchell (1992, 1993, 1995); 1995: The World Bank (1997: Table 6).
[a]Arithmetic average of France, Germany (in 1960, West Germany), Italy, and United Kingdom (1900–40, England and Wales).
[b]1910–40 Whites only, the Black rate was 181 and 132, respectively.
[c]1920.

in this respect, setting agendas, spawning global networks, and widening frames of reference.

The human rights discourse has so far been less successful in assuring the most elementary human rights, against torture, assassinations, and genocide, in some parts of the world. But the globalization of the human rights issue is a positive contribution to the equalization of rights among humans.

CONCLUSION

Taken as an analytical variable rather than as a category of interpretation, globalization, in the literal sense of referring to tendencies toward a world-wide reach or impact of social phenomena, is old and multidimensional. The first major wave of globalization is almost two thousand years old: the first spread of the world religions. The globalizing tendency itself may be toward interaction and interdependence between exogenously given and endowed actors, states, corporations, associations, and movements, or it may be heading toward global social systems, the arenas of which constitute the actors. Both kinds of globalization may involve structuralization of resources and constraints; the patterning of risks and opportunities over time; enculturation of identities, knowledge, values, and symbolic forms; and world-encompassing action, by unilateral superpowers or multilateral interaction and worldwide concerted action.

Following Amartya Sen, we took (in)equality as a multidimensional concept and related its dimensions to sociological elements and to the contents of globalization. We also found it fruitful to distinguish between (in)-equality between states (and their populations) and within states. Four mechanisms were singled out as particularly important forces of (un)-equalization: effort and productivity (attributes of actors), opportunity structures, (state) power, and communication.

So far, we found more interactive than systemic globalization, but both tendencies exist. Globalization's effects on inequality are multiple and difficult to summarize in one statement. With regard to the world distribution of income and wealth, the long-term pattern tends more to divergence than the opposite, and the recent acceleration of economic globalization has been accompanied by accelerating income differentials in the world. But intensive study of recent developments casts doubt on the thesis of a strong, uniform effect of world-market extension of opportunity structures, much more open to capital than to labor, and much more open to financial than to productive capital. Recent de-industrialization and decreased demand for low-skilled industrial labor in the most developed economies seem to derive primarily from productivity developments instead of low-wage trade competition. The successful East Asian economies also show extraordinary rates of accumulation and, given their development level, impressive productivity rises.

States maintain significant powers, and their use of them matters. Part of that power has recently been applied to promote financial and economic globalization, through lifting of capital controls and lowering of trade barriers. It would be quite misplaced to regard contemporary states as mere victims of some external globalization. Over the last thirty years inequality between states has increased strongly, while declining significantly within states, a trend not yet undone by recent intrastate unequalization. We also found that historically egalitarian societies have been more successful on the world market than more inegalitarian ones. The Scandinavian countries have shown this for about a century, and since the 1960s that pattern has been repeated by the East Asian success stories. Contrary to conventional wisdom, we also found a positive correlation between world-market dependence and competitiveness on the one hand, and welfare state generosity on the other, when comparing OECD states with a similar history.

There is as yet no concerted world power, but the concerted global action that exists—largely through UN conferences, conventions, monitoring committees, and through UN-promoted NGO (nongovernmental organization) networks—operates in an equalizing direction, with regard to human rights and its various specifications, women's rights, children's rights, the rights of ethnic minorities, etcetera.

Global communication is also a significant force of equalization, in particular the communication of medical and hygienic knowledge, manifesting itself through converging (but far from uniform) trends of vital statistics, life expectancy, and fertility. We also noticed (though sketchy) a process of cultural equalization of symbolic forms through communication, of English as a lingua franca, and of styles and taste, be they of beverages and fast food, music, clothing, or bodily comportment.

Global value systems are ancient, such as the world religions, and their content keeps changing. Currently human and citizenship rights and neoliberal economics are prominent, rather than, say, national self-determination, popular participation, and socialism. While neoliberalism tends to promote inequality, eulogizing incentives and discrediting institutions of solidarity and redistribution, the global individualism of rights has its own egalitarian dynamics, albeit different from the previous ones of nationalism, populism, and socialism. The world religions, in particular Christianity and Islam, seem also to have become concerned with equality and justice much more than previously in history.

Globalization does not necessarily mean global integration. It may just as well mean global polarization, or global conflict. On the whole, economic differentials in the world as a whole are increasing and have been doing so for more than a century. Their causes and origins are hard to identify. But the evidence available over the latest decades—concerning world trade, capital flows, and transnational labor migration—seems to indicate that the global extension of opportunity structures has had hardly any down-leveling effects; some—very unevenly located—uplifting effects; and some significant, more general, unequalizing effects.

The divergent forces appear to derive far more from the globally spiraling effects of unevenness of the actors, in terms of accumulative effort and productivity and the working of the state, than from an inherent tendency of the global system. That is, they stem from different national rates of investment, in human as well as physical capital, innovation, and different developmental conditions of the national state, more than from any world-market dynamic.

On the other hand, cultural globalization—of identifications, knowledge, values and norms, language and other symbolic forms—has strong equalizing, uplifting effects on human conditions. The globalization of mass culture and entertainment is also clearly equalizing, but whether this is uplifting or down-leveling seems a matter of taste.

Globalization does not only entail anonymous markets and satellite-radiated prepackaged mass culture. It is not synonymous with a never-ending struggle for *Lebensraum*. Globalization also includes worldwide social action and concern and direct communication. What we are facing is a globalization of options, particularly the option of more or less inequality of resources and rights.

Considering these options we should not forget a piece of wisdom from the world's most developed civilization 2,500 years ago, of millennial longevity and which might by the end of the next century become the center of the world again after a few hundred years of North Atlantic preeminence. Confucius said, " If an individual can practice five things anywhere in the world, he is a man of humanity." "May I ask what these things are?" said Zizhang. Confucius replied, "Reverence, generosity, truthfulness, diligence, and kindness. If a person acts with reverence, he will not be insulted. If he is generous, he will win over the people. If he is truthful, he will be trusted by people. If he is diligent he will have great achievements. If he is kind, he will be able to influence others" (Confucius 1993: 19).

NOTES

1. I have dealt with these issues in other contexts, most recently in "Modernities and Globalizations," an article in press.

2. The indicators used are the proportion of births unattended by trained personnel (broadly and modestly defined), the percentage of children under five who are underweight, and the percentage of women above fifteen who are illiterate.

REFERENCES

Atkinson, A., et al. (1995). *Income Distribution in the OECD Countries*. Paris: OECD.

Confucius. (1993). The Analects. In P. Buckley Ebrey, ed. *Chinese Civilization: A Sourcebook*. 2nd ed. New York: Free Press.

Frank, R., and P. Cook. (1995). *The Winner-Takes-All Society*. New York: Free Press.

Hirst, P., and G. Thompson. (1996). *Globalization in Question*. Cambridge: Polity Press.

IMF. (1988). *International Financial Statistics. Supplement on Trade Statistics.* Washington, D.C.: IMF.

———. (1996). *Direction of Trade Statistics Quarterly, September*. Washington, D.C.: IMF.

———. (1997). *World Economic Outlook May 1997*. Washington, D.C.: IMF.

Korzeniewicz, R.P., and T.P. Moran. (1997). World Economic Trends in the Distribution of Income, 1965–1992. *American Journal of Sociology* 102, no. 4: 1000–39.

Krugman, P. (1994). Competitiveness: A Dangerous Obsession. *Foreign Affairs* 73, no. 2 (March/April): 28–44.

Maddison, A. (1995). *Monitoring the World Economy 1820–1992*. Paris: OECD.

Mitchell, B.R. (1992). *International Historical Statistics: Europe 1750–1988*. 3rd ed. London: Macmillan.

———. (1993). *International Historical Statistics: The Americas 1750–1988*. 2nd edition. London: Macmillan.

————. (1995). *International Historical Statistics: Africa, Asia, Oceania 1750–1988*. 2nd edition. London: Macmillan.

OECD. (1994). *New Orientations for Social Policy*. Paris: OECD.

————. (1996). *Historical Statistics 1960–1994*. Paris: OECD.

————. (1997). *Employment Outlook July 1997*. Paris: OECD.

Sen, A. (1992). *Inequality Reexamined*. Cambridge, Mass.: Harvard University Press.

Therborn, G. (1995). *European Modernity and Beyond: The Trajectory of European Societies after World War II*. London: Sage.

Tocqueville, Alexis de. (1970). *Democracy in America*. New York: Vintage Books.

UNDP. (1996). *Human Development Report 1996*. New York: Oxford University Press.

UNICEF. (1995). *Poverty, Children and Policy: Responses for A Brighter Future*. Florence: UNICEF.

UNRISD. (1995). *States of Disarray*. Geneva: United Nations Research Institute for Social Development.

Wallerstein, I. (1974). *The Modern World System*, vol. 1. New York: Academic Press.

World Bank. (1993). *The East Asian Miracle*. New York: Oxford University Press.

————. (1995). *World Development Report 1995: Workers in an Integrating World*. New York: Oxford University Press.

————. (1997a). *World Development Report 1997*. New York: Oxford University Press.

————. (1997b). *Sharing Rising Incomes: Disparities in China*. Washington, D.C.: World Bank.

3

The State and the New Geography of Power

Saskia Sassen

The general question organizing this chapter concerns the impact of economic globalization on the territorial jurisdiction, or more theoretically, the exclusive territoriality of the nation-state. It is an effort to respond critically to two notions that underlie much of the current discussion about globalization. One is the zero-sum game: Whatever the global economy gains, the national state loses, and vice-versa. The other is that if an event takes place in a national territory it is a national event, whether a business transaction or a judiciary decision. My argument rests on an understanding of economic globalization that is quite different from many of the standard accounts that lead to these two notions.

Two key propositions organize my discussion. One of these is that the global economy needs to be produced, reproduced, serviced, financed. It cannot be taken simply as a given, or merely as a function of the power of multinational corporations and financial markets. There is a vast array of highly specialized functions that need to be executed. These have become so specialized that they can no longer be subsumed under general corporate headquarters functions. Global cities, with their complex networks of highly specialized service firms and labor markets are strategic sites for the production of these specialized functions.

The second proposition is that the global economy to a large extent materializes in national territories. This requires a particular set of negotiations that have the effect of leaving the geographic condition of the nation-state's territory unaltered, but do transform the institutional encasements of that geographic fact, that is, the state's territorial jurisdiction or, more abstractly, the state's exclusive territoriality.

My argument is that precisely because global processes materialize to a

large extent in national territories, many national states have had to become deeply involved in the implementation of the global economic system and have, in this process, experienced transformations of various aspects of their institutional structure. This would mean that the global
economy and the national state do not relate to each other as in a zero-sum
situation. My working hypothesis is that globalization is having pronounced effects on the exclusive territoriality of the national state—that is,
its effects are not on territory as such but on its institutional encasements.

The impact of economic globalization on the institutional encasement of
national territory can be illustrated with two key features of globalization,
privatization and deregulation. Privatization is not simply a change in
ownership regime; it is also a privatizing of coordination and governance
functions that shift from the public to the private corporate sector. And the
importance of private oversight institutions, such as credit rating agencies,
has increased with the deregulation and globalization of the financial markets. These agencies are now key institutions in the creation of order and
transparency in the global capital market and have considerable power
over sovereign states through their authority in rating government debt.
Finally, the rise of international commercial arbitration as the main mechanism for resolving cross-border business disputes entails a declining importance of national courts in these matters—a privatizing of this kind of
"justice." All of these developments can be captured in the image of a
shift of functions and authority from Washington's government world to
New York City's corporate world.

A NEW GEOGRAPHY OF POWER

Economic globalization represents a major transformation in the territorial
organization of economic activity and of politico-economic power. How
does the globalization of national economies reconfigure the territorial exclusivity of sovereign states, and what does this do to sovereignty and to a
system of rule based on sovereign states? Has economic globalization over
the last ten or fifteen years contributed to a major institutional discontinuity in the history of the modern state and the modern interstate system, and
particularly, in the system of rule?

To posit, as is so often done, that economic globalization simply has
brought with it a declining significance of the national state, will not do, it
seems to me. Today, the major dynamics at work in the global economy
contain the capacity to undo the particular form of the intersection of sovereignty and territory embedded in the modern state and the modern state-
system. But does this mean that sovereignty is less of a property, less of a
feature in the international system? Or that territoriality is less of a fixture?

We can begin to address these questions by examining major aspects of economic globalization that contribute to what I think of as a new geography of power. One is the much noted fact that firms can now operate across borders with ease. I will not focus on this aspect, the global footlooseness of firms, as it is well known. Indeed for many, this is what globalization is about. In my reading there are three other components in the new geography of power, and it is these I wish to examine now.

One of these components concerns the actual territories where much of globalization materializes in specific institutions and processes. And the question here is, What kind of territoriality is this? The second component of the new geography of power concerns the ascendance of a new legal regime to govern cross-border economic transactions, a trend not sufficiently recognized in the social science literature. One can see here at work a rather marked concern for various kinds of "legality" driving the globalization of the corporate economy. There has been a massive amount of legal innovation around the growth of globalization. The third component of the new geography of power is the fact that an ever-increasing number of economic activities are taking place in electronic space. This growing virtualization of economic activity, particularly in the leading information industries such as finance and specialized corporate services, may be contributing to a crisis in control that transcends the capacities of both the state and the institutional apparatus of the economy. The speed of transactions made possible by the new technologies is creating orders of magnitude, for instance in the foreign currency markets, that escape the governing capacities of private and government overseers.

Adding these three components of the new geography of power to the global footlooseness of corporate capital reveals aspects of the relation between global economy and national state that are not adequately or usefully captured in the prevalent notion of a global–national duality. This duality is conceived as a mutually exclusive set of terrains where what the global economy gains, the national economy or the national state loses. It is this type of dualization that has fed the proposition of a declining significance of the national state in a globalized economy.

Let me elaborate now on these three components of the new geography of power. I will begin with the question of the spaces of the global economy, or the strategic geography of globalization, more conceptually, the particular form of territoriality we see taking shape in the global economy today. My starting point is a set of practices and institutions: global financial markets; ascendance of Anglo-American law firms in international business transactions; the formation of the World Trade Organization (WTO); the role of credit rating agencies in international capital markets; various provisions in the General Agreement on Tariffs and Trade (GATT),

North American Free Trade Agreement (NAFTA), and other free trade agreements.

STRATEGIC SPACES: THE ASCENDANCE OF THE SUBNATIONAL

Much attention has gone to the dispersal trends associated with globalization and telematics—the off-shoring of factories, the expansion of global networks of affiliates and subsidiaries, the formation of global financial markets. What is left out of this picture is the other half of the story. This worldwide geographic dispersal of factories and service outlets takes place as part of highly integrated corporate structures with strong tendencies toward concentration in control and profit appropriation. For instance, it is well known that a very high share, about 40 percent, of international trade is actually intrafirm trade, and, according to some sources, it is even higher than that (see United Nations Conference on Trade and Development, UN-CTAD, various years).

There are two major implications here for the question of territoriality and sovereignty in the context of a global economy. First, when there is geographic dispersal of factories, offices, and service outlets in an integrated corporate system, particularly one with centralized top-level control, there is also a growth in central functions. One way of saying this is that the more globalized firms become, the more their central functions grow—in importance, in complexity, in number of transactions (Sassen 1991, 1994).

We can make this more concrete by considering some of the staggering figures involved in this worldwide dispersal and imagining what it entails in terms of coordination and management for parent headquarters. For instance, in the early 1990s U.S. firms had over 18,000 affiliates overseas; less known is the fact that German firms have even more affiliates, 19,000, up from 14,000 in the early 1980s. Or that firms such as Ford Motors, GM, IBM, and Exxon, have well over 50 percent of their workforce overseas. All of this represents a massive task of coordination and management for the firm involved. Let me clarify promptly that a lot of this has been going on for a long time and, secondly, that this dispersal does not proceed under a single organizational form—rather, behind these general figures lie many different organizational forms, hierarchies of control, and degrees of autonomy (Harrison 1994).

Of importance to the analysis here is the dynamic that connects the dispersal of economic activities with the ongoing weight and often growth of central functions. In terms of territoriality and globalization this means that an interpretation of the impact of globalization as creating a space economy that extends beyond the regulatory capacity of a single state is

only half the story; the other half is that these central functions are disproportionately concentrated in the national territories of the highly developed countries.

I should perhaps clarify that by central functions I do not only mean
top-level headquarters; I am referring to all the top-level financial, legal,
accounting, managerial, executive, and planning functions necessary to
run a corporate organization operating in more than one country, and increasingly in several countries. These central functions are partly embedded in headquarters, but also in good part in what has been called the corporate services complex, that is, the network of financial, legal,
accounting, and advertising firms that handle the complexities of operating
in more than one national legal system, national accounting system, advertising culture, etcetera, and do so under conditions of rapid innovations in
all these fields (Sassen 1991, 1994; Knox and Taylor 1995). Such services
have become so specialized and complex that headquarters increasingly
buy them from specialized firms rather than producing them in-house.
These agglomerations of firms producing central functions for the management and coordination of global economic systems are disproportionately concentrated in the highly developed countries—particularly, though
not exclusively, in the kinds of cities I call global cities. Such concentrations of functions represent a strategic factor in the organization of the
global economy, and they are situated right here, in New York, in Paris, in
Amsterdam.[1]

One argument is that it is important to unbundle analytically the fact of
strategic functions for the global economy or for global operation and the
overall corporate economy of a country. For the purposes of certain kinds
of inquiry this distinction may not matter; for the purposes of understanding the global economy, it does. Further, to operate a worldwide network
of factories, offices, and service outlets, major and minor legal innovations
are necessary, a subject I return to later.

Another instance of this negotiation between a transnational process or
dynamic and a national territory is that of the global financial markets. The
orders of magnitude in these transactions have risen sharply, as illustrated
by the U.S. $75 trillion in turnover in the global capital market, a major
component of the global economy. These transactions are partly embedded in telecommunications systems that make possible the instantaneous
transmission of money/information around the globe. Much attention has
gone to the capacity for instantaneous transmission of the new technologies. But the other half of the story is the extent to which the global financial markets are located in particular cities in the highly developed countries; indeed, the degrees of concentration are unexpectedly high. For
instance, international bank lending by countries increased from 1.9 trillion dollars in 1980 to 6.2 trillion dollars in 1991; seven countries ac-

counted for 65 percent of this total in both 1980 and 1991. What countries? Yes, the usual suspects: the United States, the United Kingdom, Japan, Switzerland, and France (Bank for International Settlements).

Stock markets worldwide have become globally integrated. Besides deregulation in the 1980s in all the major European and North American markets, the late 1980s and early 1990s saw the addition of such markets as Buenos Aires, Sao Paulo, Bangkok, and Taipei. The integration of a growing number of stock markets has contributed to raising the capital that can be mobilized through stock markets. Worldwide market value reached thirteen trillion dollars in 1995. This globally integrated stock market, which makes possible the circulation of publicly listed shares around the globe in seconds, is embedded in a grid of very material, physical, strategic places—that is, cities belonging to national territories. Again, as in the case of firms with global operations, major and minor legal innovations were necessary for the deregulation and global integration of stock markets.

The specific forms assumed by globalization over the last decade have created particular organizational requirements. The emergence of global markets for finance and specialized services, the growth of investment as a major type of international transaction, all have contributed to the expansion in command functions and in the demand for specialized services for firms.

A central proposition here is that we cannot take the existence of a global economic system as a given, but rather need to examine the particular ways in which the conditions for economic globalization are produced. This requires examining not only communication capacities and the power of multinationals, but also the infrastructure of facilities and work processes necessary for the implementation of global economic systems, including the production of those inputs that constitute the capability for global control and the infrastructure of jobs involved in this production. The emphasis shifts to the practice of global control: the work of producing and reproducing the organization and management of a global production system and a global marketplace for finance, both under conditions of economic concentration.[2]

THE STATE AND THE NEW SPACE ECONOMY

The analysis presented above points to a space economy for major new transnational economic processes that diverges in significant ways from the global-national duality presupposed in much analysis of the global economy. The shrinking capacity of the state to regulate these industries cannot be explained simply by the fact that they operate in "the global economy" rather than in the "national economy." The spatial organization of the leading information industries makes it clear that these are not mutually exclusive spaces. Rather, the globalization of finance and corporate services is embedded in a grid of strategic sites that are partly embedded in national territories. Further, firms that operate globally still require the guarantees of rights of property and contract they expect within their national territories.

But the analysis of these industries also makes it clear that insofar as transnationalization and deregulation have been a key to their growth and distinct contemporary character, they have reduced the regulatory role held by the national state until quite recently. This is illustrated by the worldwide pressure experienced by national states to deregulate their financial markets in order to allow integration into the global markets. Thus London saw its "big bang" of 1984 and Paris saw "le petit bang" a few years later under governments as diverse as the Tories in England and the Socialists in France.[3] The declining regulatory role of national states can be quite different between highly developed countries and less-developed countries. This is illustrated by the case of the December 1994 Mexican crisis and the different roles played by the U.S. and Mexican governments.

Finally, advanced information industries make it clear that unlike the prior eras of the world economy, the current forms of globalization do not necessarily contribute to reproducing or strengthening the interstate system. International finance especially reveals the extent to which the forms of internationalization evident in the last two decades have produced regulatory voids that lie beyond not only states but also the interstate system. This can be illustrated with the case of the foreign currency markets, which have reached orders of magnitude that have weakened the regulatory role of central bankers, notably the impact of concerted international action on foreign exchange rates.

Some of the features of economic globalization associated with the declining regulatory role of the state are by now well known. Globalization has contributed to a massive push toward deregulation across the board in many of the highly developed countries. Aman (1995) notes that though not all industries in a nation are equally subject to intense global competition, the existence of such competition in general contributes to an overall political context that encourages domestic regulatory reform in all industries. "Political movements and regulatory trends do not tend to discriminate among industries once the momentum for certain reforms is underway" (Aman 1995: 433).[4] The impact of global competition on the domestic politics of regulation goes well beyond the industries in which this competition is most intense. Economic globalization pushes local jurisdictions into the competition for industries that operate nationally and/or transnationally. The possibility of moving from one to another jurisdiction with lower regulatory demands, puts downward pressures on regulations across all jurisdictions—the quintessential race to the bottom. Whole countries are now engaged in this competition. (For some recent formulations in what is a vast literature see Bonacich et al. 1994; Global Crisis 1993; Bose and Acosta-Belen 1995).

In the case of finance and the advanced corporate services, globalization was a key feature of their expansion, not simply a matter of raising profits and lowering costs as with many manufacturing industries. And reducing the existing regulatory role of states was the necessary mechanism. We have seen country after country in Latin America and Asia deregulate stock markets and other financial markets to become integrated into the global financial market. The competing "jurisdictions" in this case have typically been the capital cities, as these are the ones concentrating the existing banking, financial, and top-level services sectors. (There are exceptions, such as Sao Paulo in Brazil, which is the leading financial center but not the country's capital.) There are clearly also nongeographic "jurisdictions" such as markets. However, as we examined in the first section, key aspects of many of the global financial markets are embedded in places through the material infrastructure and the work processes they require. And these places are, again, mostly leading business centers of a country. For instance, the International Banking Facilities in the United States (a sort of free zone for finance) are almost all located in New York City, though they did not have to since such facilities are not a geographic concept.

NEW LEGAL REGIMES

A second component in the new geography of power confronting national states is the emergence of new, privatized legal regimes to handle cross-border business transactions. Firms operating transnationally need to ensure that the functions traditionally exercised by the state in the national realm of the economy are available globally, notably guaranteeing property rights and contracts (Mittelman 1996, Panitch 1996, Cox 1996). To address these questions it is necessary to examine the particular forms of legal innovation that have been produced and within which much of globalization is encased, framed; and, further, how these innovations interact with the state, or more specifically, with the sovereignty of the state. These legal innovations and changes are often summarized under the notion of "deregulation" and taken as somewhat of a given—though not by legal scholars. In much social science, deregulation is another name for the declining significance of the state.

As with the discussion of territory in the global economy, my beginning point is a set of practices and minor legal forms, microhistories, which can, however, accumulate into major trends or regimes—and I am afraid are about to do so. Insofar as economic globalization extends the economy beyond the boundaries of the nation-state and hence its sovereignty, guarantees concerning property rights and contracts would appear to be threatened.

In fact, globalization has been accompanied by the creation of new legal regimes and legal practices and the expansion and renovation of some older forms that bypass national legal systems. Globalization and governmental deregulation have not meant the absence of regulatory regimes and institutions for the governance of international economic relations. Among the most important ones in the private sector today are international commercial arbitration and the variety of institutions that fulfill rating and advisory functions that have become essential for the operation of the global economy.

Over the past twenty years, international commercial arbitration has been transformed and institutionalized as the leading contractual method for the resolution of transnational commercial disputes.[5] Again, a few figures tell a quick and dirty story. There has been an enormous growth of arbitration centers. Excluding those concerned with maritime and commodity disputes—an older tradition—there were 120 centers by 1991, with another seven created by 1993; among the more recent centers created are those of Bahrain, Singapore, Sydney, and Vietnam. There were about 1,000 arbitrators by 1990, a number that had doubled by 1992 (Dezalay and Garth 1995). In a major study on international commercial arbitration, Dezalay and Garth conclude that it is a delocalized and decentralized market for the administration of international commercial disputes, connected by more or less powerful institutions and individuals who are both competitive and complementary (Dezalay and Garth 1995). It is in this regard far from a unitary system of justice, and I quote Dezalay and Garth, "organized perhaps around one great lex mercatoria—that might have been envisioned by some of the pioneering idealists of law" (Dezalay and Garth 1995; see also Carbonneau 1990).

Another instance of a private regulatory system is represented by debt security or bond rating agencies that have come to play an increasingly important role in the global economy.[6] Ten years ago Moody's and Standard and Poor had no analysts outside the United States; by 1993 they each had about 100 in Europe, Japan, and Australia. In his study of credit rating processes, Sinclair found that these agencies function as mechanisms of "governance without government" (Sinclair 1994, picking up on Rosenau 1992). He found that they have leverage because of their distinct gatekeeping functions with regard to investment funds sought by corporations and governments. In this regard they can be seen as a significant force in the operation and expansion of the global economy. And as with business law, the U.S. agencies have expanded their influence overseas; to some extent, their growing influence can be seen as both a function of and a promoter of U.S. financial orthodoxy, particularly its short-term perspective.

These and other transnational institutions and regimes do raise questions about the relation between state sovereignty and the governance of global economic processes. International commercial arbitration is basically a private justice system, and credit rating agencies are private gatekeeping systems. Along with other such institutions they have emerged as important governance mechanisms whose authority is not centered in the state. Yet they contribute to maintaining order at the top, one could say. Does the ascendance of such institutions and regimes entail a decline in state sovereignty? We are seeing a relocation of authority that has transformed the capacities of governments and can be thought of as an instance of what Rosenau has described as governance without government (1992).

We are also seeing the formation of transnational legal regimes and their penetration into national fields hitherto closed. Further, national legal fields are becoming more internationalized in some of the major developed economies. Some of the old divisions between the national and the global are becoming weaker and, to some extent, neutralized. These transnational regimes could, in principle, have assumed various forms and contents. But they are, in fact, assuming a specific form, one wherein the states of the highly developed countries play a strategic geopolitical role. The hegemony of neoliberal concepts of economic relations with its strong emphasis on markets, deregulation, and free international trade has influenced policy in the 1980s in the United States and United Kingdom and now increasingly also in continental Europe. This has contributed to the formation of transnational legal regimes that are centered in Western economic concepts.[7]

Dezalay and Garth (1995) note that the "international" is itself constituted largely from a competition among national approaches. There is no global law. Thus the international emerges as a site for regulatory competition among essentially national approaches, whatever the issue— environmental protection, constitutionalism, human rights. From this perspective "international" or "transnational" has become, in the most recent period, a form of "Americanization."[8] The most widely recognized instance of this is of course the notion of a global culture that is profoundly influenced by U.S. popular culture. But, though less widely recognized and more difficult to specify, this has also become very clear in the legal forms that are ascendant in international business transactions. Through the International Monetary Fund (IMF) and International Bank for Reconstruction and Development (IBRD) as well as GATT this vision has spread to, some would say been imposed on, the developing world.[9]

The competition among national legal systems or approaches is particularly evident in business law where the Anglo-American model of the business enterprise and competition is beginning to replace the continental model of legal artisans and corporatist control over the profession (Sinclair 1994).[10] This holds even for international commercial arbitration. Notwithstanding its deep roots in the continental tradition, especially the French and Swiss traditions, this system of private justice is becoming increasingly "Americanized."

THE DIGITALIZATION OF ECONOMIC ACTIVITY

Yet another component in the new geography of power is the growing importance of electronic space. I will address this only briefly, though there is much to be said. I want to isolate one particular issue: the distinctive challenge that the virtualization of a growing number of economic activities presents not only to the existing state regulatory apparatus but also to private sector institutions increasingly dependent on the new technologies. Taken to its extreme this may signal a control crisis in the making; this would be a type of control crisis for which we lack an analytic vocabulary.

These are questions of control that have to do with the orders of magnitude that can be achieved in the financial markets thanks to the speed in transactions made possible by the new technologies. The best example is probably the foreign currency markets, which operate largely in electronic space and have achieved volumes—a trillion dollars a day—that have left the central banks incapable of exercising the influence on exchange rates they are expected to have (though may in fact not always have had). These are questions of control that arise out of the properties of the new information technologies, notably the immense speedup of transactions they make possible, rather than out of the extension of the economy beyond the state.

The growing virtualization of economic activities raises questions of control in the global economy that not only go beyond the state but also beyond the notions of non-state–centered systems of coordination prevalent in the literature on governance.

CONCLUSION: THE STATE RECONFIGURED

In many ways the state is involved in this emerging transnational governance system. But it is a state that has itself undergone transformation and participated in legitimating a new doctrine about the role of the state in the economy. Central to this new doctrine is a growing consensus among states to further the growth and strength of the global economy.[11]

Many governments now see their responsibilities going beyond foreign policy as traditionally conceptualized and extending into world trade, the global environment, and global economic stability (Aman 1995: 437). This participation of the state in the international arena is an extremely multifaceted and complex matter that cannot be adequately addressed here. Let me just mention that some of these roles in the international arena can be seen as benevolent, e.g., in matters concerning the global environment, and others less so, e.g., the role of the governments of the highly developed countries, particularly the United States, in pushing for worldwide market reform and privatization in developing countries.

Confining the analysis here to the economic arena, the international role of the state has been read in rather diverse manners, not necessarily mutually exclusive. For instance, according to some, much of this new role of states in the global economy is dominated by a furthering of a broad neoliberal conception to the point that it represents a constitutionalizing of this neoliberal project. Others emphasize that effective international participation by national governments can contribute to the strengthening of the rule of law at the global level (Aman 1995; Young 1989; Rosenau 1992).

Yet others see participation of the state in international systems, i.e., multilateral agreements like GATT, as a loss of sovereignty because national governments have to adjust some of their policies to international standards. For instance, agreements such as GATT and institutions such as the WTO are seen by some sectors in the United States as a restriction on national sovereignty. One can see this in recent debates over the WTO and the fear of restrictions on the political autonomy of the national state; for example, the concern that it will be used to enforce GATT trade regulations to the point of overturning federal, state, and local laws since the WTO places the principle of free trade above all other considerations. This is then seen as jeopardizing a nation's right to enact its own consumer, labor, and environmental laws. It is worth noting here that many who supported GATT did not favor the WTO because they did not like the idea of binding the United States to an international dispute resolution tribunal not fully controlled by the United States; they objected to the regulatory aspects of the WTO.

An important question running through these different interpretations is whether the new transnational regimes and institutions are creating systems that strengthen the claims of certain actors (corporations, the large multinational legal firms) and correspondingly weaken the position of smaller players and of states. Ruggie has pointed out that the issue is not whether such new institutions and major economic actors will substitute for national states but rather the possibility of major changes in the system of states: "global markets and transnationalized corporate structures . . .

are not in the business of replacing states" yet they can have the potential for producing fundamental change in the system of states (Ruggie 1993: 143). What matters here is that global capital has made claims on national states and these have responded through the production of new forms of legality. The new geography of global economic processes, the strategic territories for economic globalization, had to be produced, both in terms of the practices of corporate actors and the requisite infrastructure, and in terms of the work of the state in producing or legitimating new legal regimes. Representations that characterize the national state as simply losing significance fail to capture this very important dimension and reduce what is happening to a function of the global–national duality—what one wins, the other loses. I view deregulation not simply as a loss of control by the state, but as a crucial mechanism to negotiate the juxtaposition of the interstate consensus to pursue globalization, on the one hand, and the fact that national legal systems remain as the major, or crucial instantiation through which guarantees of contract and property rights are enforced on the other.

There are two distinct issues here. One is the formation of new legal regimes that negotiate between national sovereignty and the transnational practices of corporate economic actors. The second issue is the particular content of this new regime, one that contributes to strengthening the advantages of certain types of economic actors and weakening those of others. Regarding governance, these two aspects translate into two different agendas. One is centered on the effort to create viable systems of coordination/order among the powerful economic actors now operating globally (to ensure, one could say, that the big dogs at the top do not kill each other). International commercial arbitration and credit rating agencies, as I discussed earlier, can be seen as mechanisms for creating this type of order. The second is not so much focused on how to create order at the top, but on equity and distributive questions in the context of a globally integrated economic system with immense inequalities in the profit-making capacities of firms and in the earnings capacities of households.

There is a larger theoretico/politico question underlying some of these issues that has to do with what actors gain the legitimacy for governance of the global economy and the legitimacy to take over rules and authorities hitherto encased in the national state.

NOTES

This chapter is based on chapter one of *Losing Control? Sovereignty in an Age of Globalization* (New York: Columbia University Press 1996). I want to thank the Schoff Memorial Fund for their support.

　　1. We are seeing the formation of an economic complex with a valorization

dynamic that has properties clearly distinguishing it from other economic complexes whose valorization dynamic is far more articulated with the public economic functions of the state, the quintessential example being Fordist manufacturing. Global markets in finance and advanced services partly operate through a "regulatory" umbrella that is not state-centered but market-centered. This in turn brings up a question of control linked to the currently inadequate capacities to govern transactions in electronic space.

2. The recovery of place and production also implies that global processes can be studied in great empirical detail.

3. Globalization restricts the range of regulatory options of national governments as these and many other cases, notably the Mexico and Asia crises, illustrate. Aman (1995) shows how a global perspective on domestic regulatory politics helps explain the absence of radical differences in the regulatory outcomes of different U.S. administrations over the last fifteen years. The pressures of global competition, the nature of corporate entities involved, and domestic political pressures to minimize costs and maximize flexibility militate in favor of new, more market-oriented forms of regulatory reform.

4. This spread effect can also work in the opposite regulatory direction, as was the case with reform in the New Deal era.

5. It represents one mechanism for business disputing. The larger system includes arbitration controlled by courts, arbitration that is parallel to courts, and various court and out-of-court mechanisms such as mediation. The following description of international commercial arbitration is taken from Dezalay and Garth (1995); for these authors, today "international commercial arbitration" carries a different meaning from what it did twenty years ago. It has become increasingly formal and more like U.S.-style litigation as it has become more successful and institutionalized. Today international business contracts for, e.g., the sale of goods, joint ventures, construction projects, or distributorships, typically call for arbitration in the event of a dispute arising from the contractual arrangement. The main reason given today for this choice is that it allows each party to avoid being forced to submit to the courts of the other. Also important is the secrecy of the process.

6. There are two agencies that dominate the market in ratings, with listings of U.S. $3 trillion each. They are Moody's Investors Service, usually referred to as Moody's, and Standard & Poor's Ratings Group, usually referred to as Standard & Poor. While there are several rating agencies in other countries, these are oriented to the domestic markets. The possibility of a European-based rating agency has been discussed, particularly with the merger of a London-based agency (IBCA) with a French one (Euronotation).

7. This hegemony has not passed unnoticed and is engendering considerable debate. For instance, a well-known issue that is emerging as significant in view of the spread of Western legal concepts is the critical examination of the philosophical premises about authorship and property that define the legal arena in the West (e.g., Coombe 1993).

8. All of this is not a smooth lineal progression. There is contestation everywhere, some of it highly visible and formalized, some of it not. In some countries, especially those in Europe, we see resistance to what is perceived as the American-

ization of the global capital market's standards for the regulation of their financial systems and standards for reporting financial information. Sinclair (1994) notes that the internationalization of ratings by the two leading U.S. agencies could be seen as another step toward global financial integration or as an American agenda.

9. The best-known instance of this is probably the austerity policy imposed on many developing countries. This process also illustrates the participation of states in furthering the goals of globalization, since these austerity policies have to be run through national governments and reprocessed as national policies. In this case it is clearer than in others that the global is not simply the non-national, that global processes materialize in national territories and institutions. There is a distinction here to be made, and to be specified theoretically and empirically, between international law (whether public or private law), which always is implemented through national governments, and these policies, which are part of the aim to further globalization.

10. More generally, U.S. dominance in the global economy over the last few decades has meant that the globalization of law through private corporate lawmaking assumes the form of the Americanization of commercial law (Shapiro 1993).

11. There is a growing consensus among states to further the goals of economic globalization, to the point that some see in this a constitutionalizing of this new role of states (see Panitch 1996; Cox 1987; Mittelman 1996).

REFERENCES

Aman, Alfred C. Jr. (1995). A Global Perspective on Current Regulatory Reform: Rejection, Relocation, or Reinvention? *Indiana Journal of Global Legal Studies* 2: 429–64.

Arrighi, Giovanni. (1994). *The Long Twentieth Century: Money, Power, and the Origins of Our Times*. London: Verso.

Bonacich, Edna, Lucie Cheng, Norma Chinchilla, Nora Hamilton, and Paul Ong, eds. (1994). *Global Production: The Apparel Industry in the Pacific Rim*. Philadelphia: Temple University Press.

Bose, Christine E., and Edna Acosta-Belen, eds. (1995). *Women in the Latin American Development Process*. Philadelphia: Temple University Press.

Carbonneau, Thomas, ed. (1990). *Lex Mercatoria and Arbitration*. Dobbs Ferry, N.Y.: Transnational Juris Publications.

Cohen, Michael A., Blair A. Ruble, Joseph S. Tulchin, and Allison M. Garland, eds. (1996). *Preparing for the Urban Future: Global Pressures and Local Forces*. Washington, D.C.: Woodrow Wilson Center Press (Distributed by Johns Hopkins University Press).

Coombe, Rosemary J. (1993). The Properties of Culture and the Politics of Possessing Identity: Native Claims in the Cultural Appropriation Controversy. *The Canadian Journal of Law and Jurisprudence* VI, no. 2 (July 1993): 249–85.

Cox, Robert. (1987). *Production, Power, and World Order: Social Forces in the Making of History*. New York: Columbia University Press.

Dezalay, Yves, and Bryant Garth. (1995). Merchants of Law as Moral Entrepreneurs: Constructing International Justice from the Competition for Transnational Business Disputes. *Law and Society Review* 29, no. 1: 27–64.

Drache, D., and M. Gertler, eds. (1991). *The New Era of Global Competition: State Policy and Market Power.* Montreal: McGill-Queen's University Press.

Franck, Thomas M. (1992). The Emerging Right to Democratic Governance. *American Journal of International Law,* 86, no. 1: 46–91.

Global Crisis, Local Struggles. Special Issue of *Social Justice* 20, no. 3–4, (Fall–Winter 1993).

Harrison, Bennett. (1994). *Lean and Mean: The Changing Landscape of Corporate Power in the Age of Flexibility.* New York: Basic Books.

Jacobson, David. (1996). *Rights across Borders: Immigration and the Decline of Citizenship.* Baltimore: Johns Hopkins Press.

King, Anthony. (1990). *Urbanism, Colonialism, and the World Economy: Culture and Spatial Foundations of the World Urban System.* The International Library of Sociology. London and New York: Routledge.

———, ed. (1996). *Representing the City: Ethnicity, Capital and Culture in the Twenty-First Century.* London: Macmillan.

Knox, Paul L., and Peter J. Taylor, eds. (1995). *World Cities in a World-System.* Cambridge: Cambridge University Press.

Le Debat. Le Nouveau Paris. Special Issue of *Le Debat* Summer 1994.

Mittelman, James., ed. (1996). *Globalization: Critical Reflections. Yearbook of International Political Economy,* vol. 9. Boulder, Colo.: Lynne Rienner Publishers.

Panitch, Leo. (1996). Rethinking the Role of the State in an Era of Globalization. In Mittelman, James, ed. (1996). *Globalization: Critical Reflections. Yearbook of International Political Economy,* vol. 9. Boulder, Colo.: Lynne Rienner Publishers.

Pillon, Thierry, and Anne Querrien, eds. (1995). *La Ville-Monde Aujourd'hui: Entre Virtualite et Ancrage.* Special issue of *Futur Anterieur* 30–32. Paris: L'Harmattan.

Reisman, W. Michael. (1990). Sovereignty and Human Rights in Contemporary International Law. *American Journal of International Law* 84, no. 4 (October): 866–76.

Rosenau, J.N. (1992). Governance, Order, and Change in World Politics. In Rosenau and E.O. Czempiel, eds. *Governance without Government: Order and Change in World Politics.* Cambridge: Cambridge University Press: 1–29.

Ruggie, John Gerard. (1993). Territoriality and Beyond: Problematizing Modernity in International Relations. *International Organization* 47, no. 1 (Winter): 139–74.

Salacuse, Jeswald. (1991). *Making Global Deals: Negotiating in the International Marketplace.* Boston: Houghton Mifflin.

Sassen, Saskia. (1991). *The Global City: New York, London, Tokyo.* Princeton, N.J.: Princeton University Press.

———. (1994). *Cities in a World Economy.* Thousand Oaks, Calif.: Pine Forge/Sage.

———. (1996). Losing Control? Sovereignty in an Age of Globalization. The 1995 Columbia University Leonard Hastings Schoff Memorial Lectures. New York: Columbia University Press.

Shapiro, Martin. (1993). The Globalization of Law. *Indiana Journal of Global Legal Studies* 1 (Fall): 37–64.

Sinclair, Timothy J. (1994). Passing Judgement: Credit Rating Processes as Regulatory Mechanisms of Governance in the Emerging World Order. *Review of International Political Economy* 1, no. 1 (Spring): 133–59.

Taylor, Peter J. (1995). World Cities and Territorial States: The Rise and Fall of Their Mutuality. In Paul L. Knox, and Peter J. Taylor, eds. *World Cities in a World-System*. Cambridge: Cambridge University Press: 48–62.

Trubek, David M., Yves Dezalay, Ruth Buchanan, and John R. Davis. (1993). Global Restructuring and the Law: The Internationalization of Legal Fields and Creation of Transnational Arenas. Working Paper Series on the Political Economy of Legal Change, nr. 1. Madison, Wisc.: Global Studies Research Program, University of Wisconsin.

United Nations. (1992). *World Investment Report 1992: Transnational Corporations as Engines of Growth*. New York: United Nations.

United Nations Conference on Trade and Development, Programme on Transnational Corporations. (1993). *World Investment Report 1993: Transnational Corporations and Integrated International Production*. New York: United Nations.

Young, O.R. (1989). *International Cooperation: Building Regimes for Natural Resources and the Environment*. Ithaca, N.Y.: Cornell University Press.

4

States and Capital: Globalizations Past and Present

Michael Hanagan

The term "modern" being out of favor, "global" is bidding to become the shorthand term for "the way we live now." Leading sociologists and anthropologists have backed its claim by arguing that the present period is integrally and uniquely global (Castells 1996: 66). Such versions of globalization have been attacked by those who deny that the contemporary world economy is integrally global; they argue that the expansion of global trade has increasingly been confined to a triadic trade between Western and Central Europe, North America, and a handful of Pacific Rim nations. World trade has become ever more concentrated within this triad, and large parts of the world, including Africa, the former Soviet Union, and large portions of South America, are being "delinked" and increasingly isolated from an expanding world economy (Petrella 1996: 62–83). Neither is contemporary change uniquely global; evidence of preceding periods of global expansion has been ignored (cf., Adas 1993).

Some who deny that the present period is uniquely and integrally global have developed more historically oriented theories of globalization. Many such theories emphasize larger patterns of global ebb and flow, elements of which are replicated in contemporary globalization. The logic of such analyses can be seen in Jonathan Friedman's work. Commenting on the relationship between social stratification and inflation he exclaims, "This has happened before, before the 1920s, before industrial capitalism, before the decline of the Mediterranean, perhaps before the decline of Rome and even before the disintegration of the Athenian hegemony" (Friedman 1994: 170). The major focus of inquiry becomes a group's or society's position within the pattern. Key issues become whether a nation is losing or winning hegemony, its location within long waves of economic change,

67

or place in a cycle of civilization. The danger of such analyses is that they can range over so much time and space that they lose sight of the ways in which specific historical contexts interact with and alter patterns.

In contrast, this chapter places economic and social aspects of the current wave of globalization in a narrower but more focused historical perspective. Comparing the present wave of globalization with the immediately preceding wave, it identifies the distinctive characteristics of each. Rather than focusing on the unique character of the contemporary period or locating events within recurrent or cyclical patterns of social behavior, it analyzes these globalizations as products of two independent but interrelated processes, state formation and capital accumulation. Each process has its own logic, but, at important historical moments, changing relationships between these two process exerted great influence on the two waves of globalization under consideration. Not the pattern of waves but the processes at work within them are our focus.

GLOBALIZATIONS PAST AND PRESENT

Following Charles Tilly, let us define globalization as "an increase in the geographic range of locally consequential social interaction" (Tilly 1995: 1). According to this criteria, globalization, indicated by the increased movement of both humans and commodities across continents and national boundaries, occurred in two distinct periods over the last 150 years: a first wave of globalization, 1850–1914, and a second wave of globalization, 1950 to the present. In between, the period 1914–50 might be labeled as an era of "world parochialization." Within each of the two global waves, it is useful to demarcate a turning point when previously high rates of economic growth slowed, and growth became more differentiated. Let us use the year 1873, the onset of the (first) Great Depression, as the turning point for the first wave and 1974, the beginning of the oil crisis, for the second. After 1873 and 1974, wage rates among industrialized nations tended to converge and wage differentials within individual nations to grow—with important political consequences for states (Williamson 1996).

In both periods of globalization, the transformation of communications was important. The development of television, the transistor radio, the fax machine, and the Internet are characteristic features of the contemporary global wave, but changes in communications technologies were no less revolutionary in the preceding wave. From 1867 on, the development of cables made possible rapid communication across the Atlantic. By 1914, submarine cables linked all the continents, and Marconi's new wireless was spreading. The second half of the nineteenth century saw the beginnings of the movies and the rise of the mass-circulation newspaper; in 1900 the English *Daily Mail* had a daily circulation of one million. Transmitted by submarine cables, newspaper reports allowed a mass readership to follow closely events around the world.

In both global waves transportation revolutions occurred. Before 1850, transoceanic migration was usually a one-way trip. In the period 1850–1914, return migration became common, and those Italian and Spanish farm laborers who migrated seasonally to the Argentine pampas are direct ancestors of London workers who use cheap airfares to vacation in their Caribbean homelands.

In the contemporary global wave David Harvey cites the development of passenger airlines after 1950 as an example of "time-space compression," but he cites another major instance between 1850 and 1930, due to the steamship and the locomotive (Harvey 1989). The effect of the steamship was dramatic; in 1867, the average sailing time between Europe and America was forty-four days, but a steamer could make the trip in fourteen days; by 1900 the trip was down to a week. Meanwhile competition among carriers in the "Atlantic Ferry" reduced the cost of a round-trip so that workers could commute to seasonal employment. The same technology enabled great powers to build gunboats and, by projecting their power along inland rivers, to compete in the conquest of vast colonial empires. In 1867 the opening of the Suez Canal almost halved the trip between the United Kingdom and India. On land the railroad brought a similar revolution and, by 1914, the basic railway network had been constructed in India, the United States, and Western and Central Europe (although not in Canada or Russia). By then the automobile had become an item of mass consumption in the United States.

In these two global waves the major spur to migration was economic growth and the ongoing pressure on peasant agriculture, itself caused by the growing international market in agricultural produce. In both periods, the major migrant destinations were the emerging economic giants, Germany and the United States, and the migrants themselves typically hard-pressed peasants. In 1850–1914, European peasants and rural day laborers were major contributors to European and North American factories and mines as were Chinese and Indian peasants to the plantations and mines of the Caribbean, parts of South America, and central and South Africa. Toward the end of the century, British industrial proletarians joined farm laborers in emigration. In the second wave of globalization under consideration, peasants remained the major emigrants, but sending areas changed. In the 1960s and 1970s, Irish, Spanish, Portuguese, and Yugoslav migration was insufficient to supply the rapidly growing need of the European community, and they turned to peasants in North Africa and Turkey and to residents of Britain's former colonies in the Caribbean, Africa, and

Asia. After absorbing many postwar European refugees the United States drew migrants from Central America, the Caribbean basin, and Asia. Japan turned to South Korea (Morawska and Spohn 1997: 23–62).

Both periods witnessed the emergence of transnational social movements of de-territorialized migrants and movements of Islamic fundamentalists, Palestinian nationalists, and Haitian nationalists, all having analogues in early twentieth-century Europe and America. For example, the Sons of Italy, Italia Irridenta Society, Slovak League, National Alliance of Bohemian Catholics, and American Jewish Congress were all American-based immigrant organizations that asserted a "transnational identity" in championing their homeland's cause. Each attempted to influence Woodrow Wilson's negotiations at the Versailles Conference.

In both periods of globalization, world trade increased due to the lowering of tariff barriers and then continued low effective tariff protection (the principal exception being the United States in the first period). The share of exports in world output reached a peak in 1913 not surpassed until 1970 (International Monetary Fund, IMF, 1997b: 112). And capital moved at least as easily as labor. Although proportionately heavier in the first wave, both periods saw a massive outflow of capital from developed to developing countries.[1] Only since the mid- to late 1970s has deregulation restored to investors the freedoms of the pre–World War I period when 90 percent of all foreign investments were in portfolio investments—i.e., securities acquired by investors without any control or participation in their management (Dunning 1970: 2). Even though financial deregulation did not make significant progress in most of the industrialized world until the mid-1970s, it has made up for lost time. In the last three years of the 1980s the flow of direct foreign investment measured in 1980s dollars was more than $100 billion a year, ten times as much as it had been in the first three years of the 1970s. Late nineteenth-century parallels to contemporary joint ventures abound, such as the loose agglomeration of companies used by the Paris Rothschilds to control world nickel mining and Russian petroleum refining and the Schneider group's influence in Russian metallurgy.

In both periods, transnational corporations and financial networks linking corporations across national boundaries increased. According to a 1974 study, of the eighty-five largest multinational corporations based in continental Europe, 80 percent were already in existence and 44 percent were already multinationals in 1914 (Franko 1976: 8). Such powerful multinational corporations as Bayer, Bosch, Daimler Benz, Dunlop, Lever Brothers, Nestlé, Royal Dutch Shell, Siemens, Solvay, and Unilever were already giants in the pre-1914 period. In the 1860s, the East India Railway and the Great Indian Peninsula were British companies that played a major role in building the Indian railway system and continued to run them for the Indian government. British shipping companies such as the Peninsular and Oriental Steam Navigation Company, British India, and White Star dominated international shipping, albeit with growing competition from the German Hamburg-America, the Norddeutscher Lloyd, and the French Cie. Gen. Transatlantique.

Both global waves reached turning points after which immigration and worldwide economic competition encouraged widening divisions in national wage structures between groups of highly paid and poorly paid workers. Adrian Wood and Jeffrey G. Williamson have argued forcefully that ever-increasing migration and the continued expansion of world trade have disadvantaged less skilled workers in industrialized countries and promoted the growth of wage inequality in the latter period of both global waves.[2] Currently, growing age differentials in Western Europe and the United States have attracted increased attention, and even the IMF notes that "labor markets in the advanced economies have been characterized by marked increases in wage inequality in some countries between the more skilled and less skilled, and in other countries by rises in unemployment among the less skilled" (IMF 1997a: 63). In the decades before 1914, a similar pattern of increasing income inequality is found in the United States and Europe, when income inequality in major European countries and the United States approximated the extreme inequality of contemporary Brazil or Panama (Williamson 1991: 11–12).

While the social identities of the beneficiaries of economic growth varied from one wave to the other, there is a striking similarity in the victims. One social commentator's "flex time" and "just-in-time production," when carried out for low wages and in poor working conditions, is another social commentator's "sweated labor." Sweatshops have been uncovered not only in Ho Chi Minh City and Guatemala City but in New York and London. The very terms "sweatshop" and "sweating" originated during the previous wave of globalization, and today's temporary office workers and homeworkers often reside in the same large cities, sometimes in the very same residential areas, as the casual dock laborers and artificial flower makers of a century ago.

Many of the forms of industrial production flourishing in the contemporary world and studied by industrial sociologists have late nineteenth-century predecessors. Then, as today, the garment industry was the *locus classicus* of a new form of industrial organization that emphasized quick turnover, limited inventories, and adaptability, which contemporary reformers labeled as "sweated labor." The introduction of small machines, including sewing machines available on installment plans, greatly accelerated its spread. In established garment capitals like London, New York, and Paris, a new division of labor evolved. Because of the seasonality of garments and their concern with changing fashion, initial proletarianization in the garment trade took less the form of factory industry than of an

increased division of labor and subcontracting. Employers avoided investment in costly machinery that could become obsolescent and, instead, organized decentralized but closely coordinated production in which skilled
workers labored in shops separate from those of unskilled workers. The
emigration of skilled Jewish garment workers, fleeing in response to po-
groms and Czarist oppression, provided a cheap skilled labor force in
some sectors of this industrialization. Women and children in the urban
slums were the main recruits for this new labor force, particularly women
whose own husbands were casual laborers with wages insufficient to support a family.

Both waves saw new economic powers join the world economy. Today,
Pacific Rim nations, Japan, South Korea, and Taiwan, and city states, Hong
Kong and Singapore, have fully entered the ranks of the rich nations. So,
between 1850 and 1914, a handful of industrializing powers, the United
Kingdom preeminent but followed by Belgium and perhaps France, were
joined by the United States and Germany and, later, by the Scandinavian
nations, Canada, Australasia, and, seemingly, Argentina. At the same time
that labor migration and world trade increased income inequality within
nations, they also promoted wage convergence among industrializing nations. Between 1870 and 1914 the wages of unskilled workers in Europe
and such non-European industrializers as Argentina and Canada began to
catch up with those of workers in Australia and the United States. In the
interwar period, the United States regained its lead over much of Europe,
but after 1974, even major European wage laggards, France, Italy, and
Spain, and a Latin American laggard, Argentina, began again to catch up
with the United States (Williamson 1995: 141–96).

GLOBALIZATION, 1850–1914:
CONSOLIDATED STATES AND FIXED CAPITAL

While the two great waves of globalization of the last 150 years share important common characteristics, they differ in crucial ways. Distinctive
features of globalization 1850–1914 were the development of territorially
continuous, centralized, differentiated, coercion-monopolizing "consolidated states"; rapid accumulation of fixed capital; and close links between
consolidated states and fixed capital. These links explain individual states'
ability to influence world economic development, setting limits to global
development and restricting the growth of autonomous markets for the
benefit of their citizens.

The success of capital and states in working together in the late nineteenth century confounded social commentators both then and now. States
were and have always been territorial bodies. If anything, the eighteenth-

and nineteenth-century emphasis on building territorially contiguous consolidated states was an accentuation of this territoriality. In contrast, before the mid-nineteenth century, capital concentration was distinctively nonterritorial. In the fifteenth and sixteenth centuries, Portuguese and Dutch merchants had built powerful trading empires founded on the possession of strategic fortresses and ports but mainly based on capital, commercial trading networks, superior seamanship, and naval technology.

To flourish, a close alliance between states and capital required dramatic changes in the nature of states and in the character of capital. By 1850, most states in Western and Central Europe had undergone a remarkable series of changes. States had grown incomparably stronger and yet, despite their strength, they recognized the rights of private property and of citizens, and their credible guarantees against arbitrary confiscation made them safe shelters for capital. The consolidated state created by the French Revolution and its aftermath possessed a bureaucracy that penetrated into the tiniest local community. Through taxation and conscription, it asserted increasing claims on its members but, in return, conferred legal rights to a growing number of "citizens." Finally, through education and civic rituals it promoted the growth of a common language and shared national culture. Just as important, these new consolidated states continued to exist within the so-called "Westphalian system" of militarily competitive states. Because consolidated states engaged in a battle for survival they required ever-larger financial resources to maintain their independent existence. To do so, they found it necessary to come to terms with capital and to provide it security in return for loans and financial support (Tilly 1990).

Another factor promoting the alliance of state and capital was that the new technologies of the "Second Industrial Revolution" required an enormous increase in fixed capital—capital not replaced until after a number of cycles of production such as factory buildings, factory sites, and machinery. The growth of heavy industry made capitalists more territorially conscious. Steelmaking, with its highly specialized inert machinery and long production series, was paradigmatic of industrial transformations during the so-called "Second Industrial Revolution"; the introduction of the Thomas–Gilchrist process enabled continental Europeans to use their ore deposits in high-quality steelmaking, and giant producers paid large sums to take advantage of immense opportunities. In the 1870s and 1880s, the lowered price of basic steel enabled early railways to replace rapidly deteriorating iron rails with more enduring steel rails. In coal and ore-rich areas like Upper Silesia, huge factories were erected in sparsely populated areas with little industrial tradition.

In the 1850s and 1860s, consolidated states and heavy industry began to cooperate in many ways; continental states provided financial support and encouraged banks to help native firms participate in the development of railways and military hardware. In the United States, the Civil War created a huge, governmental demand for the first fruits of the new metal technology. In Europe, use of railways to carry troops and supplies was an important element in the Prussian victories over Austria and France. The introduction of steel armor for battleships and innovations in munitions and artillery greatly increased the military's need for metal products. Troubles of large concerns reverberated throughout the economies of whole regions, and industrialists were better placed than previous smaller-scale manufacturers to request state aid. Having built new steel railways for developing countries and rebuilt the railroads of the world with steel instead of iron, leading industrial concerns found themselves with huge plants and shrinking markets. During the "Great Depression" between 1873 and 1896, giant firms struggled to regain their lost balance. Great powers such as United Kingdom, France, and Germany lobbied client states in favor of national heavy industry while foreign offices, particularly the French foreign office, encouraged private investors to favor governments, such as that of their valuable Russian allies.

Asserting its value to (and implying dependence on) the consolidated state, heavy industry demanded "protection" to guarantee home markets and so that it could compete more effectively internationally. In 1891, speaking in the name of a gigantic U.S. Steel, American industrialists played a key role in the passage of the protectionist McKinley Tariff. In 1892, in France, heavy industrialists organized in the Comité des Forges did not originate the demand for protectionism, but their rallying behind its banner insured the triumph of the protectionist Méline Tariff. In 1902, in the United Kingdom heartland of free trade, when the Birmingham industrialist Joseph Chamberlain publicly called for the Conservative Party to embrace protectionism, he echoed a sentiment with widespread support in industry.

Another aspect of this new alliance between consolidated states and capital was the growth of new forms of imperialism. The opening up of the European continent and then the world market by railways had created vast financial and industrial markets. Part of the problem for industrialists, however, was that when they invested large amounts of money outside their own nation-state, dangers of political stability and national insolvency arose. The experience of English industrialists in Latin America underlined the dangers encountered by industrialists in situations where they lacked political leverage (cf., Miller 1977a and Miller 1977b). Not so much the search for fabulous profits, but the same longing to protect fixed capital that backed protectionism also supported imperialism. In the years before 1914, metropole investment went heavily into infrastructure, mainly railroads, spreading fixed capital investments to the colonial world.

The late nineteenth century witnessed the expansion of European empires on a historically unprecedented scale. Considered as institutions, late nineteenth-century "empires" were fundamentally different than past empires. To one degree or another, all were combinations of a center consisting of a (more or less) consolidated state characterized by centralized penetration, citizenship rights and duties, and national consciousness joined with other subordinate states having a significantly lower level of centralization, citizenship rights, and duties, and more limited identity with the central state. In 1914, all the leading states and many secondary and tertiary powers, such as Belgium, Denmark, Holland, and Portugal, were empires in the sense of our definition.

The colonial empires these nations acquired exemplify the farthest limits of the relationship between consolidated states and capital. Empire extended the territorial control of European states far beyond their national boundaries. Avner Offer rightly points out that the imperial project needs to be evaluated in terms of both British national defense and capitalist profitability. To remain a great power, Britain required naval supremacy and the ports, coaling stations, and advanced communications it entailed (Offer 1993: 215–38). Although they often balked at the cost of colonies, costs they shared with the general taxpayer, businessmen supported colonial administrations that gave them privileged access to resources or constituted privileged markets. In the era of "free trade imperialism," the British Engineering Standards Association set the legal requirements for locomotives employed in the Indian railways; the standards were designed so that cheaper and more quickly delivered American locomotives could not be used in India (Headrick 1988: 82). In other areas, such as cable laying, security was used to justify reliance on British companies.

GLOBALIZATION 1850–1914 AND WORKER-CITIZENS

Every apple has its worm. For capital, the development of working-class citizenship in consolidated states posed new and long-term problems. Within the consolidated state, there developed a new kind of working class, characterized by full-time employment, clear-cut occupational assignments, and career patterns over the life cycle; at the limit, as it became more stable and more skilled, wage labor almost became a kind of fixed capital. Necessary to the state as soldiers and taxpayers and to capital as semiskilled workers, they provided the bases for the growth of powerful labor movements that imposed serious restrictions on capital accumulation—within both consolidated states and their associated empires.

If sweated temporary labor was one result of late nineteenth-century industrialization, a new kind of industrial proletariat was the result of the growth of fixed capital in the Second Industrial Revolution. Those adversely affected by industrial development in the present and past global waves have many similarities; it is the character of the beneficiaries that varies. Given their great power, industrialists had considerable freedom to choose the kinds of workers they would employ. Once capitalists had invested heavily in fixed capital, they gained so much more from the loyalty and job-specific knowledge of workers that they brought workers into supervised locales using employer-owned tools and materials, committed themselves to carry the cores of their labor forces through seasonal periods of slack, and developed an interest in collective contracts with organized labor. These tendencies spilled over into organizational and electoral strength for workers. They greatly increased the differences between sweatshops and capital-intensive firms. (Even in mining, owners put almost everyone but hewers on wages and long-term employment contracts, where previously almost everyone had operated short-term.)

Age, gender, race, national origin, marital status, and ethnicity figured prominently in the new high-wage forms of industrial organization that developed before World War I. Most employers preferred to give the newly created, stable, semiskilled jobs to adult males who had families; women's and single migrants' participation in industry was limited to lower-paying, less-skilled jobs for which demand fluctuated. Employers chose adult males partly because factory work was physically demanding and partly because they assumed that, in a free-market economy, married males would form a stable work force, insuring year-round production over a long period. Manufacturers shared with working men the feeling that married women would and should stay home to take care of children. Perhaps the most important consequence of this reconfiguration of the labor force was the declining need for unskilled labor, usually provided by women and children.

The adult, primarily male, work force in the large factories differed from previous groups of unskilled and semiskilled workers by having its own identity. Working in the same industry, year after year, they began to regard themselves as metalworkers, chemicalworkers, railwaymen, and gasworkers; further, unlike the shifting and mobile casual labor force of the earlier period, they often remained in the same geographic area for most of their lives. Trained on relatively specialized machines in large factories, semiskilled workers had much less opportunity to move from place to place than did artisans. The masculine character of much industrial work promoted an ethic of fraternalism that flourished in predominantly or exclusively male clubs, bars, and cafes. By the end of the nineteenth century, many of these male workers had begun to organize into unions and to join the labor movement.

In discussing the impact of urban citizenship on the Second Industrial Revolution, it will be helpful to focus on the United Kingdom. Not that the United Kingdom is in all respects the best example of an industrial economy of the Second Industrial Revolution—in a number of ways the United States or Germany better illustrates the technological features of this transformation—but, as the principal global power, a look at the United Kingdom best illustrates the Second Industrial Revolution in its global context. The industrial transformation of the United Kingdom was accompanied by the spread of citizenship. Following the example of the middle classes in 1832, workers took advantage of differences within ruling elites to expand their voting rights; in 1867, skilled male workers were enfranchised and in 1884, the majority of male workers. Of course, the spread of citizenship did not overcome the growing economic distinctions among citizens, but it did increase the attractiveness of electoral politics for labor and socialist parties and their conviction that real changes could be accomplished via the ballot box.

Using their citizenship rights, coalitions of male trade unionists and middle-class social reformers united in the imperial center state to politically resist the downward pressure on less skilled labor that produced sweated labor with increasing frequency after 1873. Appeals to membership in national polities played a key part in social reform. In the pre-1914 period middle-class reformers, who played an important role in the battle against "sweated industries," stressed that the spread of sweated labor would limit the expansion of the more capital intensive and better-paying jobs in industrial capitalism. Gertrude Tuckwell of the National Anti-Sweating League condemned sweating in the name of "national efficiency." According to Tuckwell, employing mothers would result in the perpetuation "of a system in which sickly, anemic workers are raising a still feebler generation whose fight for work must be appreciably weaker, who soon inevitably swell the ranks of the unemployable and disappear into the abyss" (Morris 1986: 142). An editorial in the *Daily News* took the same tack concerning sweating:

> This kind of industry is not necessary to commerce. It is contrary to commerce. It produces a class which has lost all power to maintain a reasonable rate of consumption in the home market—a class which is on the verge of pauperism and which, therefore, contributes enormously to the burden of the ratepayer—a class which lowers the average of the nation's vitality and which lays up a heritage of degeneracy for those who will follow us". (Morris 1986: 198)

Middle-class reformers were joined in their campaigns by leaders of the male-dominated trade unions, and, by applying political pressure, mainly to the Liberal Party and later to the Labour Party, they were able to accomplish substantial reforms. By 1914, capital-intensive industrialization had made real headway in its struggle with labor intensive. Trade unionists' participation in these campaigns was seldom based on the calls to "national efficiency" that so appealed to the middle classes.

Trade unionists realized that large-scale British employers had huge sums invested in machines and plants and that, in these circumstances, the right to bargain depended on preventing surplus labor from flooding markets. No Marxists, many British trade unionists lived in fear of a reserve army of the proletariat.

An enduring theme of British trade union history in the nineteenth century was the movement's determination to place as many limitations on access to the labor market as possible. To this end, male British trade unionists supported the imposition of age and hour limits on child and female labor. They supported compulsory schooling, partly for its own sake and partly because it withdrew even more labor from the market (Griggs 1983: 25). They battled for a "family wage," again, both because they believed that adult male household heads should support families but also because, under some circumstances, this demand could be used to justify removing adult women from the job market. Campaigns against female and child labor came all the easier to trade unionists, because the wives and children of craftsmen and semiskilled workers had already dropped out of the work force as a result of rising male incomes or of declining demand. The Trades Union Council supported the basic principles of the 1905 Aliens Act, which limited the entry of foreign, mainly Jewish, labor from the continent (Gainer 1972). In 1909 they won the creation of Wage Boards, which set wages in specified underpaid occupations and were designed to set wage limits within sweated industries. In 1911 they achieved state-subsidized protection for workers against unemployment and accidents in the National Insurance Act, a conquest important in its own right but also insuring that the temporarily unemployed and the family members of injured or sick workers were not forced into an overstocked labor market.

As did capitalists and generals, workers and their middle-class allies used the empire for their own purposes. In order to restrict labor supply, just as they supported immigration restriction to Britain, British trade unionists defended the right of British laborers to emigrate. As in the modern period, the years after 1880 witnessed growing rounds of joblessness due to the decline of traditional staple industries, textiles and iron, while the unskilled workers that they released were unprepared to work in the newly developing industries in chemicals and steel.

Nineteenth-century English policymakers believed that emigration ensured that unemployment would be temporary. The pre-1914 United Kingdom was a nation of emigrants. Roughly 2.4 percent of the native English population (net of returns) emigrated in the 1860s and also in the 1870s, and emigration rose sharply in the economically troubled 1880s when 3.1

percent of the population left and did not return (Baines 1985: 88). Since migration was disproportionately concentrated among the young adult population, emigration could have provided an outlet for as much as 4 or 5 percent of the labor force in each decade. More important, however, for municipal welfare programs, was the changing composition of the emigrant population. For much of the first half of the nineteenth century, rural emigration, the departure of tenants and farm laborers, had dominated the migratory stream, but in the 1880s urban migrants began to swell the tide; in bad times, urban charitable societies and even local government encouraged emigration (Baines 1985; Erickson 1994: 87–125). The urban character of emigration increased in the immediate decades after 1900.

Before 1914, groups of worker-citizens in consolidated states restricted the actions of capital. While our example was British, related processes occurred in all consolidated states. The 1850–1914 global wave was ended by World War I. The war represented the triumph of the national rivalries that were the inevitable product of the association of capital accumulation and territoriality, yet at the same time it destroyed the international economy that these same forces had long sustained. In the postwar years, the onset of the Great Depression led many countries to impose extensive capital controls in an attempt to use monetary and fiscal policy to insulate themselves from deflation and depression. While both the nationalist hostilities inspired by the war and economic policies formulated during the depression help explain the triumph of protectionism, insufficient attention has been given to the drive against foreign migrant labor begun long before the onset of war and pursued by countries uninvolved in the conflict. The Aliens Act of 1905 was only a mild British instance of such legislation. The United States banned Chinese migration in 1882; the determination to keep Australia "white" was a driving force in the movement toward federation that culminated in 1901; and the cutting of subsidies to migration in Argentina, Brazil, and Canada were all part of the same response to immigration. Economic studies suggest that political pressures to protect labor markets were almost universal and that, without the pressure of world war or depression, immigrant restriction was imposed in the New World whenever the relative position of unskilled labor in the job hierarchy was seriously threatened by immigration (Timmer and Williamson 1997).

THE GLOBAL WAVE, 1950 TO THE PRESENT: THE DECLINE OF THE WESTPHALIAN STATE SYSTEM AND CIRCULATING CAPITAL

The distinctive elements of contemporary globalization are: (1) the erosion of the Westphalian state system; (2) the growing importance of circulating capital—capital advanced at the beginning of each production cycle, including wages, raw materials, and the cost of bringing commodities to market; and (3) the loosening of the bonds linking state and capital accumulation. The increasingly onerous burden of national welfare states and labor contracts and a lessened need for state protection were important factors in this reconfiguration of economic and social power.

The subordination of European nations to Russian and American superpowers after World War II marked the end of the Westphalian system, and the collapse of the Soviet Union in 1989 put the final nail in its coffin. After 1989, for the first time in a score of centuries, no credible military threat menaces the states of western or central Europe, either individually or collectively. The announced end of conscription in France (it has already been abolished in Belgium and is scheduled for abolition in Holland) concludes a long evolution in which European states have forsaken military options within Europe. Even a once proud military alliance has been turned to the purpose of promoting markets; while NATO's current military goals are murky, admission of Eastern European states depends upon their introducing market reforms. In the 1950s and 1960s, decolonization ended the direct political control of consolidated states over large portions of the world economy and their ability to use the colonies as labor drains, strategic bases, or protected markets.

While modern states have lost the dynamic impulse driving them forward in earlier periods, they have nevertheless demonstrated a keen instinct for survival; individual Western European states abandoned the attempt to serve (as before 1914) as the principal framework for capital accumulation but banded together to expand the territory in which capital could circulate. After World War II, European states found themselves balanced precariously between the United States and the USSR; given the blood tribute it had just exacted, assertions of nationalism were widely distrusted throughout Europe. Western European states survived by adhering to a common market that brought *les trente glorieuses*, the thirty years of economic growth after World War II. That portion of Europe rebuilt under American auspices first formed itself into the European Coal and Steel Community (ECSC) serving key interests in individual nations: for Belgian political leaders, it provided subsidies for inefficient coal producers; for frightened French businessmen, access to German coal resources and the deconcentration of the German steel industry; and for Germans, control over their natural resources. The ECSC was the precursor of the Common Market and the present European Union.

Economic growth within a Common Market went a far way in restoring the damaged authority of Western European states, but it also tied them to a transnational union that limited national sovereignty in important respects. The result was what Paul Kapteyn has called the creation of a "stateless market." He notes the irony that the European states' "fear of national weakness had driven them to form a single market, but the same fear kept them from creating a state to control this market, the dramatic consequence being that sovereignty came under threat from the very forces striving to defend it" (Kapteyn 1993).

In the contemporary global wave, autonomous international financial institutions have developed, underpinned by groups of powerful states that unchained circulating from fixed capital. The pre-World War I period witnessed the flourishing of many international organizations that provided vital services for international trade, including the Universal Postal Union (1874), International Bureau of Weights and Measures (1875), and the International Labor Office (1901) (Murphy 1994). But the distinctive characteristic of contemporary transnational organizations, whether cartels of creditors, such as the World Bank or the IMF, or trade organizations, such as the WTO (GATT), is that they possess autonomous decision-making powers in vital economic areas. Giovanni Arrighi has identified the penchant for creating independent international institutions of world government rather than national institutions such as the Bank of England or UK-centered commercial networks as one of the characteristics of American political hegemony. Arrighi is not necessarily wrong, but the extent to which the declining economic power of the United States and its failing financial contribution to such institutions will enable new economic powers to replace it in these arenas remains to be seen.

The role of circulating capital has also increased because of the growing financial costs of bringing to market products of a "new international division of labour" in which "commodity production is being split into fragments which can be assigned to whichever part of the world can provide the most profitable combination of capital and labour" (Frobel, Heinrichs, and Kreye 1979: 4). Today the fourfold geographical division of labor in the electronics industry is paradigmatic. First, highly innovative research and development centers are concentrated in a handful of high-tech areas, such as Paris-Sud, the London–M4 Corridor, and Silicon Valley. Second, skilled fabrication occurs in branch plants generally in newly industrializing areas of the home country. Third, semiskilled large-scale assembly is subcontracted to low wages areas of the world such as Southeast Asia where a former source of migrant labor has become the site of sweatshops. And finally, customization of devices occurs in regional centers throughout the world, usually in the area of major electronics markets (Castells 1996: 387).

The new division of labor is characterized as much by its flexibility as by its geographic dispersal, where "flexibility" describes efforts to convert fixed into circulating capital. The contrast with late nineteenth-century heavy industry is dramatic. Where heavy industry created full-time, career employment for males over the life cycle, flexible modern industry emphasizes part-time and temporary work, mainly for women and children but sometimes even for skilled professionals. Where heavy industry built huge factories, flexible industry leases buildings and computers. Where heavy industry produced large quantities for mass consumption, flexible industry focuses on niches, limited production, and rapid turnover. Where heavy industry was predominantly national, flexible industry is transnational. Professionals in computer science and skilled technicians form part of the highly paid components of the modern labor force, but so do experts in flexibility. These last are the labor force characteristic of a global economy of circulating capital, highly paid professionals in finance, real estate, insurance, advertising, and international law (Sassen 1991).

Currently there are over one hundred stock exchanges in the world, and the growth of private capital and transnational exchange flows signify that "all states taken together . . . have suffered a loss of power *vis-à-vis* the market." (Walter 1991: 233). Finance has become independent of heavy industry. By the mid-1980s the volume of cross-border lending by banks exceeded the volume of all the international trade of the combined market economies, suggesting the extent to which speculation and manipulation have become ends in themselves (Magdoff 1992: 18). The era of organized capitalism in which a few great banks coordinated national industries to create oligopolies has been superseded by an era in which transnational corporations draw on transnational financial institutions to compete on world markets; as Lash and Urry argue, the modern era is one of "disorganized capitalism" (Lash and Urry 1987). The growing integration of the world's stock exchanges has only increased the speed with which panic can spread from one market to another around the world. As capital's relations to consolidated states have weakened so have its concerns about maintaining the stability of national labor forces or of strong national polities. As it has become economically more competitive, capital has become more politically accommodating. Capitalist investors do not fear Communist China because they can so easily and quickly leave if that is required. China's cheap labor supply and national resources represent competitive factors too important to be neglected.

In the years after 1974 as the wages of less skilled workers, or, alternatively, unemployment have increased in Europe and the United States, pressure has grown for greater immigration restriction as well as a new sensitivity toward trade negotiations. The growth of anti-immigrant political movements, attacks on immigrants, and even the defeat of President Clinton's efforts to negotiate agreements to widen NAFTA are signs of an increasing turn toward protectionism among those sections of the population affected by the reduction of barriers against the movement of capital and labor. Desperate to retain their membership at a time when globalization is undermining it, many trade unions are joining the protectionist camp.

CONCLUSION

Today in many countries, historically centers of advanced industry, battles are occurring to protect social welfare regimes and systems of industrial relations established when heavy industry predominated and the consolidated state reigned supreme. Increasingly, the Left demands that the individual state assert the rights of citizens over transnational capital; the Right demands that the state expel migrant workers. In an age when capital can electronically flee continents in nanoseconds, can national states resist transnational markets? Despite the claims of distinguished scholars, most nations simply cannot (Boyer and Drache 1996). Nine of the fifteen members states of the European Union (EU) have less than eleven million inhabitants and depend heavily on transnational trade. The most dynamic economic powers of the current globalization, Germany and Japan, depend so greatly on export that their break with international markets seems improbable; in the case of small EU nations or in the case of Japan or Germany, defying foreign markets would mean a decline in national living standards. The United States, best suited to take such a stand, becomes more dependent on exports every year. Some scholars predict the emergence of triadic trade bloc groups around the United States, the EU, and Japan, but the politics of such blocs, including the presence of rivals and the risks of incorporating economically unstable partners, are all too apparent.

While consolidated states cannot be expected to relinquish their sovereignty willingly or gracefully, they are increasingly unable to provide for the security of their citizens, and new solutions must be found. Social movements of those threatened by market expansion are going to have to confront capital not only nationally but transnationally and to create or use supranational political frameworks to regulate supranational capital. Political structures, whether very large states, associations of states, or international organizations, are necessary to redistribute resources to correct the inequities of markets. Increasingly, the most pressing challenge in contemporary politics is to develop strategies that will substitute for failing consolidated states.

Such developments are unlikely to occur without the reconstitution of an international labor movement. Labor is the political movement with the oldest international traditions, and yet, in the contemporary world, labor remains chained to a consolidated state that capital is already abandoning. Increasingly, multinational corporations and international bankers are divesting themselves of national loyalties, and, to best foster the interests of the communities in which it is rooted, labor will have to follow in their footsteps. Unlike in the past, international labor movements cannot pursue national sectional interests within the framework of an international organization but must develop a real orientation toward international change. Such an international labor movement cannot adopt the Pollyannish perspective of the political economists that immigration or expanded foreign trade never hurts, but it must realize that, by opening markets and borders selectively to countries that pursue progressive, nonexploitative developmental policies, it is encouraging the growth of a workers' world (cf., DeMartino and Cullenberg 1994). Acknowledging that market expansion is necessary, labor must also call attention to the differential impact of market expansion on society. Those who suffer through no fault of their own from strategies that promote social growth are entitled to compensation from society.

In the late nineteenth century, states and capital were bound together and, in the end, international labor had to bend to their will and become national too. In the late twentieth century, states and capital are splitting apart, with capital becoming international. Labor now has greater incentive to become international than at any time in the past.

NOTES

1. Net capital outflows measured as a percentage of GNP were about twice as high in peak years from the leading capital exporters, the United Kingdom, France, Germany, and the Netherlands, as they were in peak years of the second period from major capital exporters Germany and Japan (IMF 1997b: 113).

2. Both Wood and Williamson agree that labor-saving technological changes and increased education have also increased wage differentials but argue that their effects have been exaggerated. For a forceful statement on the contemporary period, see Wood (1994). For an interchange among economists on his argument as well as his critique of the biases inherent in the Heckscher–Olin model see Wood (1995). On education in the earlier global wave, see O'Rourke and Williamson.

REFERENCES

Adas, Michael, ed. (1993). *Islamic and European Expansion: The Forging of a Global Orde*r. Philadelphia: Temple University Press.
Arrighi, Giovanni. (1993). The Three Hegemonies of Historical Capitalism. In Stephen Gill, ed. *Gramsci, Historical Materialism and International Relations*. Cambridge: Cambridge University Press.
Baines, Dudley. (1985). *Migration in a Mature Economy: Emigration and Internal*

Migration in England and Wales 1861–1900. Cambridge: Cambridge University Press.

Boyer, Robert, and Daniel Drache, eds. (1996). *States against Markets: The Limits of Globalization*. London: Routledge.

Castells, Manuel. (1996). *The Information Age: Economic, Society, and Culture: The Rise of the Network Society, vol. 1*. Oxford: Blackwell.

DeMartino, George, and Stephen Cullenberg. (1994). Beyond the Competitiveness Debate: An Internationalist Agenda. *Social Text* 41 (Winter): 11–39.

Dunning, John H. (1970). *Studies in International Investment*. London: George Allen & Unwin Ltd.

Erickson, Charlotte. (1994). Who Were the English and Scots Emigrants to the United States in the Late Nineteenth Century? In Charlotte Erickson, *Leaving England: Essays on British Emigration in the Nineteenth Century*. Ithaca, N.Y.: Cornell University Press: 87–125.

Franko, Lawrence S. (1976). *The European Multinationals: A Renewed Challenge to American and British Bib Business*. Stamford, Conn.: Greylocks.

Friedman, Jonathan. (1994). *Cultural Identity and Global Process*. London: Sage Publications.

Fröbel, Folker, Jurgen Heinrichs, and Otto Kreye, eds. (1979). *The New International Division of Labor: Structural Unemployment in Industrialized Countries and Industrialization in Developed Countries*. Cambridge: Cambridge University Press.

Gainer, Bernard. (1972). *The Alien Invasion: The Origin of the Aliens Act of 1905*. London: Heinemann.

Griggs, Clive. (1983). *The Trades Union Congress and The Struggle for Education, 1868–1925*. Sussex: Falmer Press.

Harvey, David. (1989). *The Condition of Postmodernity*. Oxford: Blackwell.

Headrick, Daniel R. (1988). *The Tentacles of Progress: Technology Transfer in the Age of Imperialism, 1850–1949*. Oxford: Oxford University Press.

International Monetary Fund (1997a). *World Economic Outlook, May 1997*. Washington, D.C.: IMF.

———. (1997b). Annex: Globalization in Historical Perspective. In International Monetary Fund. *World Economic Outlook, May 1997*. Washington, D.C.: IMF.

Kapteyn, Paul. (1993). *The Stateless Market: The European Dilemma of Integration and Civilization*. London: Routledge.

Lash, Scott, and John Urry. (1987). *The End of Organized Capitalism*. Madison: University of Wisconsin Press.

Magdoff, Harry. (1992). *Globalization: To What End?* New York: Monthly Review Press.

Miller, Rory. (1977a). British Firms and the Peruvian Government. In D.C.M. Platt, ed. *Business Imperialism, 1840–1930: An Inquiry Based on British Experience in Latin America*. Oxford: Clarendon Press: 371–95.

———. (1977b). British Railways and the Argentine Government. In D.C.M. Platt, ed. *Business Imperialism, 1840–1930: An Inquiry Based on British Experience in Latin America*. Oxford: Clarendon Press: 395–428.

Morawska, Ewa, and Willfried Spohn. (1997). Moving Europeans in the Globalizing World: Contemporary Migrations in a Historical Comparative Perspective (1955–1994 v. 1870–1914). In Wang Gungwu, ed. *Global History and Migrations*. Boulder, Colo.: Westview Press: 23–62.

Morris, Jenny. (1986). *Women Workers and the Sweated Trades: The Origins of Minimum Wage Legislation*. Aldershot: London.

Murphy, Craig N. (1994). *International Organization and Industrial Change: Global Governance since 1850*. New York: Oxford University Press.

Offer, Avner. (1993). The British Empire, 1870–1914: A Waste of Money? *Economic History Review* XLVI, no. 2: 215–38.

O'Rourke, Kevin H., and Jeffrey G. Williamson. (1995). *Around the European Periphery 1870–1913: Globalization, Schooling and Growth*. Working Paper 5392. Cambridge, Mass.: National Bureau of Economic Research.

Petrella, Riccardo. (1996). Globalization and Internationalization: The Dynamics of the Emerging World Order. In Robert Boyer and Daniel Drache, eds. *States against Markets: The Limits of Globalization*. London: Routledge: 62–83.

Sassen, Saskia. (1991). *The Global City; New York, London, Tokyo*. Princeton, N.J.: Princeton University Press.

Sills, Barry K., and Andre Gunder Frank. (1993).World System Cycles, Crises, and Hegemonic Shifts, 1700 BC to 1700 AD. In Andre Gunder Frank and Barry K. Gills, eds. *The World System: Five Hundred Years or Five Thousand?* London: Routledge.

Tilly, Charles. (1990). *Coercion, Capital and European States, AD 990–1990*. Oxford: Blackwell.

———. (1994). *Globalization Threatens Labor's Rights*. Working Paper No. 182. New York: New School for Social Research: Center for Studies of Social Change.

Timmer, Ashley S., and Jeffrey G. Williamson. (1997). *Racism, Xenophobia or Markets? The Political Economy of Immigration prior to the Thirties*. Working Paper 5687. Cambridge, Mass.: National Bureau of Economic Research.

Walter, Andrew. (1991). *World Power and World Money: The Role of Hegemony and International Monetary Order*. New York: St. Martin's.

Williamson, Jeffrey G. (1991). *Inequality, Poverty and History: The Kuznets Memorial Lectures in the Economic Growth Center, Yale University*. Oxford: Basil Blackwell.

———. (1995). The Evolution of Global Labor Markets since 1830: Background Evidence and Hypotheses. *Explorations in Economic History* 32 (1995): 141–96.

———. (1996). *Globalization and Inequality Then and Now: The Late Nineteenth and Late Twentieth Centuries Compared*. Working Paper 5491. Cambridge, Mass.: National Bureau of Economic Research.

Wood, Adrian. (1994). *North–South Trade Employment and Inequality: Changing Fortunes in a Skill-Driven World*. Oxford: Clarendon Press.

———. (1995). How Trade Hurt Unskilled Workers. *Journal of Economic Perspectives* 9, no. 3 (Summer): pp. 5–80.

5

Class Compromise, Globalization, and Technological Change

Erik Olin Wright

Two quite contrasting images come to mind when thinking about the concept of "class compromise." The first is of two armies of roughly similar force locked in battle. There exists a balance of terror, which generates a stalemate since neither army can completely vanquish the other (or, at least, the costs of defeating the enemy are so high that it is not worth it). In such a situation the contending forces may agree to a "compromise" in the sense of an agreement to refrain from mutual damage. I will refer to this as "negative class compromise."

The second image is of two contending forces, which, in spite of their conflicts of interest, discover specific situations in which both can gain from mutual cooperation. This is not simply a situation in which there is such a sufficient balance of power between contending classes that the outcome of conflicts falls somewhere in between a complete victory or a complete defeat for either party. Rather, this situation implies that there is a possibility of a non-zero-sum game between workers and capitalists in which both parties can improve their position through various forms of positive mutual cooperation rather than simply from refraining from hurting each other. I will refer to this as a "positive class compromise."

Of course, even if such a mutually beneficial quid pro quo is feasible, this does not mean that struggle disappears—even in a non-zero-sum game there may be conflict over how the mutual gains from cooperation are to be distributed. The "compromise" in class compromise can be more or less advantageous to one class or another. Nevertheless, such non-zero-sum contexts of struggle open up possibilities for genuine compromises between antagonistic classes, compromises in which the realization of the interests of the members of one class is to some extent facilitated, rather than hindered, by the realization of the interests of another.[1]

So long as one is stuck in the game of capitalism, positive class compromises will generally constitute the most advantageous context for the improvement of the material interests and life circumstances of workers and other popular social forces. If one is interested in advancing such interests, therefore, it is important to understand the conditions that facilitate or hinder the prospects for class compromise. In this chapter I will examine the ways in which the globalization of capital and contemporary patterns of technological change affect the prospects of this kind of positive class compromise. To do this I will begin by briefly presenting a more systematic, abstract characterization of the problem of positive class compromise. This will provide the theoretical tools we need to explore somewhat speculatively the possible effects of technological change and globalization.

AN ABSTRACT MODEL OF CLASS COMPROMISE

Class compromise can be understood as a specific relationship between the associational power of workers and the interests of capitalists.[2] Both Marxists and neoclassical economists tend to see this relationship as an inverse one: increases in the power of workers negatively affect the interests of capitalists. In contrast, I will propose that this relationship has a reverse-J shape as illustrated in figure 5.1: As the associational power of workers increases, the interests of capitalists initially decline, but after some intermediate level of power, further increases in workers' power can actually be beneficial to capitalists.

This reverse-J relation can be divided into two subcomponents as illustrated in figure 5.2: a downward sloping component, reflecting the ways in which capitalists' interests are hurt by increases in working-class power, and an upward sloping component, reflecting the ways in which increases in working-class power potentially benefit capitalists. In broad terms, the downward-sloping curve reflects the ways in which increasing associational power of workers undermines the capacity of capitalists to unilaterally make decisions and control resources of various sorts, while the upward-sloping curve reflects ways in which the associational power of workers may help capitalists solve certain kinds of collective action and coordination problems. It is the existence of this upward-sloping section of the curve that creates the possibility of positive class compromise.

These components can be further disaggregated in terms of the primary institutional sites of collective action within which associational power operates and interests are constituted: the sites of exchange, production, and politics. As illustrated in figure 5.3, there is a rough correspondence between different kinds of working-class collective organizations and each of these sites of class conflict and class compromise: Trade unions are the characteristic associational form for conflict/compromise in the sphere of

Figure 5.1 Curvilinear Relationship between Working-Class Associational Power and Capitalist Class Interests

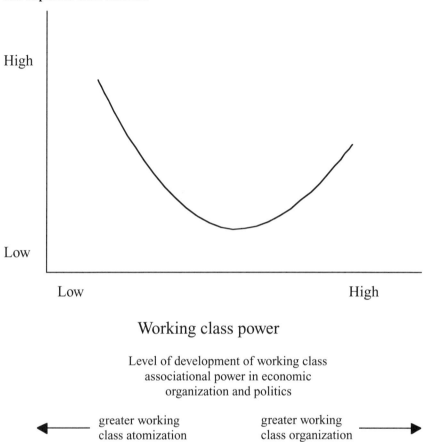

Working class power

Level of development of working class
associational power in economic
organization and politics

greater working
class atomization

greater working
class organization

exchange; works councils and related associations are the characteristic form within the sphere of production; and political parties are the characteristic form within the sphere of politics.[3] On the basis of the reasoning behind figure 5.2, increasing power of these forms of working-class association has both negative and positive effects on the material interests of capitalists. To give just one illustration here: Increasing working-class power in the form of unionization reduces the capacity of capitalists to fire labor at will and hire workers at the lowest possible wages (given market and technological constraints), but it may help solve problems in inadequate aggregate demand in consumer markets. Inadequate consumer demand represents a collective action problem for capitalists: capitalists simultaneously want to pay as low wages as possible to their own employees

Figure 5.2 Decomposition of the Relationship between Interests of Capitalists and Associational Power of Workers

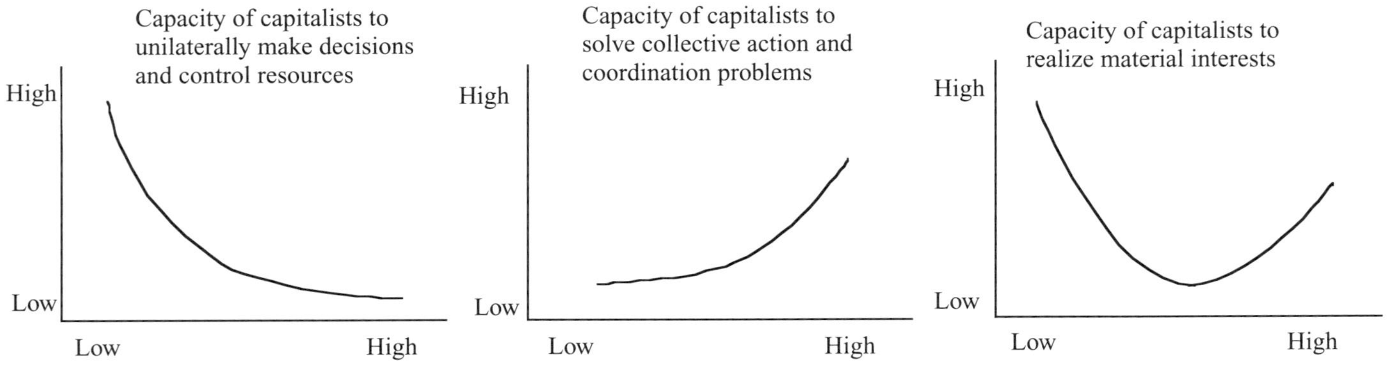
Capacity of capitalists to unilaterally make decisions and control resources
High
Low
Low
High
Capacity of capitalists to solve collective action and coordination problems
High
Low
Low
High
Capacity of capitalists to realize material interests
High
Low
Low
High

Figure 5.3   Decomposition of the Relation between Working-Class Power and Capitalist Class Interests in the Sphere of Politics, Exchange, and Production

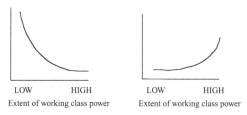

	Characteristic forms of working-class power	Capitalist class interests threatened by increasing working-class power	Capitalist class interests facilitated by increasing working-class power
Sphere of political interests	Political parties	Unilateral political influence over redistributive policies	Ability to sustain stable tripartite corporatist cooperation
Sphere of exchange	Trade unions	Unilateral ability to hire, fire, and make wage offers	Ability to restrain wages in tight labor markets; ability to sell what is produced (Keynesian effects)
Sphere of production	Work councils	Unilateral ability to control labor process and job structure	Ability to elicit complex forms of vertical and horizontal cooperation; cheaper solutions to information problems in production

and want other capitalists to pay as high wages as possible in order to generate adequate consumer demand for products. High levels of unionization, in effect, prevent individual firms from defecting from the cooperative solution to this dilemma. In conditions of tight labor markets, a strong labor movement may help capitalists to constrain wages, preventing them from rising more rapidly than productivity and thus creating inflationary pressures. Again, this is a collective action problem: individual capitalists will be tempted to defect from a wage restraint deal since offering higher wages will give them an advantage in attracting the best workers. Figure 5.3 summarizes the central ways in which variations in the power of working-class association positively and negatively affect the interests of capitalists in the spheres of exchange, production, and the state.

The graphs in figures 5.1–5.3 represent the theoretical range of possible values of working-class associational power, going from atomized, disorganized associational power to highly organized, classwide power. The historically variable institutional rules of the game under which working-class associational power is formed, however, may restrict this range to a greater or lesser extent. Electoral rules may make it very difficult for working-class parties to gain strength. Labor laws may make it difficult or easy for trade unions to grow. And laws regulating the rights of shareholders and boards of directors may make it easy or difficult for various types of works councils to gain real associational power. In any empirical investigation of class compromise, therefore, it is important to specify the region of the class compromise curves that can be described as historically excluded, as inaccessible strategically because of the nature of the institutional rules under which class conflict and class compromise take place. Of course, these rules of the game may themselves become objects of struggle and be transformed, but so long as they remain intact, they determine a more limited range of historical possibilities. Figure 5.4 illustrates such institutional exclusions for the United States and Sweden: Swedish social democracy creates a set of rules of the game in which the atomized region of the curve is largely excluded, while American liberal democracy excludes much of the positive, upward-sloping section of the curve.

TRANSFORMATIONS OF THE TERRAIN OF CLASS COMPROMISE

If the general model of class compromise we have been exploring is reasonably on target, then this suggests that the globalization of capitalism and technological changes can affect class compromise through three different routes:

(1) they can affect the basic shape of the curve;
(2) they can affect the institutional rules of the game that determine the range of institutional exclusions; and
(3) they can directly affect the associational power of workers within the strategically accessible range of possibilities.

The first of these involves the ways in which economic changes affect the functional relations depicted in figures 5.1–5.3; the second involves effects on the width of the institutional "zones of unattainability" in figure 5.4; and the third concerns the specific location within the strategic space allowed by these exclusions. Let us look at each of these in turn.

Effects on the Shape of the Curves

For purposes of understanding the changing conditions for class compromise, the critical part of the curve in figure 5.2 is the upward-sloping segment in which working-class associational power positively helps capitalists solve various kinds of collective action and coordination problems.[4] Figure 5.3 lists a range of interests of capitalists that are facilitated by increasing working-class associational power within the spheres of exchange, production, and politics. The question, then, is how globalization and technical change might affect the relationship between workers' power and capitalist interests within each of these three spheres. Figure 5.5 pres-

Figure 5.4   Working-Class Associational Power and Capitalist Interests in Liberal Democratic Capitalism (United States) and Social Democratic Capitalism (Sweden)

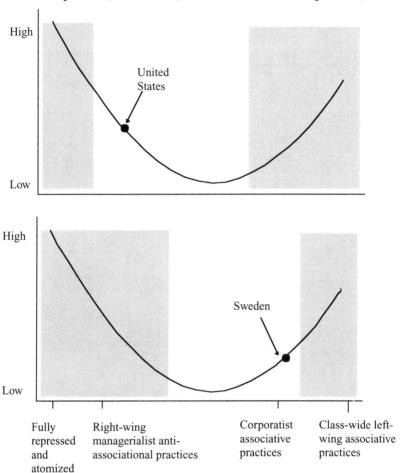

Fully repressed and atomized working class

Right-wing managerialist anti-associational practices

Corporatist associative practices

Class-wide left-wing associative practices

Degree of associational power in economic organization and politics

← greater working-class atomization   greater working-class organization →

Historically variable, institutionally excluded possibilities

Figure 5.5   Hypothesized Effects of Globalization and Technical Change on the Class Compromise Curves in the Spheres of Exchange, Production, and Politics

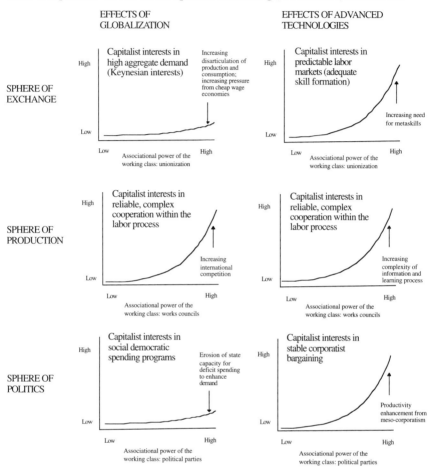

ents a set of tentative hypotheses concerning these effects. All of these hypothesized effects are highly speculative. My purpose here is less to present a well-worked-out argument for the patterns of change, than to offer some preliminary suggestions that may help to trigger a focussed discussion of the issues.

Effects of Globalization

Consider first the effects of globalization on the sphere of exchange (see the top left graph in figure 5.5). One of the standard arguments in discussions of globalization is that the increasing mobility of capital and globalization of markets has undermined the "Keynesian" solutions to macroeconomic problems in advanced capitalism. To the extent that the market for the commodities of capitalist firms is increasingly global, the realization of the economic value of those commodities depends less upon the purchasing power of workers in the countries within which those firms are located. This means that in a more deeply globalized capitalism there is a weaker positive effect on capitalist interests from high levels of unionization. While there may still be some positive value for capitalists of a strong labor movement in terms of predictable, well-ordered labor markets and possibilities of wage restraint when labor markets are tight, nevertheless, it seems that on balance globalization is likely to depress the positive slope of the curve in the upper left segment of figure 5.5.

Globalization may have quite different effects in the sphere of production. The characteristic form of working-class associational power within production are works councils. As already noted, strong works councils serve employer interests in a variety of ways: They may increase productivity through greater worker loyalty; they may help spot problems and improve quality control; and they may increase the willingness of workers to accept flexible job classifications and work assignments. Under conditions of the intensified competition that comes from increased globalization, the positive impact of each of these effects could be increased.[5] If increased competition reduces the room to maneuver for capitalists, and if there are significant untapped sources of productivity enhancement obtainable through enhanced cooperation at the point of production, then social arrangements that facilitate such cooperation—such as strong works councils—may have increasing value for capitalists.[6]

Perhaps the most commonly told story about the negative effects of globalization on the prospects of class compromise concerns the sphere of politics. Because of the heightened international mobility of capital, especially financial capital, the argument goes, the capacity of states to engage in deficit spending and other reflationary policies has eroded. One of the key ways in which a politically well-organized working class positively benefited capitalists in the past was by creating the conditions for expansive state spending programs. The reduced fiscal autonomy of the state resulting from increased globalization reduces the benefits from such policies, and thus reduces the positive slope of the class compromise curve in the sphere of politics.

Effects of Technological Change

The specific forms of technical change characteristic of the recent past may have quite different effects from globalization on the prospects for class compromise. If the arguments of theorists of "flexible specialization," "diversified quality production," "post-Fordism," and related concepts are correct, then technological changes over the past twenty years may have enlarged the scope for productivity gains obtainable by enhanced forms of cooperation between workers and managers, at least if capitalists embark on the so-called "high road" of technologically innovative systems of production and skill. If this is true, the upward-sloping portion of the class compromise curves may have moved higher.

The argument for these changes centers on transformations of the problem of skill formation, information coordination, problem solving, and adaptability under conditions of new information-processing technologies (especially as these occur within a highly competitive globalized capitalism). Various writers, among others Aoki, have argued that several things are required for firms to be able to sustain high economic performance under the conditions of these new technologies:

(1) The workers in firms need to have a high capacity for learning, problem solving, and information processing and an ability to rapidly adapt to new technologies. This means that the labor force must be characterized by "surplus skills" relative to statically defined production needs. This is required to allow for smooth and effective redeployments of labor in the face of rapid technical change. This requires a more or less continual process of skill formation and learning within production.

(2) Rigid divisions of labor and hyperspecialization need to be relaxed so that these surplus skills can flourish and be efficiently adapted to new demands under changing technical conditions of production.

(3) A fairly high level of trust is needed between labor and management so that flexibility inside of the production process can be cooperatively executed.

(4) A fairly high level of trust and cooperation is also needed between different units of production because of the complex networks of interdependency created under "flexible" conditions of production. It is not enough that workers have a capacity to solve problems and process information; they must have a willingness to cooperatively share this information across units of production.

(5) Both of these forms of trust—horizontal and vertical—are likely to be facilitated by arrangements that increase job security and thus lengthen the time horizons of the link between workers and firms.

Taken together these and other related conditions are at the core of what is often called "high road" capitalism: a capitalism that sustains for a relatively large proportion of the labor force high wages, high skills, technological advance, and reasonable job security. The question at hand then becomes whether the likelihood of creating and sustaining these conditions is enhanced or hindered by strong working-class associational power in the sphere of exchange (unions), the sphere of production (works councils), and the sphere of politics (parties).

One point is probably uncontroversial: the conditions for the productive reorganization of the labor process under diversified high-quality production are undermined by intermediate levels of working-class organization—associational practices that are continually adversarial because working-class associations are insufficiently strong to establish stable class compromises, but strong enough to keep trying. It is less clear, however, that a productivist class compromise is unobtainable under conditions of a highly atomized working class.

Two scenarios might make it possible to combine working-class atomization and sustained high performance: one depends upon fear and insecurity, the other on special cultural dispositions. Consider fear: atomized, disorganized workers might engage in the required cooperative high-performance practices if they were thoroughly convinced that a high level of enthusiastic cooperation with management was needed for the survival of the firms in which they worked and thus the protection of their jobs. Fear, rather than trust based on power, could perhaps be the glue of the needed cooperative practices. Or, alternatively, perhaps working-class associational weakness might somehow be accompanied by a set of cultural dispositions that would lead workers to enthusiastically cooperate with their employers, to trust their employers sufficiently to make the investment in surplus skills and accept reorganizations of the labor process in the direction of cooperative flexibility.

Neither of these scenarios seems very plausible. Fear may provide the basis for certain types of circumscribed cooperation, but not for the long-term acquisition of metaskills and the predictable cooperative sharing of information across productive units that requires trust that other actors will not act opportunistically. Culturally induced compliance also seems unlikely as a durable basis for cooperation in developed capitalist countries. Indeed, the tactics employers are likely to use to generate working-class weakness and atomization are also likely to generate a degree of cynicism among workers that itself undermines the very cultural dispositions that might otherwise facilitate productivist cooperation.

At least under the historical conditions of contemporary developed capitalist societies, therefore, a stable, productivist class compromise—a class compromise in the sphere of exchange to ensure the maintenance of a dynamic high-skill labor market and a compromise within production to ensure heightened vertical and horizontal cooperation—is likely to require fairly high levels of working-class associational power. Without such power workers are unlikely to have the level of trust and confidence in the long-term behavior of employers for the cooperation to be robust.[7] In game-theoretic terms, workers are unlikely to believe they can block employer opportunism unless they have some real capacity to sanction employer defections from cooperative arrangements. If this reasoning is correct, then, current economic transformations could potentially be strengthening the reverse-J curve in figure 5.2, making the upward-sloping part of the curve stronger than in previous periods in the spheres of production and exchange.[8]

It is somewhat less clear what the effect of technological change is on the shape of the class compromise curve in the sphere of politics. Traditionally, the positive effect for capitalists of strong working-class parties centered on the ways such parties facilitated the elaboration of centralized corporatist arrangements for collective bargaining and strong Keynesian state spending patterns. Some of the positive value of these institutions has been eroded by globalization as already noted. Technological change may also have weakened the utility of highly centralized forms of corporatism. If one of the concomitants of recent forms of technological change is increasing heterogeneity of the labor force both across sectors and across specific occupations, then highly centralized corporatist institutions may impede the kinds of coordination and bargaining that are most suited to enhancing productivity and capitalist interests.

On the other hand, new, much-less-centralized forms of corporatism may be increasingly important for the productive used of advanced technologies. For example, the design of effective institutions for lifelong learning and continual processes of skill (re)formation probably requires the joint inputs and coordination of state agencies, labor, and capital, and this suggests some kind of corporatist institution for working out details and forging trust and cooperation. These coordinating institutions are "corporatist" in that they are rooted in the functional representation of the key actors whose interests are at stake, but they are much more likely to be organized geographically at the local and regional level and to be differentiated to some extent along sectoral lines.[9]

While highly centralized, national forms of corporatism may have lost much of their value, these more decentralized and flexible forms of corporatism may have become increasingly useful. The question, then, is whether strong working-class political parties increase the feasibility of these sorts of arrangements. One can imagine "enlightened" capitalists trying to engineer these forms of meso-corporatism within a political context dominated by conservative, pro-business parties. Nevertheless, there are good reasons to suppose that the development and maintenance of such institutions, and above all their diffusion to the economy as a whole, would be enhanced by political parties with a strong base in the working class.

In particular, the willingness of capitalists to participate systematically in such institution building may depend upon the extent to which the low road option has been closed off. As long as the "low road" of low wages, de-skilling, and worker atomization is feasible, capitalist defections from meso-corporatist arrangements are always a temptation, and this in turn may reduce the confidence on the part of workers needed to make these institutions work most effectively. Closing off the low road option requires state interventions to raise the minimum wage to a living wage level, enforce laws on working conditions, impose constraints on factory closing, etc. Since capitalists in general want to keep their options open, it is unlikely that conservative political parties will aggressively pursue such state policies. For these reasons, working-class political strength is probably a necessary condition for enlarging and stabilizing the economic space of these kind of meso-corporatist arrangements.

If figure 5.5 accurately maps the six effects we have been discussing, then we can say the following about the overall effects of globalization and technical change on the conditions for class compromise:

(1) Globalization tends to shift the locus of class compromise toward the sphere of production, at least in the sense that the relative weight of the spheres of exchange and politics are likely to be reduced.
(2) Technological change is likely to enhance the positive effects of working-class associational power within all three spheres. The positive effects of working-class associational power on forms of cooperation and coordination between labor and capital within exchange (through the formation of metaskills), within production (through enhanced forms of cooperation over information flows and learning by doing), and within the state (through the elaboration of meso-corporatism) are all potentially enhanced by recent patterns of technological change.

Taken together, this implies that processes of class compromise within the sphere of production are likely to become increasingly central to the overall configuration of class compromise. This poses certain real dilemmas for the working class. The consumption-enhancing Keynesian mechanisms of class compromise within the sphere of exchange have an inherent macroeconomic character, which tends to spread benefits diffusely to the working class as a whole. This is particularly true when working-class associational power within politics leads to increases in the social wage rather than simply the wages of unionized workers. In contrast, production-based class compromises potentially have a more restricted scope in which the beneficial effects become contained within specific firms and sectors. Furthermore, under these technological conditions, class compromises within the sphere of exchange, by revolving around the provision of skilled-labor power, may deepen labor market divisions and exclusions rather than spread the benefits of class compromise. Productivist class compromises can thus have the effect of increasing tendencies toward economic dualism in which economic inequality between insiders and outsiders is intensified.[10] Under these conditions working-class associational power and class compromise within the political sphere become especially important. It is much more likely—if the analyses of this chapter are correct—that a production-rooted class compromise will generate benefits that diffuse throughout an economy if the political conditions for class compromise are secured through strong associational power of the working class.

Institutional Exclusions

If it is true that the globalization of capital, especially the high levels of easy international mobility of finance capital, has undermined the fiscal capacities of states to fund a generous social wage, then the institutional exclusions to the left of the trough in figure 5.1 are likely to become narrower. This, in turn, increases the incentive for the capitalist class to undermine the associational power of workers, since there is more room to move toward the peak of the capitalist utopia. The prospects of class compromise, therefore, may increasingly depend upon the way the institutional rules of the game facilitate or impede access to the upward-sloping region to the right of the trough. Specifically, in the American case, the legal rules that significantly impede union organizing and, especially, make it difficult to forge strong working-class associational practices within the sphere of production, and the political rules of the game that impede the formation of third parties can be seen as restricting the scope of potential class compromise.

The question then becomes whether the globalization of capitalism and technological change make it easier or harder to change the institutional restrictions on associational practices. I do not think there is a clear answer to this question. At the level of political debate, the forces of international competition, the global economy, and the new technical requirements of production can be enlisted both to support anti-associational laws as well as support labor law reform that would enhance the capacity for working-class organization. On the one hand, right-wing arguments about the need to eliminate government regulations and allow for a relatively unfettered market in order to compete internationally reinforces anti-associational biases. On the other hand, the arguments that high road, high performance economies require longer time horizons with durable forms of productivist cooperation suggests the need to open up more space for collective organization of employees in all spheres of social interaction. Opening up such space by changing the institutional exclusions, of course, does not in and of itself guarantee a move in the direction of more associational strength of workers, but it would improve the strategic setting in which struggles to accomplish this would take place.

The Prospects for Working-Class Associational Power within the Strategically Available Limits of Possibility

In contemporary American discussions of the choice between high road and low road capitalism—a capitalism centered on high wages, high skills, high innovation capacity, and high productivity versus a capitalism based on lower wages, declining skills, and stagnant productivity—it is often suggested that the main obstacle to the high road is capitalist myopia and ideological rigidity. Enlightenment thus seems to be the critical solution: if only capitalists would see the upward-sloping part of the curve, they would embrace it. If the class compromise curve was a full fledged J-curve rather than a reverse-J, then perhaps this would be the case. In J-curve capitalism, capitalists' own interests are best served by high levels of working-class associational power. In such a situation, when capitalists are on the downward-sloping part of the curve—the part to the left of the trough—they may not believe that the upward-sloping part of the curve even exists. Because of their limited vision, intensified by short time horizons of capital markets and pervasive intellectual confusion, capitalists may simply extrapolate in a linear manner from their immediate situation and assume that increasing working-class strength will only make things worse. If the true relationship between working-class power and capitalist interests was a strong J-curve, therefore, enlightenment of capitalists might be the key to movement in the direction of the high road.

On the other hand, if the relationship is a reverse-J, as I have argued in this chapter, then capitalist enlightenment is unlikely to do the trick, at least when the balance of power places working-class associational power in the downward-sloping part of the curve. In such a situation, even if globalization and technological change mean that capitalist interests would be furthered by the enhanced productivity of a production-centered class compromise, capitalists are generally likely to be hesitant to accept the level of working-class associational power needed to make such compromises durable. Since such associational power among workers within production inherently reduces capitalist autonomy, most capitalists most of the time will not voluntarily move to that part of the class compromise curve. The result is that, just as in the earlier era of the Keynesian class compromise within the sphere of exchange, a class compromise favorable for workers within the sphere of production is only likely as the outcome of struggle. It is not enough for capitalists to have an enlightened view of the tradeoffs they face in which they understand that the class compromise curve slopes upward with working-class associational power beyond a certain level. Enlightenment may help, but it needs to be backed by constraints, and this requires struggle.

How, then, do globalization and technological change affect the prospects for working-class struggles over associational power within the strategically accessible space of possibilities? It is hard to be optimistic. Broadly speaking, there are three effects of current economic transformations that potentially undermine the capacity of workers to struggle for enhanced associational power.

First, globalization is one aspect of a more general process of increasing marketization of social life that tends to increase heterogeneity within the labor force. The crucial dynamic here is not so much the global character of markets as such, but the increasingly pervasive and unfettered role of markets in organizing economic activities.[11] Markets are machines for accentuating inequalities. As the publicly imposed institutional constraints on the functioning of all sorts of markets—labor markets, capital markets, commodity markets, consumer markets, etcetera—has declined, economies have moved in the direction of winner-take-all lotteries, where small differences among competitors in a given market can produce huge differences in outcomes. As such differences accumulate over time, heterogeneity within markets increases. Within the labor market this is reflected in sharp rises in the levels of earnings inequalities both between occupational and educational strata and within those strata. Such heterogeneity and inequality, in turn, undermine the economic conditions for solidarity, thus making it harder to move to higher levels of working-class associational power.

Second, in combination with advanced forms of technological change, the increasing heterogeneity generated by heightened marketization has intensified tendencies toward a specific kind of dualism within developed economies in which some sectors of the labor force are in a position to forge productivist class compromises while others are not. Dualistic tendencies, of course, are not a new phenomenon. In the 1960s and 1970s there was much discussion of dual labor markets and the division between the "monopoly" and "competitive" sectors of the economy. The argument here is that the weakening of the possibilities for centralized class compromises through the state has lead to an intensification of the divisions connected to the new, technologically grounded dualism and reduced the scope for forging broader class alliances that would serve the material interests of workers in general.

Third, it is often argued that globalization increases the vulnerability of nearly all workers to job loss, either through the effects of intensified international competition or through the threat of capital mobility to low wage areas. Even if this threat is exaggerated and most job loss accompanying de-industrialization is the result of technological change rather than capital mobility, still it is the case that the belief by workers that their jobs are vulnerable because of the threat by capital to move jobs to low-wage regions undercuts their willingness to struggle for enhanced associational power. Taken together, the combination of increasing heterogeneity, deepening dualism, and decreasing job security reduces the capacity of workers to extend associational power even if the institutional exclusions were to open up new possibilities.

CONCLUSION

The core argument of this chapter can be summarized as follows. The conditions for class compromise are most favorable when the relationship between the material interests of capitalists and the associational power of workers is a reverse-J. In such conditions, while capitalists might still prefer an atomized and disorganized working class, they are more likely to accept high levels of working-class associational power. The actual capacity of workers to achieve a given level of associational power, however, depends also on the nature of the institutional rules of the game in which they mobilize. These can have the effect of truncating the reverse-J in such a way that the virtuous part of the curve becomes inaccessible, and thus class compromises favorable for workers become harder to achieve.

Current economic and political changes in advanced capitalist societies affect these relationships in a variety of complex and contradictory ways. On the one hand, globalization undermines the conditions for favorable class compromises within exchange and the state by reducing the potential Keynesian advantages to capitalists of a strong labor movement and extensive social democratic state spending. On the other hand, class compromises within production that enhance the capacity for lateral and vertical cooperation and flexibility are enhanced by the combination of technical innovations and intensified international competition. And class compromises within the spheres of exchange and the state that facilitate the productive deployment of these advanced technologies may also be strengthened, particularly if institutions of meso-corporatism are developed.

Added to these possible changes in the shape of the component class compromise curves, increased marketization (of which globalization is one dimension) appears both to have strengthened the political forces with interests in changing the institutional exclusions to make progressive class compromises more difficult, and (at the same time) to have undermined the willingness and capacity of workers to struggle for enhanced associational power within the limits of possibility strategically available.

It is commonplace these days for people on the Left to feel that the future is bleak, that the prospects for a stable, progressive class compromise are dim. If the arguments of this chapter are correct, then such pessimism really reflects only one side of a much more complex and contradictory set of processes. We live in a period where the conditions for traditional social democratic (or as others would say, "Fordist") forms of class compromise have indeed been eroding, but the potential viability of new forms of class compromise more deeply rooted in the sphere of production may have actually increased. Macro-corporatism was at the heart of advanced forms of traditional Keynesian politics of "effective demand," a politics that helped capitalists solve collective action problems around the macroeconomic demand for the products they produced. The development of new forms of meso-corporatist institutions constitutes what Joel Rogers has called the politics of "effective supply," a politics that enables capitalists to solve collective action problems in the provision of certain critical inputs into production. Technological changes have enhanced the potential benefits of such politics of effective supply, and at least within the sphere of production, the intensified competition generated by globalization may have also enhanced the potential willingness of capitalists to move toward the kinds of class compromise that make such solutions durable.

Yet, in spite of these emergent possibilities, in general the capitalist class and its political allies resist these options. Neoliberalism in its various forms remains the dominant discourse of public debate: the need for freer markets, the pathologies of state interventions, etc. Even in Europe where the old forms of class compromise had been institutionalized in the most progressive manner, there is little sympathy by capitalists for efforts at reconstructing class compromises around new forms of working-class associational power.

It thus remains the case, as in earlier eras of capitalism, that forging class compromises requires struggles. The relationship between working-class power and capitalist class interests remains a reverse-J relation, and capitalists will thus always be tempted, when historical opportunities occur, to try to move toward the capitalist utopia of weak working-class associational power. This option needs to be foreclosed in order for the new possibilities of productivist class compromises to become attractive to capitalists. Closing off this option requires state intervention, and this implies that removing the low road path of an atomized working class with relatively low wages and low skills ultimately depends upon the revitalization of a politically effective Left organized around an economic program of associational productivism.

NOTES

1. When positive class compromises occur, there will generally be aspects of negative class compromise present as well. In general, it is the costliness of pursuing a strategy of completely crushing an opponent that sets the stage for a search for arenas of mutual cooperation. This does not mean, however, that a rough balance of forces is a sufficient condition for positive class compromise. Opportuni-

ties for mutual gain may exist, but fail to be pursued because of mistrust, fear of opportunism, and other problems.

2. By "associational power" I mean power that is derived from the collective organization of workers into parties, unions, and other forms of association, rather than the power that is derived directly from their structural location in the economy.

3. This correspondence is only an "elective affinity." In particular, trade unions can be deeply and directly involved in both production and politics. When unions mobilize members to vote in electoral campaigns or when they use their resources to lobby politicians, they constitute a form of working-class associational power in the political sphere, whether or not they are closely aligned with a political party. Similarly, when unions bargain at the firm level over conditions within the labor process and play an active role in shop-floor governance through things like grievance committees, they constitute a form of associational power within production. For simplicity of exposition here I will generally assume the rough correspondence of types of association with spheres of social interaction, but the important theoretical issue is the arena within which associational power is formed and operates, not the specific form that such organizations take.

4. A fuller analysis would also consider the ways in which globalization and technical change might affect the shape of the downward-sloping segment. It could be the case, for example, that with certain technologies capitalists individually have little to gain from high levels of atomization of workers, and thus the downward-slopping curve rises less steeply to the left. Or, it could be the case that under conditions of globalization the labor market and organizational rigidities generated by even moderate working-class associational power could have a much sharper negative effect on the interests of individual capitalists, thus making the downward-sloping curve drop more sharply than in figure 5.3. I will not explore these possibilities here.

5. The extent to which the intensified competition of globalization has a positive effect on the class compromise curve may itself be a function of the technological conditions of production. Specifically, under technological conditions that foster weak interdependencies among workers within highly atomized labor processes, increased globalization may weaken the positive effects of workers associations within production. This suggests that there are probably strong interactive effects (rather than merely additive effects) of globalization and technological change on the conditions for class compromise.

6. Again, just to reiterate a point that has been made several times: work councils, like all forms of working-class associational power, also have negative effects on capitalist interests. Works councils impose various kinds of rigidities on employers that interfere with their capacity to unilaterally reorder production in the face of competitive pressures. The downward-sloping curve might therefore descend more precipitously under conditions of intensified global competition. The claim here, then, is not that the net effect of globalization is necessarily to enhance the value of institutions like works councils, but simply that the positive effects become stronger.

7. Arguments similar to these are developed at length in Aoki (1988). Aoki

argues persuasively for the Japanese case that the long-time horizons of the employment contract are crucial for the effectiveness of the more cooperative information and incentive systems in the core Japanese firms, and the stability of these long-time horizons depends significantly on working-class associational power within the enterprise. The pivot of Aoki's argument is the problem of developing within the employees of a firm (both workers and managers) high information-processing capacities and adaptive skill capacities, as well as a willingness of ordinary employees to use these capacities cooperatively. All of this requires long-time horizons, and this in turn requires significant associational power.

8. This does not mean, of course, that working-class associational power will automatically increase to take advantage of this part of the curve. Institutional exclusions may make this difficult, and in any case, capitalists may still prefer to be firmly located to the left of the trough. For all the talk of high-quality production and new forms of cooperative labor management relations, it may still be the case that the preferred option remains lower wages, unilateral control, atomized workers, and vertically imposed discipline. The sheer historical *availability* of the high road option in no way guarantees that employers will see this as their preferred strategy. The changing shape of the curve implies that the potentials for new arrangements may be changing, but this does not insure that such potentials will be realized.

9. For a discussion of the general theoretical foundations of this kind of meso-corporatism, see Cohen and Rogers (1995). These principles have been applied to an extremely interesting experiment in transforming the dynamics of labor markets in the metalworking industry in Wisconsin. The Wisconsin Regional Training Partnership (WRTP) was created in 1995 as a meso-corporatist institution, with participation of labor, capital, and the state, to try to upgrade the process of skill formation in a particular sector and transform the labor market processes that link individuals with these upgraded skills to jobs. For a discussion of this experiment, see Cohen and Rogers (1995: Rogers essay on WRTP).

10. It has often been noted that such dualism is a feature of the Japanese economy, where the lifetime employment of core workers participating in such productivist arrangements is complemented by a large number of temporary and part-time workers and workers in small firms that are largely excluded from the advantages of these forms of organization. Tendencies for such dualism also may be emerging in Germany, centering around access to the more desirable apprenticeship programs.

11. Increasing marketization is partially driven by the erosion of various forms of decommodification of labor in the form of social wages, job protections, and other forms of regulation, and partially by the intensification of competition for desirable jobs. Increasing marketization is not simply an economic phenomenon driven by economic dynamics; there is a crucial political component in the transformation of public policy around the regulation of various markets.

REFERENCES

Aoki, Masahiko. (1988). *Information, Incentives and Bargaining in the Japanese Firm.* Cambridge: Cambridge University Press.

Cohen, Joshua, and Joel Rogers. (1995). *Associations and Democracy.* London: Verso.

6

The Global Economy:
Myths or Reality?

Paul Hirst

Globalization has become the main concept in terms of which the destructive features of the modern economy are represented. It is widely accepted by academics, journalists, and politicians of all shades of opinion and in many countries that we now face the challenge of a truly globalized economy. Advanced industrial countries must respond to the intensified pressures of international competition or face relentless decline. Globalization has outlawed distinctive national strategies of macroeconomic management and social welfare. The scale of economic activity no longer corresponds to the territory of the nation-state; it is global and transnational.[1] National economies are now subsumed within supranational economic relations and processes, and they have little or no effect on global phenomena. This means that national governments have become glorified local authorities: their task is to provide those public services business wants, promote the competitiveness of local firms, and attract inward investment. Political agendas are now set by the big transnational corporations and the main international financial markets. Monetary policies that try to buck the market, high levels of direct taxation, extensive labor rights, and generous welfare payments are sure ways to render countries uncompetitive and unsuccessful. National government can act best by getting out of the way of business—by deregulating and by containing public spending.

But what if this view is wrong? If at least some nation-states are not as powerless as many politicians seem to believe? If the national economies of the advanced countries have not dissolved? If forms of supranational economic governance like the European Union (EU) do not weaken nation-states but strengthen them by extending collective control over key dimensions of economic activity? What if high levels of public spending

107

on infrastructure and on social welfare are essential underpinnings of prosperity? What if the very notion of globalization is naïve and a highly inaccurate picture of the international economy? It would then follow that in the belief that we are promoting national competitiveness, we adopt strategies based on the idea of globalization that may actually be undermining it. The rhetoric of globalization may destroy the political will to seek means to maintain output, employment, and social equity in the advanced industrial countries, to the detriment of their long-run economic performance.

In what follows I shall try to show that the picture of a recently developed and virtually ungovernable global economy based on supranational markets and footloose transnational companies is false. It will be claimed that, far from being truly global, the world economy remains dominated by the three major blocs of wealth and power, the Triad of Europe, Japan, and North America. Outside the Triad industrial growth and foreign direct investment flows are concentrated in a limited number of successful but relatively small developing countries, or in specific regions of larger countries, such as the coastal provinces of China. Together with the OECD countries, the elite of newly industrializing countries represent a small proportion of the world's population. It will also be claimed that few companies are truly transnational; rather, most are multinational and operate from a distinct base in one of the three blocs of the Triad. It will then be argued that we need to look skeptically at the huge sums that are traded daily on the world's financial markets, for they represent repeated dealing largely divorced from trade. Such financial flows do little to enhance real economic performance as represented by the production and exchange of goods and services. However, this very divorce of the markets from normal economic activity and the huge volumes traded have the potential for creating damaging instability. It is possible, however, that such markets could be made less volatile by concerted public governance on the part of the major powers.

GLOBALIZATION IS NOT NEW

If the word "globalization" were used to mean an ongoing process of the growth of international trade and investment, linking a growing number of countries in increasingly intense exchanges in an open world trading system, then there would be little that is exceptional or objectionable about it. Such a process has been going on, punctuated by the interruptions of severe economic crises and wars, for well over a century. But all too often, evidence of recent growth in international exchanges is used to justify the claim that the world economy has changed its nature. The strong version of the globalization thesis contends that national economies have simply been subsumed into world markets and that the power of such market forces either negates or renders unnecessary any possibility of effective public governance, whether by nation-states, international agreements, or supranational institutions. Thus one kind of evidence, of growing trade and investment between nations, is used to justify another kind of proposition entirely, that a timely transnational world economy has developed.

Since the early 1980s we have been in a new phase of rapid growth in world trade and spectacular growth in foreign direct investment. Everyone has shirts sewn in Manila or radios made in Thailand. Casual travelers are aware of the burgeoning construction boom transforming Asian cities like Jakarta or Kuala Lumpur with high-rise hotels and offices. Only a modern Rip van Winkle could be unaware that countries like South Korea, Taiwan, and Mexico have become major centers of manufacturing and successful exporters to the advanced countries.[2]

But such developments are not unprecedented. Since the modern international trading system developed in the second half of the nineteenth century, there have been three major phases of rapid growth in international trade and investment. The first phase was that of the Belle Epoque of 1870–1914, during which world trade and output grew steadily and in parallel at average annual rates of 3.5 percent and 3.45 percent respectively. By the late nineteenth century the whole world had become part of a developed and interconnected commercial civilization. Several of the major powers in 1913 had high trade to gross domestic product (GDP) ratios—France 35.4 percent, Germany 35.1 percent, and the United Kingdom 44.7 percent (Hirst and Thompson 1996b: 60). These ratios were either not exceeded until 1993 or were then still lower than in 1913. Capital export from the major developed economies of Europe like France and the United Kingdom, both direct and portfolio investment, reached levels relative to GDP still not exceeded today. Such export of capital helped to build the burgeoning "neo-Europes" of North America, Argentina, Australia, and South Africa. There were the Tiger economies of the Victorian era. The equivalents of Shanghai or Taipei were the explosively growing new cities like Chicago or Melbourne and rapidly expanding older foundations like Budapest, Barcelona, and Kiev.

The second major period of growth was the Great Boom that began after the Second World War and ended with the Organization of Petroleum Exporting Countries (OPEC)-induced oil price crisis of 1973. Between 1950 and 1973 world trade grew at an average annual rate of 9.4 percent, while output grew at 5.3 percent (Hirst and Thompson 1996a: 22). International trade thus grew far more rapidly than output, which was itself growing very rapidly by comparison with earlier periods. The figures for trade growth compare very favorably with those of the Belle Epoque and more than match those of the 1990s. During this period, under the Bretton Woods system of semifixed exchange rates the capital movements of most economies were strictly controlled. However, large-scale American investment and technology transfer diffused U.S. production methods and productivity levels to Europe and Japan, thus creating competition to American dominance in manufacturing. During the period several major economies enjoyed rates of growth in total factor productivity comparable to those of the Asian Tigers—for example, France at 3 percent (1950–73), Italy at 3.4 percent (1952–73), and Canada at 1.8 percent (1947–73) (Young 1994: 33).

The third period of expansion in the international economy began after the process of adjustment to the oil price shocks of 1973 and 1979. It was characterized by the liberalization of capital movements, the deregulation of the major national financial markets, and the adoption of floating exchange rates. Trade growth during this period was impressive (9 percent during 1983–90), but not greater than during the Great Boom (World Trade Organization 1995: 7). The development of rapidly growing industrial competitors like South Korea was marked, but not unusual—countries like Spain had developed from backwardness to industrial maturity in the 1950–73 period. Only those with memories and statistics that begin in the 1970s are surprised by the rapid trade growth, the emergence of new industrial powers, and the internationalization of production in the last two decades.

It should be noted that the growth in international trade and investment in the two earlier periods were not perceived as undermining the nation-state. Indeed, many modern nation-states were forged during the Belle Epoque and sustained by rapid industrial growth. Before the First World War states like Germany, Japan, and the United States sought to accelerate domestic industrial production with either active state involvement and/or tariff barriers. Countries like Germany and the United Kingdom developed systems of social insurance during this period; a rapidly internationalizing economy was not perceived as a constraint to social welfare spending.

The system of rapidly expanding trade before the First World War was made possible by a structure of international governance underwritten by the United Kingdom. It was the principal guarantor of the gold standard international monetary system, and its financial institutions, insurance companies, and merchant marines dominated world commerce. The United Kingdom was willing to pursue a policy of free trade while tolerating protectionism on the part of some of its major competitors or trading partners. Effective national policies thus had an international foundation, and even the United Kingdom was bound by the rules of the system it guaranteed.

In the post-1945 period the United States performed a similar role to that of the United Kingdom previously in creating, sustaining, and underwriting the costs of the system of international institutions that promoted monetary stability, trade openness, and growth. The period from 1950 to 1973 is the supposed heyday of autonomy in national economic policy and of Keynesian demand management. Yet such "national" policies were only possible because of and within the constraints of an effective system of supranational economic governance. The constraints, moreover, were real and often as restrictive as is the unregulated financial power of the markets today. The United Kingdom, for example, labored throughout the 1950s and 1960s under a severe balance of payments constraint that tended to cut off economic growth as the economy sucked in imports and required restrictive policies to restore external balance.

The autonomy of nation-states in the past was thus less complete and more dependent on international institutions than those who talk down the capacities of the state today suppose. Even in the post-1979 period, although there is less of a coherent architecture of institutions of international economic governance than in either the Pax Britannica or the Pax Americana, a degree of regulation has served to prevent the world trading system from being undermined by excessive volatility in the markets and to promote free trade.

The floating of exchange rates and the liberalization of capital movements led to a period of intense and destabilizing volatility in the major currencies in the early 1980s. But this free-floating period and the major imbalances between currencies it created was checked to a degree by the action of the G7 (United States, Canada, United Kingdom, Germany, France, Italy, and Japan) in the Plaza and Louvre Accords of 1985 and 1987 (Hirst and Thompson 1996a: 32–33). Since the early 1980s there has been a measure of re-regulation of the banking system and the growth of coordination between central bankers (Hirst and Thompson 1996a: 129–36). The growth of trade blocs like the EU and NAFTA (North American Free Trade Agreement) has promoted the regionalization of trade regulation, even as the new GATT (General Agreement on Tariffs and Trade) treaty and the creation of the World Trade Organization (WTO) have shown concerted interstate action to extend the scale and scope of trade liberalization measures. The world economy may be far from adequately governed; there is no hegemonic power to bear the costs of sustaining the system of international institutions, but it is minimally governed, principally by the actions of the major economic powers of the G7 and the international institutions dominated by them like the IMF (International Monetary Fund). So far this minimal governance has prevented meltdown and managed to avoid the growth-killing consequences of excessive volatility and uncertainty. How well it will respond to the crisis in Asia remains to be seen. So far the IMF seems set to repeat the errors of international policy toward Latin American debt in the 1980s, dealing with short-term debt and liquidity problems in a way that is likely to damage economic performance and, therefore, the ability to service the debt.

It may be that the various efforts at institution building like the WTO, the move to European Monetary Union, and the attempts to talk-up a new Bretton Woods-style system of managed exchange rates are all merely efforts to restore the past, to find new versions of the managed multilateralism of the post-1945 period. It might be contended in contrast that we are in fact in a period not unlike that of 1918–29, when the old powers like the United Kingdom sought unsuccessfully to reinvent the pre-1914 system. The United Kingdom returned to the gold standard in 1926, only to see the remains of the old world order destroyed in the Great Crash. Some influential commentators, like George Soros, think that the present international economic system is highly unstable and that it has within it the makings of another catastrophe like 1929 (George Soros, "The Capitalist Threat," *Atlantic Monthly* February 1997, pp. 45–58). The crisis that began in spring 1997 in the newly industrializing countries of south and east Asia strengthens this view.

In fact the most likely response to such a crisis would be to strengthen the tendencies toward the formation of economic blocs like the EU and to promote defensive competition in trade policy between them. The fact that the three blocs dominate trade and world GDP make this a distinct possibility in these circumstances. Each of the three major blocs exports about 10–11 percent of its GDP on 1993 figures and thus could easily give preference to domestic markets (Krugman 1994: 28–44). At present free trade, and the benefits it brings to domestic growth, remains the dominant orthodoxy among decision makers in the Triad. Yet promoting free trade may require greater active management of the world financial markets and of the flows of foreign direct investment (FDI) by the major powers. Free trade requires a measure of exchange rate and financial market stability, not just measures to promote market openness. Moreover, as we shall see, the concentration of FDI threatens to limit trade growth by excluding about 70 percent of the world's population. The major obstacle to such management is not ungovernable markets or the mismatch between economic relations and state territories, but very real and rather old fashioned differences of national interest between the great powers, the United States and Japan in particular.

The use of an historical perspective may lead us to realize that present developments have previous analogues, and that they are part of a series of changing conjunctures in the international economy since the 1870s. It also highlights the close interdependence between the effectiveness of the economic governance by nation-states and the international institutions that have given to such national policies their scope for action. It also reminds us that the internationalization of trade and investment is only one side of the story, that the world economy has been subject to major crises brought on by wars, the impact of trade cartels like OPEC, and the effects of weakly regulated markets (the 1929 crash). Nation-states have caused a great deal of turbulence by seeking the wrong kind of economic autonomy (autarchy) and thus prevented recovery by persisting in protectionist measures (as in the 1930s). States have thus been as influential in determining these conjunctures as have markets—long periods of growth in world trade have suddenly ended in turbulence (in 1914 and 1973). We should not be complacent, therefore, that states have lost the power to disrupt markets or that markets, left unregulated, will promote sustained growth in trade. To do so is to believe that present trends will continue indefinitely, that the world economy is an efficient self-governing system. Neither belief is justified, and supporters of an open world trading system need, somewhat paradoxically, to protect it with appropriate public institutions.

FOREIGN DIRECT INVESTMENT AND TRANSNATIONAL COMPANIES

One response to the forgoing is to say that even if the figures for trade are correct they are misleading; direct merchandise trade has become less salient since the new mobility of capital made possible by the widespread relaxation of exchange controls in the early 1980s. Foreign direct investment is an effective substitute for trade, indeed, in marketed services it is often the only way that such products can be traded internationally. Trade continues to grow more rapidly than output, but in the period 1983–90 foreign direct investment grew at over three times the rate of trade—34 percent average annual rate (Hirst and Thompson 1996c: 52). There has been a surge in foreign investment since the mid-1980s in a number of key developing countries: China, Malaysia, Mexico, Thailand, and Singapore in particular.

This may, it could be argued, explain why many developed countries have become apparently less open; since the early 1980s increasingly the localization of production through investment has replaced trade.

However FDI, important as it is, continues to circulate between the three main blocs of the Triad, the great bulk of FDI is exchanged between the rich nations. In 1981–90, 75 percent of investment flows were accounted for by the United States and Canada, the EU and EFTA (European Free Trade Association), and Japan—representing 14 percent of the world's population in 1990. If one added to this figure the nine most important developing country recipients of FDI and the eight coastal provinces of China plus Beijing then they represented another 14 percent of the world's

Table 6.1   Exports and Imports[a]

	1972	1982	1992
United States	12	19	22
Japan	19	28	17
EU 12	16	23	19
OECD[b] average			
(excluding Turkey)	40	52	48

Source: adapted from Thompson 1997, table 2.
[a]Expressed as a percentage of GDP.
[b]Organization for Economic Cooperation and Development.

population and took 16.5 percent of FDI in the same period. Thus over 90 percent of FDI was confined to just over a quarter of the world's population (Hirst and Thompson 1996a: 68).

Investment in the developing countries is not stripping the industrialized world of its capital—Paul Krugman, in a trenchant criticism of the notion of capital flight to the Third World and consequent massive job losses in the industrialized countries, pointed out that the apparently huge sum of $100 billion invested in newly industrializing countries in 1993 represented just 3 percent of investment in the industrialized Triad countries (Krugman 1996: 63). FDI thus does not alter the facts of a highly concentrated world economy centered on the three main blocs. Moreover, the blocs are centered on two nation states, Japan and the United States, and on the EU as a supranational institution of economic governance. Economy and state territory are much less out of kilter than the most enthusiastic globalizers claim. FDI could be regulated if the powers of the Triad could agree on goals and methods. FDI needs to be regulated. The distribution of the world's income is so unequal and development so concentrated in a few key states like Malaysia, that most of Africa, much of Latin America, and a good deal of South Asia remain poor and are increasingly excluded from the integrated international economy.

Some effort has to be made to boost private investment to poorer countries, rather than leave them dependent on foreign aid. One possible method would be to level a tariff on FDI flows within the Triad or to establish a common regime of tax concessions to companies from OECD countries that invest in an agreed schedule in the poorest nations. This would create a fund for investment in the poorest regions. The present danger of unregulated capital markets for developing countries is clear; countries like Thailand and Indonesia have received unsustainable flows of investment leading to overheating, bad investments, liquidity problems, and then capital flight. Markets in these circumstances seem more self-defeating than self-regulating. The longer-run danger of such "free" capital markets is that many other countries, like most of southern Africa and parts of south Asia are simply not on the map in major corporate boardrooms ("The Asian Miracle: Is It Over?" *The Economist* 1 March 1997, pp. 23–25; Frances Williams, "Asian Tigers Lose Their Bite as Exports Slump," *Financial Times*, 11 April 1997). Thus the current free flows of capital result in either unhealthy excess investment or a crippling dearth of capital in the developing countries.

Some commentators, like Susan Strange (1996), argue that a key aspect of globalization involves neither trade nor investment; it is the adoption of common practices and standards. This is facilitated by multinational companies operating in several countries making global strategic decisions and then acting locally. No transactions take place, but decisions and activities are internationalized. This is facilitated by the convergence of accounting standards, commercial law, and intellectual property rights and by the dominance of the big Anglo-American accountancy and commercial law firms.

There is some truth in this. Multinational companies do raise capital locally and use retained profits. Some companies, particularly in the service sector, work by selling franchises to local agents. Nevertheless, the stock of assets a firm holds in given countries and the key locations of its sales do matter. Firms are overwhelmingly multinational, not transnational, that is, they have a major home base in one of the Triad countries and subsidiaries and affiliates outside. They are not custodians of footloose capital but are rooted in a major market in one of the three most prosperous regions of the globe. This means that they have an interest in the prosperity of their main base and that they can be subject to regulation within it. Firms can, for example, only stage an "auction" on sweeteners from public bodies, wages, and working conditions between different countries if states and local authorities let them. Agreeing, for example, on common conditions for local development assistance in the EU, preventing competitive bidding by public bodies for firms to locate or invest, would probably reduce the overall level of public subsidy to firms and achieve the same result in development terms. Provided that public policies promote growth and are not merely punitive, then companies are unlikely to desert their main bases.

As the following tables show, most companies have an average of about two-thirds of their sales and a higher proportion of their assets in a major region like North America or Europe. These figures come from surveys that are limited in scope, and the data are far from perfect, but different sources show a similar pattern.

Not only are multinational companies de facto located in particular major industrialized countries, they actually benefit from such locations. In key U.S. export sectors—entertainment products, civil aircraft, pharma-

Table 6.2   Percentage Distribution of Multinational Corporations' Sales to Home Country/Region 1987, 1990, and 1993

	Manufacturing Services				
	1987	*1990*	*1993*	*1987*	*1993*
Canada	na	74	na	na	na
Germany	72	75	75	na	na
Japan	64	65	75	89	77
United Kingdom	66	59	65	74	77
United States	70	63	67	93	79

Source: Hirst and Thompson 1996: 96, table 4.1 (modified).

ceuticals and biotechnology, customized information technology—companies benefit from government research and development assistance, standard setting by public agencies like the FAA (Federal Aviation Administration) and FDA (Food and Drug Administration), the protection of commercial law regarding patents and trade markets, and being in key districts like Hollywood or Silicon Valley where major industries are clustered. Most major firms' senior management remain distinctly national and benefit from common understandings deriving from a similar education and participation in a national business culture.

A rootless transnational corporation would be a vulnerable entity, and it would enjoy none of the advantages of a domestic base and would have to rely solely on market performance. Many major companies have suffered difficulties, particularly during the crisis of the 1970s, and as Winfried Ruigrok points out, among the top 100 companies in the 1993 Fortune Global 500 list "virtually all appeared to have sought and gained from industrial and/or trade policies at some point. At least 20 companies . . . would not have survived . . . if they had not been saved by their governments" (Winfried Ruigrok, "Why Nationality Is Still Important," *Finan-*

Table 6.3   Percentage Distribution of Multinational Corporations' Assets to Home Country/Region 1987, 1990, and 1993

	Manufacturing Services				
	1987	*1990*	*1993*	*1987*	*1993*
Canada	na	74	na	na	na
Japan	na	na	97	77	92
United Kingdom	52	48	62	na	69
United States	67	66	73	81	77

Source: Hirst and Thompson 1996: 96, table 4.2 (modified).

cial Times, 1996). The multinational company makes good business sense; it enjoys the advantage of a solid core business in a major region of the wealthy industrial world; and it enjoys the benefit of trade and production through subsidiaries and affiliates outside the home territory. Multinational firms were responsible for about 40 percent of world output in 1990, but the share of their subsidiaries and affiliates abroad was only 7 percent, confirming the dominance of the home base (Lipsey, Blomström, and Ramstetter 1995).

ARE THE FINANCIAL MARKETS UNGOVERNABLE?

Until the liberalization of capital movements in the early 1980s governments retained a real power over the financial markets, and exchange controls limited external dealing mainly to the facilitation of trade and long-term investment. Now the daily volume of trading on the global markets exceeds $1 trillion—dwarfing the exports of the OECD countries and their daily equivalent GDP (about $40 billion) ("Survey: The World Economy," *The Economist* 7 October 1995, p. 6). In the early 1980s the reserves of the industrialized countries still exceeded the volume of daily foreign exchange dealing, but by 1995 they were less than half that volume ("Survey," p. 34). Moreover, in 1994 the total principal outstanding on trading in financial derivatives came to $20 trillion—greater than the combined GDP of North America, Western Europe, and Japan in 1993 ("Survey," p. 16).

This is generally taken to mean that central banks can no longer dictate exchange rates and control the foreign exchange markets, that interest rates and levels of inflation cannot diverge greatly from those deemed appropriate by the markets, and that states are no longer privileged borrowers in domestic capital markets, but are viewed in the same way as municipalities and companies by global markets in terms of their ability to service debt. Hence autonomy in macroeconomic policy seems to have been lost, and states can no longer control key economic variables. In some ways it might appear we are back to the world before 1914, but without a stable monetary system like the gold standard and without the international labor mobility of the earlier period to cushion economics against external shocks.

However, the picture looks a good deal more complicated when one asks to what end would states now try to manipulate the markets. Black Wednesday, when the United Kingdom was forced to leave the Exchange Rate Mechanism (ERM) by an uncontrollable wave of selling, is often cited to indicate the new powerlessness of governments. States can no longer directly change prices in the key financial markets, and the markets can place sanctions upon national polices of which they disapprove. Equally, one could respond that states have never been able in the long-run to defend exchange rates that are unsupported by real economic performance—remember Britain's devaluation in 1966 under the Bretton Woods system and that in the case of Black Wednesday the markets took two years to react to the obvious fact of a damagingly overvalued exchange rate. The United Kingdom entered in 1990 at an unsustainable target rate of 2.95 DM, when British inflation was roughly three times that of Germany. Thus the British ERM crisis is hardly a demonstration that effective public policies are impossible, since the policy in question was pursued in a stupid manner and the markets only moved once it was clear a devaluation was unavoidable. Public intervention in a crisis tends to work only if the markets want it, thus the IMF bailouts of Mexico and South Korea have been supported by foreign investors eager to secure their loans.

Equally, the failure of the first Mitterrand government has been taken to show that Keynesian expansionary policies of a radical kind are impossible. But the key questions are whether such policies can ever be effective outside a very specific conjuncture, whether they exhaust the scope for effective state action, and whether their failure is due to globalization. Keynes after all was neither in favor of reckless public borrowing nor unaware of the dangers of inflation.

Very high levels of public debt to GDP to finance government spending are ultimately unsustainable unless borrowing dramatically boosts growth. But this is now difficult to achieve; employment and output are far stickier than they were in the 1930s when significant surplus capacity remained idle and prices were falling. Boosting demand will most probably lead to accelerating imports rather than a dramatic rise in domestic production. Additional jobs and output now require significant investment and are unlikely to come on strong before a policy-induced stimulus to demand has been sourced by foreign importers. National Keynesian policies of a radical kind thus cannot be followed. The reason has less to do with the growth of global markets than with structural changes in the advanced economies that weaken the employment-generating effects of a stimulus to demand. If that is so, borrowing to sustain current expenditure on a large scale and for prolonged periods is clearly foolish, as it results in an accelerating proportion of public revenue supporting interest payments and drives up the cost of public borrowing as the state becomes more indebted.

But this does not mean states have to pursue similar policies in public expenditure, cutting to the lowest level acceptable to integrated financial markets across the globe. At the same time as world capital markets have internationalized and integrated there has been a general tendency for public expenditure to rise in the advanced world. Germany's total government expenditure rose from 32.5 percent of GDP in 1960 to 49 percent in 1995.

Yet surprisingly Japan's rose by a greater proportion but from a lower base, from 19.4 percent of GDP in 1970 to 34.9 percent in 1995 (Hirst and Thompson 1996c: 61). This is not primarily because of rising unemployment or welfare spending, which would hardly apply in the case of Japan, and between 1980 and 1990 expenditure on social protection in most of the OECD countries was relatively flat (Hirst and Thompson 1996c: 63; OECD 1994: 151). Provided a country chooses to fund current public expenditure from taxation, and the internationally traded sector of the economy remains competitive, it can sustain high levels of public provision of services and of welfare. Public policy still has a measure of autonomy, provided electorates are willing to pay the price and see the benefits of spending on infrastructure, training, and welfare. Levels of public expenditure to GDP vary across the advanced world very considerably and reflect national policy choices. In the United States public spending is 33 percent of GDP while in Sweden it is 68 percent, and those variations are not diminishing. As the *Economist* noted: " 'Wrong' hardly does justice to the claim that market forces have pushed governments into dull conformity on economic policy: the idea is ridiculous" ("The Myth of the Powerless State," *The Economist* 7 October 1995, p. 15). Moreover, high levels of public spending to GDP are not invariably evidence of economic failure and rising unemployment, for example, whilst public expenditure in Denmark remains high at 59 percent of GDP, unemployment has fallen substantially recently and external balances remain satisfactory.

Financial institutions remain key sources of investment funds for the markets. Modern capitalism is simply too big to be based on the investments of wealthy rentiers, as it is driven by the savings and provisions for the future of the broad middle classes. As table 6.4 shows there are marked differences both in the percentage of GDP devoted to pension fund assets, reflecting the balance between public and private provision, and the degree of internationalization of the assets held.

The contrast between Hong Kong and Singapore is remarkable and reflects differences in public policy. Capital markets can be limited to some extent by regulations and by tax breaks favoring domestic investment by pension funds and life insurance funds. The scope for public policy operating to localize trading by the major financial institutions is considerable, if that were seen as a desirable objective.

The huge volumes traded daily on the financial markets and the huge positions built up in the derivatives markets appear to dwarf and dominate the real economy, but one must remember what these vast sums are actually composed of. The main players are financial institutions that utilize the assets they can raise in national markets for financial products and their ability to borrow on the strength of these assets, repeatedly to "churn" large sums through the various international financial markets. Their trad-

Table 6.4   Internationalization of Pension Fund Investments

	Stock of Assets End of ($ billion)	*Percentage of GDP 1993*	*Percent International Assets (Bonds and Equities 1993)*
United States	2908.0	45.5	4
Japan	1752.7	44.6	14
Germany	254.2	13.3	3
United Kingdom	726.4	69.6	27
France (end of 1991)	199.7	15.5	5
Canada (end of 1991)	162.3	28.2	9
Hong Kong	—	—	60
Singapore	—	—	0

Source: HM Treasury 1996: tables A2.1 and A2.3.

ers either earn small margins by exploiting small and temporary imperfections between the different world market centers, or they establish positions on future market movements, suitably hedged to minimize risk if they are careful. When a given cycle of trading ends, the borrowed sums are met by market outcomes if trading has been successful, and assets are redeployed. Typically the percentage return on such vast sums is quite modest, although the profits from repeated churning can be large in total.

Institutions have to use these earnings to meet their obligations to depositors, to pensioners, and to life insurance policyholders. International trading thus recycles a substantial portion of its output back into the domestic financial system. Ultimately most of the capital used in these markets is not free-floating, but depends on national capital markets and must be returned into them. This does not mean that the international markets are unproblematic or that they can be easily controlled. People buy financial products like pensions or life insurance policies to guard against personal risks, often completely unaware that they are fuelling a very risky system of financial dealing. The international financial markets add little to real long-term economic performance, which is determined by domestic saving, productivity growth, and trade. Yet they have the ability to distribute short-term shocks around the system, and the potential—especially considering the vast obligations in the derivatives market—to produce dangerous instability. The case for regulation and stabilization is a strong one, but it will only work if the major states impose common rules on the system. The Barings and Sumitomo scandals show the dangers of failure in a fragile and interdependent system.

One solution advanced by James Tobin is to impose a small turnover tax on short-term financial movements, about 0.5 percent (James Tobin,

"Spectator's Tax," *New Economy* 1994, pp. 104–9). This would not deter the financing of trade or direct investment, but it would reduce the viability of repeated churning. Equally important are widely scouted proposals to reduce the dangers of the derivatives markets both by strengthening external regulation and the procedures within institutions: to restrict the risky over-the-counter trade, to limit market participants to banks, and to oblige players to hold substantial deposits against their positions.

At present such proposals are unlikely to be adopted, but another serious crisis may scare even conservative bankers enough to see that they are incurring incalculable and controllable risks, and it might just be possible to get the major states to coordinate regulation in that case. Increasingly effective public action to control the economy needs to be coordinated between states and, as in the case of trade openness or common economic standards, overseen or implemented by supranational bodies like the EU or the WTO. Such concerted action does not weaken states, rather, it strengthens them by stabilizing the external economic environment and giving them greater scope to pursue national policies, if national elites and electorates are willing. Times have changed, but it would be foolish to talk down the scope of national policy now, particularly by overemphasizing the policy autonomy and stand-alone economic sovereignty of states before the 1970s. As has been pointed out, at its heyday national economic management depended both on a specific economic conjuncture (rapid growth in all the major industrial economics) and on an appropriate structure of international institutions.

The current danger is that the belief that the global economy is ungovernable will induce fatalism and a bowing to the nostrums of the international financial markets and the wealthy national elites. The danger of current policies is that they favor the wealthy in the advanced countries over the broad middle-class mass and that they favor the OECD and a small number of successful developing countries over the mass of the poor of Africa, Latin America, and South Asia. Inequality limits demand and, therefore, growth, by putting structural limits to effective demand. If present attitudes among Anglo-Saxon elites prevail we shall end up with a world that is like Bourbon Naples writ large, with a wealthy aristocracy catered to by an elite of merchants and artisans and with a pauperized, underemployed mass. Modern capitalism has developed by catering to the needs of a prosperous broad middle class; it requires high levels of mass consumption to sustain its output of goods and services. Under the rhetoric of responding to international competitive pressures by cutting welfare, reducing wages, and rendering labor markets more flexible we are in danger of undermining prosperity by eating into its social foundations.[3] Those who argue this way claim that the results will be higher levels of growth and employment; sadly they are vocally resisted only by the new protectionists and those who seek to withdraw from forms of supranational economic governance like the EU (Goldsmith 1994; Greider 1997).

The option of combining trade openness with extended public governance at both national and international levels, with the aim of combining growth with fairness within and between nations, is a difficult one to argue for in today's climate, dominated as it is by free-market economic liberals on the one hand and protectionist populists on the other. Yet it remains essential. Free trade and economic growth are closely correlated in the history of the modern international economy, and protecting workers against the shocks of an open international economy is a condition not only for ensuring political support for free trade but of maintaining the prosperity on which that trade depends. Free trade may require the far greater management both of FDI and of the international financial markets—trade openness and market governance go together. The international economy remains sufficiently concentrated in the key national states for such governance to be possible if the political will and a measure of international consensus are there.

NOTES

An earlier version of this chapter appeared in *International Affairs* 73, no. 3 (1997): 409–25.

1. The most trenchant expression of this view remains Ohmae (1990) and (1996).

2. See Hirst and Thompson (1996a: ch.5) for an argument that, despite those recent and rapid changes, the fashionable notions of the early 1990s that Asian growth was unstoppable, would continue until the twenty-first century, and would lead to the Pacific Rim becoming the dominant economic center of the globe were ill-founded and short-sighted (as the present crisis has proved).

3. Dani Rodrik argues persuasively for the need to combine free trade with social protection (Rodrik 1997).

REFERENCES

Goldsmith, James. (1994). *The Trap*. London: Macmillan.

Greider, William. (1997). *One World Ready or Not: The Manic Logic of Global Capitalism*. New York: Simon and Schuster.

HM Treasury (1996). Overseas Investment and the UK. Occasional Papers No. 8.

Hirst, Paul, and Grahame Thompson. (1996a). *Globalisation in Question*. Cambridge: Polity Press.

———. (1996b). Global Myths and National Policies. *Renewal* 4, no. 2 (May 1996).

————. (1996c). Globalisation: Ten Frequently Asked Questions and Some Surprising Answers. *Soundings* 4 (Autumn).

Krugman, Paul. (1994). Competitiveness: A Dangerous Obsession. *Foreign Affairs* 74, no. 2 (March/April 1994).

————. (1996). *Pop Internationalization.* Cambridge, Mass.: MIT Press.

Lipsey, R. E., M. Blomström, and E. Ramstetter. (1995). Internationalized Production in World Output. NBER Working Paper 5385. Cambridge, Mass.: National Bureau of Economic Research.

Ohmae, Kenrichi. (1990). *The Borderless World.* London: HarperCollins.

————. (1996). *The End of the Nation State.* London: HarperCollins.

OECD. (1994). *Employment Outlook* July 1994.

Rodrik, Dani. (1997). *Has Globalisation Gone Too Far?* Washington, D.C.: Institute for International Economics.

Strange, Susan. (1996). *The Retreat of the State: The Diffusion of Power in the World Economy.* Cambridge: Cambridge University Press.

Thompson, Grahame. (1997). *International Competitiveness and Globalization.* Milton Keynes Open University.

World Trade Organization. (1995). *International Trade Trends and Statistics 1993.* Washington, D.C.

Young, Alwyn. (1994). The Tyranny of Numbers: Confronting the Statistical Realities of the East Asian Growth Experience. NBER Working Paper 4680. Cambridge, Mass.: National Bureau of Economic Research.

7

Globalization, State Sovereignty, and the "Endless" Accumulation of Capital

Giovanni Arrighi

"Times of change," remarks John Ruggie, "are also times of confusion. Words lose their familiar meaning, and our footing becomes unsure on what was previously familiar terrain" (Ruggie 1994: 553). As we seek a firmer footing in seemingly well-established notions, such as "sovereignty," we discover that their past use is itself mired in hopeless confusion. And as we coin new terms, such as "globalization," to capture the novelty of emergent conditions, we compound the confusion by carelessly pouring old wine in new bottles. The purpose of this chapter is to show that in order to isolate what is truly new and anomalous in ongoing transformations of world capitalism and state sovereignty, we must preliminarily recognize that key aspects of these transformations are either not new at all or are new in degree but not in kind.

I shall begin by arguing that much of what goes under the catch-word "globalization" has in fact been a recurrent tendency of world capitalism since early modern times. This recurrence makes the dynamics and likely outcomes of present transformations more predictable than they would be if globalization were as novel a phenomenon as many observers think. I shall then shift my focus on the evolutionary pattern that over the centuries has enabled world capitalism and the underlying system of sovereign states to become global. My contention here will be that the true novelty of the present wave of globalization is that this evolutionary pattern is now at an impasse. I shall conclude by speculating on possible ways out of this impasse and on the kinds of new world order that may emerge as a result of the recentering on East Asia of world-scale processes of capital accumulation.

GLOBALIZATION AS AN EARLY MODERN PHENOMENON

As critics of the notion of globalization have pointed out, many of the tendencies that go under that name are not new at all. The newness of the so-called "information revolution" is impressive, "but the newness of the railroad and the telegraph, the automobile, the radio, and the telephone in their day impressed equally" (Harvey 1995: 9). Even the so-called "virtualization of economic activity" is not as new as it may appear at first sight:

> Submarine telegraph cables from the 1860s onwards connected intercontinental markets. They made possible day-to-day trading and price-making across thousands of miles, a far greater innovation than the advent of electronic trading today. Chicago and London, Melbourne and Manchester were linked in close to real time. Bond markets also became closely interconnected, and large-scale international lending—both portfolio and direct investment—grew rapidly during this period. (Hirst 1996: 3)

Indeed, foreign direct investment (FDI) grew so rapidly that in 1913 it amounted to over nine percent of world output—a proportion still unsurpassed in the early 1990s (Bairoch and Kozul-Wright 1996: 10). Similarly, the openness to foreign trade—as measured by imports and exports combined as a proportion of gross domestic product (GDP)—was not markedly greater in 1993 than in 1913 for all major capitalist countries except the United States (Hirst 1996: 3–4).

To be sure, the most spectacular expansion of the last two decades, and the strongest piece of evidence in the armory of advocates of the globalization thesis, has not been in FDI or world trade but in world financial markets. "Since 1980," notes Saskia Sassen, "the total value of financial assets has increased two and a half times faster than aggregate GDP of all rich industrial economies. And the volume of trading in currencies, bonds and equities has increased five times faster." The first to "globalize" and today "the biggest and in many ways the only true global market" is the foreign exchange market. "Foreign exchange transactions were ten times larger than world trade in 1983; only ten years later, in 1992, they were sixty times larger" (Sassen 1996: 40).

In the absence of this explosive growth in world financial markets, we would probably not be speaking of globalization, and certainly not as a departure from the ongoing process of world-market reconstruction launched under U.S. hegemony in the wake of the Second World War. After all,

> Bretton Woods was a global system, so what really happened here was a shift from one global system (hierarchically organized and largely controlled politically by the United States) to another global system that was more decentral-

ized and coordinated through the market, making the financial conditions of capitalism far more volatile and far more unstable. The rhetoric that accompanied this shift was deeply implicated in the promotion of the term "globalization" as a virtue. In my more cynical moments I find myself thinking that it was the financial press that conned us all (myself included) into believing in "globalization" as something new when it was nothing more than a promotional gimmick to make the best of a necessary adjustment in the system of international finance. (Harvey 1995: 8)

Gimmick or not, the idea of globalization was from the start intertwined with the idea of intense interstate competition for increasingly volatile capital and a consequent tighter subordination of most states to the dictates of capitalist agencies. Nevertheless, it is precisely in this respect that present tendencies are most reminiscent of the Belle Époque of world capitalism of the late nineteenth and early twentieth centuries. As Sassen herself acknowledges,

> In many ways the international financial market from the late 1800s to World War I was as massive as today's. . . . The extent of the internationalization can be seen in the fact that in 1920, for example, Moody's rated bonds issued by about fifty governments to raise money in the U.S. capital markets. The Depression brought on a radical decline in this internationalization, and it was only very recently that Moody's once again rated the bonds of as many governments. (Sassen 1996: 42–43)

In short, careful advocates of the globalization thesis concur with critics in seeing present transformations as not novel except for their scale, scope, and complexity. As I have argued and documented elsewhere (Arrighi 1994), however, the specificities of present transformations can be fully appreciated only by lengthening the time horizon of our investigations to encompass the entire lifetime of world capitalism. In this longer perspective, "financialization," heightened interstate competition for mobile capital, created rapid technological and organizational change, state breakdowns, and an unusual instability of the economic conditions under which states operate. Taken individually or jointly as components of a particular temporal configuration, these are all recurrent aspects of what I have called "systemic cycles of accumulation."

In each of the four systemic cycles of accumulation that we can identify in the history of world capitalism from its earliest beginnings in late medieval Europe to the present, periods characterized by a rapid and stable expansion of world trade and production invariably ended in a crisis of overaccumulation that ushered in a period of heightened competition, financial expansion, and eventual breakdown of the organizational structures on which the preceding expansion of trade and production had been based. To borrow an expression from Fernand Braudel (1984: 246)—the inspirer of the idea of systemic cycles of accumulation—these periods of intensifying competition, financial expansion, and structural instability are nothing but the "autumn" of a major capitalist development. It is the time when the leader of the preceding expansion of world trade reaps the fruits of its leadership by virtue of its commanding position over world-scale processes of capital accumulation. But it is also the time when that same leader is gradually displaced at the commanding heights of world capitalism by an emerging new leadership. This has been the experience of Britain in the late nineteenth and early twentieth centuries, of Holland in the eighteenth century, and of the Genoese capitalist diaspora in the second half of the sixteenth century. Could it also be the experience of the United States today?

At the moment the most prominent tendency is for the United States to reap the fruits of its leadership of world capitalism in the Cold War era. Indeed, various aspects of the seeming global triumph of Americanism that ensued from the demise of the USSR are themselves widely held to be signs of globalization. The most widely recognized signs are the global hegemony of U.S. popular culture and the growing importance of agencies of world governance that are influenced disproportionately by the United States and its closest allies, such as the UN Security Council, NATO, the Group of Seven (G-7), the International Monetary Fund (IMF), the International Bank for Reconstruction and Development (IBRD), and the World Trade Organization (WTO). Less widely recognized but also significant is the ascendance of a new legal regime in international business transactions dominated by U.S. law firms and Anglo-American conceptions of business law (Sassen 1996: 12–21).

The importance of these signs of a further Americanization of the world should not be belittled. But it should not be exaggerated either, particularly for what concerns U.S. capabilities to continue to shape and manipulate to its own advantage the organizational structures of the world capitalist system. The chances are that the victory of the United States in what Fred Halliday (1983) has called the Second Cold War and the further Americanization of the world will appear in retrospect as closing moments of U.S. world hegemony, just as the United Kingdom's victory in the First World War and the further expansion of its overseas empire were preludes to the final demise of UK world hegemony in the 1930s and 1940s. As we shall see in section III of this chapter, there are good reasons for expecting the demise of U.S. hegemony to follow a different trajectory than the demise of UK hegemony. But there are equally good reasons for expecting the present, U.S.-led phase of financial expansion to be a temporary phenomenon, like the analogous UK-led phase of a century ago.

The most important reason is that the present belle epoque of financial capitalism, no less than all its historical precedents—from Renaissance Florence to the UK's Edwardian era, through the Age of the Genoese and the periwig period of Dutch history—is based on massive, system-wide redistributions of income and wealth from all kinds of communities to capitalist agencies. In the past, redistributions of this kind engendered considerable political, economic, and social turbulence. At least initially, the organizing centers of the preceding expansion of world trade and production were best positioned to master, indeed, to benefit from the turbulence. Over time, however, the turbulence undermined the power of the old organizing centers and prepared their displacement by new organizing centers endowed with the capacity to promote and sustain a new major expansion of world trade and production (Arrighi 1994).

Whether any such new organizing centers are today emerging under the glitter of the U.S.-led financial expansion remains unclear, as we shall see. But the effects of the turbulence engendered by the present financial expansion have begun to worry even the promoters and boosters of economic globalization. David Harvey (1995: 8, 12) quotes several of them, remarking that globalization is turning into "a brakeless train wreaking havoc" and worrying about a "mounting backlash" against the effects of such a destructive force, first and foremost "the rise of a new brand of populist politicians" fostered by the "mood . . . of helplessness and anxiety" that is taking hold even of wealthy countries. More recently, the Hungarian-born cosmopolitan financier George Soros has joined the chorus by arguing that the global spread of laissez-faire capitalism has replaced Communism as the main threat to open democratic society.

> Although I have made a fortune in the financial markets, I now fear that untrammeled intensification of laissez-faire capitalism and the spread of market values to all areas of life is endangering our open and democratic society. The main enemy of the open society, I believe, is no longer the communist but the capitalist threat. . . . Too much competition and too little cooperation can cause intolerable inequities and instability. . . . The doctrine of laissez-faire capitalism holds that the common good is best served by the uninhibited pursuit of self-interest. Unless it is tempered by the recognition of a common interest that ought to take precedence over particular interests, our present system . . . is liable to break down. (Soros 1997: 45, 48)

In reporting the proliferation of writings along Soros's lines, Thomas Friedman—the early booster of the idea of globalization as virtue who later invented the "brakeless train" metaphor—reiterates the view that "the integration of trade, finance and information that is creating a single global market and culture" is inevitable and unstoppable. But while globalization cannot be stopped—he hastens to add—"there are two things that can be done to it," presumably for its own good: "We can go faster or

slower. . . . And we can do more or less to cushion [its] negative effects"
(Soros 1997: I, 15).

There is much deja vu in these diagnoses of the self-destructiveness of
unregulated processes of world-market formation and related prognoses of
what ought to be done to remedy such self-destructiveness. Soros himself
compares the present age of triumphant laissez-faire capitalism with the
similar age of a century ago. In his view the earlier age was, if anything,
more stable than the present, because of the sway of the gold standard and
the presence of an imperial power, the United Kingdom, prepared to dis-
patch gunboats to faraway places to maintain the system. And yet the system broke down under the impact of the two world wars and the intervening rise of "totalitarian ideologies." Today, in contrast, the United States
is reluctant to be the policeman of the world "and the main currencies float
and crush against each other like continental plates," making the breakdown of the present regime much more likely "unless we learn from experience" (Soros 1997: 48).

> Our global open society lacks the institutions and mechanisms necessary for
> its preservation, but there is no political will to bring them into existence. I
> blame the prevailing attitude, which holds that the unhampered pursuit of
> self-interest will bring about an eventual international equilibrium. . . . As
> things stand, it does not take very much imagination to realize that the global
> open society that prevails at present is likely to prove a temporary phenome-
> non. (Soros 1997: 53–54)

Soros makes no reference to his fellow countryman Karl Polanyi's now
classic account of the rise and demise of nineteenth-century laissez-faire
capitalism. Nevertheless, anyone familiar with that account cannot help
but be struck by its anticipation of present arguments about the contradictions of globalization (on the continuing significance of Polanyi's analysis
for an understanding of the present wave of globalization, see among others Mittelman 1996). Like Friedman, Polanyi saw a slow-down in the rate
of change as the best way of keeping change going in a given direction
without causing social disruptions that would result in chaos rather than
change. He also underscored that only a cushioning of the disruptive effects of market regulation can prevent society from revolting in self-de-
fense against the market system (Polanyi 1957: 3–4, 36–38, 140–50). And
like Soros, Polanyi dismissed the idea of a self-adjusting (global) market
as "a stark utopia." He argued that no such institution can exist for any
length of time "without annihilating the human and natural substance of
[world] society." In his view, the only alternative to the disintegration of
the world market system in the interwar years "was the establishment of
an international order endowed with an organized power which would

transcend national sovereignty"—a course, however, that "was entirely beyond the horizons of the time" (Polanyi 1957: 3–4, 20–22).

Neither Soros nor Polanyi provides an explanation of why the still dominant world power of their respective times—the United States today, the United Kingdom in the late nineteenth and early twentieth centuries— stubbornly stuck to and propagated the belief in a self-adjusting global market in spite of accumulating evidence that unregulated markets (unregulated financial markets in particular) do not produce "equilibria" but disorder and instability. Underlying such stubbornness we can nonetheless detect the predicament of a declining hegemonic agency that has become overly dependent, for profits as much as for power, on a process of widening and deepening integration of world trade and finance that the hegemonic agency at the height of its power promoted and organized, but the orderly development of which it can no longer ensure. It is as if the declining hegemonic power can neither afford to jump off the "brakeless train" of unregulated financial speculation, nor reroute the train into a less self-destructive groove.

Historically, the rerouting of world capitalism into a more creative than destructive groove has been premised upon the emergence, to borrow an expression from Michael Mann (Mann 1986: 28), of new "tracklaying vehicles." That is to say, the expansion of world capitalism to its present global dimensions has not proceeded along a single track laid once and for all some five hundred years ago. Rather, it has proceeded through several switches to new tracks that did not exist until specific complexes of governmental and business agencies developed the will and the capacity to lead the entire system in the direction of broader or deeper cooperation. The world hegemonies of the United Provinces in the seventeenth century, of the United Kingdom in the nineteenth century, and of the United States in the twentieth century have all been tracklaying vehicles of this kind (cf., Taylor 1994: 27). In leading the system in a new direction, they also transformed it. And it is on these successive transformations that we must focus in order to identify the true novelties of the present wave of financial expansion.

PATHS TO GLOBALIZATION

The formation of a capitalist world system, and its subsequent transformation from being a world among many worlds to becoming the historical social system of the entire world, has been based upon the construction of territorial organizations capable of regulating social and economic life and of monopolizing means of coercion and violence. These territorial organizations are the states whose sovereignty is said to be undermined by the present wave of financial expansion. In reality, most members of the inter-state system never had the powers that states are said to be losing under the impact of the present wave of financial expansion; even the states that had those powers at one time did not have them at another time.

In any event, waves of financial expansion are engendered by a double tendency. On the one hand, capitalist organizations respond to the overac-cumulation of capital over and above what can be reinvested profitably in established channels of trade and production by holding in liquid form a growing proportion of their cash flows. This tendency creates what we may call the "supply conditions" of financial expansions: an overabundant mass of liquidity that can be mobilized directly or through intermediaries in speculation, borrowing, and lending.

On the other hand, territorial organizations respond to the tighter budget constraints that ensue from the slow-down in the expansion of trade and production by competing intensely with one another for the capital that accumulates in financial markets. This tendency creates what we may call the "demand conditions" of financial expansions. All financial expan-sions, past and present, are the outcome of the combined if uneven devel-opment of these two complementary tendencies (Arrighi 1997).

We are all very impressed, and rightly so, by the astronomical growth of capital that seeks valorization in world financial markets and by the intense competition that sets states against one another in an attempt to capture for their own pursuits a fraction of that capital. We should nonetheless be aware of the fact that at the roots of this astronomical growth there lies a basic scarcity of profitable outlets for the growing mass of profits that accumulates in the hands of capitalist agencies. This basic scarcity makes the pursuit of profit by capitalist agencies as dependent on the assistance of states as states are dependent in the pursuit of their own objectives on capitalist agencies. The dependence of capitalist agencies on states has been particularly evident in the recurrent crises that have punctuated the financial expansion, from the Latin American debt crisis of the early 1980s, through the collapse of "saving and loans" in the United States, right up to the recent East Asian financial turmoil. On all these occasions, energetic state action rescued private capital from potentially catastrophic overexpansion. And on all occasions, it is hard to imagine who else, if not states, could have done so.

Be that as it may, all past financial expansions have been moments of disempowerment of some states—including, eventually, the states that had been the tracklaying vehicles of world capitalism in the epochs that were drawing to a close—and simultaneous empowerment of other states, in-cluding the states that in due course became the new tracklaying vehicles of world capitalism. Here lies the main significance of systemic cycles of accumulation. For these cycles are not mere cycles. They are also stages in the formation and gradual expansion to its present global dimensions of the world capitalist system.

This process of globalization has occurred through the emergence at each stage of organizing centers of greater scale, scope, and complexity than the organizing centers of the preceding stage. In this sequence, city-states like Venice and transnational business diasporas like the Genoese were replaced at the commanding heights of the world capitalist system by a proto-nation-state like Holland and its chartered companies, which were then replaced by the UK nation-state, formal empire and world-encompassing informal business networks, which were in their turn replaced by the continent-sized United States, its panoply of transnational corporations and its far flung networks of quasi-permanent overseas military bases. Each replacement was marked by a crisis of the territorial and nonterritorial organizations that had led the expansion in the preceding stage. But it was marked also by the emergence of new organizations with even greater capabilities to lead world capitalism into renewed expansion than the displaced organizations (Arrighi 1994: 13–16, 74–84, 235–38, 330–31).

There has thus been a crisis of states in each financial expansion. As Robert Wade (1996) has noted, much of recent talk about globalization and the crisis of nation-states simply recycles arguments that were fashionable a hundred years ago (see also Lie 1996: 587). Each successive crisis, however, concerns a different kind of state. A hundred years ago the crisis of nation-states concerned the states of the old European core relative to the continent-sized states that were forming on the outer perimeter of the Eurocentric system, the United States in particular. The irresistible rise of U.S. power and wealth, and of Soviet power, though not wealth, in the course of the two world wars and their aftermath, confirmed the validity of the widely held expectation that the states of the old European core were bound to live in the shadow of their two flanking giants, unless they could themselves attain continental dimension. The present crisis of nation-states, in contrast, concerns the giant states themselves.

The sudden collapse of the USSR has both clarified and obscured this new dimension of the crisis. It has clarified the new dimension by showing how vulnerable even the largest, most self-sufficient, and second-greatest military power had become to the forces of global economic integration. But it has obscured the true nature of the crisis by provoking a general amnesia about the fact that the crisis of U.S. world power preceded the breakdown of the USSR and, with ups and downs, has outlasted the end of the Cold War. In order to identify the true nature of the crisis of the giant states that have been dominant in the Cold War era we must distinguish it from the long-term curtailment of national sovereignty that the globalization of the system of sovereign states has entailed for all but its most powerful members.

The principle that independent states, each recognizing the others' jurid-ical autonomy and territorial integrity, should coexist in a single political system was established for the first time under Dutch hegemony by the treaties of Westphalia. The process of globalizing the territorial organiza-tion of the world according to this principle, as Harvey (1995: 7) notes, took several centuries and a good deal of violence to complete. More im-portant, as often happens to political programs, Westphalian sovereignty became universal through endless violations of its formal prescriptions and major metamorphoses of its substantive meaning.

These violations and metamorphoses make eminently plausible Kras-ner's contention that, empirically, Westphalian sovereignty is a myth (Krasner 1997). To this we should nonetheless add that it has been no more a myth than the ideas of the rule of law; the social contract democracy, whether liberal, social, or whatever, and that, like all these other myths, it has been a key ingredient in the formation and eventual globalization of the modern system of rule. The really interesting question, therefore, is not whether and how the Westphalian principle of national sovereignty has been violated. Rather, it is whether and how the principle has guided and constrained state action and, over time, the outcome of this action has transformed the substantive meaning of national sovereignty.

When it was first established under Dutch hegemony, the principle of national sovereignty was meant to regulate relations among the states of Western Europe. It replaced the idea of an imperial–ecclesiastical authority and organization operating above factually sovereign states with the idea of juridically sovereign states that rely on international law and the balance of power in regulating their mutual relations—in Leo Gross's words, "a law operating between rather than above states and a power operating be-tween rather than above states" (Gross 1988: 54–55). The idea applied only to Europe, which was thereby instituted as a zone of "amity" and "civilized" behavior even in times of war. The realm beyond Europe, in contrast, was turned into a residual zone of alternative behaviors, to which no standards of civilization applied and where rivals could simply be wiped out (Taylor 1991: 21–22).

For about 150 years after the Peace of Westphalia the system worked very well, both in ensuring that no single state would become so strong as to be able to dominate all the others and in enabling the ruling groups of each state to consolidate their domestic sovereignty. The balance of power, however, was reproduced through an endless series of increasingly capital-intensive wars and a broadening and deepening of European expansion in the non-European world. Over time, these two tendencies altered the bal-ance of power both among states and between ruling groups and their re-spective subjects, eventually provoking a breakdown of the Westphalian system in the wake of the French Revolutionary and Napoleonic Wars (Arrighi 1994: 48–52).

When Westphalian principles were reaffirmed under British hegemony in the aftermath of the Napoleonic Wars, their geopolitical scope expanded to include the settler states of North and South America that had become independent on the eve or in the wake of the French wars. But as the geopolitical scope of Westphalian principles expanded, their substantive meaning changed radically primarily because the balance of power came to operate above rather than between states. To be sure, the balance continued to operate between states in Continental Europe, where for most of the nineteenth century the Concert of Europe and the shifting alliances among the Continental powers ensured that none of them would become so strong as to dominate all the others. Globally, however, privileged access to extra-European resources enabled the United Kingdom to act as the governor rather than a cog of the mechanisms of the balance of power. Moreover, massive tribute from its Indian empire enabled the United Kingdom to adopt unilaterally a free trade policy that, to varying degrees, "caged" all other members of the interstate system in a world-encompassing division of labor centered on itself. Informally and temporarily, but nonetheless effectively, the nineteenth-century system of juridically sovereign states was factually governed by the United Kingdom on the strength of its world-encompassing networks of power (Arrighi 1994: 52–55).

While the balance of power in the 150 years following the Peace of Westphalia was reproduced through an endless series of wars, the United Kingdom's governance of the balance of power after the Peace of Vienna produced, in Polanyi's words, "a phenomenon unheard of in the annals of Western civilization, namely, a hundred years' [European] peace—1815–1914" (Polanyi 1957: 5). Peace, however, far from containing, gave a new great impulse to the interstate armament race and to the broadening and deepening of European expansion in the non-European world. From the 1840s onwards, both tendencies accelerated rapidly into a self-reinforcing cycle whereby advances in military organization and technology sustained, and were sustained by, economic and political expansion at the expense of the peoples and polities still excluded from the benefits of Westphalian sovereignty (McNeill 1982: 143).

The result of this self-reinforcing cycle was what William McNeill calls "the industrialization of war," a consequent new major jump in the human and financial costs of war-making, the emergence of competing imperialisms, and the eventual breakdown of the United Kingdom's nineteenth-century world order, along with widespread violations of Westphalian principles. When these principles were once again reaffirmed under U.S. hegemony after the Second World War, their geopolitical scope became universal through the decolonization of Asia and Africa. But their substance was curtailed further.

The very idea of a balance of power that operates between rather than above states and ensures their factual sovereign equality—an idea that had already become a fiction under UK hegemony—was discarded even as fiction. As Anthony Giddens (1987: 258) has noted, U.S. influence upon shaping the new global order both under Wilson and under Roosevelt "represented an attempted incorporation of U.S. constitutional prescriptions globally rather than a continuation of the balance of power doctrine." In an age of industrialized warfare and increasing centralization of politico-military capabilities in the hands of a small and dwindling number of states, that doctrine made little sense either as a description of actual relationships of power among the members of the globalizing interstate system or as a prescription for how to guarantee the sovereignty of states. The "sovereign equality" upheld in the first paragraph of Article Two of the United Nations for all its members was thus "specifically supposed to be legal rather than factual—the larger powers were to have special rights, as well as duties, commensurate with their superior capabilities" (Giddens 1987: 266).

The enshrining of these special rights in the charter of the United Nations institutionalized for the first time since Westphalia the idea of a suprastatal authority and organization that restricted juridically the sovereignty of all but the most powerful states. These juridical restrictions, however, paled in comparison with factual restrictions imposed by the two preeminent state powers—the United States and the USSR—on their respective and mutually recognized "spheres of influence." The restrictions imposed by the USSR relied primarily on military–political sources of power and were regional in scope, limited as they were to its Eastern European satellites. Those imposed by the United States, in contrast, were global in scope and relied on a far more complex armory of resources.

The far-flung network of quasi-permanent overseas bases maintained by the United States in the Cold War era was, in Krasner's words, "without historical precedent; no state had previously based its own troops on the sovereign territory of other states in such extensive numbers for so long a peacetime period" (Krasner 1988: 21). This U.S.-centric, world-encompassing politico-military regime was supplemented and complemented by the U.S.-centric world monetary system instituted at Bretton Woods. These two interlocking networks of power, one military and one financial, enabled the United States at the height of its hegemony to govern the globalized system of sovereign states to an extent that was entirely beyond the horizons, not just of the Dutch in the seventeenth century, but of the Imperial United Kingdom in the nineteenth century as well.

In short, the formation of ever more powerful governmental complexes capable of leading the modern system of sovereign states to its present global dimension has also transformed the very structure of the system by gradually destroying the balance of power on which the sovereign equality of the system's units originally rested. As juridical statehood became universal, most states were deprived either de jure or de facto of prerogatives historically associated with national sovereignty. Even powerful states like the former West Germany and Japan have been described as "semisovereign" (Katzenstein 1987; Cumings 1997). And Robert Jackson (1990: 21) has coined the expression "quasi-states" to refer to ex-colonial states that have won juridical statehood but lack the capabilities needed to carry out the governmental functions traditionally associated with independent statehood. Semisovereignty and quasi-statehood are the outcome of long-term trends of the modern world system and both materialized well before the global financial expansion of the 1970s and 1980s.

THE UNITED STATES AND GLOBAL ECONOMIC INTEGRATION

What happened in the 1970s and 1980s is that the capacity of the two superpowers to govern interstate relations within and across their respective spheres of influence lessened in the face of forces that they had themselves called forth but could not control.

The most important of these forces originated in the new forms of world economic integration that grew under the carapace of U.S. military and financial power. Unlike the nineteenth-century world economic integration centered on the United Kingdom, the system of global economic integration promoted by the United States in the Cold War era did not rest on unilateral free trade or on the extraction of tribute from an overseas territorial empire. Rather, it rested on a process of bilateral and multilateral trade liberalization closely monitored and administered by the United States and its most important political allies, and on a global transplant of the vertically integrated organizational structures of U.S. corporations (Arrighi 1994: 69–72).

Administered trade liberalization and the global transplant of U.S. corporations were meant to maintain and expand U.S. world power and to reorganize interstate relations so as to contain not just the forces of Communist revolution, but also the forces of nationalism that had torn apart and eventually destroyed the nineteenth-century UK system of global economic integration. In the attainment of these objectives, as Robert Gilpin (1975: 108) has underscored with reference to U.S. policy in Europe, the overseas transplant of U.S. corporations had priority over trade liberalization. In Gilpin's view, the relationship of these corporations to U.S. world power was not unlike that of joint-stock chartered companies to British power in the seventeenth and eighteenth centuries (Gilpin 1975: 141–42).

Nevertheless, the relationship between the transnational expansion of U.S. corporations and the maintenance and expansion of the power of the U.S. state has been just as much one of contradiction as of complementarity. For one thing, the claims on foreign incomes established by the subsidiaries of U.S. corporations did not translate into a proportionate increase in the incomes of U.S. residents and in the revenues of the U.S. government. On the contrary, precisely when the fiscal crisis of the U.S. "warfare–welfare state" became acute under the impact of the Vietnam War, a growing proportion of the incomes and liquidity of U.S. corporations, instead of being repatriated, flew to offshore money markets. In the words of Eugene Birnbaum of Chase Manhattan Bank, the result was "the amassing of an immense volume of liquid funds and markets—the world of Eurodollar finance—outside the regulatory authority of *any* country or agency" (quoted in Frieden 1987: 85; emphasis in the original).

Interestingly enough, the organization of this world of Eurodollar finance—like the organizations of the sixteenth-century Genoese business diaspora and of the Chinese business diaspora from premodern to our own times—occupies places but is not defined by the places it occupies. The so-called Eurodollar market—as Roy Harrod (1969: 319) characterized it well before the arrival of the information superhighway—"has no headquarters or buildings of its own. . . . Physically it consists merely of a network of telephones and telex machines around the world, telephones which may be used for purposes other than Eurodollar deals." This space-of-flows falls under no state jurisdiction. And although the U.S. state still has some privileged access to its services and resources, this privileged access has come at the cost of an increasing subordination of U.S. policies to the dictates of nonterritorial high finance.

Equally important, the transnational expansion of U.S. corporations has called forth competitive responses in old and new centers of capital accumulation that weakened, and eventually reversed, U.S. claims on foreign incomes and resources. As Alfred Chandler (1990: 615–16) has pointed out, by the time Servan-Schreiber called upon his fellow Europeans to stand up to the "American Challenge"—a challenge that in Servan-Schreiber's view was neither financial nor technological but "the extension to Europe of an *organization* that is still a mystery to us"—a growing number of European enterprises had found effective ways and means of meeting the challenge and of themselves becoming challengers of the long-established U.S. corporations even in the U.S. market. In the 1970s, the accumulated value of non-U.S. (mostly Western European) foreign direct investment grew one and one-half times faster than that of U.S. foreign direct investment. By 1980, it was estimated that there were over 10,000 transnational corporations of all national origins, and by the early 1990s more than three times as many (Stopford and Dunning 1983: 3; Ikeda 1996: 48).

This explosive growth in the number of transnational corporations was accompanied by a drastic decrease in the importance of the United States as a source, and an increase in its importance as a recipient, of foreign direct investment. The transnational forms of business organization pioneered by U.S. capital, in other words, had rapidly ceased to be a "mystery" for a large and growing number of foreign competitors. By the 1970s, Western European capital had discovered all its secrets and had begun outcompeting U.S. corporations at home and abroad. By the 1980s, it was the turn of East Asian capital to outcompete both U.S. and Western European capital through the formation of a new kind of transnational business organization—an organization that was deeply rooted in the region's gifts of history and geography and combined the advantages of vertical integration with the flexibility of informal business networks (Arrighi, Ikeda, and Irwan 1993).

No matter which particular fraction of capital won, the outcome of each round of this competitive struggle was a further increase in the volume and density of the web of exchanges that linked people and territory across political jurisdictions both regionally and globally. This tendency has involved a fundamental contradiction for the global power of the United States—a contradiction that has been aggravated rather than mitigated by the collapse of Soviet power and the consequent end of the Cold War. On the one hand, the U.S. government has become prisoner of its unprecedented and, with the collapse of the USSR, unparalleled global military capabilities. These capabilities remain essential, not just as a source of "protection" for U.S. business abroad, but also as the main source of the lead of U.S. business in high technology both at home and abroad.

On the other hand, the disappearance of the Communist "threat" has made it even more difficult than it already was for the U.S. government to mobilize the human and financial resources needed to put to effective use or just maintain its military capabilities. Hence the divergent assessments of the actual extent of U.S. global power in the post–Cold War era.

"Now is the unipolar moment," a triumphalist commentator crows. "There is but one first-rate power and no prospect in the immediate future of any power to rival it." But a senior U.S. foreign policy official demurs, "We simply do not have the leverage, we don't have the influence, the inclination to use military force. We don't have the money to bring the kind of pressure that will produce positive results any time soon." (Ruggie 1994: 553)

THE FUTURE OF GLOBALIZATION

The true peculiarity of the present phase of financial expansion of world capitalism lies in the difficulty of projecting past evolutionary patterns into the future. In all past financial expansions, the old organizing centers' declining power was matched by the rising power of new organizing centers capable of surpassing the power of their predecessors not just financially but militarily as well. This has been the case of the Dutch in relation to the Genoese, of the British in relation to the Dutch, and of the Americans in relation to the British.

In the present financial expansion, in contrast, the declining power of the old organizing centers has been associated not with a fusion of a higher order but with a fission of military and financial power. While military power has become centralized further in the hands of the United States and its closest Western allies, financial power has become dispersed among a motley ensemble of territorial and nonterritorial organizations which, de facto or de jure, cannot even remotely aspire to match the global military capabilities of the United States. This anomaly signals a fundamental break with the evolutionary pattern that has characterized the expansion of world capitalism over the last 500 years. Expansion along the established path is at an impasse—an impasse that is reflected in the widespread feeling that modernity or even history is coming to an end, that we have entered a phase of turbulence and systemic chaos with no precedent in the modern era (Rosenau 1990: 10; Wallerstein 1995: 1, 268), or that a "global fog" has descended upon us as we blindly tap our way into the third millennium (Hobsbawm 1994: 558–59). While the impasse, the turbulence, and the fog are all real, a closer look at the extraordinary economic expansion of the East Asian region over the last thirty years can give some insights into the truly new kind of world order that may be emerging at the edges of the impending systemic chaos.

To be sure, the significance of the East Asian economic expansion has not gone unchallenged. Thus, according to Paul Krugman, the reliance of East Asian economic expansion in the 1980s on heavy investment and big shifts of labor from farms into factories, rather than productivity gains, makes it resemble the economic expansion of the Warsaw Pact nations in the 1950s. "From the perspective of the year 2010, current projections of Asian supremacy extrapolated from recent trends may well look almost as silly as 1960s-vintage forecasts of Soviet industrial supremacy did from the perspective of the Brezhnev years" (Krugman 1994: 78).

But a recent comparative analysis of rates of economic growth since the 1870s by the Union Bank of Switzerland (UBS) contradicts Krugman's assessment. The UBS report finds "nothing comparable with the [East] Asian economic growth experience of the last three decades." Other regions grew as fast during wartime dislocations (e.g., North America during the Second World War) or following such dislocations (e.g., Western Europe after the Second World War). But "the eight-percent plus average annual income growth set by several [East] Asian economies since the late 1960s is unique in the 130 years of recorded economic history." This growth is all the more remarkable in having been recorded at a time of overall stagnation or near stagnation in the rest of the world, and in having "spread like a wave" from Japan to the Four Tigers (South Korea, Taiwan, Singapore, and Hong Kong), from there to Malaysia and Thailand, and then on to Indonesia, China, and, more recently, to Vietnam (Union Bank of Switzerland 1996: 1).

Moreover, what distinguishes most clearly the East Asian economic expansion of the 1980s from that of Warsaw Pact nations in the 1950s is the extraordinary advance of East Asia in global high finance. The Japanese share of the total assets of *Fortune*'s top fifty banks in the world increased from 18 percent in 1970, to 27 percent in 1980, to 48 percent in 1990 (Ikeda 1996). As for foreign exchange reserves, the East Asian share of the top ten central banks' holdings increased from 10 percent in 1980 to 50 percent in 1994 (*Japan Almanac* 1993 and 1997). Clearly, if the United States no longer has "the money to bring the kind of pressure that will produce positive results"—as the previously quoted senior U.S. foreign policy official deplored—East Asian states, or at least some of them (most notably Japan, Hong Kong, Singapore, and Taiwan), have all the money they need to keep at bay the kind of pressure that is driving states all over the world—the United States included—to yield to the dictates of increasingly mobile and volatile capital.

An overabundance of capital, of course, brings problems of its own, as witnessed by the collapse of the Tokyo stock exchange in 1990–92 and the more devastating financial crisis that swept the entire East Asian region in 1997. For all their devastation, however, these crises (and the other crises that in all likelihood will hit East Asia in the years to come) in themselves are no more a sign of a roll-back of East Asian financial power vis-à-vis the United States than Black Thursday on Wall Street in 1929 (and the devastation of the U.S. economy that ensued) was a sign of a roll-back of U.S. financial power vis-à-vis Britain. As Braudel has pointed out in discussing the financial crisis of 1772–73—which began in London but reflected an ongoing shift of world financial supremacy from Amsterdam to London—"any city which is becoming or has become the centre of the world-economy, is the first place in which the seismic movements of the system show themselves." As further and more compelling evidence in support of this hypothesis, he notes that the crisis of 1929–31 began in New York but reflected an ongoing shift of world financial supremacy from London to New York (Braudel 1984: 272).

Braudel does not explain why this should have been so. A good part of the explanation, however, can be inferred from Geoffrey Ingham's observation that in the 1920s the United States had not yet developed the capacity to replace the United Kingdom as the organizing center of the global economy, in spite of its spectacular advances in production and capital accumulation. At that time, the U.S. financial system was in no position to produce the necessary international liquidity through a credit-providing network of banks and markets. "London had lost its gold, but its markets remained the most important single center for global commercial and financial intermediation" (Ingham 1994: 41–43).

Mutatis mutandis, similar considerations apply to London vis-à-vis Amsterdam in the 1770s, and to Tokyo and other East Asian financial centers vis-à-vis New York and Washington in the 1990s. The very speed, scale, and scope of capital accumulation in the rising centers clashes with the latter's limited organizational capabilities to create the systemic conditions for the enlarged reproduction of their expansion. Under these circumstances, the most dynamic centers of world-scale processes of capital accumulation tend to become the epicenters of systemic instability. In the past, this instability was an integral aspect of the ongoing structural transformations of world capitalism that several decades later resulted in the establishment of a new hegemony. Whether the present instability centered on East Asia is the harbinger of a future East Asian world hegemony remains to be seen. But whether it is or not, for now it validates rather than invalidates the hypothesis of an ongoing shift of the epicenter of world-scale processes of capital accumulation from the United States to East Asia.

Ironically, this shift originated in major U.S. encroachments on the sovereignty of East Asian states at the onset of the Cold War. The unilateral military occupation of Japan in 1945 and the division of the region in the aftermath of the Korean War into two antagonistic blocs created, in Bruce Cumings's words, a U.S. "vertical regime solidified through bilateral defense treaties (with Japan, South Korea, Taiwan and the Philippines) and conducted by a State Department that towered over the foreign ministries of these four countries."

All became semisovereign states, deeply penetrated by U.S. military structures (operational control of the South Korean armed forces, Seventh Fleet patrolling of the Taiwan Straits, defense dependencies for all four countries, military bases on their territories) and incapable of independent foreign policy or defense initiatives. . . . There were minor demarches through the military curtain beginning in the mid-1950s, such as low levels of trade between Japan and China, or Japan and North Korea. But the dominant tendency until the 1970s was a unilateral U.S. regime heavily biased toward military forms of communication." (Cumings 1997: 155)

Within this "unilateral U.S. regime" the United States specialized in the provision of protection and the pursuit of political power regionally and globally, while its East Asian vassal states specialized in trade and the pursuit of profit. This division of labor has been particularly important in shaping U.S.–Japanese relations throughout the Cold War era right up to the present. As Franz Schurmann (1974: 143) wrote at a time when the spectacular economic ascent of Japan had just begun, "[freed] from the burden of defense spending, Japanese governments have funneled all their resources and energies into an economic expansionism that has brought affluence to Japan and taken its business to the farthest reaches of the globe." Japan's economic expansion, in turn, generated a "snowballing" process of concatenated, labor-seeking rounds of investment in the surrounding region, which gradually replaced U.S. patronage as the main driving force of the East Asian economic expansion (Ozawa 1993: 130–31; Arrighi 1996: 14–16).

By the time this snowballing process took off, the militaristic U.S. regime in East Asia had begun to unravel as the Vietnam War destroyed what the Korean War had created. The Korean War had instituted the U.S.-centric East Asian regime by excluding Mainland China from normal commercial and diplomatic intercourse with the non-Communist part of the region, through blockade and war threats backed by "an archipelago of American military installations" (Cumings 1997: 154–55). Defeat in the Vietnam War, in contrast, forced the United States to readmit Mainland China to normal commercial and diplomatic intercourse with the rest of East Asia, thereby broadening the scope of the region's economic integration and expansion (Arrighi 1996).

This outcome transformed, without eliminating, the previous imbalance of the distribution of power resources in the region. The rise of Japan to industrial and financial powerhouse of global significance transformed the previous relationship of Japanese political and economic vassalage vis-à-vis the United States into a relationship of mutual vassalage. Japan continued to depend on the United States for military protection. But the reproduction of the U.S. protection-producing apparatus came to depend ever more critically on Japanese finance and industry. At the same time, the reincorporation of Mainland China in regional and global markets brought back into play a state whose demographic size, abundance of entrepreneurial and labor resources, and growth potential surpassed by a good margin that of all other states operating in the region, the United States included. Within less than twenty years after Richard Nixon's mission to Beijing, and less than fifteen after the formal reestablishment of diplomatic relations between the United States and the People's Republic of China (PRC), this giant "container" of human resources already seemed poised to become again the powerful attractor of means of payments it had been before its subordinate incorporation in the European-centered world system.

If the main attraction of the PRC for foreign capital has been its huge and highly competitive reserves of labor, the "matchmaker" that has facilitated the encounter of foreign capital and Chinese labor is the Overseas Chinese capitalist diaspora.

> Drawn by China's capable pool of low-cost labor and its growing potential as a market that contains one-fifth of the world's population, foreign investors continue to pour money into the PRC. Some 80 percent of that capital comes from the Overseas Chinese, refugees from poverty, disorder, and communism, who in one of the era's most piquant ironies are now Beijing's favorite financiers and models for modernization. Even the Japanese often rely on the Overseas Chinese to grease their way into China. (Kraar 1993: 40)

In fact, Beijing's reliance on the Overseas Chinese to ease Mainland China's reincorporation in regional and world markets is not the true irony of the situation. As Alvin So and Stephen Chiu (1995: ch. 11) have shown, the close political alliance that was established in the 1980s between the Chinese Communist Party and Overseas Chinese capitalists made perfect sense in terms of their respective pursuits. The alliance provided the Overseas Chinese with extraordinary opportunities to profit from commercial and financial intermediation, while providing the Chinese Communist Party with a highly effective means of killing two birds with one stone: to upgrade the domestic economy of Mainland China and at the same time to promote national unification in accordance to the "One Nation, Two Systems" model.

The true irony of the situation is that one of the most conspicuous legacies of nineteenth-century Western encroachments on Chinese sovereignty is now emerging as a powerful instrument of Chinese and East Asian emancipation from Western dominance. An Overseas Chinese diaspora had long been an integral component of the indigenous East Asian tribute-trade system centered on imperial China. But the greatest opportunities for its expansion came with the subordinate incorporation of that system within the structures of the European-centered world system in the wake of the Opium Wars. Under the U.S. Cold War regime, the diaspora's traditional role of commercial intermediation between Mainland China and the surrounding maritime regions was stifled as much by the U.S. embargo on trade with the PRC as by the PRC's restrictions on domestic and foreign trade. Nevertheless, the expansion of U.S. power networks and Japanese business networks in the maritime regions of East Asia provided the diaspora with plenty of opportunities to exercise new forms of commercial intermediation between these networks and the local networks it controlled. And as restrictions on trade with and within China were relaxed, the diaspora quickly emerged as the single most powerful agency of the economic reunification of the East Asian regional economy (Hui 1995).

It is too early to tell what kind of political-economic formation will eventually emerge out of this reunification and how far the rapid economic expansion of the East Asian region can go. For what we know, the present rise of East Asia to the most dynamic center of processes of capital accumulation on a world scale may well be the preamble to a recentering of the regional and world economies on China as they were in pre-modern times. But whether or not that will actually happen, the main features of the on-going East Asian economic renaissance are sufficiently clear to provide us with some insights into its likely future trajectory and implications for the global economy at large.

First, the renaissance is as much the product of the contradictions of U.S. world hegemony as of East Asia's geo-historical heritage. The contradictions of U.S. world hegemony concern primarily the dependence of U.S. power and wealth on a path of development characterized by high protection and reproduction costs—that is, on the formation of a world-encompassing, capital-intensive military apparatus on the one side, and on the diffusion of wasteful and unsustainable patterns of mass consumption on the other. Nowhere have these contradictions been more evident than in East Asia. Not only did the Korean and Vietnam Wars reveal the limits of the actual power wielded by the U.S. warfare–welfare state. Equally important, as those limits tightened and expansion along the path of high protection and reproduction costs began to yield decreasing returns and to destabilize U.S. world power, East Asia's geo-historical heritage of comparatively low reproduction and protection costs gave the region's governmental and business agencies a decisive competitive advantage in a global economy more closely integrated than ever before. Whether this heritage will be preserved remains unclear. But for the time being the East Asian expansion has the potential of becoming the tracklaying vehicle of a developmental path more economical and sustainable than the U.S. path.

Second, the renaissance has been associated with a structural differentiation of power in the region that has left the United States in control of most of the guns, Japan and the Overseas Chinese in control of most of the money, and the PRC in control of most of the labor. This structural differentiation—which has no precedent in previous hegemonic transitions— makes it extremely unlikely that any single state operating in the region, the United States included, will acquire the capabilities needed to become hegemonic regionally and globally. Only a plurality of states acting in concert with one another has any chance of bringing into existence an East Asian-based new world order. This plurality may well include the United States and, in any event, U.S. policies toward the region will remain as important a factor as any other in determining whether, when, and how such a regionally based new world order would actually emerge.

Third, the process of economic expansion and integration of the East Asian region is a process structurally open to the rest of the global economy. In part, this openness is a heritage of the interstitial nature of the process vis-à-vis the networks of power of the United States. In part, it is due to the important role played by informal business networks with ramifications throughout the global economy in promoting the integration of the region. And in part, it is due to the continuing dependence of East Asia on other regions of the global economy for raw materials, high technology, and cultural products. The strong forward and backward linkages that connect the East Asian regional economy to the rest of the world augur well for the future of the global economy, assuming that the economic expansion of East Asia is not brought to a premature end by internal conflicts, mismanagement, or U.S. resistance to the loss of power and prestige, though not necessarily of wealth and welfare, that the recentering of the global economy on East Asia entails.

Finally, the embedding of the East Asian economic expansion and integration in the region's geo-historical heritage means that the process cannot be replicated elsewhere with equally favorable results. Adaptation to the emergent East Asian economic leadership on the basis of each region's own geo-historical heritage—rather than misguided attempts at replicating the East Asian experience out of context, or even more misguided attempts at reaffirming Western supremacy on the basis of a flawed assessment of the actual power wielded by the U.S. military–industrial complex—is the most promising course of action for non-East Asian states. Whether this is a realistic expectation is, of course, an altogether different matter.

NOTE

I would like to thank Beverly Silver, David Smith, Dorie Solinger, and Steven Topik for very useful comments on an earlier version of this chapter.

This chapter also appeared in *State and Sovereignty in the Global Economy.* D. Smith et al., eds. (Routledge, in press).

REFERENCES

Arrighi, Giovanni. (1982). A Crisis of Hegemony. In S. Amin, G. Arrighi, A.G. Frank, and I. Wallerstein. *Dynamics of Global Crisis*. New York: Monthly Review Press: 55–108.

———. (1994). *The Long Twentieth Century: Money, Power and the Origins of Our Times*. London: Verso.

———. (1996). The Rise of East Asia: World-Systemic and Regional Aspects. *International Journal of Sociology and Social Policy* 16, no. 7/8: 6–44.

———. (1998). Financial Expansions in World Historical Perspective: A Reply to Robert Pollin. *New Left Review*, forthcoming.

————, Satoshi Ikeda, and Alex Irwan (1993). The Rise of East Asia: One Miracle or Many? In R.A. Palat, ed. *Pacific-Asia and the Future of the World-System.* Westport, Conn.: Greenwood Press: 41–65.

Bairoch, Paul, and R. Kozul-Wright. (1996). Globalization Myths: Some Historical Reflections on Integration, Industrialization and Growth in the World Economy. United Nations Conference on Trade and Development Discussion Paper # 113.

Braudel, Fernand. (1984). *The Perspective of the World.* New York: Harper and Row.

Chandler, Alfred. (1990). *Scale and Scope: The Dynamics of Industrial Capitalism.* Cambridge, Mass.: Belknap Press.

Cumings, Bruce. (1997). Japan and Northeast Asia into the Twenty-First Century. In P.J. Katzenstein and T. Shiraishi, eds. *Network Power: Japan and Asia.* Ithaca, N.Y.: Cornell University Press: 136–68.

Frieden, Jeffry A. (1987). *Banking on the World: The Politics of American International Finance.* New York: Harper and Row.

Friedman, Thomas. (1997). Roll Over Hawks and Doves. *The New York Times,* Feb. 2, I: p. 15.

Giddens, Anthony. (1987). *The Nation State and Violence.* Berkeley: California University Press.

Gilpin, Robert. (1975). *U.S. Power and the Multinational Corporation.* New York: Basic Books.

Gross, Leo. (1988). The Peace of Westphalia, 1648–1948. In R.A. Falk and W.H. Hanrieder, eds. *International Law and Organization.* Philadelphia: Lippincott: 45–67.

Halliday, Fred. (1983). *The Making of the Second Cold War.* London: Verso.

Harrod, Roy. (1969). *Money.* London: Macmillan.

Harvey, David. (1995). Globalization in Question. *Rethinking Marxism* 8, no. 4: 1–17.

Hirst, Paul. (1996). Global Market and the Possibilities of Governance. Paper presented at the Conference on Globalization and the New Inequality, University of Utrecht, November 20–22.

Hobsbawm, Eric. (1994). *The Age of Extremes: A History of the World, 1914–1991.* New York: Vintage.

Hui, Po-keung. (1995). Overseas Chinese Business Networks: East Asian Economic Development in Historical Perspective. Ph. D. diss., Department of Sociology, State University of New York at Binghamton.

Ikeda, Satoshi. (1996). World Production. In T.K. Hopkins, I. Wallerstein et al. *The Age of Transition: Trajectory of the World-System 1945–2025.* London: Zed Books.

Ingham, Geoffrey. (1994). States and Markets in the Production of World Money: Sterling and the Dollar. In S. Corbridge, R. Martin, and N. Thrift, eds. *Money, Power and Space.* Oxford: Blackwell.

Jackson, Robert. (1990). *Quasi-States: Sovereignty, International Relations, and the Third World.* Cambridge: Cambridge University Press.

Japan Almanac (Various Years). Tokyo: Asahi Shimbum Publishing Co.

Katzenstein, Peter. (1987). *Policy and Politics in West Germany: The Growth of a Semisovereign State.* Philadelphia: Temple University Press.

Kraar, Louis. (1993). The New Power in Asia. *Fortune*, October 31: 38–44.

Krasner, Stephen. (1988). A Trade Strategy for the United States. *Ethics and International Affairs* 2: 17–35.

———. (1997). Sovereignty and Its Discontents. Paper presented at the Conference on "States and Sovereignty in the World Economy," University of California, Irvine, Feb. 21–23.

Krugman, Paul. (1994). The Myth of Asia's Miracle. *Foreign Affairs* LXXIII, no. 6: 62–78.

Lie, John. (1996). Globalization and Its Discontents. *Contemporary Sociology* 25, no. 5: 585–87.

McNeill, William. (1982). *The Pursuit of Power: Technology, Armed Forces and Society since A.D. 1000*. Chicago: University of Chicago Press.

Mann, Michael. (1986). *The Sources of Social Power. Vol. I: A History of Power from the Beginning to A.D. 1760*. Cambridge: Cambridge University Press.

Mittelman, James H., ed. (1996). *Globalization: Critical Reflections*. Boulder, Colo.: Lynne Rienner.

Ozawa, Terutomo. (1993). Foreign Direct Investment and Structural Transformation: Japan as a Recycler of Market and Industry. *Business & the Contemporary World* 5, no. 2: 129–50.

Polanyi, Karl. (1957). *The Great Transformation: The Political and Economic Origins of Our Time*. Boston: Beacon Press.

Rosenau, James. (1990). *Turbulence in World Politics: A Theory of Change and Continuity*. Princeton, N.J.: Princeton University Press.

Ruggie, John. (1994). Third Try at World Order? America and Multilateralism after the Cold War. *Political Science Quarterly* 109, no. 4: 553–70.

Sassen, Saskia. (1996). *Losing Control? Sovereignty in an Age of Globalization*. New York: Columbia University Press.

Schurmann, Franz. (1974). *The Logic of World Power: An Inquiry into the Origins, Currents, and Contradictions of World Politics*. New York: Pantheon.

So, Alvin Y., and Stephen W.K. Chiu. (1995). *East Asia and the World-Economy*. Newbury Park, Calif.: Sage.

Soros, George. (1997). The Capitalist Threat. *The Atlantic Monthly* 279, no. 2: 45–58.

Stopford John M., and John H. Dunning. (1983). *Multinationals: Company Performance and Global Trends*. London: Macmillan.

Taylor, Peter. (1991). *Territoriality and Hegemony, Spatiality and the Modern World-System*. Newcastle upon Tyne, UK: Department of Geography, University of Newcastle upon Tyne.

———. (1994). Ten Years that Shook the World? The United Provinces as First Hegemonic State. *Sociological Perspectives* 37, no. 1: 25–46.

Union Bank of Switzerland. (1996). The Asian Economic Miracle. *UBS International Finance* (Zurich) 29: 1–8.

Wade, Robert. (1996). Globalization and Its Limits: The Continuing Economic Importance of Nations and Regions. In S. Berger and R. Dore, eds. *Convergence or Diversity? National Models of Production and Distribution in a Global Economy*. Ithaca, N.Y.: Cornell University Press.

Wallerstein, Immanuel. (1995). *After Liberalism*. New York: The New Press.

Part II
Income Inequality and Flows
of Money and Goods

8

Income Inequality and Flows of Money and Goods: Introduction

Nico Wilterdink

Inequality is rising in the Western world. After decades of democratization, leveling of incomes, and emancipation of the working classes, the differences between the rich and the poor are growing again in most if not all Western societies. The tendency started some fifteen to twenty years ago and does not seem to have ended.

According to a now widespread idea, this increase of inequality is connected to processes of globalization—forces in the world economy that are beyond the control of national states and tear the socioeconomic groups within these states apart. On the evolving integrated world markets, workers in the rich countries are confronted with increasing competition from other countries, and capital owners can move their wealth easily to wherever the returns are expected to be the highest.[1]

This "globalization thesis" has met with several criticisms. Some scholars have pointed out that globalization is not a recent phenomenon, but should be conceived—if it has any meaning at all—as an age-long historical process with different stages or waves. As Arrighi, Hirst, and Hanagan make clear in the first part of this book, it was particularly the period 1850–1914 that saw a huge increase of world trade and international capital flows. Globalization as such is too broad a concept to give a satisfactory explanation for the growth of income inequality in Western states since about 1980.

This criticism should be conceived not as a refutation of the globalization thesis, but rather as a plea for historical specification. Not only are the processes subsumed under this concept in the 1980s and 1990s quite different from those a century before (if only because of the advances in information, communication, transportation, and production technologies in the course of these hundred years), they also impinge on very different societies. One essential difference, or set of differences, pertains to the nature and dynamics of state organizations. In the late nineteenth century the growth of international trade and capital movements went hand in hand with the strengthening of state functions, whereas today's globalization is connected to a weakening of state controls coupled with efforts to cut back on social expenditures, which had vastly expanded in the previous period.

A second criticism has been put forward by economists who find the statistical basis for the supposed connection weak or absent (Krugman 1994: 145 ff.; Berman et al. 1994; cf., Burtless 1995). Some defend an alternative explanation: it is not international trade but technological change that is largely responsible for the recent growth of income inequality through its impact on the demand for different types of labor. Modern high technology, by substituting robots and computers for simple work tasks, depresses the demand and therefore the wages for low-skilled workers, whereas the same process pushes up the demand for highly educated specialists.

The three contributions that follow are part of the ongoing debate on the possible connections between globalization and growing inequality. Each in their own way, they give new support to, and shed new light on, the thesis that globalization processes do contribute to the inequality in Western nation states that has been growing since about 1980. John Schmitt points out that technological change cannot explain convincingly the dramatic increase of wage inequality in the United States since the late 1970s coupled with a real wage decline for the majority of wage-earners; at best, it can explain only part of this development. The alternative explanation, which stresses growing international trade, is also only partial. The suggestion that both explanations are mutually exclusive is misleading, Schmitt argues, as "technology" and "trade" are interconnected. Moreover, growing international trade is part of wider globalization processes, which also include immigration, vast capital flows, and increasing relocation options for employers who thereby weaken unions' bargaining power and put a negative pressure on workers' wages.

When wages in general decline relative to other types of income, the growth of income inequality might be connected to changes in the functional distribution of income, i.e., the relative proportions of wages and capital income in total income. In their investigation of changes in income inequality in the Netherlands since the First World War, Jan Reijnders and Jan Luiten van Zanden stress the importance of this source of income inequality. As wage inequality hardly changed in the Netherlands since the beginnings of the 1980s, the growth in overall income inequality that did occur has to be explained differently. The authors find a strong correlation between changes in Dutch personal income inequality and changes in the share of capital income in total income in the period 1914–93; as the share of capital income went up, income inequality increased, and vice versa. The results of their regression analysis show clear connections of these intertwined developments with indicators of economic conditions and power relations, but the nature of the connections is somewhat different for the prewar period (1914–39) and the postwar period (1945–93). It is only in the second period that an increase of income inequality and the share of capital income can be related to a decreasing degree of unionization of the labor force. This is particularly relevant for the period since 1983. It is also in this period that the increasing international integration of capital markets pushed up capital income. As Reijnders and van Zanden conclude, these connections are not specific to the Netherlands, but have a much wider significance.

As Nico Wilterdink suggests in chapter eleven, these findings may be interpreted in terms of a power-interdependence model of socioeconomic inequality, in which the ownership and the control of capital are regarded as power resources. The growing international mobility of physical and financial capital gives its owners and managers increasing power advantages and therefore income advantages in relation to groups and organizations that are much more bound to national territories, in particular organized labor and national governments. Available data show a strong growth of foreign direct investments (FDI) in the world economy, particularly since the second half of the 1970s. However, the empirical evidence for the supposed relation between the internationalization of capital, specified as the growth of FDI, and increasing income inequality is only weak. Insofar as there is such a relation, it apparently does not "work" on the level of separate national states; there is no positive correlation between the openness of a national economy defined in terms of FDI-flows and FDI-stock related to GDP and the degree of income inequality, nor between changes in these respects. This is in line with the results of earlier studies that found no positive connection (rather a negative one) between income inequality and openness of the national economy defined in terms of import and export relative to gross domestic product (GDP) (Gottschalk and Joyce 1991; Rodrik 1997).

Taken together, these chapters raise several questions and suggest several lines of further investigation. They show both similarities and differences in income inequality trends in Western nations—an overall tendency of growing inequality since the 1980s (with a few exceptions) together with strong variations in timing and degree. This raises the question of what the normal or typical development is. To be more specific, does the U.S. development represent an advanced stage of what happens or will happen in all prosperous societies, or is it exceptional? Comparative data show that the degree to which income inequality has grown in the United

States in the last two decades has been quite extraordinary, and that the United States is the exception rather than the rule in its strong and continuous increase of wage inequality.[2] This specific development cannot be explained only in terms of unspecific processes such as globalization (or, in particular, the growth of international trade) or technological change. Institutional characteristics peculiar to the United States, such as the relatively low degree of unionization and the highly decentralized nature of wage bargaining, should be added to the explanation; it is under these conditions that globalization processes (growth of international trade, increasing capital mobility, growing immigration) and other, related forces directly impinging on the labor market (technological and organizational innovations) have led to substantially growing wage disparities.

On the other hand, the fairly high stability of wage inequality in the Netherlands, noted by Reijnders and van Zanden, is less exceptional than it might seem. It is found in most other Western European countries as well and can be connected to a high degree of centralization and coverage in collective wage bargaining (Hartog 1996). The high stability in the distribution of the bulk of wage incomes appears not to rule out increasing income inequality in general, however, which means that the causes of increasing inequality must lie elsewhere. Other (possible) sources of growing income inequality are the growth of capital income; the growth of top labor incomes that are not, or only imperfectly, covered by the wage statistics;[3] the growing income disparities among the self-employed; and the relative lowering of transfer income levels. Whereas the last-mentioned source is dependent on political decision making, the other ones are largely independent from governmental control and institutionalized labor relations.

This leads to the hypothesis that the primary sources of the general tendency of growing income inequality in economically advanced societies since the 1980s are the increase of capital income relative to labor income and the increase of top labor incomes, particularly managers' incomes, relative to other labor incomes. Furthermore, it may be hypothesized that these increases reflect a power shift in favor of the owners and managers of large concentrations of capital (large shareholders, executives and directors of financial and nonfinancial corporations, managers of investment funds), which in turn is connected to and can partly be explained by the growing international mobility of physical and financial capital. These hypotheses suggest further statistical research on trends in income distribution as well as social research on changing institutions and corporate structures.

The suggested hypotheses, while focussing on general trends and similarities, do not deny the continuing importance of differences between countries (cf., Crouch and Streeck 1997). The consequences of globalization or, in particular, the growing mobility of capital, depend on nation specific institutions rooted in particular histories and vary accordingly. Moreover, globalization itself, however defined, is partly determined by political decisions taken in the framework of evolving institutional structures on national and international levels.

Research in this field is necessarily interdisciplinary; it combines and crosses the borders of economics, sociology, political science, and economic history. The following chapters, one by an economist, the second by an economist and an economic historian, and the third by a sociologist, give some ideas on how to pursue this interdisciplinary endeavor.

NOTES

1. The publications in which these ideas have been set forth range from detached scholarly work to popular and normative accounts. See e.g., Harrison and Bluestone 1990; Reich 1991; Wood 1994; Thurow 1996; and Rodrik 1997.

2. According to OECD statistics, the only other OECD country that exhibits such a strong and continuous increase of wage inequality in the period 1980–95 is the United Kingdom. [OECD 1996: 61–62 (table 3.1)]

3. The OECD wage statistics compare the upper earnings limits of the ninth, fifth, and first deciles of workers, which means that the earnings in the tenth (upper) decile are excluded from the comparison (OECD 1996: 61–62). Besides, the wage statistics do not cover the non-salary earnings by managers, such as the (often very large) extra incomes through stock options. There are many indications that top management incomes have increased very strongly in absolute and relative terms since the 1980s. (See e.g., Wilterdink 1995.)

REFERENCES

Berman, Eli, et al. (1994). Changes in the Demand for Skilled Labor within U.S. Manufacturing: Evidence from the Annual Survey of Manufactures. *The Quarterly Journal of Economics*: 367–97.

Burtless, Gary. (1995). International Trade and the Rise of Earnings Inequality. *Journal of Economic Literature* XXXIII: 800–16.

Crouch, Colin, and Wolfgang Streeck, eds. (1997). *Political Economy of Modern Capitalism*. London: Sage.

Gottschalk, Peter, and Mary Joyce. (1991). Changes in Earnings Inequality—An International Perspective. The Luxembourg Income Study. Working Paper 66.

Harrison, Bennett, and Barry Bluestone. (1990). *The Great U-Turn*. New York: Basic Books [1988].

Hartog, Jan. (1996). Dutch Income Inequality in International Perspective. Paper presented at the conference "Globalisation and the New Inequality," Utrecht, Nov. 1996.

Krugman, Paul. (1994). *Peddling Prosperity*. New York: Norton.

OECD. (1996). *Employment Outlook 1996*. Paris: OECD.

Reich, Robert. (1991). *The Work of Nations*. New York: Vintage Books [1992].

Rodrik, Dani. (1997). *Has Globalization Gone Too Far?* Washington, D.C.: Institute for International Economics.

Thurow, Lester C. (1996). *The Future of Capitalism*. New York: William Morrow.

Wilterdink, Nico. (1995). Increasing Income Inequality and Wealth Concentration in the Prosperous Societies of the West. *Studies in Comparative International Development* 30 (Fall): 3–23.

Wood, Adrian. (1994). *North–South Trade, Employment, and Inequality*. Oxford: Clarendon Press.

9

Inequality and Globalization: Some Evidence from the United States

John Schmitt

After initial hesitation in some quarters, nearly all economists now agree that wage inequality has increased substantially in the United States since the late 1970s. Most of the analyses of the changing U.S. wage structure have focused on changes over time in relative wages. Workers in the ninetieth percentile of the wage distribution or workers with a four-year university degree, for example, have always earned substantially more than workers in the tenth percentile of the distribution or those who have not earned a high school degree. In 1995, however, the difference in these relative wages was much larger than it was in 1979. The current economic debate in the United States now centers on whether technology or trade is the driving force behind this rising inequality. An impartial assessment of the state of the economic debate in the United States would conclude that economic opinion there believes that skill-biased technological change is the fundamental force behind recent changes in the wage structure, with globalization playing at most a modest role and perhaps no role at all in widening inequality.

In this context, this chapter has two main goals: first, to shift the analysis of recent developments in the U.S. wage structure away from widening relative wages toward the stagnation and decline in real wage levels; and second, to question the usefulness of the current "technology versus trade" debate. The chapter has four sections. The first briefly reviews developments in the U.S. wage distribution since 1979. The second critiques the terms of the technology versus trade debate. The third section analyzes some of the theory and evidence on the impact of globalization on the U.S. wage structure. The final section reflects on the implications of the U.S. evidence for the debate over globalization in Europe.

DEVELOPMENTS IN THE U.S. WAGE STRUCTURE SINCE 1979

Almost without exception, analyses of changes in the wage structure since the end of the 1970s have concentrated on widening relative wages. This emphasis on relative wages, while useful and important, has, however, diverted attention from the broad stagnation and deterioration in real wage levels.

Panel (a) of table 9.1 reports one standard measure of wage inequality, the "90-10 differential," for data from the Current Population Survey for the years 1979, 1989, and 1996 (the first two years are business cycle peaks; the last is well into the current economic recovery). The 90-10 differential is the ratio of the wage of a worker in the ninetieth percentile of the wage distribution to that of a worker in the tenth percentile of the distribution. For men, the ratio increased from 3.67 in 1979 to 4.23 in 1989 and then to 4.45 by 1996.[1] The rate of growth in the 90-10 differential was lower in the first half of the 1990s (0.03 points per year, on average) than it had been in the 1980s (0.06 points per year). For women, the 90-10 differential increased from 2.71 to 3.85 between 1979 and 1989 and then grew further to 4.02 by 1996. Note, however, that the level of inequality among women workers was well below that of men in all three years and that inequality increased much more slowly for women in the 1990s (0.02 points per year) than it had in the 1980s (0.11 points per year).

The numbers in panel (a) of table 9.1 are well-traveled ground. What is just as striking, but has received far less attention, however, are the trends

Table 9.1   Wage Structure[a] in the United States, 1979–96

				Annualized Change	
	1979	*1989*	*1996*	*1979–89*	*1989–96*
a) Wage Inequality					
Men 90th/10th	3.67	4.23	4.45	0.06	0.03
Women 90th/10th	2.71	3.85	4.02	0.11	0.02
b) Hourly Wage Levels					
Men 90th	$24.62	$24.80	$24.55	0.07%	− 0.14%
Men 50th	13.66	12.41	11.51	− 0.91	− 1.03
Men 10th	6.71	5.86	5.52	− 1.27	− 0.83
Women 90th	$15.78	$18.36	$19.34	1.63%	0.76%
Women 50th	8.58	9.07	8.93	0.57	− 0.22
Women 10th	5.82	4.76	4.81	− 1.82	0.16

Source: Economic Policy Institute; analysis of Current Population Survey Outgoing Rotation Group.

[a]1995 dollars.

in wage levels reported in panel (b). Even as relative wages of male workers in the ninetieth percentile skyrocketed, the real wage levels of ninetieth percentile workers were virtually stagnant, growing at annual rates of 0.07 percent during the 1980s and falling 0.14 percent in the first half of the 1990s. The rise in 90 – 10 differential since the end of the 1970s, then, is due almost entirely to the sharp decline in real wages for workers at the tenth percentile. The hourly wage of male workers at the tenth percentile fell 1.27 percent per year on average in the 1980s and 0.83 percent per year in the 1990s. Even the median male worker has seen his wages fall by about 1 percent per year since 1979 (– 0.91 percent per year in the 1980s, accelerating slightly to – 1.03 percent per year in the 1990s).

For women, the story is more complicated. The rise in the 90-10 differential in the 1980s was the result of both rising real wages for women in the ninetieth percentile (1.63 percent annual rate) and falling real wages for women in the tenth percentile (– 1.82 percent). The deceleration in the growth of the 90-10 differential in the 1990s reflects a halving of the annual growth rate in real wages for women at the ninetieth percentile (0.76 percent) and small positive growth (0.16 percent) in wages for women at the tenth percentile (which may be related to increases in the federal minimum wage in 1990 and 1991). The "median woman" experienced positive wage growth in the 1980s (0.57 percent), but has been losing ground in the 1990s (– 0.22 percent).

Table 9.2 makes clear that a four-year university degree was not sufficient to protect against stagnating and even falling wages.[2] Panel (a) reports data for university-educated workers of all ages. As a group, university-educated men, like men at the ninetieth percentile of the wage distribution had roughly stagnant wages between 1979 and 1995, with an

Table 9.2 Hourly Wages[a] for U.S. Workers with Four-Year College Degrees, 1979–95

				Annualized Change	
	1979	*1989*	*1995*	*1979–89*	*1989–95*
(a) All College-Educated					
Men	$19.43	$19.54	$19.55	0.06%	0.01%
Women 90th/10th	12.42	14.02	14.84	1.29	0.97
(b) Graduates, 1–5 Years Experience					
Men	$14.04	$13.86	$12.54	– 0.13%	– 1.59%
Women	11.24	12.51	11.55	1.13	– 1.28

Source: Economic Policy Institute; analysis of Current Population Survey Outgoing Rotation Group.
[a]1995 dollars.

annual growth rate of 0.06 percent in the 1980s, slowing to 0.01 percent in the 1990s. University-educated women's wages grew faster (1.29 percent per year in the 1980s, slowing to 0.97 percent per year in the 1990s), but from levels far below those of their male counterparts. Panel (b) shows wage data for recent university graduates (those with only one to five years of labor market experience). Wages for recent, male university graduates fell 0.13 percent per year, on average, between 1979 and 1989 and then at a much steeper 1.59 percent annual rate between 1989 and 1995. Recent, female university graduates fared better in the 1980s, with a 1.13 percent annual growth rate over the decade, but have been hit hard since 1989, when wages began falling at a 1.28 percent annual rate.

Another side effect of the focus on relative wages (and, as I shall discuss later, of the emphasis on skill-biased technological change) is the tendency to view most of the wage inequality problem as one of educational "haves" (those with a four-year university degree or more) and the educational "have nots" (the three-fourths of the U.S. workforce without a four-year university degree). In fact, only a little less than half of the increase since 1979 in the male 90 – 10 differential is due to changes in the returns to formal education and work experience; changes in education and work experience differentials account for just 40 percent of the rise in the female 90-10 differential over the same period.[3] These numbers establish that most of the increase in overall inequality in the last twenty years does not stem from growing differences between education groups, but rather from widening differences within education groups. The data then clearly suggest that most of the recent increase in inequality is not related to workers' "skills," at least as they are typically measured by economists.[4]

THE "TECHNOLOGY VERSUS TRADE" DEBATE

The "technology versus trade" debate has been at the center of recent discussions of the causes of the rising wage inequality documented above (see e.g., Freeman 1995). Before analyzing the role of globalization in inequality, I would like to present three objections to this particular framing of the inequality debate.

First, no *prima facie* case exists that technology has played any role in widening wage inequality since 1979. Most of the research that has found a relationship between technology and changes in the wage structure has relied on indirect measures of technology, often nothing more than a residual in an econometric specification. The research that has demonstrated that technology affects the wage structure (something that should not be too controversial) has not shown that technological change had a bigger impact in the 1980s and 1990s than it did in the 1970s. If technology has not had a larger impact in the 1980s and 1990s—either because technological progress occurred more rapidly or because it became more biased against less-skilled workers—then it is not likely that technology was responsible for the significant changes in the wage structure evident after the late 1970s.[5]

The developments outlined above in the U.S. wage structure are inconsistent with the belief that an acceleration in skill-biased technological change is responsible for the recent rise in wage inequality. What kind of skill-biased technological change leaves the wages of the most-skilled male workers, those at the ninetieth percentile of the wage distribution and those with a four-year university degree, virtually unchanged over a twenty-year period? What kind of skill-biased technological change sees the real wages of recent university graduates male and female—in many ways, those most comfortable with much of the new computer technology—falling about one percent per year, even as the growth in the share of university graduates decelerates? How can skill-biased technological change explain the 50 percent or more of overall wage inequality that is not related to workers' formal education or job experience? Finally, what kind of technological change is it that can completely rearrange the U.S. wage structure but have no effect on the growth rate in economy-wide labor productivity, which has averaged just one percent or so per year since the mid-1970s?

A second objection to the technology versus trade debate is that trade represents only one aspect of a much broader process of globalization. The focus on trade in final goods discourages a discussion of the much more complex process of globalization, which also includes international outsourcing, "threat effects" associated with international relocation of production, foreign direct investment, foreign portfolio investment, multilateral and bilateral lending, private international lending, immigration, trade-induced changes in technology, and other factors.

Third, the trade–technology dichotomy also sweeps to one side changes in labor and product market institutions that have contributed to wage inequality. The United States since 1979 has embraced a wide range of economic policy changes that have almost without exception reduced the bargaining power of workers with respect to their employers. The Federal Reserve Board has, since Paul Volcker's tenure as chairman, become much tougher on inflation (though the Fed has become far more lenient than European central bankers—a key, often overlooked aspect of the "U.S. model"). The real value of the minimum wage fell about 30 percent during the 1980s and even after increases in 1990, 1991, 1996, and 1997 still stands at a level about 20 percent below where it was in 1979. Private sector unionization rates declined about ten percentage points during the 1980s, with unions now representing only about 12 percent of workers in the private sector. Product market deregulation (in airlines, trucking, telecommunications, and other industries) also reduced wages in many major industries. Separately, these measures have all served to varying degrees to reduce the levels or the rates of growth of real wages. Together, they probably account for most of the changes since the end of the 1970s in the U.S. wage structure.

Seen in this context, globalization is largely just another of the institutional changes since the late 1970s that have worked to liberalize markets and to undermine the bargaining power of workers. The complex bilateral and multilateral agreements that were the necessary precondition for any meaningful process of globalization were government policies—not inexorable, exogenous forces. These agreements, which have generally dealt as much with the terms of making foreign direct and portfolio investments as with trade in goods, opened domestic product and labor markets to foreign competition, generally in ways detrimental to the economic interests of workers.

THEORY AND EVIDENCE ON GLOBALIZATION, WAGES, AND EMPLOYMENT IN THE UNITED STATES

Economic theory suggests that the broad process of globalization should affect U.S. wages through a variety of channels. A comprehensive review of the theoretical underpinnings and the empirical evidence for each channel is beyond the scope of this chapter. This section seeks only to sketch some of the relevant thinking and report some of the direct evidence that suggests a significant role for globalization in recent changes in the wage structure.

Much of the U.S. literature has concentrated on the direct impact of increased volumes of trade in final goods on the wages and employment of opportunities of U.S. workers, particularly those in production jobs or with less than a four-year university degree. Sachs and Shatz (1994), for example, conclude that changes in net export shares between 1979 and 1989 lowered manufacturing employment in the United States by 5.9 percent relative to what it would have been if net export shares had remained at their 1979 level throughout the decade of the 1980s. Rising shares of trade with developing countries were responsible for the vast majority of the job losses, which were disproportionately concentrated among production workers. Saeger (1995) estimates that the increase in U.S. trade with low-wage countries between 1970 and 1990 reduced the manufacturing share of total U.S. employment by about 2.7 percentage points over the same period.

Many trade economists, however, have objected to the use of trade volumes to measure the impact of trade on wages and employment. They argue that standard trade theory (the Stolper–Samuelson theorem in a Heckscher–Ohlin framework) suggests that trade affects domestic wages and the distribution of domestic employment by changing goods prices (see, for example, Lawrence and Slaughter [1993]). Schmitt and Mishel (1996) estimate that trade-induced changes in domestic prices were responsible for 6–20 percent of the increase during the 1980s in the university–nonuniversity wage differential in manufacturing and 35–100 percent of the smaller increase over the same period in the nonproduction–production workers differential. Sachs and Shatz (1994) and Krueger (1995) find broadly similar results, though they offer different interpretations of their potential significance.

Trade can also affect less-skilled manufacturing workers by giving firms opportunities to outsource less-skill intensive work to low-wage countries and then later import intermediate products for subsequent processing. Feenstra and Hansen (1996), for example, show imported manufacturing inputs more than doubled as a share of total inputs in manufacturing between 1972 and 1990 (from 5.3 percent to 11.6 percent).

Immigration is another mechanism through which globalization may affect the domestic income distribution. Documented immigration to the United States has raised the share of foreign-born workers from 4.7 percent of all workers in 1970 to about 7.9 percent of the total in 1990. While recent immigrants tend to include a greater share of university graduates than in the native population, they are also almost two times more likely than natives to have less than a high school degree.[6] All else constant, the increase in the labor supply should depress wages; the increase in the relative supply of less-skilled workers suggests that the wage depressing effects should be strongest for the lowest paid workers.

Relatively little research exists on a host of other aspects of globalization and the domestic wage distribution. Large-scale capital flows—short-term and long-term; private, bilateral, and multilateral lending and development assistance; foreign direct investment; foreign portfolio investment; and others—change the geographical distribution of employment opportunities. They also facilitate employer strategies based on relocation and outsourcing (real or threatened) in wage bargaining. Even expanding exports can put pressure on the wages of domestic workers if employers can argue credibly that pay levels must fall in order to maintain competitiveness in export markets. Rising trade volumes and falling manufactured goods prices can also affect the type and pace of technological development, making it difficult to separate trade and technology effects. Finally, as the traded sector sheds and adds labor, the labor market becomes a transmission mechanism that conveys the effects of globalization to the nontraded sector.

THE "U.S. VERSUS EUROPE" DEBATE

The differences between the political debate over globalization in Europe and in the United States are striking. Capital in both areas seeks open economies with a minimum of social protections, but faces different obstacles in achieving these goals. Europe has relatively open economies with extensive social protections; the United States has a relatively closed economy (though exposure to low-wage countries is much higher than in Europe)[7] with only minimal social protections. In the current European political climate, a reduction in openness (except perhaps with respect to immigration) seems unlikely, but the future of the welfare state is the subject of intense political debate; in the current U.S. political climate, any expansion of social protections is probably politically impossible, but the degree of openness to the international economy is a major political question.

These differences in political terrain have shaped very different debates over globalization. In Europe, where economies appear irreversibly open and social insurance programs are generous, but under attack, conservatives governments in Germany, France, and elsewhere have argued that the welfare state is an unaffordable luxury in the new, global economy.[8] Some Europeans, concerned about safeguarding social protection systems, have responded that this argument amounts to little more than using the idea of globalization to justify dismantling the welfare state.[9] In the United States, where social protections are minimal and a substantial portion of the population opposes most attempts to further open the U.S. economy, mainstream politicians and economists have argued that international economic forces will bring large, rapid, and broadly shared increases in the standard of living and have ridiculed those on the U.S. Left and Right who have argued that globalization would undermine the national standard of living.

Where in these two debates does the truth lie? A brief review of trade theory and the empirical evidence from the United States suggests that globalization should have and has had a significant impact on economic inequality there. Nothing about the mechanisms through which trade affects inequality in the United States suggests that the impact should be different in Europe, assuming that Europe chooses to engage the international economy in a similar manner. Rhetoric about the incompatibility of the global economy and the traditional welfare state has resonance because the globalization threat is credible. At the same time, those in Europe who downplay the role of globalization in inequality have convincingly argued that the idea of globalization, particularly as it is framed by conservative governments in Europe, can disempower social movements seeking to reduce inequality: in the face of an overwhelming and inexorable process of globalization, resistance seems futile.

The principal lesson for Europe from the recent U.S. experience is that economic inequality is the result of a broad deterioration in the social and economic institutions that previously acted to protect and improve the living standards of the majority of the population. Globalization has played an important role, but that role has often been misunderstood. The globalization process is part of a conscious government policy—unilateral reductions in tariff and nontariff barriers, complex bilateral and multilateral trade and investment agreements, the active promotion of export-led growth strategies in developing countries, and others—not simply, or even primarily, a consequence of shadowy, uncontrollable, external economic forces. In this sense, the liberalization of international trade and investment has not been so much an independent cause of rising inequality as yet another mechanism (along with restrictive macroeconomic policy, a lower minimum wage, reduced union power, deregulated product markets, and so on) through which powerful political forces have been able to impose greater economic inequality. In this context, the political debate in both the United States and Europe should focus not so much on the current effects of globalization, but rather the future terms of globalization.

CONCLUSION

The precipitous rise in wage inequality in the United States since the end of the 1970s is now a well-established fact. The debate over what has caused the new inequality, however, continues. Recent research in the United States has concentrated on the relative responsibility of trade versus technology, with most economists probably assigning a much larger weight to technology. Both the framing of the debate (as exclusively between trade and technology) and the early consensus that technology is the primary culprit, however, are unfortunate. The technology thesis sits uncomfortably with the simple observation that real wages for workers at the top of the wage distribution (ninetieth-percentile male workers or university-educated males) have been stagnant for two decades. Rising wage inequality has not been the result of a process in which technologically driven demand for high-skilled workers has bid up the real wages of workers at the top of the distribution, while leaving those without those same skills behind. The data instead make clear that something has pulled the bottom out of the wage distribution, dragging down the wages of workers in the middle and the bottom, while workers near the top have barely managed to hold their own.

At face value, foreign trade with low-wage countries is a better candidate than technology to explain these developments in the overall wage distribution. Concentration on trade alone, however, obscures much of the real cause of stagnating and declining wages. First, the process of global-ization is much more complex than the volume of international trade in manufactures, with most recent trade agreements more concerned about the rules of investment than those for the exchange of goods and services. Research on a variety of channels through which the broader globalization process affects employment opportunities and wages in the United States (trade volumes, trade prices, outsourcing, immigration, and others) sug-gests a substantial role for international economic forces. Economists have made few inroads in measuring the impact of other potentially important aspects of globalization, particularly those that have to do with a wide range of capital flows.

Second, by pitting trade against technology, the current debate has de-nied the role in rising inequality played by a host of changes to product and labor markets including the tight monetary policy (the 1980s more than the 1990s); tight fiscal policy (the 1990s more than the 1980s); the decline in the real value of the minimum wage; the fall in union member-ship rates; the deregulation of product markets in areas of the economy where less-educated workers historically earned high wages (like airlines, trucking, telecommunications); and others. These institutional changes have played a major role in the upheaval in the U.S. wage distribution dur-ing the past two decades.

Finally, even those economists in the debate who have argued that trade has had an important negative impact on the U.S. economy have tended to analyze trade (and, even more so, globalization) as an exogenous force beyond the control of national economies. When viewed as the liberaliza-tion of international capital, product, and labor markets, however, the globalization process becomes both a conscious policy that defines the na-tional terms of engagement with the world economy and an obvious com-plement to a long list of domestic, free-market policies.

NOTES

1. The 1996 figure for male workers is down slightly from 4.53 in 1995.

2. The coding for educational attainment in the Current Population Survey changed in 1992, making wage comparisons between 1989 and 1996 by education level more difficult. The analysis here uses information from a brief period of over-lap from the old and new coding to put the new data on a basis consistent with the earlier data. See Webster (1996) for details.

3. See Mishel, Bernstein, and Schmitt (1996: tables 3.24 and 3.25).

4. The preceding analysis of real wage levels has relied on the Consumer Price Index (CPI-U-X1) to compare real wage levels over time. Recently, a commission appointed by the U.S. Senate Finance Committee (SFC, 1996) has argued that the CPI overstates price increases by about 1.1 percentage points per year relative to a

"truc" cost-of-living measure. If true, the growth in real wage levels in tables 9.1 and 9.2 would be understated by 1.1 percentage points per year, undermining much of the argument presented here. Nevertheless, this chapter, consistent with the practice of the vast majority of U.S. economists, continues to use the CPI for several reasons.

First, any adjustment to the CPI would have no effect on the analysis of relative wages and inequality. Second, it appears that the SFC named the commission not primarily out of concern with the accuracy of the CPI, but rather because the SFC believed that a determination that the CPI overstated inflation would help to reduce the federal government deficit by lowering annual cost-of-living adjustments for Social Security recipients and by slowing down the indexation of income tax brackets. Apparently with this goal in mind, the SFC chose to staff the commission with five economists, all of whom had previously stated that the CPI significantly overstated inflation. Economists who had argued that the CPI did not overstate inflation or who believed that any overstatement was small were not included. Third, the SFC's proposed quality adjustments, which account for most of the proposed bias, are subjective and speculative. Madrick (1997a, 1997b), for example, has questioned the commission's failure to consider any cases in which the quality of consumer goods may have deteriorated, such as retail services, transportation (especially due to congestion), education, medical insurance, and other areas. Fourth, many of the criticisms of the CPI would probably apply to European price indices. Given that real wages have risen steadily across the full European wage distribution, comparable adjustments to European price indices would suggest that real wage growth has been even faster than previously believed, leaving the relative U.S.–European differences unaffected. Finally, Baker (1997) has conducted a careful review of the commission's findings and concludes that the commission's evidence is just as supportive of the idea that the CPI understates increases in the cost-of-living. He argues compellingly that the more rapid rates of wage growth suggested by the commission's estimate imply improbably low historical levels of wages and income. For example, applying an adjusted-CPI based on the biases suggested by the commission to nominal data for family income would suggest that half of all U.S. families in 1960 lived below the current poverty level.

5. For a full discussion of these ideas and evidence that the impact of technology on the wage structure has not changed significantly between the 1970s and the 1990s, see Mishel and Bernstein (1996).

6. The data are from Borjas (1994).

7. UNCTAD (United Nations Conference on Trade and Development) data cited by the OECD (1995: table 3.5), for example, show that developing country imports as a share of consumption of manufacturing goods in North America almost doubled from 2.3 percent in 1980–81 to 4.3 percent in 1990–91; in European Union countries, the share was virtually unchanged at 2.7 percent over the same period.

8. Rodrik (1997) contains an excellent discussion of the complex relationship between the development of the welfare state and processes of globalization.

9. See, for example, Loïc Wacquant's presentation to the Conference on "Globalisation and the New Inequality" at Utrecht University, November 22, 1996.

REFERENCES

Baker, Dean. (1997) forthcoming. Does the CPI Overstate Inflation? An Analysis of the Boskin Commission's Report. In Dean Baker, ed. *Getting Prices Right: The Debate over the Accuracy of the Consumer Price Index.* Armonk, N.Y.: M.E. Sharpe.

Borjas, George. (1994). The Economics of Immigration. *Journal of Economic Literature* 32: 1667–1717.

Feenstra, Robert, and Gordon Hanson. (1996). Globalization, Outsourcing, and Wage Inequality. *American Economic Association Papers and Proceedings* 86, no. 2: 240–45.

Freeman, Richard B. (1995). Are Your Wages Set in Beijing? *Journal of Economic Perspectives* 9, no. 3 (Summer): 15–32.

Krueger, Alan. (1995). Labor Market Shifts and the Price Puzzle Revisited. Industrial Relations Section, Princeton University.

Lawrence, Robert, and Matthew Slaughter. (1993). International Trade and American Wages in the 1980s: Giant Sucking Sound or Small Hiccup? *Brookings Papers: Microeconomics* 2: 161–223.

Madrick, Jeff. (1997a). The Cost of Living: A New Myth. *New York Review of Books*, March 6: 19–23.

———. (1997b). The Cost of Living: An Exchange. *New York Review of Books*, June 26: 65–67.

Mishel, Lawrence, and Jared Bernstein. (1996). Inside the Black Box: Estimating Technology's Impact on Wage Inequality Trends, 1973–94. Economic Policy Institute.

———, and John Schmitt, ed. (1996). *The State of Working America 1996–97.* Armonk, N.Y.: M.E. Sharpe.

Organization for Economic Cooperation and Development. (1995). *Linkages: OECD and Major Developing Economies.* Paris: OECD.

Rodrik, Dani. (1997). *Has Globalization Gone Too Far?* Washington, D.C.: Institute for International Economics.

Sachs, Jeffrey, and Howard Shatz. (1994). Trade and Jobs in U.S. Manufacturing. *Brookings Papers on Economic Activity* 1: 1–84.

———. (1995). International Trade and Wage Inequality in the United States: Some New Results. Economics Department, Harvard University.

Saeger, Steven S. (1995). Trade and Deindustrialization: Myth and Reality in the OECD. Economics Department, Harvard University.

Schmitt, John, and Lawrence Mishel. (1996). Did International Trade Lower Less-Skilled Wages during the 1980s? Standard Trade Theory and Evidence. Economic Policy Institute Technical Paper.

Senate Finance Committee. (1996). Toward a More Accurate Measure of the Cost of Living. Final Report to the Senate Finance Committee from the Advisory Commission to Study the Consumer Price Index. Washington, D.C.: United States Senate.

Webster, David. (1996). Wage Analysis Computations. In Lawrence Mishel, Jared Bernstein, and John Schmitt, eds. *The State of Working America 1996–97.* Armonk, N.Y.: M.E. Sharpe.

10

Globalization and the New Inequality: A Classical View

Jan Reijnders and Jan Luiten van Zanden

The current international debate about the changes in the distribution of income during the 1980s and early 1990s has focused largely on changes in the labor market. The literature about the "declining middle" and the recent rise in inequality of the income distribution has concentrated on changes in the supply and demand for different kinds of labor, and on institutional and political developments that have affected the position of different groups of laborers (see, for example, the contributions to Danziger and Gottschalk 1993). This debate has been mainly waged by Anglo-Saxon scholars, for the obvious reason that the upswing in inequality has been particularly marked in the United States and the United Kingdom. Changes in the distribution of income on the European continent have been much less dramatic, although in a number of European countries a trend toward greater inequality can also be observed. In the Netherlands this certainly is the case: according to the estimates of the Central Bureau of Statistics (CBS) the inequality of the distribution of disposable income began to increase after 1983 and continues to do so since. At the same time, changes in the structure of wages are very small indeed: a recent Organization for Economic Cooperation and Development (OECD) survey showed that the Netherlands was one of the few countries in which earnings dispersion did not increase during the 1980s. The same survey showed that the college premium, which is considered to be a major source of rising inequality in the United States and the United Kingdom, in fact fell in the Netherlands during the 1980s (OECD 1995). More detailed evidence published by the CBS showed that various measures of the "skill premium" had declined almost continuously between 1969 and 1993 (CBS 1996). In short, the Dutch upturn in income inequality seems to be abnormal, as changes in relative earnings are not able to explain it.

This chapter therefore focuses on the classical determinants of the (recent) changes in income inequality. We argue that changes in the functional distribution of income—between wages and profit income (or operating surplus)—should be taken into account in an explanation of the recent changes in the distribution of income over households. We will show that there is a close relationship between these two concepts of income distribution: the changes in the share of operating surplus total income run parallel to the changes in the inequality of the distribution of income over households. This conclusion is the result of an analysis of the long-term changes in income inequality during the twentieth century (specifically, 1914–93). Next, the determinants of the changes in the personal distribution of income are analyzed, which leads to the conclusion that factors related to the functional distribution of income—in fact, related to the economic position and relative strength of capital and labor—are able to explain long-run changes in the personal distribution of income satisfactorily. This analysis results in a somewhat different perspective on the recent upturn in inequality, and on the role globalization has played in it. It is concluded that globalization, which is defined within this framework as a strong increase in international mobility of capital and of goods—whereas the mobility of labor has remained limited—has contributed to the undermining of the bargaining power of labor. On the other hand the relative position of capital—of the shareholder for example—has certainly improved as a result of this process of globalization. In this way globalization has contributed to the rise of the "new inequality" of the 1980s and 1990s.

PERSONAL VERSUS FUNCTIONAL DISTRIBUTION

The analyst of the development of income distribution in the Netherlands can profit from the fact that this subject has attracted considerable attention in that country and has been addressed by scholars such as Hartog, Veenbergen, de Meere, and the statisticians of the Netherlands Central Statistical Office (Hartog and Veenbergen 1978; Hartog 1979; CBS 1994a and 1994b). They provided the empirical material on which the present analysis is built. The image that we synthesized out of the available empirical material is presented in figure 10.1 (solid line).[1]

The figure contains the sequence of Theil coefficients—a measure of the inequality of the personal income distribution—pertaining to the dispersion of after tax incomes in the Netherlands in the period 1914–93. Inspection of the graph shows that the new inequality that is characteristic of the 1980s and early 1990s is only one reversal in a sequence of ups and downs that seem to be superimposed upon a general downward trend, that is a tendency toward more equality. After the pronounced peak that coincides

Figure 10.1 Inequality Measures of Personal and Functional Income Distribution in the Netherlands, 1914–93

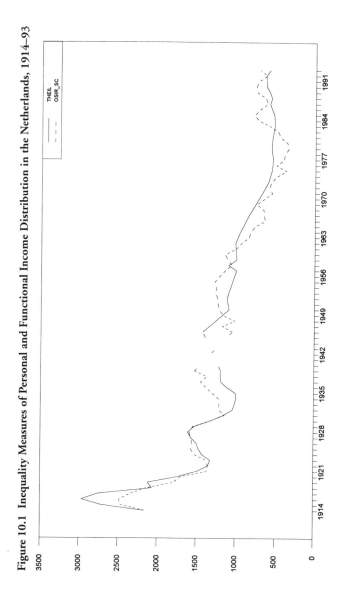

with the First World War a fall in inequality sets in that continued throughout the depression of 1920–23 to reach a local minimum in 1923. During the boom in the second half of the 1920s, inequality slowly increased, reaching a peak in 1928. The depression of the 1930s again led to a fall, which made way for another slight rise following the economic recovery of 1935–36. Between the world wars, therefore, we encounter a close correlation between economic development and income inequality: Economic growth is accompanied by an increase in inequality, and both depression periods (1920–23 and 1929–35) exhibit a striking fall (see also de Meere 1983; Schultz 1968).

The first data after the Second World War reveal a new peak in inequality. This is remarkable because wealth inequality sharply declined during the war (Wilterdink 1984), and there is some evidence that this was also the case with wage–income inequality (Weststrate 1984). Independent estimates made by T. Paul Schultz (1968), based on the same sources, do indeed show a fall in income inequality between 1939 and 1946, which continues after 1946. There is therefore some reason to doubt the initial increase of the Theil index after 1945.

According to Hartog's figures, the distribution of income maintained a more or less stable level in the period from 1950 to 1965, with inequality somewhat less than in 1938–39. On the other hand, the CBS figures show quite a marked fall in inequality from 1962 onward, a fall that continued into the first half of the 1970s. About ten years of stability followed, after which a slight increase in inequality can be registered, starting in 1983. Between 1983 and 1991 the Theil coefficient rose by 20 percent from .137 to .165. Thus the long-term fall in income inequality that had run through the twentieth century seems to have come to an end halfway through the 1980s (Wilterdink 1993).

As was said before, much of the current international debate about the new inequality is cast in terms of (changes in) the characteristics and positions of individuals or small groups of individuals. In our view, however, there is a lot to gain if the changes in the (in)equality are analyzed against the background of the long-term changes in the distribution of income that are tied to economic development in general and to the changing balance of power between socioeconomic groups that goes along with this. This implies that we will investigate the possibility of explaining the changes in the personal distribution on the basis of factors pertaining to the functional distribution of income.

The intuitive plausibility of such an approach may be illustrated by aligning an indicator that typically relates to functional income distribution to the Theil representation of the personal distribution. This comparison is included in figure 10.1, where the ratio of the operating surplus to domestic product[2] (dotted line) is scaled[3] with the sequence of Theil coef-

Figure 10.2 Factors Determining Functional and Personal Income Distribution

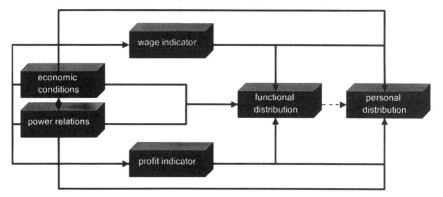

ficients of after tax income. It is obvious that this operating surplus to income ratio (OSIR)—in spite of its somewhat different dynamics—traces the contours of the development of the Theil sequence. This implies that the course of the operating surplus ratio may be expected to play an important role in the explanation of the movements of the Theil sequence over time. It may also imply that the set of variables that can explain movements of the operating surplus can also explain movements of the personal distribution of income.

The idea behind this can be illustrated by means of the framework outlined in figure 10.2. There are two sets of fundamental conditions that determine a set of intermediate variables indicating the rewards of productive factors (labor and capital), namely the economic circumstances and the power relations within society as a whole and between socioeconomic classes. In turn, these factor rewards interact with and are accentuated by the fundamental factors to produce the functional distribution of income. Our proposition now is that the latter also applies to the personal distribution of income. Accordingly, the functional and personal distributions are different expressions of one and the same process, i.e., they are the products of a similar interaction and accentuation of factor rewards and basic conditions (as indicated by the dotted arrow between the functional and personal distribution).

This proposition may be tested empirically by regression analysis. To this end we have to operationalize the various categories by attaching specific empirical time series to them. For the personal and functional distribution, this has in fact already been done. The personal distribution is expressed as the sequence of Theil coefficients (THEIL) and the sequence of operating surplus to income ratios (OSIR). With regard to the wage indicator there is a straightforward choice, namely the real wage level (RWAGE).

The choice of the profit indicator is not as straightforward as that. In this respect we have to content ourselves with a very indirect indicator, namely the real level of security prices (RVSECUR). As indicators of the balance of social and political power we use the degree of unionization of the labor force (ORG) and an index combining the number of enfranchised citizens and their attendance rates at the national elections (ELECT). As indicators of economic conditions we use a volume index of gross domestic product (GDPVL), a price index of gross domestic product (GDPPL), and the rate of unemployment (UNEMP). The latter can be said to be a dual indicator. On the one hand it is an economic indicator that signifies economic conditions. On the other hand it is an indicator of the socioeconomic position of the working class and consequently is an expression of the balance of socioeconomic power.

Our analysis of the functional to personal distribution relation is done in two stages. The first stage stresses the element of continuity and assumes that the pre- and postwar eras are a single expression of one and the same process. Accordingly we will try to establish the relationship between the explanatory variables and the functional and personal distributions for the period 1914–93 as a whole. In the second stage the analysis considers the pre- and postwar periods separately. This allows for the inclusion of special characteristics of the generating mechanism, that is for the assumption that the relations between the explanatory variables and functional and personal level of distribution can vary according to the circumstances that are typical for the pre- and postwar periods as such. Apart from the allowance for changes in the interrelation between factors, it is also possible to introduce extra explanatory variables for the postwar period (such as factors relating to state interference in the economic process and the influence of the social security system) that were very important in the postwar period as opposed to their relative insignificance in the prewar situation.

STAGE ONE: THE PERIOD 1914–93 AS A WHOLE

Subsequently the relations implicit in the "cascade" of figure 10.2 are put to the test. The relations between the basic conditions and factor rewards fall outside the scope of our present analysis. We therefore immediately proceed to the interrelations pertaining to functional and personal distribution as such.

In the tests a back-stepwise procedure is followed. First, all regressors that are considered relevant are introduced into the regression. In the next steps all regressors that prove not significant at the 5 percent level are deleted one at a time. Only the last stage, that is the regression with all insignificant variables removed, is discussed. To avoid spurious results due to trend correlation, the data that require such transformation are detrended.[4] The result of regressing the operating surplus to income indicator against the variables relating to economic conditions and the social and political power indicators are shown in table 10.1. The results of the regression are what one would expect. Capital's share increases on an increase of the real value of securities and decreases on an increase of the real wage. Obviously the volume growth of GDP favors capital's share, whereas the intuition that unemployment goes at the expense of labor's share is affirmed by the positive sign of the unemployment level.

The value of the Durbin–Watson statistic, however, gives us something to worry about. With seventy usable data and, apart from the intercept, four regressors, a Durbin–Watson of 0.85 implies a positive autocorrelation of residuals, a circumstance not uncommon to economic time series (Thomas 1997: 296). Apart from a true autoregression of residuals, this may indicate that the regression model is poorly specified. Since it is not our intention to present a perfect dynamic model of the sequence, we will accept as a working hypothesis that the autoregression is due to underspecification and consequently that some unknown related factor is responsible for this. Instead of hunting for this related factor we content ourselves with a repair measure that provides for the explicit estimation of this autoregressive factor and accordingly to correct the significance levels of the regressors included in the model. Estimation of a model including an autoregressive factor[5] results in the figures in table 10.2. Apart from the improvement of the R-square and Durbin–Watson statistics, and the adjustment of the significance levels, the results are similar to the OLS case above.

Having established the relations between basic conditions, factor rewards, and the functional distribution of income, we can proceed with the test of our basic proposition that these sets of variables are also eligible to explain the personal distribution (see table 10.3). The outcome is perfectly

Table 10.1   Dependent Variable X_OSIR—Estimation by Stepwise Annual Data from 1914:01 to 1993:01

Usable Observations	70	Degrees of Freedom	65
Centered R**2	0.884377	R Bar**2	0.877262
Durbin–Watson Statistic	0.852043		

Variable	Coeff	Std Error	T-Stat	Signif
1. Constant	− 0.067079704	0.011917146	− 5.62884	0.00000042
2. X_RWAGE	− 0.639469412	0.056571361	− 11.30377	0.00000000
3. X_RVSECUR	0.146414280	0.012916901	11.33509	0.00000000
4. L_UNEMP	0.061860801	0.006811251	9.08215	0.00000000
5. X_GDPVL	0.302477776	0.094000287	3.21784	0.00201553

Table 10.2   Dependent Variable X_OSIR—Estimation by Hildreth–Lu Annual Data from 1915:01 to 1993:01

Usable Observations	69	Degrees of Freedom	64
Centered R**2	0.922745	R Bar**2	0.917916
Durbin–Watson Statistic	2.186266		

Variable	Coeff	Std Error	T-Stat	Signif
1. X_RWAGE	− 0.683637988	0.087097376	− 7.84912	0.00000000
2. X_RVSECUR	0.091814095	0.025060038	3.66377	0.00050626
3. X_GDPVL	0.485840249	0.129438448	3.75345	0.00037842
4. L_UNEMP	0.030241258	0.010367323	2.91698	0.00486960
5. RHO	0.858304131	0.075952778	11.30050	0.00000000

Table 10.3   Dependent Variable X_THEIL—Estimation by Hildreth–Lu Annual Data from 1915:01 to 1993:01

Usable Observations	71	Degrees of Freedom	65
Centered R**2	0.907387	R Bar**2	0.900263
Durbin–Watson Statistic	1.746155		

Variable	Coeff	Std Error	T-Stat	Signif
1. Constant	1.960145573	0.385548900	5.08404	0.00000336
2. X_RWAGE	− 0.658623873	0.112868992	− 5.83530	0.00000019
3. X_RVSECUR	0.131186100	0.036579413	3.58634	0.00064304
4. L_ELECT	− 0.324943507	0.064106736	− 5.06879	0.00000356
5. X_GDPVL	0.462858189	0.186096743	2.48719	0.01545141
6. RHO	0.649360095	0.085505921	7.59433	0.00000000

compatible with our proposition. The factors explaining the course of the functional and personal distribution of income are strikingly similar; the coefficients of the real wage, the real value of securities, and GDP are almost the same in the two regressions. The exception to this rule is the role played by unemployment and by the share of the population that takes part in elections. Unemployment does not turn up as an important factor that determines the development of the personal distribution of income; ELECT does. At present we are not able to explain these results satisfactorily; a closer look at the two subperiods may provide some of the answers.

STAGE TWO: SUBPERIODS

1914–39

The analysis in the preceding section focused on the period 1914–93 as a whole; the assumption was that the basic relations between the relevant variables remain virtually the same. On the basis of historical experience, however, one would expect that this does not actually hold. The Second World War forms a watershed in socioeconomic relations that probably fundamentally changed the operational and distributional parameters of the economy. The possible changes in the functioning of the economy before and after the war are already visible in figure 10.1. The prewar period seems to be characterized by violent fluctuations along a strong downward trend in inequality. By contrast, the postwar period is characterized by a smooth undulation around a moderately downward-sloping trend in inequality.

To investigate the possible differences in the underlying mechanism that determine changes in income distribution we repeat the previous tests for distinct periods (see table 10.4). The results are similar to the ones pertaining to the period 1914–93 in the sense that the real wage, unemployment, and GDP volume indicator are represented here and have the same sign. The real value of securities has dropped out to be replaced by the price index, which signalizes that rising prices raise capital's share at the expense of labor's share and vice versa. The really surprising results relate to the explanation of the course of the Theil coefficients as shown in table 10.5. The real wage, the value of securities, and the electorate index are the same as before. The problem is that the signs of the unionization index and the unemployment rate appear to be counterintuitive. One would have expected that the unionization index would have the same sign as the democratic participation index. An increase of either one of them would indicate an increase of the balance of power in favor of labor. Likewise one would expect that a rise in rate of unemployment would lead to an increase of inequality because rising unemployment rates go along with declining income of the unemployed and a weakening of the labor's market force. The latter problem is probably explained by the fact that the unemployment variable acts as an index of business fluctuations: when profit income

Table 10.4   Dependent Variable X_OSIR—Estimation by Stepwise Annual Data from 1914:01 to 1939:01

Usable Observations	26	Degrees of Freedom	22
Centered R**2	0.963517	R Bar**2	0.958542
Durbin–Watson Statistic	1.997404		

Variable	Coeff	Std Error	T-Stat	Signif
1. X_RWAGE	−0.862642644	0.037831547	−22.80220	0.00000000
2. L_UNEMP	0.033372494	0.002843406	11.73680	0.00000000
3. X_GDPVL	0.556793586	0.048720984	11.42821	0.00000000
4. X_GDPPL	0.046763893	0.008612306	5.42989	0.00001873

declined sharply during the two depressions (1921–23 and 1929–33)—resulting in a modest reduction of inequality at first—unemployment went up rapidly as well. De Meere (1983) discusses this relationship more in detail. He concluded that the inequality of the personal distribution of income declined during the first years of the depression of the 1930s as a result. This might explain the counterintuitive result that high unemployment "causes" a decline in inequality.

1945–93

If the prewar situation is characterized by violent movements and the postwar period by a relatively smooth development one must expect to find at least some differences in the operating mechanism behind changes in the distribution of income. Testing the determinants of the functional distribution leads to the results in table 10.6. Compared to the same analysis for the prewar situation the constellation remains more or less the same as far as factor rewards and the influence of the volume and price development of GDP are concerned. The main differences are that the unemployment indicator has disappeared and is replaced by the two "power" indicators that obviously operate in favor of labor's share.

The test for the Theil sequence is seriously affected by serial correlation. The insertion of the autocorrelation coefficient in the estimation absorbs a high proportion of the explanatory power and "crowds out" the other explanatory variables (see table 10.7). It appears therefore that the smooth downward course of the Theil sequence until the early 1980s mainly depends on nominal GDP growth. The changed sign of the election variable signals the asymmetry between the increase of democratic participation that coincides with the socioeconomic emancipation of the working classes and the decreasing interest in democratic participation that is ac-

Table 10.5   Dependent Variable X_THEIL—Estimation by Stepwise Annual Data from 1914:01 to 1939:01

Usable Observations	26	Degrees of Freedom	20
Centered R**2	0.956713	R Bar**2	0.945891
Durbin–Watson Statistic	2.490620		

Variable	Coeff	Std Error	T-Stat	Signif
1. X_RWAGE	− 0.886121368	0.150136414	− 5.90211	0.00000899
2. X_RVSECUR	0.190260802	0.063947664	2.97526	0.00748075
3. L_ORG	0.269349738	0.067837066	3.97054	0.00075369
4. L_ELECT	− 0.206865370	0.060978847	− 3.39241	0.00289151
5. L_UNEMP	− 0.101114950	0.036449485	− 2.77411	0.01170767

Table 10.6 Dependent Variable X_OSIR—Estimation by Stepwise Annual Data from 1946:01 to 1996:01

Usable Observations	44	Degrees of Freedom	37
Centered R**2	0.965113	R Bar**2	0.959455
Durbin–Watson Statistic	2.030565		

Variable	Coeff	Std Error	T-Stat	Signif
1. Constant	3.551536783	0.525761761	6.75503	0.00000006
2. X_RWAGE	− 0.683951194	0.081883360	− 8.35275	0.00000000
3. X_RVSECUR	0.131361257	0.017324968	7.58219	0.00000000
4. L_ORG	− 0.287314097	0.057061474	− 5.03517	0.00001265
5. L_ELECT	− 0.315633527	0.106624222	− 2.96024	0.00533863
6. X_GDPVL	0.329111868	0.135461099	2.42957	0.02008931
7. X_GDPPL	0.285010524	0.057880205	4.92415	0.00001783

centuated by the downward shift in participation rates that followed the 1967 abolition of the compulsory attendance at elections. All in all, these results are not very satisfactory and do not help us very much in understanding the underlying mechanism. We therefore broadened the analysis by taking into account the role of social security.

To assess the impact of this centrally organized redistribution mechanism a series relating to social security (SC)[6] is introduced. Reassessment of the regression of x_OSIR including the social security indicator among the regressors does not bring about anything, because the contribution of l_SC is not significant. The functional distribution of income is not affected by the secondary redistribution inherent in the social security system. Social security, however, does affect the personal distribution. Reassessment of x_THEIL in the light of l_SC leads to the results[7] in table 10.8. From the sign of the social security indicator it is clear that the sys-

Table 10.7 Dependent Variable X_THEIL—Estimation by Hildreth–Lu Annual Data from 1947:01 to 1993:01

Usable Observations	46	Degrees of Freedom	42
Centered R**2	0.935237	R Bar**2	0.930611
Uncentered R**2	0.935252	T × R**2	43.022
Durbin–Watson Statistic	1.930124		

Variable	Coeff	Std Error	T-Stat	Signif
1. X_GDPVL	− 0.581073518	0.195055257	− 2.97902	0.00478916
2. X_GDPPL	− 0.557119148	0.138321633	− 4.02771	0.00023114
3. L_ELECT	0.011804970	0.005357951	2.20326	0.03311409
4. RHO	0.823092997	0.091293075	9.01594	0.00000000

tem performs its redistributive tasks as expected. The dummy obviously picks up the shadow of a trend in l_SC. The signs of the factor reward indicators remain as expected. A rising real wage fosters equality, whereas a rise in the real value of securities leads to greater inequality. The earlier mentioned change of sign of the election indicator also applies to this case.

CONCLUSION: THE NEW INEQUALITY OF THE 1980S AND 1990S

What does this exercise in explaining long-term trends in the development of the inequality of Dutch income distribution teach us about the determinants of the new inequality? In order to answer this question, we have taken a closer look at the recent rise in income inequality. As stated in the introduction of this chapter, in the Anglo-Saxon literature this phenomenon is usually explained out of increases in relative wages, the result of changes in relative scarcities of different types of labor. For the Netherlands this interpretation does not seem to hold, because the structure of relative wages has not changed very much.

The most consistent result of this attempt to explain long-run changes in income inequality was that there existed a very close relationship between the personal and the functional distribution of income. This is also very much the case for the recent upturn in inequality: both the Theil coefficient and the share of operating surplus in income began to move up during the 1980s. The fluctuations in the latter have been more erratic, but the trends were essentially the same.

A second conclusion is that changes in the Theil index can be explained rather well using a small number of variables that are related to the functional distribution of income: the real wage and the real value of shares

Table 10.8   Dependent Variable X_THEIL—Estimation by Stepwise Annual Data from 1946:01 to 1993:01

Usable Observations	44	Degrees of Freedom	38
Centered R**2	0.941040	R Bar**2	0.933282
Durbin–Watson Statistic	1.600392		

Variable	Coeff	Std Error	T-Stat	Signif
1. Constant	− 3.443667665	0.913430976	− 3.77004	0.00055510
2. X_RWAGE {2}	− 0.409578099	0.061834273	− 6.62380	0.00000008
3. X_RVSECUR {2}	0.081222958	0.016833785	4.82500	0.00002290
4. L_ELECT	0.712502830	0.144365986	4.93539	0.00001624
5. L_SC	− 0.237696136	0.040970312	− 5.80167	0.00000107
6. T_DUMMY	0.007167746	0.000868964	8.24861	0.00000000

contributed in general strongly to changes in the Theil index, as did (for the period as a whole) the degree of political participation and the growth of GDP. During the postwar period expenditure on social security also contributed to the explanation of changes in the personal distribution of income.

Within this framework it becomes possible to explain the sudden change of course in the Theil index after 1983. The following reasons come to mind.

(1) The 1970s and early 1980s were years of low (and declining) profitability of Dutch industry, which contributed to the poor economic performance of the period; during the 1980s profitability was restored again, which was the result of (a) government policies to lower the taxes and premium burden on the private sector, (b) wage moderation by the trade unions, and (c) an improvement of international competitiveness as a result. This is the most obvious explanation for a U-turn in the share of capital in income.

(2) The position of the trade unions was greatly weakened by (a) the rise in unemployment after 1974 and (b) the fall in union density in the same period; the "offensive" policies adopted by the unions in the 1970s, aimed at redistributing income toward the lower incomes, were abolished as a result, and they were forced to change course and concentrate on wage moderation (and the restoration of profitability in industry).

(3) The same U-turn occurred in Dutch politics. During the 1970s redistributive policies were high on the agenda (especially between 1973 and 1977), but after 1983 a moderate "supply side" approach came to dominate, and policymakers in general advocated the lowering of social benefits and charges, the lowering of minimum wages, the increase in flexibility of labor markets, and so on. The declining political participation in these years may be seen as a factor that contributed to this change in policies.

(4) Finally, the position of capital was strengthened as a result of globalization. One significant aspect of this process was the enormous increase in the internationalization of capital markets during the 1980s, which resulted in a huge increase in international capital flows. This integration of international capital markets has put more pressure on companies to improve their performance, especially in the short term; downsizing in order to increase profitability and push up share prices has been one of the consequences of this new trend. In short, the globalization of capital markets has strengthened the position of shareholders (and managers). Labor, on the other hand, has not profited from a comparable development; it has remained relatively immobile, and its relative position vis-à-vis capital has weakened. As a result of these changes in the relative position of capital and labor, real wages have stagnated, and real share prices have gone up enormously since 1983. Obviously these developments are not restricted

to the Netherlands, as the contribution of John Schmitt to this volume shows. We have tried to show that these changes are able to explain the "new inequality" of the 1980s and 1990s in the Netherlands.

APPENDIX 1: LIST OF VARIABLES AND ABBREVIATIONS

ELECT	Election index: index combining the number of enfranchised citizens and their attendance rates at the national elections (proxy for power relations)
GDPPL	Price level of gross domestic product (indicator of economic conditions)
GDPVL	Volume of gross domestic product (indicator of economic conditions)
ORG	Degree of unionization of the labor force (proxy for power relations)
OSIR	Operating surplus to income ratio (expresses functional distribution)
OSIR_SC	OSIR scaled to the level of THEIL
RVSECUR	Real value of securities (proxy for factor reward of capital)
RWAGE	Real wages (factor reward for labor)
SC	Ratio of social charges to wages and salaries (indicator of the impact of social security and collective unemployment and health insurance)
THEIL	Theil coefficients (express personal distribution)
UNEMP	Unemployment rate (dual indicator: proxy for power relations at the same time proxy for economic conditions)

APPENDIX 2: SOURCES, LINKING, AND TRANSFORMATION OF DATA

Since the objective of this chapter is to study long-term patterns our endeavor was to create the longest possible time series. We could not afford to have significant discontinuities in the material. Therefore we linked series wherever logically possible and bridged small gaps by interpolation wherever necessary. The only exception to this rule is the discontinuity coinciding with the Second World War. In our view it is inconceivable that this gap can be filled in a logically acceptable way.

The sources of the data are discussed in detail in Soltow and van Zanden (1997: ch. 8). The most important series are:

THEIL: Theil coefficient

1914–58   Normalized Theil coefficient based upon income after deduction of income taxes. Source: Hartog 1979: 4, table 1
1959–84   Theil coefficients of disposable income. Source: de Kleijn and van de Stadt 1987
1985–91   Theil coefficients of disposable income. Source: Jeurissen 1994: 10, table 8; Jeurissen 1994: 46, table 18
1992–93   Theil coefficients of disposable income. Own calculations based upon CBS 1994b: 49, table 6.5

The Hartog, de Kleijn and van de Stadt, and Jeurissen series have different levels. This difference can be explained by the fact that Hartog applies a correction to adjust for changes in the number of intervals (Hartog 1979: 4). The series merely differ by a multiplicative factor. The multiplicative link is established in 1959.
The small gaps in the Hartog index are bridged by linear interpolation.

OSIR: Operating surplus/Net Domestic Product (factor cost)

1914–20   van de Bie 1995.
1921–86   van Bochove and Huitker 1987: 6ff, table H1
1986–95   CBS (Central Statistical Office), Statline (Internet), table 6363natr00.

Other series: see Soltow and van Zanden 1997.

NOTES

1. For the construction of indices, see the appendix on Sources, Linking, and Transformation of Data.
2. This is the ratio of non-labor income to net domestic product at factor cost, the complement of the labor share.
3. Scaling is obtained by the linear regression of the operating surplus to income series on the Theil sequence.
4. Detrending is obtained by fitting the model $y_t = gt + f_i \cos(2''(t + *)/f_i))$ to the logarithms of the data. The growth rate g and the (amplitude, phase, and periodicity) parameters of two cyclical components are estimated simultaneously. Next the trend gt is subtracted. Variables that have been detrended are marked with an x_ in front of their names. Series that are not detrended are log-transformed in order to bring them on equal footing with the detrended ones. They are prefixed with l_. The customary growth-rate transformation is considered inadequate for our purpose because it results in a loss of information regarding long-term patterns (Reijnders 1990: 246 ff).

5. Usually Cochrane Orcutt is applied. In case of missing values we use Hildreth–Lu.

6. That is the ratio of social charges to wages and salaries. The series starts in 1921. The break between the prewar and postwar level is such that the series can not be detrended in a fashion comparable to the other series. For this reason the series is only log-transformed. To capture the influence of a possible shadow of a trend, a time dependent dummy T_DUMMY is introduced into the regression.

7. There is a technical problem here because the GDP indicators are strongly correlated with SC. To avoid awkward results, the GDP indicators are deleted from the regression. Time lags have been included for the factor reward indicators because this improves the results in terms of Durbin–Watson.

REFERENCES

Arts, W., and P. van Wijck. (1991). The Dynamics of Income Inequality in a Representative Democracy. *Rationality and Society* 3 (1991): 317–42.

———. (1994). De lange termijn dynamiek van de Nederlandse inkomensverdeling. In H. Flap and M.D. van Leeuwen, eds. *Op lange termijn*. Hilversum: Verloren: 37–60.

Bie, R. van de. (1995). *Een doorlopende groote roes*. Amsterdam: Thesis Publishers.

Bochove, C.A. van, and T.A. Huitker. (1987). Main National Accounting Series 1900–1986. CBS occasional paper, no. NA-017. The Hague: Netherlands Central Bureau of Statistics.

CBS. (1994a). Personele inkomensverdeling 1991. In *Supplement Sociaal-economische maandstatistiek*, 94/4, The Hague: Netherlands Central Bureau of Statistics.

———. (1994b). Inkomen en vermogen. In *Sociaal-economische maandstatistiek*, 94/12. The Hague: Netherlands Central Bureau of Statistics.

———. (1996). *Tijdreeksen arbeidsrekeningen 1969–1993: Ramingen van het opleidingsniveau*. Voorburg/Heerlen: Netherlands Central Bureau of Statistics.

Danziger, S., and P. Gottschalk, eds. (1993). *Uneven Tides: Rising Inequality in America*. New York: Russell Sage Foundation.

Hartog, J. (1979). Income Taxes and the Distribution of Income in the Netherlands 1914–1973. Discussion paper. Institute for Economic Research, Erasmus University Rotterdam.

———, and J.G. Veenbergen. (1978). Dutch Treat: Long-run Changes in Personal Income Distribution. *De Economist* 126, no. 4: 521–49.

Jeurissen, P.C.J. (1994). Personele inkomensverdeling 1991. In *Supplement Sociaal-economische maandstatistiek*, 94/4. The Hague: Netherlands Central Bureau of Statistics.

Kleijn, J.P. de, and H. van de Stadt. (1987). Inkomensniveau en Inkomensongelijkheid 1959–1989. In *Supplement Sociaal- economische maandstatistiek*, 87/6. The Hague: Netherlands Central Bureau of Statistics.

Mccrc, J.M.M. de. (1979). Inkomensgroei en ongelijkheid te Amsterdam 1877–1940. *Tijdschrift voor Sociale Geschiedenis* 13 (1979): 3–46.

———. (1983). Long-term Trends in Income and Wealth Inequality in the Netherlands 1808–1940. *Historical Social Research* 27 (1983): 8–37.

OECD. (1995). *Income Distribution in OECD Countries*. Paris: OECD.

Reijnders, J. (1990). *Long Waves in Economic Development*. Aldershot: Edward Elgar.

Schultz, T.P. (1968). Secular Equalization and Cyclical Behavior of Income Distribution. *The Review of Economics and Statistics* 50 (1968): 259–76.

Soltow, L., and J.L. van Zanden. (1997). *Income and Wealth Inequality in the Netherlands Sixteenth–Twentieth Centuries*. Amsterdam: Het Spinhuis.

Thomas, R.L. (1997). *Modern Econometrics*. Harlow: Addison-Wesley.

Tinbergen, J. (1975). *Income Distribution, Analysis and Policies*. Amsterdam: North-Holland.

Weststrate, C. (1984). *Economic Policy in Practice: The Netherlands 1950–1957*. Amsterdam: Stenfert Kroese.

Wilterdink, N. (1984). *Vermogensverhoudingen in Nederland*. Amsterdam: Arbeiderspers.

———. (1993). *Ongelijkheid en interdependentie*. Groningen: Wolters-Noordhoff.

Zanden, J.L. van, and R.T. Griffiths. (1989). *Economische Geschiedenis van Nederland in de twintigste eeuw*. Utrecht: Het Spectrum.

11

The Internationalization of Capital and Trends in Income Inequality in Western Societies

Nico Wilterdink

Since the 1980s, the trend of equalization of living conditions within Western societies seems to have stopped or even reversed. During the greater part of this century, socioeconomic inequality diminished; with ongoing industrialization and the growth of productivity, wage incomes tended to grow more than capital incomes, and wage incomes on the lower occupational levels more than those on the higher ones (Brenner et al. 1991). Expanding welfare state arrangements diminished the risks of poverty. The equalization trend took place not only in periods of economic growth, but also in times of stagnation and crisis, like the depression in the 1930s and the two world wars. It was precisely in these periods of crisis that the groundwork was laid for what came to be known as the welfare state. This system, with its egalitarian consequences, expanded in the 1950s and 1960s under the impact of fast economic growth (Flora and Heidenheimer 1981).

In the 1970s, the first indications of discontinuity with respect to this long-term trend of economic expansion and equalization became manifest. The "oil crisis" of 1973 marked the transition to a new phase in the history of Western capitalism, in which economic growth slowed down, mass unemployment again became a chronic problem, national governments started to cut on social expenditures, and industrial firms under the impact of growing international competition restructured their activities toward "post-Fordist" flexibility. As firms spread their production more and more internationally, the mobility of physical capital grew, whereas the growth of international financial transactions, stimulated by the liberalization of markets, was even higher (Dicken 1992). These transformations were accompanied by political and ideological changes: a growing belief in free-market forces as the basis of a well-functioning economy and a concomitant increasing skepticism or even hostility toward all kinds of government regulation. It also meant a growing acceptance of socioeconomic inequality, which actually increased in the majority of the highly industrialized countries since about 1980.

As this short and schematic description suggests, all these changes are causally interrelated. It is difficult to specify empirically, however, how these changes are interrelated. In this chapter I will focus on two (supposed) changes in this complex: the increase of income inequality in Western national societies, and the internationalization or "globalization" of capital, i.e., the growth of international direct investment flows.

A causal relation between these two processes can be hypothesized on different theoretical grounds. My starting point is a sociological power-interdependence model, which assumes that income and wealth inequalities are to be viewed as based on and manifestations of power-(inter)dependence relations between individuals and collectivities (Wilterdink 1995). International mobility of capital makes its owners and managers less dependent on other relevant actors in a given national state—workers, labor unions, local and national governments—and therefore is a source of power with respect to these actors. The more internationally mobile capital is, the larger the power of its owners and managers with respect to other relevant actors, which becomes manifest in relatively larger incomes accruing to them and, in general, a higher degree of intrastate income inequality. More specifically it is to be expected that an increase of the international mobility of capital will lead to (a) an increase of capital income compared to labor income, (b) an increase of management incomes compared to the incomes of other company employees, (c) an increase of the incomes of private company employees compared to the incomes of public officials, and (d) an increase of labor incomes compared to government-regulated transfer incomes.

These general statements need empirical testing. The questions to be dealt with in this chapter are (1) What is the evidence for a tendency of growing income inequality in Western countries since the beginnings of the 1980s? and (2) To what extent and how can this tendency be related to the increasing international mobility of capital? After dealing with these questions I will interpret the possible link between the two processes by viewing them in the wider context of economic, political, and ideological changes.

GROWING INCOME INEQUALITY: IS IT A GENERAL TENDENCY?

The statement that the distribution of personal incomes has become more unequal in Western societies after 1980 is supported by a large mass of data, but not all the evidence for all these societies points in this direction.

The clearest and strongest evidence has been found for the United States, where incomes started to diverge in the middle of the 1970s. For the United Kingdom, too, the statistics indicate a substantial increase of income inequality in the 1980s. For most other Western countries the evidence for this tendency is weaker. On the basis of an Organization for Economic Cooperation and Development (OECD) survey (Atkinson, Rainwater, and Smeeding 1995a) and other sources[1] we can give the following overview of recent changes in the distribution of disposable family incomes within Western nation-states.

Australia:	increase of inequality 1981–95
Belgium:	slight increase of inequality 1983–92
Canada:	decrease of inequality 1971–82, slight increase 1982–91
Denmark:	decrease of inequality until 1985, some increase 1985–87
Finland:	decrease of inequality 1966–81, no clear change 1981–92
France:	slight decrease of inequality 1970–79, slight increase 1979–89
Germany (West):	slight decrease of inequality until 1983, slight increase 1983–92
Ireland (Republic):	slight decrease of inequality 1973–87, increase 1987–94
Italy:	decrease of inequality 1967–82, no clear change 1982–91
The Netherlands:	decrease of inequality until 1983, increase 1983–95
New Zealand:	increase of inequality 1982–92
Norway:	no clear change 1970–86, slight increase of inequality 1986–89
Portugal:	no clear change 1980–90
Spain:	decrease of inequality 1980–90
Sweden:	decrease of inequality until 1981, increase 1981–91
United Kingdom:	decrease of inequality until 1977, strong increase 1977–95
United States:	decrease of inequality 1930–50, near stability 1950–75, strong increase 1975–95

We can conclude from this overview that income inequality started to increase—after a period of decrease—in most Western countries (thirteen out of the seventeen mentioned) somewhere in the 1970s or 1980s.[2] They include all the major Western national economies, with the (possible) exception of Italy. Among these countries, however, there appears a considerable variation in timing and degree. For countries on the European continent (France, Germany, Sweden, the Netherlands, Belgium) the tendency is slight or moderate compared to the United Kingdom and the United States, where it also started at an earlier date. In Denmark and Norway, the period for which the deleveling tendency has been found started only relatively late (in the second half of the 1980s) and comprises only a few years until the last year of coverage—too short to say whether it reflects an incidental fluctuation or a basic trend reversal.

The expectation of growing inequality is not supported by the available data for four out of the seventeen countries. For three countries (Italy, Finland, Portugal) there are no clear indications of a tendency in any direction, whereas the income distribution in Spain seems to have become less unequal in the 1980s. Two of these four countries, Spain and Portugal, have a relatively low level of prosperity, as indicated by their per capita gross domestic product (GDP), and a relatively high income inequality. Both countries, moreover, made the transition from a right-wing dictatorship to a parliamentary democracy in the 1970s. These specific conditions might explain the absence of a deleveling tendency in the income distribution in these countries; both are in a stage of "modernization" in which the forces leading toward more equality are (still) at least as strong as the inequality enhancing forces. More generally, it is safe to assume that the impact of the internationalization of capital on income inequality depends on intrastate processes such as the stage of industrialization and changes in the political system.

It should also be kept in mind that the statistical data on which the trend assessments are based are only rough indications of the actual incomes. In particular, property income and the incomes of the self-employed are notoriously underreported.[3] Given the positive correlation between these incomes and total personal income, the actual degree of income inequality will be underestimated. This underestimation can be expected to be stronger the less reliable the income data in a given country are (due, for example, to a relatively high degree of tax evasion) and the larger the proportion of property income in personal income. When property income increases relative to other kinds of income, as has happened in recent years, it generally leads to an underestimation of the growth of inequality. It is quite likely, therefore, that the overall tendency of increasing income inequality in Western societies since about 1980 is actually stronger than is indicated by the available statistics.

Among the countries that do exhibit a tendency of growing income inequality we may roughly distinguish between an Anglo-Saxon pattern (the United States, the United Kingdom) and a European-continental pattern (in particular the countries of the European Union apart from the United Kingdom). According to the first pattern, the growth of income inequality has started at an early date and has been quite dramatic; it comprises a substantial increase of wage inequality and a growth of poverty and material inse-

curity among those who do not have paid jobs. In the second case, the in
crease of income inequality has started at a later date and has been moderate
until now; wage inequality has hardly increased, and although poverty has
spread, its extension has been limited by a still strongly developed welfare
state. It has to be noted that Canada conforms to this last pattern, whereas
Australia approaches more nearly the Anglo-Saxon pattern.

Before examining the possible reasons for this variation, we will look at
the connection between growing socioeconomic inequality and the increasing mobility of investment capital on a general level.

INTERNATIONAL INVESTMENTS AND
TRANSNATIONAL COMPANIES

The focus here will be on foreign direct investments (FDI) rather than
portfolio investments, i.e., on investments by companies in other countries
than their home country, which give them control over economic activities
in these countries. In this way, companies become transnational. They enhance their geographical flexibility and autonomy; extend their networks
of control; and therefore increase, at least potentially, their power with respect to groups and organizations tied to a particular territorial state, including national governments and labor unions.

After the Second World War the total amount of foreign direct investment in the world economy has grown dramatically. The estimated total
FDI flow tripled from $4 billion in 1960 to $12 billion in 1970; in 1980 it
had risen to an estimated total of about $52 billion, in 1990 to $232 billion,
and in 1995 to $318 billion. For the period 1960–95 as a whole the yearly
FDI flow grew nominally seventy-eight-fold, which comes to an annual
average growth of 13.2 percent. This is about four times the growth of
world production in the same period.[4]

Part of this growth can be attributed to the expansion of Japanese and
other non-Western firms. Whereas these firms contributed less than 2 percent to the total FDI flow in 1960, this percentage has risen to approximately 22 percent in 1995, of which 7 percent is by Japanese firms.[5] Nevertheless, the expansion of FDI flows from Western countries has also
been very strong; the annual nominal growth for these countries in
1960–95 is 12.5 percent, not much less than the annual growth of 13.2
percent for the world as a whole. In other words, the growing mobility of
capital in the world economy during the last decades largely reflects the
international expansion of Western-based firms, in spite of the growing
importance of Japan and a few other economies.

The growth rate of the total FDI flow accelerated in the three decades
after 1960. In the first half of this period (1960–75) the average annual
nominal growth was 13.6 percent; in the second half (1975–90) it was 15.4

percent. The difference in the relative growth rate, i.e., compared to the nominal growth of total world production, is much larger: 3 percent annual growth in 1960–75, 6 percent in 1975–90. It was in this second period that socioeconomic inequality in most Western countries started to increase.

However, both the nominal and the relative growth rate of FDI flows did not increase continuously, as can be seen in the following table. It appears that the nominal and relative growth of FDIs accelerated in two specific periods: the second half of the 1970s and—even more—the second half of the 1980s. Growth stagnated in the years in between, the first half of the 1980s. This fluctuation can be considered as part of the business cycle. In the beginning of the 1980s not only foreign but also domestic investments shrunk, and unemployment rose in most Western countries. From about 1983, when Western economies recovered in terms of profits, investments, output, and—later and to a lesser degree—employment FDIs expanded abundantly. From 1985 to 1990 the mobility of international capital and the transnationalization of corporations increased to a particularly unprecedented degree.

All in all we may conclude that the tendency of growing income inequality in Western societies since about 1980 has been preceded by an acceleration in the growth of FDIs by Western-based companies after 1975. But a clear time correlation between the two trends cannot be found. In most Western countries income disparities started to increase when the growth of FDIs was very low or even negative. We may hypothesize that the start of the trend reversal in the income distribution was connected to economic recession: the recession of 1980–83 in Europe and the recession of 1973–75 in the United States. When profits and investments fell in these years, production stagnated or declined, unemployment rose, unions lost bargaining power, and companies and governments took measures to cut labor costs. This led to an increase of income inequality, particularly when companies started to restore their profit margins. The subsequent eco-

Table 11.1 Nominal and Relative Annual Growth of Total Foreign Direct Investment Flow

	Nominal Growth	*Relative Growth*[a]
1960–70	11.6	3.2
1970–75	17.6	2.9
1975–79	20.5	6.3
1979–85	0.6	− 2.2
1985–90	31.5	16.5
1990–95	6.5	1.7

Note: In percentages.
[a]Compared to total world production.

nomic recovery, however, did not lead to a new reversal in the income distribution trend: income inequality continued to grow. It is this continuation that might be related to the increasing international mobility of capital as shown by the figures on FDIs.

ECONOMIC OPENNESS AND INCOME INEQUALITY: AN INTERNATIONAL COMPARISON

From the thesis that economic internationalization leads to more inequality it might be inferred that there is a positive correlation between the degree of internationalization of a national economy and the degree of income inequality at a given time (when national economies on a similar level of economic development are compared). In other words, the more open the economy, the more inequality. Openness could be defined in terms of the amount of foreign trade relative to GDP,[6] but according to the assumptions of this chapter the amount of capital export and import is the more relevant variable. The degree of internationalization or openness of a given national economy can be defined then as the capital stock invested by domestic firms in other countries plus the capital stock invested in the country by foreign firms relative to gross national product (GNP).

It is not easy to compare the degree of income inequality of different countries, since the statistical definitions of income vary from country to country and different criteria of inequality may lead to different results. Here nine Western countries are selected for comparison: Australia, Canada, France, (West) Germany, Italy, the Netherlands, Sweden, the United Kingdom, and the United States. Even though a precise assessment of the relative degree of income inequality of these nine countries in a given year is very difficult, the evidence that, e.g., Sweden now has a more equal income distribution than the United States is overwhelming. On the basis of several estimates[7] we may rank the countries with respect to personal income inequality at the end of the 1980s as follows:

Highest inequality: United States
Second: Australia, Italy, United Kingdom
Third: Canada, France, Germany
Lowest inequality: the Netherlands, Sweden.

Table 11.2 spells out the relative openness of these countries in terms of FDI stock relative to GNP.[8] From table 11.2 it appears that there is no clear correlation between openness to foreign capital (inward stock) or the orientation of domestic firms to foreign investment (outward stock) or the combination of both with income inequality. If we dichotomize between high and low openness and high and low inequality, there are four logical

Table 11.2   FDI Stock of Nine Countries, 1989

	Inward Stock	*Outward Stock*	*Total*
United States	7.4 (5)	7.8 (7)	15.2 (6)
Australia	26.0 (1)	9.6 (5)	35.6 (3)
Italy	5.3 (7)	4.6 (9)	9.9 (9)
United Kingdom	19.4 (3)	23.1 (2)	42.5 (2)
Canada	18.7 (4)	12.9 (4)	31.6 (4)
France	4.9 (8)	7.1 (8)	12.0 (8)
Germany	5.8 (6)	9.2 (6)	15.0 (7)
The Netherlands	22.2 (2)	35.3 (1)	57.5 (1)
Sweden	4.1 (9)	13.8 (3)	17.9 (5)

Note: In percentages of GNP; the numbers in parentheses indicate the rank order.

possibilities, and all of these actually occur. The combination of high openness and high inequality (as theoretically expected) occurs in the case of the United Kingdom and Australia. Italy, however, combines high inequality with low openness, and for the United States high inequality also goes together with a relatively low degree of openness. Sweden shows the theoretically expected combination of low inequality and low openness. The Netherlands, on the other hand, exemplifies low inequality together with high openness.

A comparison of changes in income distribution and FDI flows in different countries might lead to clearer results. It could be expected that a higher growth of FDI inflows and outflows will lead to a stronger increase of income inequality. As indicated, there has been considerable variation among Western countries in the extent to which income inequality increased in the course of the 1980s. Taking again the same nine countries, we can rank them in this respect as follows.[9]

Highest increase in income inequality: United States
Second: United Kingdom
Third: Australia
Fourth: The Netherlands, Sweden
Fifth: France, Germany
No apparent increase: Canada, Italy.

Table 11.3 gives the growth of FDI outflows and inflows with respect to these countries from the middle of the 1970s.[10] Again, no clear pattern appears from this table. The growth of FDI has been high for all countries. On the whole, it has not been higher in countries with a relatively strong increase in income inequality. The growth of FDI outflow from the United States has even been strikingly low compared to that in the other countries.

Table 11.3   Growth of FDI Inflows and Outflows, 1974–90

	Inflow	*Outflow*	*Total*
United States	17.8	6.4	10.9
United Kingdom	13.5	11.4	12.4
Australia	16.1	15.2	15.4
The Netherlands	12.8	13.3	13.1
Sweden	26.5	22.7	23.4
France	12.5	20.9	17.1
Germany	7.9	16.0	13.5
Canada	12.1	11.5	11.7
Italy	12.0	19.9	15.1

Note: Average annual increase, in percentages.

We have to conclude that variations in the amount of FDI cannot explain between-countries variations in income distribution and its change over time. This is not to say that international capital movements do not have an impact on the income distribution within national states, or, more specifically, are not an important factor in the tendency of increasing income inequality since about 1980. The statistical evidence supporting this thesis is rather weak, however. And insofar as the thesis is valid, it apparently does not "work" on the level of separate nation-states. In order to explain between-countries variations in income distribution and its changes we have to look to more specific factors, such as the institutional arrangements of the welfare state.

DISCUSSION

Globalization is not an all-determining force, sweeping away the differences between national states or making political decisions at that level irrelevant. Nationally specific institutional characteristics still explain a good deal of the variations in the degree of income inequality among Western societies. High social benefits levels, progressive taxation, and relatively centralized and regulated ("corporatist") bargaining between labor unions and employers' organizations are all connected with a relatively low income inequality (Kalb et al. 1997: 24–25). This might give support to the voluntaristic idea that an egalitarian income policy on the national level is still possible.

The question, however, is to what extent such a policy is possible, given the ongoing internationalization of capital. To answer this question, different types of income should be distinguished. To the extent that capital is internationally mobile, capital markets are globally integrated, and firms are organized transnationally, returns to capital in different places converge. The same processes facilitate tax evasions and put pressure on governments to lower the taxes on capital income. For these reasons it is to be expected that capital incomes will be determined increasingly by global markets rather than national institutions. A similar tendency is observable for top management incomes, for which the standards tend to converge across national boundaries as firms become more transnational. Both types of incomes have risen considerably relative to other incomes in recent years, thus contributing to the growth of income and wealth inequality.

On the other hand, the bulk of wage incomes and, even more, transfer incomes are still to a large extent determined by national institutions and policies. But these institutions and policies are not autonomous; they are in turn influenced by international developments. As the international mobility of capital increases, the capacity of a country to attract productive investments becomes a central political consideration. One possible option is to cut on social expenditures, which drive up, through taxes and premium payments, the investors' costs of labor.

Given the goals of economic growth, prosperity, and full employment, national governments might try to adapt to the internationalization of capital by privatization, deregulation of labor markets, cutting on welfare spending, and the lowering of tax rates for companies and high-income groups, resulting in increasing inequality. This policy has been pursued to a greater or lesser degree by many governments since the 1980s. In particular, the United States has been taken as the model for this policy: it combines a highly deregulated, "flexible" labor market; a tax system that is quite favorable for the rich; and relatively low welfare spending and, as a result, has a strongly increased and high income inequality with a relatively low rate of unemployment. On the other hand, mass unemployment has become an endemic problem in Western European countries such as France and Germany, with their much more regulated economies, stronger labor unions, more generous welfare systems, and less inequality. This suggests a dilemma between job growth and low unemployment on the one hand, and some degree of collective material security and social justice on the other (cf., Esping-Andersen 1996).

However, whether this is an inevitable dilemma is questionable. The institutional characteristics that contribute to a relatively egalitarian income distribution—high social benefits, a progressive tax system, strong labor unions, and centralized bargaining—do not necessarily lead to low economic performance and high unemployment. Nor is there a clear negative correlation between wage inequality and unemployment among Western countries (Franzmeyer et al. 1996; OECD 1996). To be more specific, the strong U.S. job growth since the 1980s has not been accompanied, and cannot therefore be explained, by high economic growth; on the contrary, the average U.S. growth-rate of GNP and productivity has been lower than that of most other Western economies. Rather than jobless growth the result has been more jobs without growth; or, to put it more precisely, the outcome has been the combination of more jobs, lower wages, and longer work-hours for the majority of the population (Mishel and Schmitt 1995).

On the other hand, a country such as Norway suggests that it is still possible to combine economic growth and low unemployment (4.9 percent in 1996) with a fairly generous welfare system—though with some cutbacks in recent years—and a relatively low and more or less stable income inequality (OECD 1997; Hagen and Hippe 1993). This has been achieved by a country whose population has chosen to remain outside the European Union. Norway has of course the advantage of its large oil fields, but this could have contributed to high unemployment as well.

Another case in point—and another example of a "small open economy" (Katzenstein 1985)—is the Netherlands. This country, while maintaining extensive welfare arrangements and a relatively egalitarian income distribution, has achieved a remarkably strong employment growth since 1983 (1.8 percent per year in 1983–96, which is about the same as in the United States) resulting in a relatively low unemployment rate (6.7 percent in 1996, compared to 11.3 percent in the European Union as a whole). This outcome has been preceded, and at least partly produced, by a series of step-by-step reforms on the basis of cooperation between the national government, employers, and labor unions; these include wage moderation, the lowering of the minimum wage-level, the stimulation of part-time jobs and labor market flexibility, the privatization of some social insurances, and selective cuts in government and welfare expenditures (Visser and Hemerijck 1997). These measures contributed to the increase of income inequality and material insecurity, but only to a moderate degree. Thus, the "Dutch model" suggests pragmatic solutions by steering a midway between the rigid defense of established social rights and harsh reforms giving free reign to the international market.

This model has its limitations too, however. On the one hand, it did not prevent increasing inequality; on the other, it did not solve the unemployment problem. The Dutch unemployment rate is only low in comparison to that of neighboring countries and has remained particularly high among specific groups, such as ethnic minorities. The model's success, moreover, partly depends on the fact that it has not been followed by other European countries. Thus, the policy of wage moderation has brought the labor costs in the Netherlands appreciably below the German level, but this comparative advantage will stop as soon as German unions accept a similar wage reduction.

This illustrates the risks of a competition "down to the bottom" under the impact of the internationalization of capital. Long-run solutions to the problems of unemployment and increasing inequality can only come from concerted actions on different levels—local, national, regional (such as European), and global—by governments, labor unions, and other organizations. Until now, international economic cooperation has been mainly directed to the opening of markets and the stimulation of international trade and capital movements. It is time that more cooperative efforts on an international scale be directed toward other goals: employment, labor relations, social security, coordinated taxation, and degrees of socioeconomic inequality within and between political communities, which are not too far removed from notions of social justice and fairness.

NOTES

1. Atkinson, Rainwater, and Smeeding (1995b); Atkinson (1995). For the Scandinavian countries also: Ringen and Uusitalo (1990). For France: Oberti (1993). For Canada: The Distribution of Income in Canada, *Child & Family* (obtained from the Internet, March 1998). For Germany: Bedau et al. (1987); Schluter (1996: table 3). For Ireland: Barrett et al. (1997). For the Netherlands: Central Bureau of Statistics, *Sociale Maandstatistiek* May 1992, February 1993, December 1994, February 1997. For New Zealand: Le Heron and Pawson (1996: 96). For the United Kingdom: HMSO, *Social Trends*, several years. For the United States: Mishel and Mishel (1995).

2. The same holds true for the major industrialized non-Western national economy, Japan: whereas income inequality in this country tended to decrease in the 1960s and 1970s (Mizoguchi et al. 1980), it increased after 1980 (Atkinson, Rainwater, and Smeeding 1995a).

3. This appears very clearly by comparing the personal income data (based on surveys or taxes) with aggregate national account statistics. See e.g., Smeeding and Schmaus (1990, in particular table 1.4).

4. Sources: Group of Thirty (1984: 4); OECD (1994: I, 118); United Nations (1993: table 14); United Nations (1994: 12); United Nations (1996: table I.1). In so far as different sources give different data, in general the highest ones have been taken as the basis for the trend assessment. As FDI flows are recorded only incompletely, the published data underestimate their real size. This underestimation is probably larger for the earlier years, which would mean that the calculated growth of FDI is exaggerated to some extent. On the other hand, new forms of transnational expansion of corporations that are not comprised in the FDI definition, such as franchising deals and licensing agreements, have developed in recent years. Cf., Strange (1996: 46–48).

5. In 1990 the share of non-Western firms in total FDI outflows was even higher: approximately 25 percent, of which 22 percent was by Japanese firms alone. After their spectacular growth in the 1980s, Japanese investment outflows declined dramatically in the years 1991–93. Sources: see note 4.

6. Which is the more usual definition. According to this definition, there is no positive correlation between (the increase of) openness and (the increase of) in-

come inequality. See Gottschalk and Joyce (1991); and Therborn, this volume. This corresponds with the results of the analysis in this chapter.

7. SCP (1992: 402–3); Atkinson, Rainwater, Smeeding (1995b: table 3). These sources use the data of the Luxembourg Income Study (LIS), which purports to maximize the comparability of the income data on different nations. The bases for the comparison are disposable household incomes.

8. Data derived from United Nations (1993: 82 ff).

9. Sources: see notes 1 and 6. Cf., also Sawyer (1976).

10. Data derived from: OECD (1994: I, 118–19).

REFERENCES

Atkinson, A.B. (1995). Income Distribution in Europe and the United States. Economics Discussion Paper 103, Nuffield College, Oxford.

Atkinson, A.B., L. Rainwater, T.M. Smeeding. (1995a). *Income Distribution in OECD Countries: Evidence from the Luxembourg Income Study*. Paris: OECD.

———. (1995b). Income Distribution in European Countries. DAE Working Papers. Cambridge: University of Cambridge, Department of Applied Economics.

Barrett, Alan, et al. (1997). The Earnings Distribution and Returns to Education in Ireland, 1987–89. CEPR Discussion Paper 1679.

Bedau, Karl-Dietrich, et al. (1987). Die Einkommenslage der Familien in der Bundesrepublik Deutschland in den Jahren 1973 und 1981. Deutscher Institut für Wirtschafsforschung. Beiträge zur Strukturforschung, Heft 97.

Brenner, Y.S., H. Kaelble, M. Thomas, eds. (1991). *Income Distribution in Historical Perspective*. Cambridge/Paris: Cambridge University Press/Editions de la Maison des Sciences de l'Homme.

Dicken, Peter. (1992). *Global Shift: The Internationalization of Economic Activity*. London: Paul Chapman.

Esping-Andersen, G. (1996). After the Golden Age? Welfare State Dilemmas in a Global Economy. In G. Esping-Andersen, ed. *Welfare States in Transition: National Adaptations in Global Economies*. London: Sage: 1–31.

Flora, Peter, and Arnold J. Heidenheimer, eds. (1981). *The Development of Welfare States in Europe and America*. New Brunswick/London: Transaction Books.

Franzmeyer, Fritz, et al. (1996). *Employment and Social Policies under International Constraints*. A Study for the Ministerie van Sociale Zaken en Werkgelegenheid (SZW) of the Netherlands by the Deutsches Institut für Wirtschaftsforschung in Berlin. 's-Gravenhage: Vuga.

Gottschalk, Peter, and Mary Joyce. (1991). Changes in Earnings Inequality—An International Perspective. The Luxembourg Income Study. Working Paper 66.

Group of Thirty. (1984). *Foreign Direct Investment*. New York.

Hagen, K., and J.M. Hippe. (1993). The Norwegian Welfare State: From Post-War Consensus to Future Conflicts? In A. Cohen Kiel, ed. *Continuity and Change: Aspects of Contemporary Norway*. Oslo: Scandinavian University Press.

Kalb, Don, et al. (1997). The Conundrum of Globalization: Inequality, Marginality and Policy Imperatives in Advanced Welfare States. AWSB Research Papers 97/01. Utrecht: AWSB.

Katzenstein, Peter J. (1985). *Small States in World Markets*. Ithaca, N.Y.: Cornell University Press.

Le Heron, Richard, and Eric Pawson, eds. (1996). *Changing Places: New Zealand in the Nineties*. Auckland: Longman Paul.

Mishel, Lawrence, and Jared Bernstein. (1995). Income Deterioration and Inequality in the United States. In Lawrence Mishel and John Schmitt, eds. *Beware the U.S. Model: Jobs and Wages in a Deregulated Economy*. Washington, D.C.: Economic Policy Institute: 101–32.

Mishel, Lawrence, and John Schmitt, eds. *Beware the U.S. Model: Jobs and Wages in a Deregulated Economy*. Washington, D.C.: Economic Policy Institute.

Mizoguchi, Toshiyuki, et al. (1980). Over-time Changes in the Size Distribution of Household Income under Rapid Economic Growth: The Japanese Experience. In K. Ohkawe and B. Key, eds. *Asian Socioeconomic Development*. Tokyo: University of Tokyo Press: 233–66.

Oberti, Marco. (1993). Economic Inequality. In M. Forsé et al. *Recent Social Trends in France 1960–1990*. Frankfurt: Campus/Montreal & Kingston: McGill-Queen's University Press: 141–46.

OECD. (1994). *The OECD Jobs Study: Evidence and Explanations*. 2 vols. Paris: OECD.

———. (1996). *Employment Outlook 1996*. Paris: OECD.

———. (1997). *Employment Outlook 1997*. Paris: OECD.

Ringen, Stein, and Hannu Uusitalo. (1990). Income Distribution and Redistribution in the Nordic Welfare States. *International Journal of Sociology* 20, no. 3: 69–91.

Sawyer, Malcolm. (1976). *Income Distribution in OECD Countries*. OECD Economic Outlook. Occasional Studies (July 1976).

Schluter, Christian. (1996). Income Mobility in Germany: Evidence from Panel Data. Distributional Analysis Research Programme. Discussion Paper 17. London School of Economics.

Sociaal en Cultureel Planbureau. (1992). *Sociaal en Cultureel Rapport 1992*. Rijswijk.

Smeeding, Timothy, and Günther Schmaus. (1990). The LIS Database: Technical and Methodological Aspects. In T.M. Smeeding et al., eds. *Poverty, Inequality and Income Distribution in Comparative Perspective: The Luxembourg Income Study (LIS)*. New York: Harvester/Wheatsheaf: 1–19.

Strange, Susan. (1996). *The Retreat of the State: The Diffusion of Power in the World Economy*. Cambridge: Cambridge University Press.

United Nations. (1993). *World Investment Directory 1992. Vol. III: Developed Countries*. New York.

———. (1994). *World Investment Report 1994*. New York/Geneva.

———. (1996). *World Investment Report 1996*. New York/Geneva.

Visser, Jelle, and Anton Hemerijck. (1997). *A Dutch Miracle: Job Growth, Welfare Reform and Corporatism in the Netherlands*. Amsterdam: Amsterdam University Press.

Wilterdink, Nico. (1995). Increasing Income Inequality and Wealth Concentration in the Prosperous Societies of the West. *Studies in Comparative International Development* 30 (Fall): 3–23.

Part III

Flows of People

12

Flows of People: Globalization, Migration, and Transnational Communities

Richard Staring

International migration is often seen as a core element of globalization processes. Many are quick to add that contemporary immigration has entered a new, unique phase, one that distinguishes itself from earlier periods of migration. This has urged some to speak of the "age of migration," while others introduce the concept of "the New Migration" (Castles and Miller 1993; Koser and Lutz 1998). There are, however, opposing views and ideas on the uniqueness of contemporary migration patterns and the number of people involved. Löfgren, for instance, argues that the great waves of migration happen not so much nowadays, but were concentrated during the period from the latter part of the nineteenth century up to World War I (Löfgren 1996: 56). He is a proponent of more historical perspectives on international migration and argues for a focus upon its significance within different historical periods instead of thinking in quantitative terms of more or less. The question then is how contemporary migration differs from earlier periods of migration, and how the relationship between international migration and globalization can be classified. We will therefore first consider contemporary migration flows in comparison with those of a century ago and try to ascertain the uniqueness of each. We will proceed by describing the relationship between globalization, economic restructuring, and international migration as it relates to Saskia Sassen's influential theory on global cities and the discussion that theory evoked. Finally, some alternative and additional arguments for explaining international migration patterns will be presented.

THE GLOBALIZATION OF MIGRATION

In his global immigration overview, Maurice Davie (1936) extensively describes immigration to the United States between 1820 and 1930. Immigration to the United States during this period is above all a European affair, as more than 85 percent of the immigrants came from countries such as Russia, Italy, Ireland, and the United Kingdom. Among the other countries mentioned, only five percent came from Mexico, some Asian countries, and the West Indies. Half a century later, the situation has reversed, as most new immigrants to the United States have a Hispanic or Asian background, and only a minority comes from European countries. Another recent geographical change in sending countries has been described for Europe by K. Koser and H. Lutz, who point to the recent arrival of immigrants—and refugees—from countries like the former Yugoslavia, the former Soviet Union, and central European countries (Koser and Lutz 1998: 2). Furthermore, the traditional composition of sending and receiving countries is increasingly blurred. Within southern Europe, traditional labor-exporting countries like Italy, Greece, and Spain have also become receiving countries (Hugo 1995: 401).

If we take a closer look at the number of people involved in international migration some prudence in making generalizations seems wise. For instance, observations that the number of immigrants to the United States is currently at an all-time high are not quite correct, as is illustrated in table 12.1. Especially if we take the number of immigrants as a percentage of the population, it becomes obvious that the largest influx of immigrants took place during the first decades of this century. The contemporary immigrant population in the United States is 10 percent of the total popula-

Table 12.1   Immigration to the United States, 1820–1996

1820–30	143,439	1911–20	5,735,811
1831–40	599,125	1921–30	4,107,209
1841–50	1,713,251	1931–40	528,431
1851–60	2,596,214	1941–50	1,035,039
1861–70	2,314,824	1951–60	2,515,479
1871–80	2,812,191	1961–70	3,321,677
1881–90	5,246,613	1971–80	4,493,314
1891–1900	3,687,564	1981–90	7,338,062
1901–10	8,795,396	1991–96	6,146,215

Sources: 1993: INS (1993). 1994: as cited in *Immigration and Illegal Aliens: Burden or Blessing* (1995: 4). The figures based for the fiscal years 1994–96 are published in *Migrant News,* January 1997. In 1994, 804,416; 1995, 720,461; and 1996, 915,900 immigrants settled legally in the United States.

tion, whereas it accounted for 15 percent of the total during the immigration waves at the beginning of this century (Krikorian 1998). Koser and Lutz (1998) conclude that one could claim that Europe received the largest number of immigrants, but only in the rather brief time span directly after World War II. One wonders whether this observation can be confirmed when a longer time span is considered.

Unfortunately, official data only partially mirror reality, as it tends to reflect the formal, documented part of immigration. Both undocumented immigrants who enter a host country illegally, and the so-called "visa-overstayers" are neglected within these data. For 1995, the Immigration and Naturalization Service (INS) estimated the total number of undocumented immigrants in the United States at five million, but others claim that such estimates are far too exaggerated.[1] For Europe, the number of illegal immigrants was estimated at somewhere around 2.6 million (Castles and Miller 1993: 79).

According to those scholars who stress the uniqueness of contemporary international migration, migration flows are first of all becoming more global in scope as more countries are involved in long-distance migration. Ever more countries, as well as people, are involved in and affected by international migration. Second, contemporary migration flows can be characterized as increasingly diverse (Castles and Miller 1993: 8; Campani 1995: 547; cf., Champion 1994; Pugliese 1993). This diversity expresses itself in the economic, cultural, and social background of the persons involved in international migration. Furthermore, different types of immigrants, such as refugees, asylum-seekers, undocumented migrants, family reunifiers, professionals, entrepreneurs, and labor immigrants are often simultaneously present in many immigration countries (Cohen 1995: 3; Champion 1994). Within all this diversity, undocumented immigrants and refugees are becoming a more prominent and growing category worldwide (Champion 1994; Miller 1995; Koser and Lutz 1998). With the growing participation of women in labor migration flows, the "feminization of migration" has also been coined as an important characteristic of contemporary migration (Castles and Miller 1993: 8; Phizacklea 1998).

Those scholars who downplay the uniqueness of contemporary migration flows are less inclined toward sweeping statements and are often equipped with a longer historical perspective. Historian Moch for instance, in a study that links migration with historical change in Europe from 1650 onward, argues that migration processes are grounded in large-scale changes in landholding patterns, employment demands, demographic trends, and the location of capital (Moch 1992: 7). She refers to Immanuel Wallerstein, who perceives (international) migration as the intrinsic outcome of the development and expansion of the capitalist world market since the sixteenth century (cf., Massey et al. 1993: 444; Phizacklea 1998).

For the twentieth century, Moch concludes that in comparison with earlier migration flows, the migrant home, as well as state intervention and the control of international migration, will be distinctive elements (Moch 1992: 161). In *Controlling Immigration*, Cornelius, Martin, and Hollifield discuss these last two key elements of contemporary migration patterns. The authors observe an increasing similarity among industrialized, labor-importing countries in the policy instruments chosen for controlling immigration, and they envision a greater gap between the goals of these migration policies and their outcomes. Although industrialized countries increasingly try to control immigration by further tightening entry restrictions, the authors argue that governments have a difficult time overcoming internal economic interests and "push" pressures in the sending countries. This seemingly powerless position governments find themselves in is accompanied by a sensitivity for the general public opinion concerning the consequences of the influx and settlement of immigrants for the identity and unity of nation-states (Cornelius, Martin, and Hollifield 1994: 3–6). How should Western governments, for instance, respond to the presence of Moslem immigrants and their quest for Islamic schools and other religiously motivated needs? Or how should they deal with large proportions of the population that speak a foreign language, as is the case in California? As most developed countries nowadays must be characterized as multiethnic, the presence of immigrants has definitely set the issue of national culture versus multiculturalism at the top of the political agenda (Staring, van der Land, Tak, and Kalb 1997).

A final element frequently put forward refers to the influence of improved, faster, and cheaper transportation opportunities and communication facilities on international migration. Instead of undertaking the long sea journey to Ellis Island—like most European immigrants to the United States until far into the 1950s—one can nowadays fly from the Old Continent to New York City in eight hours. At the beginning of the nineteenth century the sea journey from Europe to America could last—depending on weather conditions—from one to three months, and it was often accompanied by serious dangers. The introduction of the steamship decreased the duration of the journey around 1900 to less than ten days (Handlin 1951), but this still compares poorly with contemporary travel. In his contribution to this volume, Portes emphasizes the communication and traveling opportunities that facilitate and encourage the origin and continuation of transnational immigrant communities. Nevertheless, one should not overestimate the value of modern travel, because available opportunities and utilized opportunities are two different matters. Many undocumented immigrants and refugees are restricted to the informal services of smugglers and traffickers and have to face time-consuming and dangerous journeys comparable to those of their predecessors. Current images of rickety boats filled with Haitians, Cubans, Albanians, or Kurds entering their imagined paradises are manifold.

Although one has to be careful when generalizing contemporary migration flows, especially with regard to the number of people involved, there are enough relevant characteristics to distinguish international migration within the late twentieth century from that of earlier periods. Among the most prominent described above are the numbers of cultures that are involved in international migration. The resulting intensity and density of transnational linkages are also made possible by improved communication and travel opportunities. The entrance and settlement of immigrants has not only led to comparable restrictive migration regimes of capitalist welfare states, but also to the development of multiethnic societies. The visibility of the mainly nonwhite immigrants in most Western countries, their involvement in entrepreneurship, and their distinctive cultures and religions have influenced the identities of welfare states. Seen in this perspective, processes of globalization have not only changed the economies and cultures of Third World countries, but they have also restructured the cultures of Western welfare states.

ECONOMIC RESTRUCTURING AND
INTERNATIONAL MIGRATION

A long research tradition exists that relates international migration to economic forces. More than a century ago, Ernest Ravenstein was the first to develop general laws concerning international migration. He perceived the movement of people as the relocation of capital. Ravenstein was also one of the first scientists to attribute central importance to the economic motive in migration. As he stated "nothing can compare with the desire inherent in most men to 'better' themselves in material respects" (Ravenstein 1889: 286). Since then, in most theories of international migration economic motives play an important role in explaining and interpreting the movement of people. It does not seem exaggerated to state that within the migration discipline there is a preoccupation with labor and capital as determinants of the origin and direction of migration flows.

One of the migration theories most frequently referred to in the context of neoclassical economics is Everett Lee's "theory of migration," in which he perceives migration as the interplay between factors in countries of origin and destination, intervening obstacles, and personal factors (Lee 1969: 288). In his perspective, migration is the result of an unbalanced exchange of goods or an unbalanced allocation of production factors. Both of these phenomena lead to wage differences, which ultimately lead to migration, as individuals from areas with low wages migrate to countries with higher wages. People are seen accordingly as rational and calculating human beings that make rational choices in their search for better (economic) conditions (cf., Borjas 1989). Migration then is primarily the outcome of conscious and voluntary choices made by individuals, and a migration flow is the cumulation of all these calculating individuals. Migration restores the equilibrium and, according to this optimistic view, it simultaneously contributes to the development of the sending countries. Push and pull factors determine the size and the direction of the migration flows. Adherents of this model also take intervening obstacles, for instance travel expenses or distance, into account as personal factors that can influence the individual decision to migrate (Lee 1969; Öncü 1990: 177–79).

This image of immigrants as rational decision makers has been severely criticized by scholars who could not adequately explain contemporary migration patterns using this framework. Opponents refer to the theory's implication that migration flows would originate from the poorest Third World countries, while research indicates that migrants in general originate from countries with more intermediate wage levels. The poorest countries hardly engage in international migration. Besides, the migrants are usually not the poorest people from these countries, but rather those with some resources (Portes 1995: 20). It is therefore hard to maintain that migration flows are the spontaneous outcome of wage differentials or global economic inequalities (Portes and Rumbaut 1990: 224). Neoclassical theories are also not capable of explaining the directions of migration flows. Why are certain migration flows directed at certain specific countries and others of comparable economic standing neglected? Migration flows on a macro level are the result of historical relationships between sending and receiving countries, be it of a political, economical, or cultural nature. Economic restructuring results in a reorientation of the economy of the sending countries and a diffusion of (Western) consumption patterns in the peripheral countries (Portes and Rumbaut 1990). As traditional economies are reshaped and consumption patterns not met, international migration becomes one of the possible household strategies to fulfill these newly perceived needs.

One theory, in which several elements of the criticisms sketched above are incorporated, is elaborated by Saskia Sassen. In her various publications on "global cities" (Sassen 1988, 1991, 1994) she employs a helicopter view on globalization and economic restructuring in relationship to international migration.[2] According to Sassen, one of the consequences of the relocation of production to peripheral countries is the countermovement of labor from Third World countries to the advanced economies. This process promises to offer an explanation for the origin and direction of long-distance migration from the periphery to the core countries. When households in the periphery are exposed to Western modes of production and Western consumption aspirations, and simultaneously lack the means to implement them, emigration becomes a viable alternative and solution to these disruptions (Portes 1995: 21). According to Sassen, it is in global cities that the central role of control and management of the newly emerging global economic system is played out (Burgers 1995: 365). Global cities, which often evolve from their old mercantile functions as natural harbors and ports, are the centers of (economic) power, finance, communication, and transport, and are often the locations of transnational corporations headquarters (cf., Cohen 1997: 165–67). For Sassen, however, these global cities are not only multifunctional or multiple centers, but also main destinations for immigrants. In global cities the specific economy generates not only high-level, specialized jobs, but also a vast amount of low-level, often informal, and unattractive, poorly paid jobs. Jobs at the lower end of the occupational structure are created in specific sectors such as cleaning, catering, and security. Furthermore, the polarized occupational structure of these cities gives rise to a growing informal sector in which migrants often participate (Burgers 1995: 365). Although most sectors of production have been relocated outside the global city, some—mostly garment and fashion industries—remain and can survive, due to the presence of (illegal) immigrants (Cohen 1995: 168; Waldinger 1996: 15). This specific, hourglass-shaped occupational structure of global cities creates a demand for immigrant labor willing to fulfill the 3D-jobs: dirty, dangerous, and demeaning (see also chapter 13 in this section). Moreover, the sheer number of immigrants who settle down in these global cities creates a new demand for businesses that offer ethnic products and services such as schools, newspapers, and broadcasting stations. This implies additional jobs for immigrants from these communities.

The work of Sassen has not only been embraced by many scholars, but it has also evoked much discussion among her colleagues. The outcome of empirical research on the field of migration suggests that economic restructuring and social polarization within cities fails to serve as an adequate explanation for international migration flows and its continuation even in times when there are only a few jobs left. Two of the three contributions to this section on the relationship between internal migration and processes of globalization—the chapter by Light, Kim, and Hum and the chapter by Burgers—can be located in this ongoing debate on the work of Sassen and her findings on social polarization in global cities. In a review article, *The Global City and the Universal Suburb*, Burgers (1995) wonders what has happened to Los Angeles as a "global city." In *Mobility of Labor and Capital*, Sassen (1988) presents Los Angeles—among other major cities—as a prime example of a global city. However, in her later work this Southern California city disappears from the list. The chapter by Light, Kim, and Hum sheds some light on this unresolved question. They

take Greater Los Angeles in the period of 1970–90 as a case for the influence of globalization on this region, which has witnessed the greatest influx of immigrants in the United States since 1965. The authors conclude
that although global restructuring has affected this region, it has influenced
immigration to Los Angeles less than expected. Global restructuring can
sufficiently explain the acceleration of Hispanic immigration into the Los
Angeles region in a context where real wages and self-employment incomes for immigrants decline. Migration network theory, the authors con-
clusively argue, can explain this process. Spill-over migration due to chain
or network-driven migration exceeds the consequences and effects of
globalization.

Burgers, in his contribution to this section, is also skeptical about the
explanatory power of Sassen's polarization thesis. Analyzing data on unemployment and educational level for major Dutch cities, he finds that social polarization takes place between employed and unemployed Dutch
and not—as Sassen argues—within the labor market. Burgers then focuses
more specifically upon the labor market position of (undocumented) immigrants in these cities, and fails to find any functional relationship between
the presence of immigrants and the "pulls" of the postindustrial urban
labor market. According to Burgers, social polarization can take different
shapes depending on the type of welfare state. He proposes a three-layered
model of the effects of global processes and the way they are appropriated
by the local. Beside institutional factors, he includes the historical trajectories of individual cities and immigrant networks in this model.

It is striking that Burgers and Light, Kim, and Hum can not sufficiently
explain the presence and the continuing influx of immigrants with the demand for immigrant labor created by restructured urban economies. In
their own ways, they conclude that they have to seek additional explanations to deal with the urban realities they are facing. In both chapters, the
authors find the issues resolved in part by the existence of social networks
that link sending and receiving countries. In the following section we will
deal more specifically with these social networks of international migration.

SOCIAL NETWORKS IN A TRANSNATIONAL CONTEXT

Considering the critique concerning the economic restructuring thesis it
seems that economic motives, whether on macrostructural or microstruc-
tural levels, fail to explain international migration as it unfolds and continues. Massey et al. argue that "the conditions that initiate international
movement may be quite different from those that perpetuate it across time
and space. . . . New conditions that arise in the course of migration, come

to function as independent causes themselves" (Massey et al. 1993: 448). Among the most important new conditions are the social networks that connect immigrants with their fellow countrymen and the people left behind. The grounding of social networks across national boundaries is one of the key notions amid the new conditions. Boyd states that

> social networks based on kinship, friendship and community ties are central components in migration system analysis. Social networks mediate between individual actors and larger structural forces. They link sending and receiving countries. And they explain the continuation of migration long after the original impetus for migration has ended. (Boyd 1989: 661)

Although never as popular and central as nowadays, social networks in different disguises and notions have long played a role in interpreting migration. In particular, scholars who are studying international migration on a meso or micro level—often accompanied with more qualitative research methods—constantly remind us of the central importance of migrant networks as a key in understanding migration (cf., Hammar et al. 1997). Thomas and Znaniecki (1918), in their classic study on Polish peasants in America, draw attention to the importance of transnational family relations and community ties for the increase of the newly established Polish communities in the United States. Siu, (1953) in his study of Chinese immigrants in Chicago, gives numerous examples of the strength of these linkages for the arrival of newcomers. He also makes us aware of the controlling potentials of these networks, as they not only successfully promote immigration even when restrictive legislation exists, but are also capable of deterring potential immigrants. In the early 1960s, Price elaborated the concept of chain migration (Price 1963). He also stresses the fact that migration can be a self-sustaining process, as earlier migrants—even in times of economic depressions—recruit and encourage those network members who were left behind to follow them (Price 1963: 122). According to Price, chain migration focuses on the contacts of immigrants with relatives and friends in their home countries as an important source of further immigration. He writes, "with semi-literate peasant peoples intimate direct conversation and visible signs of success in the form of gold watches or brand-new clothes and shoes have had even more spectacular effects than letters from abroad" (Price 1963: 108). According to Price, the influence of relatives and friends accounted for 94 percent of the immigrants who entered the United States from 1908 to 1910 (Price 1963: 109), and recent research among immigrants confirms this conclusion.

Among the contributors to this section, Portes deals most thoroughly with social networks. Much of his earlier work underlines the relevance of these networks for immigration, for instance, in *Immigrant America*, writ-

ten in collaboration with Rumbaut. The authors' views on the relevance of
social networks are best reflected in the following citation.

> More than a movement that follows automatically the push and pull of eco-
> nomic conditions, labor migration should be conceptualized as a process of
> progressive network building. Networks connect individuals and groups dis-
> tributed unevenly across space, maximizing their economic opportunities
> through multiple displacements. (Portes and Rumbaut 1990: 232)

In his contribution to this section, Portes elaborates upon his earlier work
on social networks in a transnational, globalized context. Like Light, Kim,
and Hum and Burgers, Portes describes the social networks of immigrants
as a key in understanding contemporary immigration. He focuses on and
expounds the concept of "transnational communities," diverging, however, from the original work of Basch, Glick Schiller, and Blanc-Szanton
on transnational immigrant communities by limiting the definition of
transnational migrants. In his view not all immigrants who maintain relationships with their home country should be labeled as transmigrants, only
those whose transnational activities constitute a major part of their occupations on a regular basis. Portes perceives the rise of transnational entrepreneurs as one of the popular responses to global restructuring. Their success
depends upon geographically extended, dense, and solidary networks, and
upon improved transportation and communication facilities. By presenting
a range of empirical data on transnational communities, Portes displays
their cumulative character: what begins as an economic initiative can ultimately have a severe political, social, and cultural impact in both sending
and receiving societies. Although his examples are mainly drawn from the
United States, this by no way means that his findings are restricted to this
continent. It would be interesting to discern whether such processes can
also be observed in a European context.

  According to Light et al. and Burgers, global restructuring theories belong primarily to the category of demand-driven explanations, which emphasize pull factors for the continuance of immigration to Western urban
centers. They have little regard for the other side of the story, the push
elements that are situated in the sending countries. Social networks simultaneously function on both ends of the process; it is not surprising therefore that they are increasingly put forward to explain the continuation of
migration flows. However, many questions still remain with regard to the
push side, and further research is needed. The influences of cultural globalization processes on peripheral countries, in relationship to the perceived
opportunities of these countries' populations, are among the most important. The cultural influence of globalization and its appropriation on a local
level within these peripheral regions, combined with the inclusive and ex-

clusive capacities of transnational networks, may result in a growing awareness of opportunity in distant parts of the world. Unfortunately, these opportunities all too often must be characterized as false. Many immigrants, who have successfully mobilized the social capital of their networks, increasingly find themselves in a hostile environment where they are excluded from full citizenship.

NOTES

1. Estimations of the number of illegal immigrants living in the United States vary between three and five million.

2. The following section on Sassen draws heavily on Burgers's review article (1995) on Sassen.

REFERENCES

Borjas, George J. (1989). Economic Theory and International Migration. *International Migration Review* 23, no. 3: 457–85.

Boyd, Monica. (1989). Family and Personal Networks in International Migration: Recent Developments and New Agendas. *International Migration Review* 23, no. 3: 638–71.

Burgers, Jack. (1995). The Global City and the Universal Suburb, Recent Issues in Urban Sociology. A Review Article. *Netherlands Journal of Housing and the Built Environment* 10, no. 4: 363–73.

Campani, Giovanna. (1995). Women Migrants: From Marginal Subjects to Social Actors. In Robin Cohen, ed. *The Cambridge Survey of World Migration.* Cambridge: Cambridge University Press: 546–50.

Castles, Stephen, and Mark J. Miller. (1993). *The Age of Migration: International Population Movements in the Modern World.* Houndmills: Macmillan.

Champion, A.G. (1994). International Migration and Demographic Change in the Developed World. *Urban Studies* 31, no. 4-5: 653–77.

Cohen, Robin. (1995). Prologue. In Robin Cohen, ed. *The Cambridge Survey of World Migration.* Cambridge: Cambridge University Press: 1–9.

Cornelius, Wayne A., Philip L. Martin, and James F. Hollifield, eds. (1994). *Controlling Immigration. A Global Perspective.* Stanford, Calif.: Stanford University Press.

Davie, Maurice R. (1936). *World Immigration: With Special Reference to the United States.* New York: Macmillan.

Hammar, T., G. Brochmann, K. Tamas, and T. Faist. (1997). *International Migration, Immobility and Development: Multidisciplinary Perspectives.* Oxford: Berg.

Handlin, Oscar. (1951). *The Uprooted: The Epic Story of the Great Migrations That Made the American People.* New York: Grosset and Dunlap.

Hugo, Graeme. (1995). Illegal International Migration in Asia. In Robin Cohen, ed. *The Cambridge Survey of World Migration*. Cambridge: Cambridge University Press: 397–402.

Immigration and Naturalization Service. (1993). *Statistical Yearbook of the Immigration and Naturalization Service*.

Koser, K., and H. Lutz. (1998). The New Migration in Europe: Contexts, Constructions and Realities. In K. Koser and H. Lutz, eds. *The New Migration in Europe: Social Constructions and Social Realities*. Houndmills: Macmillan: 1–20.

Koser, Khalid. (1997). Social Networks and the Asylum Cycle: The Case of Iranians in the Netherlands. *International Migration Review* 31, no. 3: 591–611.

Krikorian, Mark. (1998). Will Americanization Work in America? *Freedom Review* 28, no. 3.

Landes, Alison, Cornelia Blair, and N. Jacobs, eds. (1995). *Immigration and Illegal Aliens: Burden or Blessing?* Wylie, Texas: Information Press.

Lee, Everett S. (1969). A Theory of Migration. In J.A. Jackson, ed. *Migration*. Cambridge: Cambridge University Press: 282–97.

Löfgren, Orvar. (1996). Taking the Back Door: On the Historical Anthropology of Identities. In Don Kalb, Hans Marks, and Herman Tak, eds. Historical Anthropology: The Unwaged Debate. *Focaal, Journal for Anthropology* 26/27: 53–58.

Massey, Douglas M., J. Arango, G. Hugo, A. Kaoaouci, A. Pellegrino, and J. E. Taylor. (1993). Theories of International Migration: A Review and Appraisal. *Population and Development Review* 19, no. 3: 431–66.

Miller, Mark J. (1995). Illegal Migration. In Robin Cohen, ed. *The Cambridge Survey of World Migration*. Cambridge: Cambridge University Press: 537–40.

Moch, Leslie Page. (1992). *Moving Europeans: Migration in Western Europe since 1650*. Bloomington: Indiana University Press.

Öncü, Ayse. (1990). International Labour Migration and Class Relations. In Alberto Martinelli and Neil J. Smelser, eds. *Economy and Society: Overviews in Economic Sociology*. London: Sage Publications: 175–203.

Phizacklea, Annie. (1998). Migration and Globalization: A Feminist Perspective. In K. Koser and H. Lutz, ed. *The New Migration in Europe: Social Constructions and Social Realities*. Houndmills: Macmillan: 21–38.

Portes, Alejandro. (1995). Economic Sociology and the Sociology of Immigration: A Conceptual Overview. In Alejandro Portes, ed. *The Economic Sociology of Immigration: Essays on Networks, Ethnicity, and Entrepreneurship*. New York: Russell Sage Foundation: 1–41.

———, and Ruben G. Rumbaut. (1990). *Immigrant America: A Portrait*. Berkeley: University of California Press.

Price, Charles A. (1963). *Southern Europeans in Australia*. Melbourne: Oxford University Press.

Pugliese, E. (1993). Restructuring of the Labour Market and the Role of Third World Migrations in Europe. *Environment and Planning D—Society and Space* 11: 513–22.

Ravenstein, Ernest G. (1889). The Laws of Migration. *Journal of the Royal Statistical Society* 52: 241–301.

Sassen, Saskia. (1988). *The Mobility of Labor and Capital: A Study in International Investment and Labor Flow*. London: Cambridge University Press.

———. (1991). *The Global City: New York, London, Tokyo*. Princeton, N.J.: Princeton University Press.

Siu, Paul C.P. (1987). *The Chinese Laundryman: A Study of Social Isolation*. New York: New York University Press. Originally presented as thesis (Ph.D.), University of Chicago, 1953.

Staring, Richard, Marco van der Land, Herman Tak, and Don Kalb. (1997). Localizing Cultural Identity. In Richard Staring, Marco van der Land, and Herman Tak, eds. Globalization/Localization: Paradoxes of Cultural Identity. *Focaal, Journal for Anthropology* no. 30–31: 7–22.

Thomas, William I., and Florian Znaniecki. (1996). *The Polish Peasant in Europe and America: A Classic Work in Immigration History*. Edited by Eli Zaretsky. Chicago: University of Illinois Press [originally published 1918–20].

Waldinger, Roger. (1996). *Still the Promised City? African Americans and New Immigrants in Postindustrial New York*. Cambridge, Mass.: Harvard University Press.

13

Globalization, Vacancy Chains, or Migration Networks? Immigrant Employment and Income in Greater Los Angeles, 1970–90

Ivan Light, Rebecca Kim, and Connie Hum

In the broadest sense, globalization refers to all processes that incorporate the peoples of the world into a single world society (Nederveen Pieterse 1994: 161). These processes are economic, cultural, and political.[1] However, in the restricted economic sense used here, globalization means movement toward a globally integrated market for labor and capital, especially the latter. Global restructuring is economic globalization in process. Global restructuring theory accounts for a multiplicity of linked changes worldwide in terms of the resurgent power of financial capital in a world with ever fewer barriers to trade. At the core, restructuring theory calls attention to local economic changes produced by resource shifts in the globalized market. In that global market, capital flows freely across international boundaries in response to profit incentives and labor, more inhibited, flows more freely than before (McLean Petras 1983: 48–49; see also Zolberg 1991). One could dub this scenario the production of the local by the global.

Global restructuring theory proclaims the supremacy of big capital. The agents of global restructuring are transnational corporations and money-center banks that, spanning continents, reallocate jobs and work among them in response to profit incentives and are indifferent to political or cultural loyalties or boundaries (Bornschier and Stamm 1990). These transnational corporations and banks are the dominant actors in the globalized economy. Additionally, restructuring theory claims that profit incentives

217

have created an international urban hierarchy centered upon three world cities and a number of supporting major cities. From these supreme organizing nodes, London, Tokyo, and New York in Sassen's influential account, transnational business corporations reach out to control the regional economies they penetrate.[2] As a result, local and regional economies operate more than previously as players in an international script written by distant financiers.[3]

From this core claim, restructuring theory extracts three key propositions. First, restructuring theory proposes that in the newly globalized world, multinational and transnational corporations strip production jobs away from high-priced workers in developed countries, assigning their tasks instead to newly opened factories in cheap-labor countries of the Third World (White and McMahon 1995: 50). Second, as job exportation unravels, transnational corporations center financial control, producer services, and advanced technology in Japan, Western Europe, and the United States (Savitch 1990: 151; Scott and Storper 1992: 3–4, 11). Third, both these changes alter the income structure of these developed countries (Sassen 1988: 22–23, 136). That is, the expansion of these highly paid sectors increases the number and share of the most affluent in these countries while redundant ex-production workers increase the number and share of the poor.[4] The middle class dwindles in size while the numbers of the wealthy and of the poor increase.[5]

GLOBALIZATION, MIGRATION, AND INFORMALIZATION

Moore and Pinderhughes (1993: xxvii) declare that "The growth of an informal economy is part and parcel of late twentieth-century economic restructuring." This judgment epitomizes restructuring theory, which explains the growth of informal economies in the developed countries as a by-product of newly polarized income distributions arising from global restructuring (Sassen 1990: 484–85; Sassen-Koob 1989: 70).[6] Continuing, restructuring theorists explain immigration too in terms of growing effective demand for cheap labor.[7] At the top of the income distribution, newly rich, so the argument proceeds, dual earner households need servants, gardeners, and nannies (Wrigley 1997: 117–39). Immigrants from poor countries will take these low-wage jobs; unemployed native workers will not (Waldinger 1995: 12–29). These immigrant workers receive no social security benefits, no employer-paid health care. Their wages are not reported to tax officials, and their job tenure is casual. Therefore, underpaid employees of rich households cannot afford mainstream products and services that require a mainstream income. Like the newly impoverished natives of the ex-middle class, dismissed from their production jobs, they look for discounted goods produced and sold in the informal sector. Like the rich, the immigrant poor buy clothing manufactured in the informal sector. Unlike the rich, who buy them in fancy boutiques, the workers of the informal sector and the distressed ex-middle class natives buy garments manufactured in the informal sector from informal sector vendors on street corners and at swap meets.

Figure 13.1 shows how globalization theorists explain both immigration and informalization. Their explanation is linear (Frey 1996–97: 26). First, global restructuring changes the income structure of the advanced countries, increasing the number and share of the wealthy in total income while diminishing the income share of the poor but increasing their number. The hourglass income distribution creates demand for low-priced goods the poor can afford, as well as for personal services the rich wish to buy. Responding to the new demand for personal services as well as for informal production workers, immigrants from poor countries swarm into the great cities of the developed world where they serve both purposes. Much of this production is informal. Whether they work for wealthy households or for industrial sweatshops, the immigrant poor receive substandard pay and benefits, often paid in cash. However, in this view, globalization-induced changes in demand completely explain immigration and informalization.[8] In a nutshell, restructuring theory maintains that "the foreign investment that drives economic globalization" emanates from world cities whose economic characteristics "create a strong demand for immigrant labor" (Massey et al. 1993: 446).

CRITIQUE OF RESTRUCTURING THEORY

Restructuring theory parsimoniously links economic processes in the advanced and developing countries, thus crafting a coherent vision of a global master process of which local immigration and informalization are by-products. No wonder restructuring theory has enjoyed wide popularity. However, as arguments have matured, restructuring theory has attracted criticism of basically four types. Formal criticism addresses globalization's overemphasis upon global structure at the expense of local agency as well as its economism and linear determinism.[9] Here economism means overemphasis upon market forces to the neglect of cultural, social, and

Figure 13.1 Globalization, Immigration, and Informalization

Global restructuring ➜ Hourglass Income Distribution ➜

Demand for Cheap Labor ➜ Immigration from Third World ➜ Informalization political responses to market forces (see Fernandez-Kelly and Garcia 1989; Fligstein 1997). Determinism means the utter elimination of political choice and of immigrant agency.[10] Thus, Logan and Swanstrom observe that the global restructuring literature represents markets as natural forces separable from and superior to national and local states.[11] Instead, they insist that "a great deal more [political] discretion exists to shape economic and urban restructuring than is commonly believed" (Logan and Swanstrom 1990: 5–6). Kloosterman declares that interregional differences prove that restructuring does not determine urban outcomes (Kloosterman 1994: 468). Marxist critics have taken a similar tack. Gottdiener and Komninos wish to escape "one-dimensional, deterministic explanations" in order to forge "approaches that consider political and cultural as well as economic dimensions" (Gottdiener and Komninos 1989: 8).

A second criticism complains that restructuring theory claims to explain immigration that is actually produced by related but different causes. Waldinger's version of this complaint objects that "shifts in the availability of native workers" engender "vacancies which immigrants fill" (Waldinger 1992: 100). Like the globalization theorists whom he criticizes, Waldinger proposes real increases in demand for cheap labor. However, Waldinger does not agree that an increase in demand for cheap labor explains immigration. In Waldinger's view, immigrants fill the structural vacancies in American cities rather than native-born blacks because, thanks to their social networks, immigrants outcompete the native blacks in American labor markets. But for this surprising competence, American labor markets would recruit needed cheap labor from black communities, in which case global restructuring would not have engendered immigration to the United States from Latin America and Asia. Therefore, in a strict sense, Waldinger argues, global restructuring did not cause the immigration of Third World people to the United States.

Another version of this complaint turns upon the intermediating role of immigrant employers in expanding initial demand for immigrant labor (Light, Bernard, and Kim 1997). Immigrant employers account for a large share of total immigrant employment in destination cities. In the garment industry of Los Angeles, a major immigrant industry, 85 percent of immigrant workers have immigrant employers (Light et al. 1997). Similarly, immigrant employers hire one-third of all immigrant workers in San Diego (Cornelius 1997: 9). When immigrant employers hire immigrant workers, they expand demand for these workers beyond what the unaided American economy would have provided. However, to obtain this result, foreign entrepreneurs, themselves the prior product of immigration, secondarily expand initial American demand. This sequence implies that immigrations sometimes expand initial labor demand as they develop, thus permitting more immigrants to stay than otherwise could have done so. In that case, because of the contingent role of immigrant employers, global restructuring alone can not have caused all the immigration of Third World people.

Third, global restructuring need not exclude all other causes of immigration to developed countries and, in some versions of the theory, does not. True, restructuring theory's principal architect, Saskia Sassen, has taken a consistently hard line on this point. "It is the economy rather than the immigrants which is producing low-wage jobs" (Sassen 1991: 302).[12] However, other restructuring theorists have acknowledged that restructured demand in the metropoles causes some of the Third World immigration, but did not cause all or even most of it. Thus, writing of Los Angeles, Ong and Blumenberg (1996) noted that an immigration-driven "increase in the relative and absolute number of low-earning workers" had contributed seriously to the growth of wage inequality. From this observation, they concluded that global restructuring's influence on earnings inequality arose "through supply-side changes" rather than just through demand-driven processes as in Sassen's version of globalization theory (Sassen 1991: 314, 322).

Ong and Blumenberg's conclusion opens the question of just how autonomous supply-side influences might obtrude into global restructuring. In a promising answer, Massey and his colleagues (1993: 448) have observed that, "the conditions that initiate international movement" need not "perpetuate it." That is, just as eating precedes and induces but does not cause digestion so global restructuring may initiate migrations that, once underway, owe their continuation and expansion to causes that did not engender them. In this case, path-dependent causalities offer more satisfactory explanatory models than simple ones. Pursuing their idea, Light (1998) has proposed the concept of "spillover migration" to explain how a migration earlier set in motion by global restructuring might outgrow and surpass its parent. Spillover immigrations occur when the motor of a continuing immigration switches from the demand to the supply side in midstream. In immigration spillovers, demand conditions trigger a migration, but immigrant social networks thereafter expand and continue it. What began because of novel demand conditions continues or expands because social networks lower the social, economic, and emotional cost of migration.[13] As the migration network matures, growth of the immigrant labor force in the target destination saturates the newly restructured demand, causing declining incomes and conditions in the informal sector because immigration continues or accelerates despite declining real wages. The informal sector then expands, despite declining conditions, because maturing migration networks partially or wholly compensate for the declining income. In spillover migrations, declining incomes at the bottom end result from labor markets saturated by network-driven migration rather than from the strong and stable labor demand of the host economy.[14]

WHAT IS DEMAND-DRIVEN MIGRATION?

To illustrate and amplify these criticisms, we review below the extensive globalization research on Los Angeles, seeking to understand what economic effects global restructuring theory can and cannot explain. Since global restructuring presupposes demand-driven immigration, our points of departure are dual. One is a theoretical explication of what a demand-driven migration would entail; another is an empirical look at whether Los Angeles really experienced a demand-driven migration between 1970 and 1990. The Los Angeles case does not, we submit, resemble the demand-driven migration that global restructuring theory requires or that Waldinger's ethnic succession model requires. Rather, the evidence suggests, migration to Los Angeles changed motors from the demand side to the supply side as initial labor demand evaporated and migration networks matured. In this metropolitan case, an important one for global restructuring theory, evidence points to the need for more complex models of migration and informalization than global restructuring theory delivers.[15]

What, after all, does demand-driven migration require? Global restructuring theorists have not even raised this question, much less answered it. However, as long as they remain demand-driven, migrations are insatiable consumers of migrant labor. Insatiability arises because, as the receiving economy grows, partially because of immigrant labor, the demand for additional immigrants grows apace. The more immigrants enter the demand-driven economy, the more the economy grows; and the more the economy grows, the more immigrants the economy demands. Key indicators of stable demand for immigrant labor are stable real wages and relative wages that keep pace with those of native-born workers. Another is a low and stable rate of unemployment among immigrants. In the past, when the demand-driven phase of an immigration has ended, real wages of immigrant workers have declined because earlier cohorts of immigrant workers partially or fully saturated labor demand. As labor markets approach saturation, the real and relative wages of immigrants fall. In fully saturated labor markets, a theoretical extreme case, the real wages of recent immigrants would reach zero and their unemployment would reach 100 percent. Declining real and relative wages of immigrants are a sign that immigrant labor niches are deteriorating. Therefore, whatever else may cause them, immigrations that continue in the face of declining real wages are not demand-driven.

Two historic examples frame this issue independent of Los Angeles, the case in evidence here. During the Great Migration of European whites to the United States, between 1880 and 1914, real wages of the native whites declined about ten percent. Although the wages of European immigrants, male and female alike, were consistently higher than, or as high as, those of the native whites, their real wages declined too (Hill 1975: 58–59; Blau 1980: 37; Shergold 1976: 459–60; Norby Fraundorf 1978: 219). This decline suggests that European immigrants continued to arrive in the United States in great number after their real wages had begun to decline. Evidently, even the robust economy of the United States could not absorb all the immigrant labor that arrived without wage declines. However, precisely that absorption defines demand-driven immigration. Therefore, in a strict sense, the Great Migration of European whites was not demand-driven in its second phase even if it was demand-driven in the first phase. After the demand-driven phase ended, and real wages began to decline, something other than demand continued the Great Migration.

A second example tells a comparable story. During the interwar migration of five million native blacks from the American South to northern, central, and western cities—a major transformation of American society in the twentieth century—the earliest black migrants received real wages as high as those paid later black migrants until 1929 (Harrison 1991: vii). In that depression year, demand for urban labor collapsed. The real wages of black migrants naturally dropped, remaining low until 1942 when war production began. Black migration from the South declined drastically at the beginning of the Great Depression in response to declining real wages and rising unemployment. The coordinated decline of real wages and of interstate black migration signaled a real demand-driven migration because when the demand slackened, the migration slackened too. War production hugely increased the real wages of Southern blacks, raising them well past what blacks had received before the Great Depression. War production also reinvigorated a black migration from the South (Trotter and Lewis 1996: 251; Groh 1972: 60). When the war ended in 1945, demand for production workers slowed, and the real wages of migrant black workers declined through 1970 (Groh 1972: 113; Henri 1975). Nonetheless, the black migration that the Second World War had initiated continued unabated until 1970, despite the decline in real wages after 1946.[16]

Postwar black interstate migration rolled on for twenty-four years after real wages of interstate migrants dropped. Abrupt declines in labor demand (caused first by depression and later by peace) reduced real wages for black migrants from the South. Therefore, judging by its decline after 1929 and recrudescence in 1942, the internal migration of blacks from the South was only demand-driven up to 1945. The interstate migration had switched motors by 1946, and so interstate black migration continued until 1970 despite declining real wages. Noting the discrepancy, Groh attributes the postwar continuation of interstate black migration to technological change in agriculture, a classic migration push.[17] In any case, like the migration of the European whites that had preceded it, the interstate migration of Southern blacks passed through a demand-driven phase into a second phase when the motor of migration changed. Neither of these historical migrations remained demand-driven throughout their entire duration; their demand-driven phase ended, and real wages declined, but migration continued anyway. These historic examples suggest that current migrations may also continue after their demand-driven phase has ended for reasons that do not derive from labor demand.

LOS ANGELES RESTRUCTURES

Los Angeles had undergone twenty-five years of well-documented restructuring by 1990 (Lopez-Garza 1989; Soja 1987; Light 1988: 69–74). Indeed, this global restructuring was, according to Ong and Blumenberg, "more extensive in Los Angeles than in the rest of the United States" (Ong and Blumenberg 1996: 323). As is already well understood, in this quarter century of painful transition, heavy manufacturing industry left Southern California for the Pacific Rim, leaving behind high technology, the aerospace and defense industries, and immigrant-staffed sweatshops.[18] The real wages of manufacturing workers stagnated and declined in the protracted, industrial egress, widening the gap between rich and poor (Ong and Blumenberg 1996: 312; see also Soja, Morales, and Wolff 1987; Soja 1989). New jobs in service industries employed many persons displaced from manufacturing but usually at much lower wages (Scott 1988). As elsewhere, ostentatious, newly rich millionaires became more prominent on the high end of the income distribution and desperately poor, unskilled immigrants at the low end.[19]

In this Southern California region, where feverish globalization was underway for twenty-five years, we wish to ascertain whether migration was actually demand-driven throughout the period. The two largest groups of immigrants were Latinos and Asians. These two groups accounted for 83 percent of international migrants in the Los Angeles region in 1990 (Sabagh and Bozorgmehr 1996). Between 1970 and 1990, the foreign born also increased from 11 percent to 32 percent of the population of Los Angeles County (Sabagh and Bozorgmehr 1996: 85). Except for non-Hispanic whites, whose immigration peaked early and then declined, all the immigrant groups in Southern California have continued to field very large immigration cohorts in every five-year period. In the specific case of Mexicans, the largest immigrant group, the immigration cohorts grew consistently in size between 1950 and 1989, reaching their maximum in 1989. Yet, as we shall show, all this immigration has continued in the face of declining real incomes for immigrants. In this respect, of course, Southern California was not unique, for, as Borjas has shown, age-adjusted immigrant cohorts received successively lower wages relative to natives in every decade since 1950 (Borjas 1989: 21–37).

Comparing four ethno-racial groups in Southern California, Light and Roach found that the wages of whites in the private sector increased 3.92 fold in the twenty-year period; wages of blacks increased more than those of whites; wages of Asians (immigrant and nonimmigrant) increased as much as those of whites; but the wages of Hispanics increased only 72 percent as much as did the wages of whites (Light and Roach 1996: 200). This result indicates falling real wages for Hispanics, but not for Asians. However, research directed specifically at immigrant Latinos and immigrant Asians finds that both Asian immigrants and Latino immigrants experienced declining real incomes and increased unemployment over the twenty-year period in Los Angeles and its region.[20] Cheng and Yang undertook a cohort analysis of Asian immigrants who arrived in Southern California in the 1960s, 1970s, and 1980s. Summarizing their results, they declare the evidence indicates "erosion" of the Asian immigrants' economic welfare in this period.

> Compared with subsequent cohorts at comparable periods of time, the 1960s cohort seems to have done somewhat better in the first decade of residence. . . . Moreover, the 1980s cohort seems to be doing worse than the 1970s cohort at the end of the first decade of residence. (Cheng and Yang 1996: 323)

Lopez, Popkin, and Telles undertook a similar, cohort analysis of the earnings of Salvadoran, Guatemalan, and Mexican immigrants in Los Angeles, comparing real earnings in three successive periods (Lopez, Popkin, and Telles 1996: 299). Their evidence compares mean earnings of immigrant Salvadoran, Guatemalan, and Mexican men aged twenty-five to sixty-four in 1975–79, 1980–84, and 1985–89. All three Latino groups show continuous decline in 1989-dollar earnings over each successive period. Overall declines were between 30 percent and 40 percent of initial real wages. Ong and Blumenberg find that real hourly compensation in the private sector of Los Angeles increased only 14.5 percent between 1969 and 1989 compared to an increase of 98 percent between 1948 and 1969. However, among immigrants, they find, real wages actually declined 13 percent between 1970 and 1980 (Ong and Blumenberg 1996; see also Schimek 1989). Studying three cohorts of Mexican immigrants to Los Angeles, Ortiz also finds evidence of declining real wages between 1970 and 1990. Mexican immigrants of the 1960s cohort, she writes,

> saw their real earnings advance steadily from the beginning to the end of the period. . . . More disturbing is the fate of subsequent cohorts, who not only

slipped further behind native whites with each decade but failed to recapture the very modest earnings of their predecessors." (Ortiz 1996: 257)

RESTRUCTURING SELF-EMPLOYMENT

Self-employment offers another test of globalization's economic impact on Greater Los Angeles. Under a regime of global restructuring, job-exporting regions increase self-employment for two reasons. First, self-employment increases because the exportation of production jobs strips native-born workers of secure, high-wage production jobs, encouraging them to undertake self-employment as a survival strategy. We call this jobs-export self-employment. It is a defensive form of self-employment that protects living standards of displaced workers. However, a second, equally genuine increase in globalization-induced self-employment is positive, not defensive. This positive increase arises from expansion of incorporated self-employment, the highest income sector of the entire labor market, in reflection of the enhanced demand for high-income professional/technical workers that restructuring notoriously brings (Allen and Turner 1997: 188).

However, we must distinguish these two globalization-driven increases in self-employment from network-driven increases in self-employment. Network-driven increase in self-employment is neither positive nor attributable to globalization. Network-driven increases occur when redundant immigrants, having saturated labor markets in the destination economy, turn in desperation to low income self-employment, especially in the informal sector. When this process occurs, heavy immigrant influx overwhelms demand for entrepreneurs, driving down the average economic returns of entrepreneurship. This result is similar to the increase among displaced native production workers, whose jobs were exported; however, the increase of self-employment among immigrants is network-driven.

Rates of incorporated and unincorporated self-employment did increase in Southern California between 1970 and 1990, a period of intense global restructuring. Combining all four major ethno-racial categories, Light and Roach report that aggregate self-employment increased 2.29 fold in the twenty years, whereas the general labor market increased only 1.80 fold (Light and Roach 1996: 196). Incorporated self-employment and unincorporated self-employment both increased. The increase in incorporated self-employment occurred among all ethno-racial categories and promoted the absolute and proportional growth of the highest income stratum in each, thus contributing to income polarization, the telltale symptom of globalization. Increases in unincorporated self-employment were less universal. Among the native born, increases in self-employment outstripped increases in wage employment among whites and Hispanics. Rates increased faster among women than among men (table 13.1). Among the foreign born, increases in self-employment outstripped increases in wage employment among white men and women, Asian men, and Hispanic men and women.

The financial return of incorporated self-employment kept pace with the wages of private-sector workers among whites and blacks, but not among Asians and Hispanics. Among Hispanics, the income of the incorporated self-employed increased only 73 percent as much as did Hispanic wage income in the private sector. However, the income gains of the unincorporated self-employed were appreciably better than the income gains of the unincorporated self-employed. Among all four ethno-racial categories, the earnings of the unincorporated self-employed failed to keep pace with earnings of co-ethnic wage earners in the private sector (Light and Roach 1996: 201). The discrepant earnings trajectories of the incorporated and the unincorporated self-employed suggest that growth in high-end demand, a product of globalization, permitted the incorporated sector to absorb newcomers without declining incomes. This is demand-driven entrepreneurship. In contrast, the uniformly declining incomes of the unincorporated self-employed suggest supply-driven increases that overwhelmed demand for marginal entrepreneurs, driving down their average incomes. The two groups whose unincorporated self-employment increased the most in number (whites, Hispanics) increased their self-employment earnings less than the two groups (Asians, blacks) whose numbers increased least. Light and Roach attribute the increased supply of white entrepreneurs to jobs export, and the increased supply of Hispanic entrepreneurs to network-driven saturation of labor markets.

HUMAN CAPITAL

Immigrant earnings might decline because later immigrant cohorts had lower average educational levels than earlier cohorts. Because income increases with education, declining educational levels should produce declining incomes. In this case, changes in average educational levels (rather than the saturation of labor markets) might account for declining real incomes of immigrants. In point of fact, the mean educational levels of Asian immigrants in Los Angeles and in the United States did decrease between 1970 and 1990, but the mean educational levels of Hispanic immigrants were stable or increased only slightly (Borjas 1990: 231–32). One might suppose that the Asian case repels explanation in terms of market saturation whereas the Hispanic case supports it.

However, the interpretation of declining educational levels is not sim-

Table 13.1   Wage Employment and Self-Employment in 1990 by Ethno-Racial Category, Nativity, and Gender

	Number, 1990		Index, 1970–90	
	Employees	*Self-Employed*	*Employees*	*Self-Employed*
Native Whites				
Men	1,374,026	261,693	108	150
Women	1,150,660	123,124	151	280
Total	2,524,686	384,817		
% Women	45.6	40.0		
Foreign Whites				
Men	125,983	42,955	124	210
Women	102,924	14,366	145	197
Total	228,907	57,321		
% Women	44.9	25.1		
Native Blacks				
Men	185,518	14,103	153	150
Women	200,050	7,336	201	179
Total	385,568	21,439		
% Women	51.2	34.2		
Native Asians				
Men	50,231	6,819	209	105
Women	45,190	2,941	264	226
Total	95,421	9,760		
% Women	47.3	30.1		
Foreign Asians				
Men	204,690	44,605	984	1438
Women	185,950	23,213	1074	n.a.
Total	390,640	67,818		
% Women	47.6	34.2		
Native Hispanics				
Men	265,110	21,797	191	245
Women	223,708	10,028	271	627
Total	488,818	31,825		
% Women	45.7	31.5		
Foreign Hispanics				
Men	631,527	50,624	659	817
Women	381,434	23,309	746	1793
Total	1,012,961	73,933		
% Women	37.6	31.5		

Source: U.S. Census of 1990, 5 percent public use sample.

ple.[21] After all, if successive immigrant cohorts display lower educational levels, we must invoke progressive saturation to field a demand-driven explanation. Progressive saturation arises when the first immigrant cohort saturates the highest-level demand in the destination economy, then gives way to a second cohort, lower in educational level, which saturates a lower-level demand. In turn, that second cohort gives way to a third cohort, still less educated, which saturates a still lower-level demand. In this way, a demand-driven economy could successively attract immigrants ever lower in human capital, paying each cohort less than its better-educated predecessor. However, although progressive saturation is a plausible explanation of declining educational levels among immigrants, progressive saturation does not fit global restructuring theory. According to restructuring theory, globalization increases opportunities at the top and at the bottom of the reception economy without saturating either the top or the bottom. If progressive saturation occurs, with erosion spreading down the ladder, and educational levels decline, global restructuring cannot explain it.[22]

Moreover, declining cohort quality usually results from network migration (Massey et al. 1993: 453). Networks produce declining cohort quality when initially high-level cohorts, who responded directly to demand, later promote the entry of less-qualified kin. By assigning stronger priorities to family reunification than does either Australia or Canada, U.S. immigration law encourages precisely this outcome. That is, when initial immigrants qualify for admission because of needed occupational skills, the immigrant cohort that arises has high educational levels. When this skilled cohort later applies for family reunification, the people they sponsor have lower educational levels than their sponsors. In this way, migration networks, amplified by the U.S. immigration code, drive down the average educational level of successive migration cohorts. To the extent that the U.S. immigration law amplifies and expands migration networks, increasing their contribution to total migration, the laws of the United States (and not global restructuring) account for continuing migration. To the extent that migration networks would have operated independent of the law's enhancement, migration networks (not globalization) account for the continuing migration. Either way, a demand-driven globalization theory cannot explain declining cohort quality.

Turning now to the Hispanic immigrants, whose average educational level in Southern California was low but stable, we find that global restructuring cannot explain this outcome either. First, Allen and Turner conclude that "employment restructuring did not precede immigration" in Southern California. On the contrary, "the presence and prospects of low-wage immigrant labor encouraged job growth" that took advantage of the labor supply. This judgement reverses the temporal priorities that globalization theory requires (Allen and Turner 1997: 186).[23] Second, since Hispanic real incomes are declining and Hispanic educational levels are stable, we cannot escape the deterioration of the Hispanic immigrants' economic status. The same human capital is earning less money. Deteriorating economic status implies saturation of market demand, whereas global restructuring requires a strong and insatiable demand for low-wage labor. Even if global restructuring once opened new demands to immigrants in the early 1970s, low-level as well as high-level, saturation of those new demands would signal the end of demand-driven immigration. When demand is saturated, a demand-driven immigration ends unless it substitutes another motor. Since immigration to Southern California either accelerated or continued at the same level in the face of declining real wages, then something other than demand now drives the immigration. That something could plausibly be a network-driven migration that, in conjunction with Mexico's economic crisis, continued when demand was saturated.

CONCLUSION

Global restructuring explains many features of Southern California's economic trajectory between 1970 and 1990. Declining wages in manufacturing industries; the egress of a million native-born whites from the region; increased self-employment by whites, and especially by white women; and across-the-board increases in incorporated self-employment, all these phenomena global restructuring easily explains. Waldinger's vacancy chains are compatible with globalization to the extent that globalization-induced room at the top turned into new demand for cheap labor thanks to ethnic succession. However, neither vacancy chains nor global restructuring, both demand-driven explanations, explain the acceleration of Hispanic immigration despite declining real wages and declining self-employment incomes for immigrants. Even when we take account of cohort quality, whether declining or stable, no demand-driven theory can explain why immigrant influx accelerates as real incomes decline. On the other hand, migration network theory can explain such a process, and, furthermore, we know that network migration organized all the immigrants to Southern California in every year of this period. For example, 70 percent of immigrant workers in San Diego found their current job "through social networks—relatives or friends employed at the same firm where they now work" (Cornelius 1997: 14). Migration networks are compatible with strong immigrant influx in the face of declining real incomes, but global restructuring theory is not.

Without wishing to dismiss globalization, whether as theory or process, we propose that globalization theorists have extended their reach beyond their grasp. Possibly their explanation fit the 1970s. However, in Southern

California, immigration to the region rather quickly saturated initial demand, and immigration's motor switched to the migration network. At least in Southern California, and, we suspect, much more broadly in the developed countries, migration is now and has for fifteen years been network-driven. The crucial evidence for this claim is the declining real and relative wages of the newly arriving immigrants. If the migration were demand-driven, immigrant real wages would have remained stable rather than having dropped. This decisive theoretical point has several policy implications. First, migration has saturated host country demand and now runs on its own momentum, responsive to processes that originate outside the labor-importing countries. If this is true, then economic arguments for the advantageousness of the immigration to the labor-importing country no longer apply. Network-driven migrations into saturated labor markets are more economically advantageous to the immigrants than to the reception country.

Second, as Sassen has observed, the "primacy of immigration" over globalization would suggest that policymakers could reduce immigration to slow or even "eradicate" informalization (Sassen 1997: 228–29). After all, if globalization's appetite for low-wage labor has already been sated, then resistance to what has become a spillover migration does not challenge global restructuring, a possibly quixotic endeavor. Especially in the United States, whose family reunification laws are so generous, immigration laws amplify and expand network migration. Less generous immigration laws could reduce network-driven immigration, thus reducing informalization. The possibilities for legal control of immigration are considerably brighter if the globalization juggernaut would not thereby be frustrated.

Third, if network-driven, the existing migration cannot be expected to extinguish itself. If left to itself, network-driven migrations may potentially continue even beyond the point at which economic conditions in destination metropoles are as bad as those in the originating villages. That is, before migration networks disintegrate, wages in Mexico or Central American must be better than those in Los Angeles, not just the same. This intriguing possibility arises because migration networks can make it easier to migrate in search of a job in New York or Los Angeles than to find a job in one's homeland. Therefore, until conditions are appreciably worse in the destination than in the homeland, migrants will continue to prefer the easy path of the migration network to the harder path of finding a job in their home neighborhood.

Finally, if the migration to Los Angeles has become network-driven, then wealthy employers of immigrant labor could pay more to their nannies, servants, and gardeners than they now do without undo economic hardship to themselves or to the economy. After all, they once did pay more until the saturation of labor markets drove down real and relative wages of immigrants. Although the declining wages of immigrants bene-fited their American employers, the declining real wages of immigrants have themselves imposed uncompensated costs upon the state of Califor-nia and upon California taxpayers. The taxpayers and the state of Califor-nia pay for the medical care that low-wage immigrants cannot buy from their pay packets. At this juncture, the fiscal needs of the state come into collision with the private advantage of employers of low-wage immigrant labor. In a conflict of this nature, the possibilities for immigration reduc-tion are much greater than they would be if the state's fiscal need contra-dicted imperatives of globalization.

NOTES

1. "Culture is increasingly global" (Boli and Thomas 1997: 172).
2. The transnational corporations continue to control much of the end product and to reap the profits associated with selling in the world market. The internation-alization and expansion of the financial industry has brought growth to a large number of smaller financial markets, a growth which has fed the expansion of the global industry. But top-level control and management of the industry has become concentrated in a few leading financial centers, notably New York, London, and Tokyo. (Sassen 1991: 5; see also Sassen 1997: 229–30)
3. "Global forces and transnational flows are becoming more and more domi-nant at the national and local levels" (Knight 1989: 25).
4.

The world economy is managed from a relatively small number of urban cen-ters in which banking, financing, administration, professional services, and high-tech production tend to be concentrated . . . Poorly educated natives resist taking low-paying jobs at the bottom of the occupational hierarchy, creating a strong demand for immigrants . . . Native workers with modest educations cling to jobs in the declining middle, migrate out of global cities, or rely on social insurance programs for support. (Massey, Arango, Hugo, Kaoaouci, Pellegrino, and Taylor 1993: 447)

5. This is still Sassen's view.

The rapid growth of the financial industry and of highly specialized services generates not only high level technical and administrative jobs but also low wage unskilled jobs. There is further an indirect creation of low wage jobs induced by the presence of a highly dynamic sector with a polarized income distribution. It takes place in the sphere of consumption. . . .The expansion of the high income work force, in conjunction with the emergence of new cul-tural forms in everyday living, has led to a process of high income gentrifica-tion that rests, in the last analysis, on the availability of a vast supply of low wage workers. The increase in the numbers of expensive restaurants, luxury housing, luxury hotels, gourmet shops, boutiques, French hand laundries, and special cleaners . . . illustrates this trend. (Sassen 1997)

6. See also Sassen-Koob (1985: 255). For a critical evaluation of the polarization thesis, see Hamnett (1994: 401–24).

7. "The expansion of the high-income work force, in conjunction with the emergence of new cultural forms in everyday living, has led to a process of high-income gentrification, which rests, in the last analysis, on the availability of a vast supply of low-wage workers" (Sassen 1991: 279; see also: pp. 281, 282).

8. "The presence of large immigrant communities then can be seen as mediating in the process of informalization rather than directly generating it: The demand side of the process of informalization is therewith brought to the fore" (Sassen 1991: 282).

9. "Larger translocal economic forces have far more weight than local policies in shaping urban economies" (Sassen 1990: 237). This view is widely held. "Global forces and transnational flows are becoming more and more dominant at the national and local levels" (Knight 1989: 25).

10. On agency in globalization, see Dicken (1992: 121).

11. For someone who says exactly this, see Peterson (1981).

12.

Elsewhere (Sassen 1988), I have argued at length that the large influx of immigrants into the United States from low-wage countries over the last fifteen years, which reached massive levels in the 1980s, cannot be understood separately from this restructuring. The expansion in the supply of low-wage jobs generated by major growth sectors is one of the key factors in the continuation of ever-higher levels of the current immigration. (Sassen 1991: 315–16)

13. To illustrate the argument, consider a town with a new suburban factory and expensive public transport. When the factory opens, it pays workers a generous $5 per day, but the bus fare is $3. After paying the bus fare, workers net $2 for a day's work. Later, the transit authority reduces bus fares from $3 to $1. This reduction permits additional workers to seek jobs at the factory, which lowers its wages from $5 to $3 in response to labor surplus. Nonetheless, workers continue to come even though the factory lowered wages 40 percent, and workers still net $2 for a day's work. In this illustration, the reduced bus fare stands for the migration network that lowers the social, emotional, and financial costs of migration.

14. "The polarization thesis, as it effects growth at the bottom end of the occupational and income distributions, may be contingent on the existence of large-scale ethnic immigration and a cheap labor supply" (Hamnett 1994: 408).

15. "The tendency towards polarization should manifest itself more clearly in larger cities than in nations as a whole. Polarization should be especially articulated in these larger cities, not only because deindustrialization has hit urban areas hardest, but also because both types of services are spatially concentrated there" (Kloosterman 1994: 469).

16. This continuation prompted Sydney Walton to declare the continuing migration economically irrational (Walton 1994: 38).

17. "By the mid-1950s the war booms had run their course but the new migra-

234 people a year

tion had not; it was holding at near-record levels of some 150,000 people a year. A new element was involved. Technology was forcing out those who still remained on the farm" (Groh 1972: 60).

18. "Since 1965, Los Angeles has experienced an almost complete destruction of its Fordist industries, once the largest cluster west of the Mississippi " (Soja 1996: 439); see also Allen and Turner (1997: 185).

19. "The new industrial complex has contributed to a transformation in the social structure of major cities where it is concentrated. This transformation assumes the form of increased social and economic polarization" (Sassen 1991: 329). See also: Haeusermann and Kraemer-Badoni (1989: 344).

20. The wage gap for Mexican immigrants increased in California as well as in Los Angeles, but the gap increased less in the state than in Los Angeles. Mexican immigrant men's wages declined from 67 percent of white men's wages in 1960 to 60 percent in 1980 (Vernez 1993: 150).

21. For a summary of the cohort quality debate, see Borjas (1996: 72–80).

22. Reyneri (1997) observes that migration chains notoriously exaggerate opportunities in the destination economy, promoting more immigration than the destination economy can actually absorb. As a result, immigrants anticipate a rosier job supply than actually exists in their destination. In this case, demand does not drive the migration. Rather, the illusion of demand drives the migration. That illusion is a product of the migration network, so the migration network (not the reception economy) is actually driving demand in this situation. One cannot salvage demand-led immigration by phantom demand.

23. The authors add, "The effect of this labor surplus has been to depress wages, not only for immigrants themselves but also for those born in the United States" (Allen and Turner: 197).

REFERENCES

Allen, James P., and Eugene Turner. (1997). *The Ethnic Quilt*. Los Angeles: Center for Geographical Studies of California State University at Northridge.

Blau, Francine D. (1980). Immigration and Labor Earnings in Early Twentieth Century America. *Research in Population Economics* 2: 21–41.

Boli, John, and George M. Thomas. (1997). World Culture in the World Policy: A Century of Interorganizational Non-Governmental Organization. *American Sociological Review* 62: 171–90.

Borjas, George J. (1989). Immigrant and Emigrant Earnings: A Longitudinal Study. *Economic Inquiry* 27: 21–37.

———. (1990). *Friends or Strangers*. New York: Basic.

———. (1996). The New Economics of Immigration. *The Atlantic* XXXX, November: 72–80.

Bornschier, Volker, and Hanspeter Stamm. (1990). Transnational Corporations. In Alberto Martinelli and Neil J. Smelser, eds. *Economy and Society*. Newbury Park, Calif.: Sage.

Cheng, Lucie, and Philip W. Yang. (1996). Asians: The Model Minority Deconstructed. In Roger Waldinger and Mchdi Bozorgmehr, eds. *Ethnic Los Angeles.* New York: Russell Sage.

Cornelius, Wayne. (1997). The Structural Embeddedness of Demand for Immigrant Labor: New Evidence from San Diego and Japan. Presentation to the Research Seminar of the Center for U.S.–Mexican Studies University of California-San Diego, January 15, 1997.

Dicken, Peter. (1992). *Global Shift: The Internationalization of Economic Activity.* New York: Guilford Press.

Fernandez-Kelly, M. Patricia, and Anna M. Garcia. (1989). Informalization at the Core: Hispanic Women, Homework, and the Advanced Capitalist State. In Alejandro Portes, Manuel Castells, and Lauren A. Benton, eds. *The Informal Economy.* Baltimore: Johns Hopkins University.

Fligstein, Neil. (1997). Is Globalization the Cause of the Crises of Welfare States? Paper presented at the Annual Meeting of the American Sociological Association, Toronto, August 1997.

Frey, William H. (1996–97). Immigration and the Changing Geography of Poverty. *Focus* 18: 24–28.

Gottdiener, Mark, and Nicos Komninos. (1989). Introduction. In Mark Gottdiener and Nicos Komninos, eds. *Capitalist Development and Crisis Theory: Accumulation, Regulation and Spatial Restructuring.* New York: St Martin's.

Groh, George W. (1972). *The Black Migration.* New York: Weybright and Talley.

Haeusermann, Hartmut, and Thomas Kraemer-Badoni. (1989). The Change of Regional Inequality in the Federal Republic of Germany. In Mark Gottdiener and Nicos Komninos, eds. *Capitalist Development and Crisis Theory: Accumulation, Regulation and Spatial Restructuring.* New York: St Martin's.

Hamnett, Chris. (1994). Social Polarisation in Global Cities: Theory and Evidence. *Urban Studies* 31: 401–24.

Harrison, Alferdteen. (1991). *Black Exodus: The Great Migration from the American South.* Jackson: University Press of Mississippi.

Henri, Florette. (1975). *Black Migration: Movement North, 1900–1920.* New York: Anchor.

Hill, Peter J. (1975). Relative Skill and Income Levels of Native and Foreign Born Workers in the United States. *Explorations in Economic History* 12: 58–59.

Kloosterman, Robert C. (1994). Double Dutch: Polarization Trends in Amsterdam and Rotterdam after 1980. *Regional Studies Association* 30: 467–76.

Knight, Richard. (1989). The Emergent Global Society. In Richard V. Knight and Gary Gappert, eds. *Cities in a Global Society.* Newbury Park, Calif.: Sage.

———, and Gary Gappert, eds. (1989). *Cities in a Global Society.* Newbury Park, Calif.: Sage.

Light, Ivan. (1988). Los Angeles. In *The Metropolis Era. Vol. 2. Mega-Cities.* Beverly Hills: Sage: 69–74.

———. (1998, forthcoming). Globalization and Migration Networks. In Jan Rath and Robert Kloosterman, eds. *Migration and the Garment Industry in Europe and North America.* London: Macmillan.

———, and Elizabeth Roach. (1996). Self-Employment: Mobility Ladder or Economic Lifeboat? In Roger Waldinger and Mehdi Bozorgmehr, eds. *Ethnic Los Angeles.* New York: Russell Sage Foundation.

Light, Ivan, Richard Bernard, and Rebecca Kim (1997). Immigrant Incorporation in the Garment Industry of Los Angeles. *International Migration Review*: 5–25.

Logan, John R., and Todd Swanstrom. (1990). Urban Restructuring: A Critical View. In John Logan and Todd Swanstrom, eds. *Beyond the City Limits*. Philadelphia: Temple University.

Lopez, David, Eric Popkin, and Edward Telles. (1996). Central Americans: At the Bottom, Struggling to Get Ahead. In Roger Waldinger and Mehdi Bozorgmehr, eds. *Ethnic Los Angeles*. New York: Russell Sage Foundation.

Lopez-Garza, Marta. (1989). Immigration and Economic Restructuring: The Metamorphosis of Southern California. *California Sociologist* 12: 93–110.

McLean Petras, Elizabeth. (1983). The Global Labor Market in the Modern World Economy. In Mary M. Kritz, Charles B. Keely, and Silvano M. Tomasi, eds. *Global Trends in Migration*. New York: Center for Migration Studies.

Massey, Douglas, Joaquin Arango, Graeme Hugo, Ali Kaoaouci, Adela Pellegrino, and J. Edward Taylor. (1993). Theories of International Migration: A Review and Appraisal. *Population and Development Review* 20: 431–66.

Moore, Joan, and Raquel Pinderhughes. (1993). Introduction. In Joan Moore and Raquel Pinderhughes, eds. *The Barrios: Latinos and the Underclass Debate*. New York: Russell Sage Foundation.

Nederveen Pieterse, Jan. (1994). Globalization as Hybridization. *International Sociology* 9: 161–84.

Norby Fraundorf, Martha. (1978). Relative Earnings of Native- and Foreign-Born Women. *Explorations in Economic History* 15: 211–20.

Ong, Paul, and Evelyn Blumenberg. (1996). Income and Racial Inequality in Los Angeles. In Allen J. Scott and Edward W. Soja, eds. *The City: Los Angeles and Urban Theory at the End of the Twentieth Century*. Los Angeles: University of California.

Ortiz, Vilma. (1996). The Mexican-Origin Population: Permanent Working Class or Emerging Middle Class? In Roger Waldinger and Mehdi Bozorgmehr, eds. *Ethnic Los Angeles*. New York: Russell Sage Foundation.

Peterson, Paul E. (1981). *City Limits*. Chicago: University of Chicago.

Reyneri, Emilio. (1997). The Informalization of Migrant Labour: Oversupply of Illegal Migrants or Pull-Effect by the Underground Receiving Economy? The Italian Case. Paper presented at the University of Warwick International Conference on Globalization, Migration, and Social Exclusion, May 31, 1997.

Sabagh, Georges, and Mehdi Bozorgmehr. (1996). Population Change: Immigration and Ethnic Transformation. In Roger Waldinger and Mehdi Bozorgmehr, eds. *Ethnic Los Angeles*. New York: Russell Sage Foundation.

Sassen, Saskia. (1988). *The Mobility of Labor and Capital: A Study in International Investment and Labor Flow*. Cambridge: Cambridge University Press.

———. (1990). Beyond the City Limits: A Commentary. In John Logan and Todd Swanstrom, eds. *Beyond the City Limits*. Philadelphia: Temple University.

———. (1990). Economic Restructuring and the American City. *Annual Review of Sociology* 16: 465–90.

———. (1991). *The Global City: New York, London, Tokyo*. Princeton, N.J.: Princeton University Press.

————. (1997). Immigration in Global Cities. Hp Feb. 6, 1997. Online. Available at http://www.interplan.org/immig/im01001.html. Oct. 22, 1997.

————. (1997). The Informal Economy: Between New Developments and Old Regulations. *Yale Law Review* 103: 2289–304.

Sassen-Koob, Saskia (1985). Capital Mobility and Labor Migration: Their Expression in Core Cities. In Michael Timberlake, ed. *Urbanization in the World Economy*. Orlando, FL: Academic Press.

————. (1989). New York City's Informal Economy. In Alejandro Portes, Manuel Castells, and Lauren A. Benton, eds. *The Informal Economy*. Baltimore: Johns Hopkins University.

Savitch, H.V. (1990). Post-Industrialism with a Difference: Global Capitalism in World-Class Cities. In John Logan and Todd Swanstrom, eds. *Beyond the City Limits*. Philadelphia: Temple University.

Schimek, Paul. (1989). Earnings Polarization and the Proliferation of Low-Wage Work. In Paul Ong, ed. *The Widening Divide: Income Inequality and Poverty in Los Angeles*. Los Angeles: Graduate School of Architecture and Urban Planning of the University of California.

Scott, Allen J. (1988). *Metropolis*. Berkeley: University of California.

————, and Michael Storper. (1992). Industrialization and Regional Development. In Michael Storper and Allen J. Scott, eds. *Pathways to Industrialization and Regional Development*. London: Routledge.

Shergold, Peter R. (1976). Relative Skill and Income Levels of Native and Foreign Born Workers: A Reexamination. *Explorations in Economic History* 13: 459–60.

Soja, Ed. (1989). *Postmodern Geographies*. London: Verso.

Soja, Edward W. (1987). Economic Restructuring and the Internationalization of the Los Angeles Region. In Michael Peter Smith and Joe R. Feagin, eds. *The Capitalist City*. London: Basil Blackwell.

————. (1996). Los Angeles, 1965–1992. In Allen J. Scott and Edward W. Soja, eds. *The City: Los Angeles and Urban Theory at the End of the Twentieth Century*. Los Angeles: University of California.

————, Rebecca Morales, and Goetz Wolff (1987). Industrial Restructuring: An Analysis of Social and Spatial Change in Los Angeles. In Richard Peet, ed. *International Capitalism and Industrial Restructuring*. Boston: Allen and Unwin.

Trotter, Joe W., and Earl Lewis. (1996). *African Americans in the Industrial Age*. Boston: Northeastern University.

Vernez, Georges. (1993). Mexican Labor in California's Economy. In Abraham F. Lowenthal and Katrina Burgess, eds. *The California-Mexico Connection*. Stanford, Calif.: Stanford University.

Waldinger, Roger. (1992). Taking Care of the Guests: The Impact of Immigrants on Services—An Industry Case Study. *International Journal of Urban and Regional Research* 16: 92–113.

————. (1995). *Still the Promised Land? African Americans and New Immigrants in New York, 1940–1990*. Cambridge, Mass.: Harvard University.

Walton, Sidney F. Jr. ZBC (1994). *A Geomical Solution to the Problem of Haphazard Black Migration*. San Ramon, Calif.: San Ramon Valley Counseling, Consultation, and Education Services.

White, Sammis B., and William F. McMahon. (1995). Why Have Earnings Per Worker Stagnated? *Journal of Urban Affairs* 17: 33–51.

Wrigley, Julia. (1997). Immigrant Women as Child Care Providers. In Ivan Light and Richard Isralowitz, eds. *Immigrant Entrepreneurs and Immigrant Absorption in the United States and Israel.* Aldershot, UK: Ashgate: 117–39.

Zolberg, Aristide R. (1991). Bounded States in a Global Market: The Uses of International Labor Migrations. In Pierre Bourdieu and James S. Coleman, eds. *Social Theory for a Changing Society.* Boulder, Colo.: Westview.

14

A World of Difference: Between the Global and the Local

Jack Burgers

GLOBALIZATION AND SOCIAL INEQUALITY

For some time now, the local consequences of globalization have been an object of fascination in urban sociology. Cultural, socioeconomic, and political issues are analyzed in a framework of what Giddens (1981: 91) has called the increasing "time-space distanciation": the process whereby societies are "stretched" over longer spans of time and place. The notion of globalization seems to refer to at least two phenomena: the growing mobility of capital and consumer goods on the one hand, and increasing long-distance migration on the other.

During the last decades, the economies of the Western countries have changed profoundly. Increasingly, manufacturing industries in the Western countries have suffered from competition from low-wage countries. As a result, they have been automated, relocated, or closed down altogether. Decreasing employment in the manufacturing industries has, according to authors from various intellectual traditions, contributed to greater social inequality in Western cities (cf., Bluestone and Harrison 1982; Wilson 1987, 1996; Harvey 1989; Mollenkopf and Castells 1991).

The demographic aspect of globalization is the spectacular growth of long-distance migration. In 1990, the International Organization for Migration estimated the number of migrants, both legal and illegal, around the world to be more than eighty million. For the year 1992 the estimate already amounted to 100 million (Castles and Miller 1993: 4). In addition to its rapid acceleration, long-distance migration has an unprecedented geographical dispersal. More and more countries and regions are affected by it in one way or another. Western countries are becoming multicultural and multiethnic societies because of the influx of people from countries outside the economic core area. In many cases, these minority groups are confronted with severe problems in making a living in their new surroundings. Their labor market position is very weak; they seem to be the modern-day proletariat of the emerging postindustrial society. The growth of the number of migrants from economic peripheral areas in advanced economies also seems to contribute to social inequality.

Because both economic and demographic change can be explained by globalization—growing mobility of capital and consumer goods and growing mobility of people, respectively—it is tempting to relate the two in one theoretical framework. This is what Saskia Sassen, in a number of publications (1988, 1991, 1994), has done. Sassen contends that today we are witnessing a new phase in an ongoing process of "internationalization." This new phase consists of the internationalization of production sites through foreign investment, which explains both the origin and direction of long-distance migration from the Third World to the First. According to Sassen, we should not make the mistake of viewing long-distance migration as a domestic phenomenon, be it in terms of countries of origin or of countries of destination. It is not the poverty, overpopulation, or economic stagnation of Third World countries per se that generates migration. Nor are the economic opportunities of the rich countries in themselves sufficient explanations as "pull factors." Rather, countries of origin and destination are directly related in one way or the other. In the case of the United States, economic, military, and diplomatic policies in foreign countries have triggered migration from these countries to the United States. Globalization presupposes locations that operate as loci of control. Globalization is essentially the relocation of production activities by transnational corporations. Put another way: it is a centralized practice of decentralization. The role of control and management of the newly emerging global economic system is played by major cities, which Sassen designates as "global cities." Global cities are "cities that are strategic sites in the global economy because of their concentration of command functions and high-level producer-service firms oriented to world markets; more generally, cities with high levels of internationalization in their economy and in their broader social structure" (Sassen 1994: 154). These global cities are key destinations for migrants. The most important reason for the vast majority of new migrants to settle down in global cities is the fact that the particular economy of these cities not only generates high-level, specialized jobs, but also a vast number of low-wage jobs. The presence of low-wage, unattractive jobs in an environment with so many highly skilled and well-paid jobs should not be read as an anachronism. The very presence of specialized services and corporate headquarters, where the attractive jobs are to be found, is an important source of low-wage jobs, both directly and indirectly. The direct effect is through jobs at the lower end of the occupational structure created within the specialized sectors (cf., catering, security, cleaning, etcetera). The indirect effect is through the ancillary sectors and the consumption structure underlying the lifestyles of the growing number of high-income professionals. This kind of employment gives rise to a growing informal economic sector. Because of this peculiar occupational structure, global cities are polarized or dual cities.

In this chapter I will show that in the Dutch situation the economic and demographic aspects of globalization are less strongly interrelated than we might expect when using Sassen's theoretical scheme. In section two, I will argue that there certainly is a tendency of polarization in the big Dutch cities. But this polarization is basically a divide between the employed and the unemployed. There is no strong evidence for a polarization within the labor market related to globalization. Unemployment has struck especially within minority groups. Apparently, urban labor demand cannot possibly explain the growing number of migrants in big cities. In section three, I will present some data on illegal migrants in Rotterdam to show that even the most compliant migrant workers—the undocumented immigrants—do not in great numbers and to a large extent engage in informal economic activities that cater either to the postindustrial growth sectors or the individual households of the urban professional class. I will argue that the factor that can help to explain this divergence from Sassen's theory on globalization and polarization is the specific character of the Dutch welfare state. Using Dutch data and building on Sassen's notion of the relation between globalization and polarization, I will, in section four, present the contours of an analytical model that links globalization and individual life-chances. I will argue that besides institutional factors, social and ethnic networks and the specific social and economic trajectories of individual cities need to be taken into account.

POLARIZATION AND THE LABOR MARKET IN THE BIG DUTCH CITIES

As Chris Hamnett (1994) has shown, the labor market in the main cities in the Netherlands does not show a trend toward polarization. The dominant trend is one of professionalization and upgrading. The average educational level of the people employed has been rising for a number of years, and the number of jobs at the upper end of the employment structure has grown not only absolutely but in relative numbers as well. If we look at the income distribution, the picture is more complicated. Kloosterman (1996), comparing wage classes, has shown that there is a slight overall tendency toward polarization in the cities of Amsterdam and Rotterdam. But there are important differences among cities and economic sectors. In the case of Amsterdam and Rotterdam, the "exposed" sectors—those most prone to globalization—seem to be upgrading instead of polarizing (Kloosterman 1996). Hamnett (1996) has shown for London that income polarization has occurred since the end of the 1980s but argues that, in terms of explanation, changing employment rates are more important than occupational differences. Apparently, there is no clear-cut relationship between income polarization and an emerging postindustrial employment structure. For the Dutch case, polarization is, more than anything else, a divide between being employed or unemployed. This divide correlates strongly with educational level and ethnicity.

In 1992 there were 303,000 officially registered unemployed in the Netherlands. The real number was probably much higher. Many thousands of people who lost their jobs were, by creative use of the national disability assurance, declared physically disabled to work. It can be assumed that people who perceive of their chances finding jobs as very small, do not register themselves as looking for work.

Of the grand total of 303,000 officially registered unemployed for the Netherlands in 1992, 26 percent lived in the four main cities, while only 13 percent of the Dutch population between ages fifteen and sixty-five did so (Burgers and Dercksen, 1993).

If we look at the educational level of the unemployed, we get almost a perfect mirror image of the pattern we see among the employed. Figures 14.1 and 14.2 depict the educational levels of both categories. While the growth in employment was concentrated at the upper end of the employment structure requiring high educational levels, the unemployed in the cities are poorly schooled, if at all. When we look at educational levels of the total population between ages fifteen and sixty-five in the Dutch cities, a slightly polarized pattern emerges, as table 14.2 shows. Although there are notable differences between the four cities, all have both a higher pro-

Table 14.1   Unemployment in the Four Main Cities and the Netherlands, 1992

	Population Aged 15–64	*Labor Force*	*Registered Unemployed N*	*Registered Unemployed %*
Amsterdam	508,000	374,000	35,000	9.4
Rotterdam	392,000	256,000	24,000	9.5
The Hague	297,000	205,000	13,000	6.5
Utrecht	168,000	125,000	7,000	5.5
Netherlands	1,0436,000	7,254,000	303,000	4.2

Source: Central Bureau for Statistics.

Figure 14.1   Educational Level of the Working Population of Amsterdam, Rotterdam, The Hague, and Utrecht, 1992

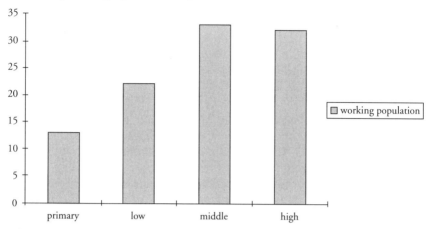

Source: van der Wouden 1996
Note: In thousands

Figure 14.2   Educational Level of the Unemployed in Amsterdam, Rotterdam, The Hague, and Utrecht, 1992

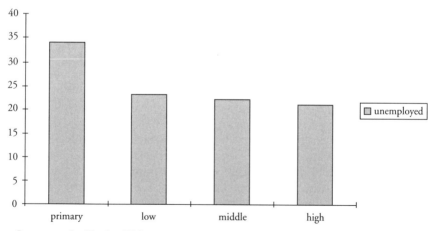

Source: van der Wouden 1996
Note: In thousands

Table 14.2   Educational Level of the Population Aged between Fifteen and Sixty-five, 1991

	Amsterdam %	Rotterdam %	The Hague %	Utrecht %	The Netherlands %
Primary or Less	14	19	18	15	12
Higher and Academic	34	21	26	35	20

Source: Central Bureau for Statistics.

portion of poorly educated people and a higher proportion of people trained professionally and scientifically. So when we include the unemployed in our analysis, the distribution of educational levels in cities is slightly polarized.

What can be said about the position of migrants in this respect? The Dutch big cities are not only polarized in terms of the incidence of high quality jobs and poorly educated unemployed. The socioeconomic divide is, to an important degree, ethnically polarized. In Rotterdam more than 10 percent of the population aged between fifteen and sixty-five was registered as looking for a job (not all of them out of work) in 1993. For the ethnic minority population (comprised of the four important groups in the Netherlands, the Surinamese, the Antillians, the Turks, and the Moroccans), the percentage unemployed was over 25 percent. Of the indigenous Dutch unemployed in Rotterdam, 9 percent was out of work for longer than a year in 1993. For the four minority groups mentioned above, the ratio of long-term unemployed amounted to more than 30 percent (Municipality of Rotterdam 1994).

Looking at the city of Amsterdam, we get the same picture. As table 14.1 showed, in 1992 the rate of unemployment was 9.4 percent, more than twice as high as the national rate of 4.2 percent. The minorities are clearly in a much worse position than the indigenous Dutch. Whereas the rate of officially registered unemployment of the Dutch amounted to 6.2 percent, the rates for the minorities ranged from 18.6 percent for the Antillians to 26.7 percent for the Turks. As to the educational levels of the unemployed, the ethnic minorities again stand out negatively. Of the total number of unemployed, 29 percent have only primary education. For the Surinamese and Antillians the percentage is 38 and for the Turks and Moroccans 64 (Municipality of Amsterdam 1993).

We may conclude that when we look at Dutch cities, there is an evident trend toward social polarization. But the crucial divide is not so much situated in the labor market as Sassen suggests, but separates people holding jobs and people depending on welfare. The question rises: How can it be that the process of globalization, causing both economic and demographic restructuring, apparently results in different types of social inequality in cities in different countries? I would suggest that institutional factors are of decisive importance here. The work of Esping-Andersen (1990, 1993) is helpful to understand the role these factors play. Esping-Andersen has shown that social polarization appears in different guises in different countries, depending on their specific social history and welfare state arrangements. The way in which the global process of economic restructuring manifests itself at the level of the everyday lives of individual people is strongly influenced by institutional arrangements. In corporatist welfare states, as for instance the Netherlands and Germany, relatively many less-educated people are excluded from both private and public jobs. High minimum wages reduce their profitability as a labor force in the private sector. Because there is little employment created for low-skilled workers in the public sphere, the income of a large number of people at the lower end of the social hierarchy takes the form of a welfare check. That is why corporatist states, as the Netherlands, are characterized by relatively low rates of labor market participation.

MIGRATION AND POLARIZATION: ETHNIC MINORITIES AND THE LABOR MARKET

The Dutch experience raises an interesting point as to the relation between migration and economic restructuring. The ongoing concentration of minority groups in Dutch cities is, at least in any direct sense, unrelated to the supply of jobs. On the contrary, the jobs suited for low-skilled people, as many members of immigrant minority groups are, are increasingly moving out of the cities (van der Wouden 1996). The concentration of minority groups in the Dutch big cities is not the result of a job motivated in-migration of members of minority groups, but of a housing-motivated out-migration of indigenous well-to-do households during roughly the past three decades.

In terms of globalization, the relation between the internationalization of the economy and long-distance migration is of great importance. The social and economic position of undocumented immigrants forms the ultimate test, I would argue, for any direct relationship between economic restructuring and long-distance migration. One could argue that the highly regulated Dutch labor market gives rise to many informal economic activities. And it might very well be that migrant workers, more than other groups, are employed in the informal sector. If this would be the case, it would be especially true for undocumented workers. They are not entitled to the blessings of the relatively benevolent Dutch welfare state and could therefore be expected to be dependent on whatever labor is offered, either formally or informally. Undocumented migrants could do the low-skill work that is made impossible or unnecessary for other groups by institutional factors.

In an ongoing research project in the city of Rotterdam we interviewed 175 undocumented migrants. One of the things we wanted to know was how these people manage to survive and make a living. Inspired by the work of Sassen on global cities, we ventured the hypothesis that illegal immigrants would be dependent on low-skilled jobs for their livelihood and that they would find these jobs in the informal service sector. In so far as there would turn out to be any informal industrial production in Rotterdam—for instance in sweatshops in the garment industry—we expected to find undocumented immigrants there as well. This hypothesis, however, was only partially supported by the results of our inquiry. Some jobs that offer illegal immigrants the opportunity to earn money were situated in traditional sectors: agriculture and horticulture (about 20 percent of the undocumented migrants that had a job); others were in traditional industrial sectors as the port, construction, and illegal garment sewing shops (about 16 percent). Undocumented immigrants, as expected, also join the growing service sector proletariat: cleaners, assistants in retail shops and markets, workers in bars or restaurants, prostitutes, and casual workers in private homes (about 45 percent of those employed). Less than one in every ten migrants who earn some money, does so by drug trafficking; we have no clear indication that crime rates for undocumented migrants diverge from those found among immigrants with a valid stay permit. Those who work, in many cases, do not hold jobs that could be called regular, neither in terms of job security nor the number of working-hours. Many of the working undocumented migrants are employed by compatriots that are legal inhabitants of the Netherlands. The work they do is not so much dependent on the globalizing sectors of the urban economy, but on the presence of minority communities in Dutch cities. Many entrepreneurial activities in this sphere are catering to the ethnic community in which they are embedded.

Yet the most striking observation concerning the livelihood of undocumented immigrants in Rotterdam is that more than one-third of them do not have a job at all. Some are supported by relatives or friends. Others make a living in criminal activities, especially in the trafficking of drugs. We have to conclude that current developments in the structure of employment of big cities such as Rotterdam provide at best only a partial explanation for the way in which illegal immigrants support themselves. Until now the category of the undocumented unemployed has hardly been described in the literature on illegal immigrants.[1] The large proportion of unemployed illegal immigrants in Rotterdam shows unequivocally that the restructuring of urban labor markets is by no means the only explanation for long-distance migration. During our interviews, many illegal immigrants indicated that their original intention was to go "West" or "North" without knowing exactly what their destination eventually would be and lacking even basic information about the country of their destination. It was most surprising to find how little information undocumented immigrants have about the possibilities in the city of their destiny. In any event, their actual labor market position clearly falsifies any simple, functional relationship between economic restructuring and long-distance migration as suggested by Saskia Sassen. Although (perceived) economic opportunity may have triggered migration at an earlier date—in the era of the guest workers—once set in motion, migratory flows have a dynamic and logic of their own (cf., Light, Kim, and Hum 1997). Postindustrial labor market needs in modern-day Rotterdam cannot explain neither the arrival nor the social position of undocumented immigrants.

Paradoxically, the effect of institutional factors is very manifest even in the case of people who are legally not part of Dutch society. The jobs at the bottom of the labor market that are situated within the public sphere are, of course, not available to undocumented migrants. Probably more important for the opportunities of undocumented migrants on the labor market is the effect of the high minimum wage level in the Netherlands. Because many labor-intensive economic activities in the private sector have become too expensive for many private households, there has come into being a large informal sector, especially in the sphere of home repair and maintenance. Many people active in these informal activities also hold jobs in the formal sector (cf., Renooy 1990). Undocumented migrants often lack the assets to compete on this informal labor market. On top of that, they have to compete with newcomers to the labor market for low-paid jobs, be it in the formal or the informal economy. Young people and women are filling the vacancies in the lower-paid segments of the service industries (Kloosterman and Elfring 1991).

BY WAY OF CONCLUSION: A MODEL TO ANALYZE THE LOCAL EFFECTS OF GLOBALIZATION

Using data on Dutch cities, two conclusions can be drawn. First, the growing mobility of capital and consumer goods, on the one hand, and the growing mobility of people, on the other, seem to be at least partially autonomous processes. Both the ongoing concentration of migrants in Dutch cities and the presence of undocumented migrants in the Netherlands can hardly be attributed to any needs of the postindustrial urban labor market. Second, as far as globalization leads to polarization, it can have different guises depending on the specific institutional context in which polarization manifests itself. Polarization can take the form of a bifurcating labor market in one institutional setting and a simultaneous upgrading of the job structure and growing unemployment in another. One could conceive of the institutional context—different types of welfare states, that is—as a mediating variable between the global and the local. One could use the metaphor of a prism breaking entering light to grasp the role of institutional factors in influencing the way in which globalization impinges on the life chances of people in specific social contexts. Using this metaphor, the question rises if there are other variables that could play a role comparable to institutional factors. Looking at the data on Dutch cities at least two variables come to mind (Burgers 1996b).

First, significant differences can be discerned among individual cities. Within the same institutional context, there can be major differences among cities as to the local consequences of global restructuring. Table 14.1, for instance, shows that there are marked differences in terms of unemployment between Dutch cities. Although all four cities have higher levels of unemployment than the national rate, Amsterdam and Rotterdam stand out as concentration points of unemployment. But there are also important differences between Amsterdam and Rotterdam. Rotterdam is a traditional industrial city, while Amsterdam is much more a service city. We can illustrate this by the number of people working in the different economic sectors.

The service character of Amsterdam's economy also shows in the level of education of the population. Although, as I stated before, both cities show a polarizing tendency compared with the national figures, the share of the higher educated in the occupational population in Amsterdam is much higher than in Rotterdam: 34 versus 21 percent (see table 14.1). The more service-oriented employment structure of Amsterdam apparently attracts more professionals than the more traditional industrial employment structure of Rotterdam. It is also possible that Amsterdam is a more interesting place to live for professionals than Rotterdam. The Amsterdam housing stock and morphological structure offer more possibilities for gentrification. In a survey of directors and presidents of large corporations

Table 14.3   Job Holders in Amsterdam and Rotterdam According to Economic Sector, 1989–91

	Manufacturing and Agriculture %	*Trade and Distribution %*	*Services %*
Amsterdam	15	27	58
Rotterdam	22	29	49
The Netherlands	30	25	44

Source: Central Bureau for Statistics.

in Rotterdam, the unattractive character of Rotterdam as a place of residence was often mentioned as a reason for the low degree of involvement of the economic elite with the city in which they are operating (Engbersen 1991). Besides housing opportunities, cultural amenities in Amsterdam might play an important role. The arts thrive in Amsterdam, while Rotterdam's image in this respect is rather bleak. Thus, while there is a common framework of postindustrial urban restructuring with respect to shifts in the composition of employment, the outcomes also seem to be contingent on the positions cities occupy in the global urban system (Kloosterman 1996).

Besides institutional and the specific urban contexts, there is still a third factor that plays an intermediary role between the global and the local. I am referring to specific social categories and networks people are embedded in. Cross and Waldinger (1992) have shown that in London and New York different ethnic groups occupy different niches in the urban labor market. For the Dutch situation there are clear differences between minority groups in terms of rates of unemployment, self-employment and entrepreneurial activities, housing situation and segregation, engagement in criminal activities, linguistic abilities, etcetera. Changing social and economic opportunities due to the globalization of economic activities will have different consequences for different ethnic and social groups. Different causes triggering migration will result in different types of migrants who will, in their turn, differ in terms of assets that are of importance for their opportunities in western postindustrial urban labor markets. An increasing part of the in-migration in the Netherlands during the 1990s consisted of a highly differentiated category of refugees. They were not attracted in the first place by the economic opportunities the Netherlands might offer. It is not clear yet how many of them want and/or have the opportunity to stay permanently in the country in which they found asylum. But it is clear that there are huge differences in the assets they bring to the Dutch labor market.

Concluding, I would propose a three-layer model for a comparative analysis of the local effects of globalization. In between the global—the growing mobility of capital, consumer goods, and people—and the local— the life chances of individual people in specific urban contexts—there are intervening variables that, precisely because the world is increasingly unified in terms of economic and demographic exchange, might very well magnify already existing differences. Empirical research has to show whether globalization flattens out differences between places and people or magnifies them. But it is very clear that in terms of the effects of globalization on life chances and social inequality, the institutional, urban, and social contexts can make a world of difference.

NOTE

1. Not in the scientific literature, that is. T. Coraghessan Boyles's novel on illegal migrants in California—*Tortilla Curtain*—gives both an accurate and moving account of the problems undocumented migrants face in finding a job.

REFERENCES

Bluestone, B., and B. Harrison. (1982). *The De-industrialization of America.* New York: Basic Books.

Burgers, Jack. (1996a). The Global City and the Universal Suburb: Recent Issues in Urban Sociology. *Netherlands Journal of Housing and the Built Environment* 10: 363–73.

———. (1996b). No Polarisation in Dutch Cities? Inequality in a Corporatist Country. *Urban Studies* 33 (1996): 99–106.

———, and Willem Dercksen. (1993). Stedelijke problemen en sociaal beleid. *Bestuurswetenschappen* 47: 438–49.

Burgers, Jack, and Engbersen, G. (1996). Globalization, Immigration, and Undocumented Immigrants. *New Community* 22: 619–37.

Castles, Stephen, and Mark J. Miller. (1993). *The Age of Migration: International Population Movements in the Modern World.* London: Macmillan.

Central Bureau for Statistics. (1989). *Regionaal statistisch zakboek 1989.* 's-Gravenhage.

Cross, Malcolm, and Roger Waldinger. (1992). Migrants, Minorities, and the Ethnic Division of Labor. In Susan Fainstein et al., eds. *Divided Cities: New York and London in the Contemporary World.* London: Blackwell.

Engbersen, G., et al. (1991). Civic Responsibility. Over de betrokkenheid van ondernemers bij de economische en sociale ontwikkeling van Rotterdam. Leiden/Utrecht: Rijksuniversiteiten.

Esping-Andersen, G. (1990). *The Three Worlds of Welfare Capitalism.* Cambridge: Cambridge University Press.

———, ed. (1993). *Changing Classes: Stratification and Mobility in Post-Industrial Societies.* London: Sage.

Giddens, Anthony. (1981). *A Contemporary Critique of Historical Materialism.* Oxford: Polity Press.

Hamnett, Chris. (1994). Social Polarisation in Global Cities: Theory and Evidence. *Urban Studies* 31: 401–25.

———. (1996). Social Polarisation, Economic Restructuring and Welfare State Regimes. *Urban Studies* 33: 1407–30.

Harvey, David. (1989). *The Condition of Postmodernity.* London: Basil Blackwell.

Kloosterman, R.C. (1991). Stedelijke arbeidsmarktparadoxen: het Amsterdamse voorbeeld. In O. Atzema, M. Hessel, and H. Zondag. (1991). *De werkende stad.* Utrecht: Elinkwijk.

———. (1996). Double Dutch: Polarization Trends in Amsterdam and Rotterdam after 1980. *Regional Studies* 30, no. 5: 467–76.

————, and T. Elfring. (1991). *Werken in Nederland*. Schoonhoven: Academic Service. Light, I., R. Kim, and C. Hum. (1997). Globalization Effects on Employment in Southern California, 1970–1990. Paper presented at the University of Warwick Conference on Globalization. May 26.

Mollenkopf, John H., and Manuel Castells, eds. (1991). *Dual City: Restructuring New York*. New York: Russell Sage Foundation.

Municipality of Amsterdam. (1993). *Amsterdam in cijfers: Jaarboek 1993*. Amsterdam.

Municipality of Rotterdam. (1994). *Kerngegevens Arbeidsmarkt Rijnmond 1993*. Rotterdam.

Renooy, P. (1990). *The Informal Economy*. Amsterdam: Regioplan.

Sassen, Saskia. (1988). *The Mobility of Labor and Capital: A Study in International Investment and Labor Flow*. Cambridge: Cambridge University Press.

————. (1991). *The Global City: New York, London, Tokyo*. Princeton, N.J.: Princeton University Press.

Wilson, W. (1996). *When Work Disappears: The World of the New Urban Poor*. New York: Knopf.

Wilson, William Julius. (1987). *The Truly Disadvantaged: The Inner City, the Underclass, and Public Policy*. Chicago: University of Chicago Press.

Wouden, H.C. van der. (1996). *De beklemde stad: Grootstedelijke problemen in demografisch en sociaal-economisch perspectief*. Rijswijk: Sociaal en Cultureel Planbureau.

15

Globalization from Below: The Rise of Transnational Communities

Alejandro Portes

The aphorism "capital is global, labor is local" lies at the base of an edifice built continuously during the last half century. From different theoretical quarters, this edifice has been celebrated as the final triumph of free trade and economic rationality or denounced as the tomb of proletarian consciousness and national liberation. Whatever the outlook, the narrative that follows portrays an increasingly bound global economy with capital—in the form of direct corporate ventures or portfolio investment—crisscrossing the earth in search of accumulation. The success of these initiatives is generally correlated inversely with the economic autonomy achieved by national states and the social and economic prerogatives earned by local labor. For the most part, however, the momentum acquired by global capitalist expansion is such as to sweep away everything in its path, confining past dreams of equality and autonomous national development to the dustbin of history.

The process of capital going abroad in search of valorization is, of course, nothing new and is indeed the cloth from which numerous accounts of the evolution of the capitalist world-system have been fashioned. What is new in the contemporary period are the modalities and intensity of the process, driven by technological improvements in communications and transportation. Today instantaneous investments and disinvestments are made in the bourses of remote Asian and Latin American countries, and, as Castells (1980) puts it, a garment design conceived in New York can be transmitted electronically to a factory in Taiwan and the first batches of the product received in San Francisco in a week's time. The advantages of the process seem to be entirely on the side of those best able to avail themselves of the new technologies, thus turning globalization into the final apotheosis of capital against its adversaries, be they state managers or organized workers.

Yet, as social scientists professionally trained to look at the dialectics of things, we understand that a social process of this magnitude cannot be all one-sided. By its very momentum, the process is likely to trigger various reactions giving rise to countervailing structures. In the end, the technology-driven revolution that we are witnessing at century's end may not usher in the era of unrestrained global capitalism after all, but a new form of the struggle of exchange versus use values and of the formal rationality of law versus the substantive rationality of private interests.

As a contribution to this analysis, I attempt in this chapter to give theoretical form to the concept of transnational communities, as a less noticed but potentially potent counter to the more visible forms of globalization described in the recent literature. I embark in this task not without some hesitation since the concept of transnationality, like that of globalization itself, threatens to become part of one of those passing fads that grip social scientists' attention for a while only to fade into oblivion. I believe, however, that there is enough real substance here to make the effort worthwhile. If successful, the concept may actually perform double duty as part of the theoretical arsenal with which we approach the world-system structures, but also as an element in a less-developed enterprise, namely the analysis of the everyday networks and patterns of social relationships that emerge in and around those structures. The latter goal belongs properly in the realm of a midrange theory of social interaction that I will attempt to at least outline in the following comments.

THE ONSET OF TRANSNATIONAL NETWORKS

The actual working-class response to the globalization of capitalist production has been more subtle than the creation of international trade unions or the attempt to get national states to impose labor standards on Third World exports. Both attempts have proven ineffective because the competitive realities of the world economy undermine any incipient class solidarity along national lines, leaving the field clear to footloose capitalist investment. Reasons for the futility of these efforts have been dealt with at length elsewhere (Portes 1994). Instead, what common people have done in response to the process of globalization is to create communities that sit astride political borders and that, in a very real sense, are "neither here nor there" but in both places simultaneously. The economic activities that sustain these communities are grounded precisely on the differentials of advantage created by state boundaries. In this respect, they are no different from the large global corporations, except that these enterprises emerge at the grassroots level and their activities are often informal.

A group of social anthropologists who pioneered in the identification of this process and the attempt to make theoretical sense of it put their findings as follows:

> We define "transnationalism" as the processes by which immigrants forge and sustain multi-stranded social relations that link together their societies of origin and settlement. We call these processes transnationalism to emphasize that many immigrants today build social fields that cross geographic, cultural, and political borders . . . An essential element . . . is the multiplicity of involvements that transmigrants sustain in both home and host societies. We are still groping for a language to describe these social locations. (Basch, Glick Schiller, and Blanc-Szanton 1994: 6)

The puzzled attitude of these authors toward this emergent phenomenon is understandable when we begin to grasp the bewildering array of activities that it comprises and the potential social and economic weight that it possesses. In this and the following sections, I will try to make three main points: (1) The emergence of transnational communities is tied to the logic of capitalism itself. They are brought into play by the interests and needs of investors and employers in the advanced countries. (2) These communities represent a distinct phenomenon at variance with traditional patterns of immigrant adaptation. (3) Because the phenomenon is fueled by the dynamics of globalization itself, it has greater growth potential and offers a broader field for autonomous popular initiatives than alternative ways to deal with the depredations of world-roaming capital.

Let us begin by looking at the origins of these communities. As the preceding quote indicates, they are composed primarily of immigrants and friends and relatives of immigrants. Public opinion in the advanced countries has been conditioned to think that contemporary immigration stems from the desperate quest of Third World peoples escaping poverty at home. In fact, neither the poorest of the poor migrate, nor is their move determined mainly by individualistic calculations of advantage.[1] Instead contemporary immigration is driven by twin forces that have their roots in the dynamics of capitalist expansion itself. These are, first, the labor needs of First World economies, in particular the need for fresh supplies of low-wage labor, and second, the penetration of peripheral countries by the productive investment, consumption standards, and popular culture of the advanced societies.

Contrary to widespread perceptions, immigrants come to the wealthier nations less because they want to than because they are needed. A combination of social and historical forces has led to acute labor scarcities in these economies. In some instances, these are real absolute scarcities such as the dearth of industrial workers in Japan and the deficit in certain professions, like nursing and engineering in the United States. In other instances, however, the scarcity stems from the culturally conditioned resistance of native-born workers to accept the low-paid menial jobs commonly performed by earlier migrants (Piore 1979; Gans 1992; Portes and Guarnizo 1991). The list of such stigmatized occupations is large and includes, among others, agricultural stoop labor, domestic and other personal services, restaurant kitchen work, and garment sweatshop jobs (Sassen 1989).

Because of trade union and public opposition, the continuation of the immigrant labor flow has often taken place surreptitiously, under various legal subterfuges. In the United States, public outcry at the volume of unauthorized migration led to the passage of the 1986 Immigration Reform and Control Act, or IRCA. This piece of legislation reflects with notable clarity the resilient need for immigrant labor and the enduring power of employer associations. Instead of reducing the volume of immigration, the 1986 law actually increased it through several ingenious loopholes.[2]

By 1990, the foreign-born population of the United States had reached almost twenty million, the largest absolute total in the century (Fix and Passel 1991; Rumbaut 1994). The legislated loopholes of the IRCA plus new generous provisions of the 1990 Immigration Act virtually guarantee that this absolute number and the proportion that immigrants represent in the total U.S. population will increase significantly by the century's end. In Germany and France, despite official termination of the foreign guest-worker program in the 1970s, immigrant communities have continued growing ceaselessly through a variety of legal loopholes and clandestine channels (Zolberg 1989; Hollifield 1994). Today, Germany has a foreign population of seven million or roughly 9 percent of the total, a proportion quite similar to that in the United States (Münz and Ulrich 1995; Bade 1995). Even in ethnically homogenous Japan, labor scarcity has prompted a variety of legal subterfuges including the use of foreign company "trainees" and visa overstayers to perform line industrial jobs. By 1990, the foreign-born population of Japan numbered about 1.1 million, still an insignificant proportion of the total population, but expected to more than double during the next decade (Cornelius 1992, 1994).

The other side of the equation is the effects of the globalization process in the supply of potential immigrants. The drive of multinational capital to expand markets in the periphery and, simultaneously, to take advantage of its reservoirs of labor has had a series of predictable social consequences. Among them are the remolding of popular culture on the basis of external forms and art forms and the introduction of consumption standards bearing little relation to local wage levels (Alba 1978). This process simultaneously pre-socializes future immigrants in what to expect of their lives abroad and increases the drive to move through the growing gap between local realities and imported consumption aspirations. Paradoxically, the process does not so much affect the very poor in peripheral societies, as it does working- and middle-class sectors that are frequently the most exposed to marketing messages and cultural symbols beamed from the centers (Grasmuck and Pessar 1991; Portes and Bach 1985).[3] The fundamental point is that contemporary core-bound immigration is not an optional process, but one driven by the structural requirements of advanced capitalist accumulation. As such, the presence of Third World immigrants in cities of the developed world can be confidently expected to endure and expand. These groups provide, in turn, the raw material out of which the phenomenon of transnational communities develop.

THE RISE OF TRANSNATIONAL ENTERPRISE

The continuation of a de facto open immigration policy is prompted by employers' demand for fresh sources of low-wage labor in the advanced countries, while the relocation of production facilities abroad is motivated by a similar demand by certain industrial sectors. Peripheral workers who become employed under these various arrangements are not simply exploitable objects, but can become aware of the logic of these processes and the constraints that they create for personal mobility. Itzigsohn (1994) has shown how workers in the Dominican Republic become informal entrepreneurs in order to avoid the drudgery and minimal remuneration of work in the industrial export sector. In the Dominican context, the informal economy becomes, paradoxically, a means of popular resistance against the designs of foreign capital.[4]

Many immigrant workers too soon become aware that the pay and labor conditions in store for them in the advanced world do not go far in promoting their own economic goals. To bypass the menial dead-end jobs that the host society assigns them, they must activate their networks of social relationships. Immigrant social networks display two characteristics that those linking domestic workers generally do not have. First, they are simultaneously dense and extended over long physical distances. Second, they tend to generate solidarity by virtue of generalized uncertainty. Exchange under conditions of uncertainty creates stronger bonds among participants than that which takes place with full information and impartially enforced rules.

This sociological principle, established both in field studies and experimental observation, applies particularly well to immigrant communities (Kollock 1994). Their economic transactions both internal and with outsiders tend to occur with little initial information about the trustworthiness of exchange partners and the character and reliability of state regulation. This high uncertainty creates the need to "stick together" and to stay with the same partners, regardless of tempting outside opportunities, once their trustworthiness has been established.

Geographically extended, dense, and solidary networks can put into play a number of economic initiatives. In one such instance, highlighted by Sassen (1994), they lead to long-distance labor markets where job opportunities in far away locations are identified and appropriated. In another, described by Zhou (1992), they lead to pooling resources to lower consumption costs and produce enough savings for business or real estate acquisition. In a third, extensively studied by Light (1984) and his associates (Light and Bonacich 1988), they lead to the emergence of informal credit associations where pooled savings are allocated on a rotating basis. A fourth such initiative consists of appropriating the price and information differentials between sending and receiving countries through the creation of transnational enterprises.

This fourth strategy is not necessarily incompatible with the others, but is distinct in that it depends on transactions that occur regularly across political borders. To be feasible, such transactions require extraordinarily resilient networks to insure timely supplies, deliveries, and payments under conditions where little or no external regulation exists. Grassroots transnational enterprise benefits from the same set of technological innovations in communications and transportation that underlie large-scale industrial restructuring. A class of immigrant transnational entrepreneurs that shuttles regularly across countries and maintains daily contact with events and activities abroad could not exist without these new technologies and the options and lower costs that they make possible. More generally, this form of popular response to global restructuring does not emerge in opposition to broader economic forces, but is driven by them. Through this strategy, labor (initially immigrant labor) joins the circles of global trade, imitating and adapting, often in ingenious ways, to the new economic framework.

However, this parallel between the strategies of dominant economic actors and immigrant transnational enterprise is only partial. Both make extensive use of new technologies, and both depend on price and information differences across borders, but while corporations rely primarily on their financial muscle to make such ventures feasible, immigrant entrepreneurs depend entirely on their social capital (Guarnizo 1992; Zhou and Bankston 1994). The social networks that underlie the viability of such popular initiatives are constructed through a protracted and frequently difficult process of immigration and adaptation to a foreign society that gives them their distinct characteristics. In turn, the onset of this economic strategy tends to strengthen such networks. Thus transnational entrepreneurs expand and thicken, in a cumulative process, the web of social ties that make their activities possible. This cumulative growth of networks and firms grounded simultaneously in two countries eventually leads to a qualitatively distinct phenomenon. This qualitative change, that represents the terminal point of my inquiry, may best be ushered by some examples from the recent literature.

THE CONSTRUCTION OF TRANSNATIONAL COMMUNITIES

There exists today in the Dominican Republic literally hundreds of small and medium enterprises that are founded and operated by former immigrants to the United States. They include small factories, commercial establishments of different types, and financial agencies. What makes these enterprises transnational is not only that they are created by former immigrants, but that they depend for their existence on continuing ties to the United States. A study of 113 such firms conducted in the late 1980s found that their mean initial capital investment was only $12,000, but that approximately half continued to receive periodic capital transfers from abroad averaging $5,400. Moneys were remitted by kin and friends who remained in the United States but were partners or co-owners of the firm. In addition to capital, many firms received transfers in kind, producer goods, or commodities for sale (Portes and Guarnizo 1991:16).

In the course of fieldwork for this study, the authors found a second mechanism for capital replenishment, namely owners' periodic trips abroad to encourage new potential immigrant investors. These trips are also used by factory owners and managers to sell part of their production. Proprietors of small garment firms, for example, regularly travel to Puerto Rico, Miami, and New York to sell their wares. It is common practice to have a prearranged verbal agreement with buyers abroad, including small clothing stores. On their way back to the Dominican Republic, the informal exporters fill their empty suitcases with inputs needed for business such as garment designs, fabrics, and needles.

To the untrained eye, these loaded-down international travelers appear as common migrants visiting and bearing gifts for their relatives back home. In reality, they are engaged in a growing form of transnational informal trade. The information requirements for this dense traffic are invariably transmitted through kin and friendship networks spanning the distance between places of origin and destination. By the same token, it is clear that the men and women who operate these firms are not "return immigrants" in the traditional sense of the term. Instead, they made use of their time abroad to build a base of property, bank accounts, and business contacts from which to organize their return home. The result is not final departure from the United States, but rather a cyclical back-and-forth movement through which the transnational entrepreneur makes use of differential economic opportunities spread across both countries (Portes and Guarnizo 1991: 21–22).

There is a remarkable disparity between the dynamism of transnational enterprise and governmental misunderstandings or ignorance of the phenomenon. Officials of the Dominican and U.S. governments are mostly interested in the size and channeling of immigrant remittances and appear unaware of the intense entrepreneurial activity going on underneath. In the capital city of Santo Domingo, research conducted during the last two years reveals how returned immigrants have pioneered a number of business lines based on ideas and skills learned in the United States. These include fast-food home delivery, computer software and video stores, the selling and rental of cellular phones, automobile detailing, and many others. Meanwhile, executives of the Dominican construction industry admit that many of their firms could not survive without demand for second homes and business space generated by Dominicans abroad. Entire new sections of the city, especially toward the west and near the international airport, have been built with the immigrants in mind.[5] Popular lore has designated this population with a distinct name—*Dominicanos ausentes* (absent Dominicans) or *Dominican yorkers* (because of their concentration in New York City). They loom increasingly large in the tourism, garment, electronics, construction, and entertainment sectors of the local economy. By and large, the Dominican state in the past has been indifferent and generally unaware of these developments (Guarnizo 1994).

A similar story, but with a unique cultural twist, is told by David Kyle (1994) in his study of the Otavalan indigenous community in the highlands of Ecuador. Traditionally, the region of Otavalo has specialized in the production and marketing of clothing, developing and adapting new production skills since the colonial period under Spain. During the last quarter of a century or so, Otavalans have taken to traveling abroad to market their colorful wares in major cities of Europe and North America. By so doing, they appropriate the exchange value pocketed elsewhere by middlemen between Third World indigenous producers and final consumers. After years of traveling abroad, they have also brought home a wealth of novelties from the advanced countries, including newcomers to their town. In the streets of Otavalo, it is not uncommon to meet European women attired in traditional indigenous dress—the wives of transnational traders who met them and brought them back from their long-distance journeys.

During the same period, semipermanent Otavalan enclaves began to appear abroad. Their distinct feature is that their members do not make their living from wage labor or even local self-employment but from the commercialization of goods brought from Ecuador. They maintain a constant communication with their hometown in order to replenish supplies, monitor their *telares* (garment shops), and buy land. The back-and-forth movement required by this trade has turned Otavalans into a common sight, not only at the Quito airport but also at street fairs in New York, Paris, Amsterdam, and other large cities. According to Kyle, Otavalans have even discovered the commercial value of their folklore, and groups of performers have fanned throughout the streets of First World cities in recent years.

The sale of colorful ponchos and other woolens, accompanied by the plaintive notes of the *quena* flute, has been quite profitable. The economic success of these indigenous migrants is evident in their near universal refusal to accept wage labor abroad and in the evident prosperity of their town. Otavalo is quite different in this respect from other regions in the Andean highlands. Its Indian entrepreneurs and returned migrants comprise a good portion of the local upper strata, reversing the traditional dominance of white and mestizo elites.

Like the Dominican Republic, El Salvador is a country profoundly influenced by the transnational activities of its expatriate communities. In this case, out-migration was initially prompted by a violent civil war that sent enough Salvadorans out of the country to decisively alter the country's economic and social fabric. By 1996, remittances totaled approximately $1.26 billion, exceeding the sum total of the country's exports (Landolt 1997). The influence of Salvadoran transnational enterprises goes well beyond this figure. Major travel and package delivery firms have grown out of small informal concerns to service the manifold needs of the immigrant community and their counterparts at home. Immigrant capital has funded everything from new "Tex-Mex" food stands in the capital city of San Salvador to well-stocked computer software and video stores in the capital and in provincial cities such as San Miguel.[6]

In turn, Salvadoran banks and major businesses have come to see the large immigrant concentrations in cities like Los Angeles as a new market and a means of rapid expansion. Thus, the Constancia Bottling Company, a beer and soft drinks concern, set up a plant in Los Angeles to cater to the needs of the immigrant population. Similarly, the Salvadoran Chamber of Industry and Construction (CASALCO in the Spanish acronym) has held real estate fairs in Los Angeles, seeking to expand the already sizable demand for new housing by Salvadorans abroad. As in the Dominican Republic, expatriates have also acquired a new name in Salvadoran culture, *el hermano lejano* (the distant brother). Having access to the solidarity and resources of such "brothers" has become a vital means of survival, not only for families but for entire communities.

Because of their experiences of a harsh civil war and perhaps because of its mostly rural backgrounds, Salvadorans abroad maintain strong emotional ties with their hometowns. Dozens of *comites de pueblo* (town committees) have been created in Los Angeles; Washington, D.C. and Houston to support the respective communities and advance local development projects. Landolt (1997: 20) summarizes the developmental significance of such efforts:

> Like the contrast between families that receive remittances and those that do not, municipalities that receive this "grassroots transnational aid" *versus* those that do not highlight the economic relevance of collective remittance strategies. Towns with a hometown association abroad commonly have paved roads and electricity. Their soccer teams have better equipment, fancier outfits, and perhaps even a well-kept field where they practice.

A final example involves immigrant communities of considerably greater economic power. The very growth of Asian communities in the United States, particularly the Chinese, has created opportunities for moneyed entrepreneurs from Taiwan and Hong Kong to invest profitably in the United States and, in the process, become themselves part of the transnational community. Smith and Zhou (1995) explain how the rapid growth of Chinese home ownership in the New York suburb of Flushing has been largely financed by new Chinese banks established with Taiwanese and Hong Kong capital. The rapidly growing Chinese population in Flushing and adjacent cities in the borough of Queens is very much oriented to home ownership but lacks the knowledge of English and credentials necessary to seek credit from mainstream institutions. To meet the burgeoning demand for housing loans processed in their own language, local entrepreneurs have gone to Taiwan and Hong Kong to pool capital for new banks, and new immigrants have come to the United States bearing the necessary resources. As a result, Chinese-owned banks in Flushing proliferated. Although small by conventional standards, they serve simultaneously the economic interests of the immigrant community and of their overseas investors.

Three thousand miles to the West, the city of Monterey Park, California, has been transformed into the "first suburban Chinatown" largely by the activities of well-heeled newcomers (Fong 1994). Many Taiwanese and Hong Kong entrepreneurs established businesses in the area less for immediate profit than as a hedge against political instability and the threat of a Chinese Communist takeover. Opening a new business in the United States facilitates obtaining permanent residence permits, and many owners bring their families along to live in Monterey Park, while they themselves continue to commute across the Pacific.

The activities of the "astronauts," as these entrepreneurs are dubbed locally, adds a new layer of complexity to the transnational community. In this instance, returned immigrants do not invest U.S.-accumulated savings in new enterprises at home; rather, immigrants bring new capital to invest in firms in the United States. The birth of a child on American soil guarantees U.S. citizenship and anchors the family definitively in their new setting. As a result of the twin processes of successful investments and citizenship acquisition, Chinese immigrants have moved swiftly from the status of marginal newcomers in Monterey Park to the core of the city's business class (Fong 1994).

I have dwelled on these examples at some length to give credibility to a phenomenon that, when initially described, strains the imagination. A multitude of similar examples could have been used, as illustrated in the pioneering collection by Basch and her collaborators (Basch, Glick Schiller, and Blanc-Szanton 1994). The central point that these multiple examples illustrate is that, once started, the phenomenon of transnationalization acquires a cumulative character expanding not only in numbers but in the qualitative character of its activities. Hence, while the original wave of these activities may be economic and their initiators can be properly labeled transnational entrepreneurs, subsequent activities encompass political, social, and cultural pursuits as well.

Alerted by the initiatives of immigrant entrepreneurs, political parties and even governments establish offices abroad to canvass immigrant communities for financial and electoral support. Not to be outdone, many immigrant groups organize political committees to lobby the home government or, as in the case of multiple Salvadoran and Dominican immigrant initiatives, to influence the local municipality on various issues. To provide yet another example, Mexican immigrants in New York City have organized vigorous campaigns in support of public works in their respective towns. Smith (1992) tells about the reaction of the Ticuani (Puebla) Potable Water Committee upon learning that the much awaited tubing has arrived and, with it, the final solution to the town's water problem. They immediately made plans to visit the new equipment:

> On first sight, this is no more than an ordinary civic project. Yet when we consider certain other aspects of the scene, the meaning becomes quite different. The Committee and I are not standing in Ticuani, but rather on a busy intersection in Brooklyn. The Committee members are not simply going to the outskirts of the town to check the water tubes, but rather they are headed to JFK airport for a Friday afternoon flight to Mexico City, from which they will travel the five hours overland to their pueblo, consult with the authorities and contractors, and return by Monday afternoon to their jobs in New York City. (Smith 1992: 1)

Churches and private charities have joined this movement between home country and immigrant community with a growing number of initiatives involving both. Finally, the phenomenon acquires a cultural veneer as home performers and artists use the expatriate communities as platforms to break into the First World scene and as returnee artists popularize cultural forms learned abroad. The end result of this cumulative process is the transformation of the original pioneering economic ventures into transnational communities, characterized by dense networks across space and by an increasing number of people who lead dual lives. Members are at least bilingual; move easily between different cultures; frequently maintain homes in two countries; and pursue economic, political, and cultural interests that require a simultaneous presence in both. It bears repeating that the onset of this process and its development is nurtured by the same forces driving large-scale capitalist globalization. Marx describes the proletariat as created and placed into the historical scene by its future class adversaries, so global capitalism has given rise to the conditions and incentives for the transnationalization of labor.

It is important to note, however, that not all immigrants are involved in transnational activities, nor is everyone in the countries of origin affected by them. The sudden popularity of this term may make it appear as if everybody is "going transnational," which is far from being the case. In this sense, little is gained, by the relabeling of immigrants as "transmigrants" since the new term adds nothing to what is already known. It is preferable to reserve the term "transnational" for activities of an economic, political, and cultural sort that require the involvement of participants on a regular basis as a major part of their occupation. Hence, the Salvadoran merchant who travels regularly back home to replenish supplies or the Dominican builder who comes periodically to New York to advertise among his compatriots is a transnational entrepreneur; the immigrant who buys one of those houses or who travels home yearly bearing gifts for his family and friends is not. Reasons for the emergence of this novel phenomenon and its bearing on international and domestic inequalities are explored next.

THE STRUCTURE AND CONSEQUENCES OF TRANSNATIONALIZATION

If conditions confronting today's immigrants bore some similarity to those faced by their U.S.-bound European predecessors at the turn of the century, it is likely that they would not have moved so decisively in the direction of transnational enterprise as a means of survival or mobility. That earlier era featured two significant conditions distinct from those today.

They are, first, a plethora of relatively well-paid wage jobs in industry and, second, costly and time-consuming long-distance transportation. The first condition militated against widespread entrepreneurial ventures and gave rise over time to stable working-class ethnic communities. Most Poles and Italians in the United States became workers and not entrepreneurs because labor market opportunities in the American industrial cities where they arrived made this an attractive option. By contrast, today's uncertain and minimally paid service sector jobs strongly encourage immigrants to seek alternative economic paths.

Communications and transportation technologies were such as to make it prohibitive for turn-of-the-century immigrants to make a living out of bridging the cultural gap between countries of origin and destination or lead simultaneous lives in both. No trans-Pacific commuting was possible. No means were available for Polish peasants to check how things were going at home over the weekend and be back in their New York jobs on Monday. Although some activities that could be dubbed "transnational" according to a strict definition of the term did occur among earlier European immigrants, the present process is characterized by three features. First, the near-instantaneous character of communication across national borders and long distances; second, the numbers involved in these activities; and third, the fact that, after a critical mass is reached, they tend to become "normative."

Airplanes, telephones, fax machines, and electronic mail facilitate contact and exchange among common people on a scale incommensurate with what could be done a century earlier. For this reason, and given the economic, political, and cultural incentives to do so, more immigrants and their home country counterparts have become involved in transnational activities. Once the process begins, it can become cumulative so that, at a given point, it can turn into "the thing to do" not only among the pioneers, but even among those initially reluctant to follow this path. Immigrant communities like Monterrey Park near Los Angeles and highly transnationalized towns in El Salvador and the Dominican Republic have begun to approach this stage.

It bears repeating that grassroots transnational enterprises are not set up in explicit opposition to the designs of large banks and corporations. What the world-ranging activities of these major actors do is to provide examples, incentives, and technical means for common people to attempt a novel and previously unimagined alternative. By combining their new technological prowess with mobilization of their social capital, former immigrant workers are thus able to imitate the majors in taking advantage of economic opportunities distributed unequally in space.

The long-term potential of the transnationalization of labor runs against growing international inequalities of wealth and power as well as intranational ones in the countries of out-migration. What the process does, above all, is to weaken a fundamental premise of the hegemony of corporate economic elites and domestic ruling classes. That premise, noted at the start of this chapter, is that labor and subordinate classes remain "local," while dominant elites are able to range "global." So far the process has not run its course to the extent of threatening Third World labor supplies for runaway multinationals or the abundance of immigrant workers for employers in the advanced world. It has gained sufficient momentum, however, to earn the attention of authorities in small countries like El Salvador and in states of large countries like Mexico that have initiated policies designed to control or co-opt these grassroots ventures.

If, in the long run, transnational enterprise can become an equalizing force, in the short term, it can have the opposite effect. Reasons have already been noted by Landolt (1997) in her comment about growing disparities between sending localities that possess a committee among its migrants abroad and those that do not. Pioneering transnational entrepreneurs who have become successful favor their own families and perhaps their home communities, but also seek to restrict competition from others. Successful political activists who have mobilized support among immigrants strengthen their own parties at home, while trying to prevent others from gaining access to the same resources. Hence, to the extent that the process of transnationalization is short-circuited by the regulatory or co-optive activities of established elites, it may simply incorporate a minority of successful entrepreneurs into these elite ranks, while continuing to exclude others. Inequalities among Third World families and local communities would be exacerbated, not reduced by the transnational activities of immigrants.

There is reason, however, to be optimistic about the long-term effects of this phenomenon. Despite the predictable, indeed inevitable co-optive and control activities of sending governments and transnational corporations, the process of capitalist globalization is so broadly based and has generated such momentum as to continuously nourish its grassroots counterpart. Every new attempt to market wireless telephones, Internet access, or cheaper airline tickets in less-developed countries and every effort of employers in New York or Los Angeles to resupply themselves with new pools of docile migrant labor strengthens this feedback process. The targets of such initiatives are not simply "customers" or " laborers," but individuals capable of reacting creatively to the new situation in which they find themselves. Multinational elites and national governments may believe that the process of transnationalization is still too feeble to pose any significant challenge to the status quo. In reality, the tiger may have already left the cage, and there would be little point in closing it after him.

NOTES

An earlier version of this essay was published in W.P. Smith and R.P. Korczenwicz, *Latin America in the World Economy* (Westport, Conn.: Greenwood Press, 1996): 151–68.

1. This statement cannot be fully justified here without hopelessly derailing the reader's attention from the central focus of the analysis. The argument has been documented fully in several earlier writings. See Portes (1978) and Portes and Böröcz (1989).

2. Some 2.5 million formerly unauthorized aliens were legalized under the IRCA. Subsequent legislation contained generous provisions for newly legalized immigrants to bring their relatives. More importantly, the IRCA retained a large loophole allowing for the continuation of the unauthorized flow by requiring employers to check prospective workers' documents but not to establish their validity. Predictably, a massive fraudulent documents industry sprang up to service the new immigrants and their employers (Bach and Brill 1991). More recent legislative attempts to control immigration, such as Proposition 187 in California and a new act enacted by the U.S. Congress in 1996 promised to fare no better (Portes and Rumbaut 1996: ch. 8).

3. Sassen (1988) has developed a variant of this argument where runaway industries located in peripheral export zones stimulate out-migration by pre-socializing their work forces in First World cultural practices. Most of the labor force in these industries is formed by young people who are commonly dismissed after a few years. The combination of the skills and aspirations learned during their employment with their economic redundancy converts them into a ready pool for future migration. Sassen provides little empirical evidence, but subsequent research in a number of Latin American countries indicates that Sassen's thesis has some validity. See Pérez-Sainz (1994); Itzigsohn (1994).

4. Past analyses of the informal sector in peripheral countries have shown it to be an efficient tool for decreasing costs and increasing flexibility in the utilization of labor by large formal firms (Portes and Walton 1981; Benería 1989). These analyses assumed a regulatory framework, enforced by the state, which protected workers and simultaneously constrained employers. That framework has largely evaporated in the new export production zones where workers are subjected to much harsher conditions. It is this surrender of the regulatory powers of the state that is redefining the character and meaning of popular informal enterprise in many Third World cities.

5. Based on interviews conducted by the author and by a research team headed by Professor Carlos Dore of the Latin American School of Social Sciences (FLACSO) in the Dominican Republic during the fall of 1996.

6. This brief summary is based on interviews with informants in the Salvadoran communities of Washington, D.C. and Los Angeles and in two major sending cities in El Salvador—San Salvador, the capital, and San Miguel. Interviews were conducted by a field team led by Patricia Landolt of Johns Hopkins University and Luis E. Guarnizo of the University of California—Davis in cooperation with FUNDE, a Salvadoran nongovernmental research organization. The Salvadoran research team was led by Mario Lungo and Sonia Baires. These interviews are part of a comparative project led by the author. For more detailed presentation of these results see Baires and Landolt (1997).

REFERENCES

Alba, Francisco. (1978). Mexico's International Migration as a Manifestation of Its Development Pattern. *International Migration Review* 12 (Winter): 502–51.

Bach, Robert L., and Howard Brill. (1991). Impact of IRCA on the U.S. Labor Market and Economy. Report to the U.S. Department of Labor. Institute for Research on International Labor. Binghamton: State University of New York.

Bade, Klaus J. (1995). From Emigration to Immigration: The German Experience in the Nineteenth and Twentieth Centuries. Paper presented at the German-American Migration and Refugee Policy Group. American Academy of Arts and Sciences, Cambridge, Mass. March 23–26.

Baires, Sonia, and Patricia Landolt. (1997). Transnationalism: The Case of El Salvador. Final Report to the Project on Transnational Communities. Department of Sociology, Johns Hopkins University.

Basch, Linda G., Nina Glick Schiller, and Cristina Blanc-Szanton. (1994). *Nations Unbound: Transnational Projects, Post-colonial Predicaments, and De-territorialized Nation-States*. Langhorne, Penn.: Gordon and Breach.

Benería, Lourdes. 1989. Subcontracting and Employment Dynamics in Mexico City. In A. Portes, M. Castells, and L. Benton, eds. *The Informal Economy: Studies in Advanced and Less Developed Countries*. Baltimore: Johns Hopkins University Press: 173–188.

Castells, Manuel. (1980). Multinational Capital, National States, and Local Communities. I.U.R.D. Working Paper. University of California, Berkeley.

Cornelius, Wayne A. (1992). Controlling Illegal Immigration: Lessons from Japan and Spain. Working paper. Center for U.S.–Mexico Studies, University of California, San Diego.

———. 1994. Japan: The Illusion of Immigration Control. In P.L. Martin, W.A. Cornelius, and J.F. Hollifield, eds. *Controlling Immigration: A Global Perspective*. Stanford, Calif.: Stanford University Press: 375–410.

Fix, Michael, and Jeffrey S. Passel. (1991). The Door Remains Open: Recent Immigration to the United States and a Preliminary Analysis of the Immigration Act of 1990. Working Paper. The Urban Institute and the Rand Corporation.

Fong, Timothy P. (1994). *The First Suburban Chinatown: The Remaking of Monterey Park, California*. Philadelphia: Temple University Press.

Gans, Herbert. (1992). Second-Generation Decline: Scenarios for the Economic and Ethnic Futures of the Post–1965 American Immigrants. *Ethnic and Racial Studies* 15 (April): 173–92.

Grasmuck, Sherri, and Patricia Pessar. (1991). *Between Two Islands: Dominican International Migration*. Berkeley: University of California Press.

Guarnizo, Luis E. (1992). One Country in Two: Dominican-Owned Firms in the United States and the Dominican Republic. Ph.D. dissertation. Department of Sociology, Johns Hopkins University.

———. (1994). Los "Dominican Yorkers": The Making of a Binational Society. *Annals of the American Academy of Political and Social Science* 533: 70–86.

Hollifield, James F. (1994). Immigration and Republicanism in France. In P.L. Martin, W.A. Cornelius, and J.F. Hollifield, eds. *Controlling Immigration: A Global Perspective*. Stanford, Calif.: Stanford University Press: 143–75.

Itzigsohn, Jose A. (1994). The Informal Economy in Santo Domingo and San Jose: A Comparative Study. Ph.D dissertation. Department of Sociology, Johns Hopkins University.

Kollock, Peter. (1994). The Emergence of Exchange Structures: An Experimental Study of Uncertainty, Commitment, and Trust. *American Journal of Sociology* 100 (September): 313–45.

Kyle, David. (1994). The Transnational Peasant: The Social Structures of Economic Migration from the Ecuadoran Andes. Ph.D. dissertation. Department of Sociology, Johns Hopkins University.

Landolt, Patricia. (1997). Transnational Communities: An Overview of Recent Evidence from Colombia, Dominican Republic, and El Salvador. Report. Program in Comparative and International Development, Department of Sociology, Johns Hopkins University (Manuscript).

Light, Ivan. (1984). Immigrant and Ethnic Enterprise in North America. *Ethnic and Racial Studies* 7 (April): 195–216.

———, and Edna Bonacich. (1988). *Immigrant Entrepreneurs: Koreans in Los Angeles 1965–1982*. Berkeley: University of California Press.

Münz, Rainer, and Rolf Ulrich. (1995). Changing Patterns of Migration, the Case of Germany, 1945–1994. Paper presented at the German-American Migration and Refugee Policy Group, American Academy of Arts and Sciences, Cambridge, Mass. March 23–26.

Pérez-Sainz, Juan Pablo. (1994). *El dilema del Nahual*. San José: FLACSO Editores.

Piore, Michael. (1979). *Birds of Passage*. Cambridge, Mass.: Cambridge University Press.

Portes, Alejandro. (1978). Migration and Underdevelopment. *Politics and Society* 8: 1–48.

———. (1994). By-passing the Rules: The Dialectics of Labour Standards and Informalization in Less Developed Countries. In W. Sensenberger and D. Campbell, eds. *International Labour Standards and Economic Interdependence*. Geneva: Institute for Labor Studies, ILO: 159–76.

———, and Robert L. Bach. (1985). *Latin Journey: Cuban and Mexican Immigrants in the United States*. Berkeley: University of California Press.

Portes, Alejandro, and József Böröcz. (1989). Contemporary Immigration: Theoretical Perspectives on Its Determinants and Modes of Incorporation. *International Migration Review* 23 (Fall): 606–30.

Portes, Alejandro, and Luis E. Guarnizo. (1991). Tropical Capitalists: U.S.-Bound Immigration and Small Enterprise Development in the Dominican Republic. In S. Díaz-Briquets and S. Weintraub, eds. *Migration, Remittances, and Small Business Development: Mexico and Caribbean Basin Countries*. Boulder, Colo.: Westview Press: 101–31.

Portes, Alejandro, and Rubén G. Rumbaut. (1996). *Immigrant America: A Portrait*. 2nd ed. Berkeley: University of California Press.

Portes, Alejandro, and John Walton. (1981). *Labor, Class and the International System*. New York: Academic Press.

Rumbaut, Rubén G. (1994). Origins and Destinies: Immigration to the United States since World War II. *Sociological Forum* 9, 4: 583–621.

Sassen, Saskia. (1988). *The Mobility of Labor and Capital: A Study in International Investment and Labor Flow*. New York: Cambridge University Press.

———. (1989). New York City's Informal Economy. In A. Portes, M. Castells, and L.A. Benton, eds. *The Informal Economy: Studies in Advanced and Less Developed Countries*. Baltimore, MD: Johns Hopkins University Press: 60–77.

———. (1994). Immigration and Local Labor Markets. In A. Portes, ed. *The Economic Sociology of Immigration: Essays in Networks, Ethnicity, and Entrepreneurship*. New York: Russell Sage Foundation: 87–127.

Smith, Christopher, and Min Zhou. (1995). Flushing: Capital and Community in a Transnational Neighborhood. Manuscript. New York: Russell Sage Foundation.

Smith, Robert C. (1992). Los ausentes siempre presentes: The Imagining, Making, and Politics of a Transnational Community between New York City and Ticuaní, Puebla. Manuscript. Institute for Latin American and Iberian Studies, Columbia University.

Zhou, Min. (1992). *New York's Chinatown: The Socioeconomic Potential of an Urban Enclave*. Philadelphia: Temple University Press.

Zhou, Min, and Carl L. Bankston. (1994). Entrepreneurship: An Alternative Path to Economic Mobility for Asian Americans. In I. Natividad, ed. *Asian American Almanac*. Columbus, OH: Gale Research, Inc.

Zolberg, Aristide R. (1989). The Next Waves: Migration Theory for a Changing World. *International Migration Review* 23 (Fall): 403–30.

Part IV

Beyond the Mosaic: Globalization and Cultural Identity

16

Beyond the Mosaic: Questioning Cultural Identity in a Globalizing Age

Don Kalb and Marco van der Land

Culture is deeply and thoroughly implicated in the social shifts associated with globalization, and it is so in multiple and manifold ways. How deeply, how thoroughly, and how multiple, we are only gradually starting to learn, certainly where it concerns culture as lived identity, which is what this chapter is about.

But even when our theoretical reach is still hampered, popular awareness of culture's deep involvement in globalization has been widespread. It has probably helped to boost the new academic fields of cultural and postcolonial studies, including their ramifications within their mother social science and humanities disciplines. It has also provoked fearful reactions, first of all from the nationalist Right almost everywhere, but from the American, South American, and Asian Left as well. Why is our theoretical reach still hampered? We probably find it so hard to envision culture and globalization with more efficacy because somewhere on the road toward the establishment of the social sciences in the course of the nineteenth and twentieth centuries, some basic insights in key social and historical phenomena have been lost.

These insights can probably be excavated and must be recovered. But as yet they lay buried under a social science heritage that has been profoundly shaped by the experience of nationalism and the formation of nation-states everywhere in the world between 1789 and the 1970s. This experience has led us to think that what matters basically in questions of culture is what one could call "horizontal" difference: difference vis-à-vis territorial others and opponents; ethnic and national distinctions; and the territorial borders and symbolic boundaries between such multiple particularities. In the birthact of the social sciences, as well as in historiography and literature, a view was inscribed of a global mosaic of human cultures. The social sciences now gained their raison d'être by describing and explaining what went on, and what had to be going on, within any single part of the mosaic, that is within the boundaries. Sociology since Spencer, Weber, and Durkheim explained the differentiation of social spheres (state, economy, society, culture) within the leading modern countries, while anthropology studied the lack of such differentiation in the gradually colonized non-state societies. But by becoming so caught up with the internal set-up of the constituent parts, the social sciences in the twentieth century failed to grasp how and why the parceling up had proceeded in the first place, and in what ways culture had been involved. Moreover, they had lost the earlier interest of the political economists such as Smith, Ferguson, and Marx in the whole wider and uneven world-encompassing capitalist transformation from which the parts of the mosaic gained form and aspiration.

As a consequence, the social science heritage up to the 1960s had at worst naturalized culture as a field of territorially engraved or socially embodied differences (what Clifford Geertz, 1998, calls "pointillism") and at best studied the role of culture in the modernization process within any single unit or groups of units. But the place of culture in relation to the making of the mosaic itself, and in relation to its capitalist dynamics of development, had been little questioned. Accordingly, the social sciences are nowadays not particularly well equipped to study the unraveling of the mosaic in the course of current globalizations, let alone the pervasive as well as elusive role of culture therein. Their guiding questions still inevitably reflect their original preoccupations. Issues of cultural homogeneity versus heterogeneity loom large on their list of priorities.

From the 1960s on, some scholarly renegades, within Marxism broadly conceived as well as in Weberian or older world-historical traditions, from Immanuel Wallerstein (1974, 1980) to Eric Wolf (1982), from Roland Robertson (1992) to William McNeill (1991, 1993), have started to reinsert the study of nations, cultures, and civilizations within wider world history and within the development of the world-system. They started to place the various human particulars in relation to the "universal." By so doing they gave a highly needed impulse to more universal and transnational approaches to the human condition of national particularism.

But, interestingly, their record on culture was mixed. Their work was powerfully enabling, but either their treatment of culture in relation to world capitalism was somehow epiphenomenal, as in the case of Wallerstein and Wolf, or culture was for all practical purposes limited to the exchange between great traditions over long periods of time. The long-term global perspectives that were needed to restore the necessary broad view over centuries of human history, understandably, did not allow the close-up painting of culture as everyday identity in action that anthropology and the first practitioners of cultural studies had taught us to look for. Also, the heritage of the human sciences had made a point of perceiving culture and political economy as opposite pieces of the pie, whereas, obviously, they were inseparably intertwined in the course of such large-scale social transformations. Consequently, any contemporary work that aspires to a deeper understanding of cultural process within the current waves of globalization, though inevitably building on these authors' achievements, must find new ways of posing questions and finding answers that are pertinent to the current conjuncture.

Let us first briefly indicate which sorts of new questions we think should be asked but are as yet rarely posed, then discuss the ways the social sciences have in fact concerned themselves with culture and globalization and introduce the contributions that follow.

The English language features some words that are still powerfully reminiscent of the intricate interconnections between culture and identity on the one hand and power and appropriation on the other, at the start of the capitalist system. Think of the conceptual relation expressed by such a pair as property and propriety.[1] Think of the hugely suggestive double meaning of the notion of customs.[2] The early English vernacular, apparently, was highly sensitive to such perennial interweavings of power and identity and did not yet comfortably delegate such events to different spheres of life, described by different jargons and tended by different specialisms.

These symbolic condensations hint at what can and should be asked about cultural identities in the current era of globalization. Globalization, as the first section of this book amply underscores, implies quite a meaningful shift in the locus of social power from national states to transnationally operating capitalist agencies. It means an intensification of capitalist dynamics to the detriment of national modes of regulation and integration. This shift, of course, works out differently in different locations, nor are its outcomes simply predictable. Nevertheless, the direction of change in global power balances is indisputable. And with it occur such things as new debates about property rights, civic rights, welfare entitlements, family responsibilities and kin-forms, gender, work and labor, etc. Again, they do so differently on different levels (local, national, regional, global), and differently in different locations, depending on power relationships, institutional heritage, and on the particular local relation toward global capital flows. But globalization is everywhere associated with such contestations and the ensuing social changes, and everywhere are social identities fully implicated in the restructuring of such basic social arrangements in favor of capitalist interests, which are everywhere expressing themselves in obsessions with commodification, productivity, profitability, and pecuniary accountability. Social identities are not only implicated in the receiving end of such equations, but also in the possible responses any population can conceive of, in any claims on states and capital that social movements can articulate and implement. What the question of cultural identity and globalization therefore requires is a recovered critical attention to issues of property and propriety, global capitalist accumulation, and localized everyday life. Such questions are only beginning to be asked; work on them seems necessary.[3]

The question of culture and globalization that has recently attained most attention among social scientists and the wider public is, of course, the issue of whether globalization is implying increased homogenization or not. This is a question that springs logically from the received wisdom of the global mosaic of national cultures and consequently provokes strong and opposite normative responses. This is also the question that Kloos, Warde, and Löfgren address in this section. Their contributions crosscut in particular ways with the paradigms that can be discovered in this wider literature.

One body of work employs what one could call a "conversational paradigm." It emphasizes the emergence of a world society and a global culture. Authors in this paradigm do not necessarily imply that such a global culture is homogeneous, but they do emphasize that everyone, each nation, each civilization, and each group, nowadays has to position itself in relation to this wider and pluralistic global cultural environment. Cultural identities in the global age therefore necessarily develop in tandem with each other, they claim. Examples of this vision can be found in the work of cultural sociologists such as Roland Robertson (1992) and Malcolm Waters (1995), world-historian William McNeill (1991, 1993), and partly in the writings of the anthropologist Ulf Hannerz (1992, 1996), who has coined the notion of a "global ecumene."

Now conversation in itself does not tell everything about the possible outcomes. While McNeill sees the continued expression of national differences mainly as a "smoke screen" for a growing universality of culture, both Robertson and Waters believe in the spread of an ethical relativism and liberal pluralism as a consequence of globalization. Hannerz's notion of the global ecumene also connotes the softening of cultural antagonisms, though he is much more keenly aware of the new forms of heterogeneity that are emerging within nations, certainly in the "soft states" of the less-developed world. He has proposed that we see cultural process in globalization analogous to the emergence of creole languages, which mix lexicons and grammatical structures from different origins into one localized vernacular.

At this point, Hannerz's work moves into what can be called the "creative consumption paradigm," which is mainly based on anthropology (see for example Staring et al. 1997), subaltern studies, and the early British work in cultural studies. Creolization of pre-existing cultures happens because differently located groups with different histories, needs, and experiences appropriate the opportunities and commodities offered by the world market in distinct ways, thus continuously producing cultural expressions and identities of their own. In his vision, this leads to a new fragmentation of earlier national cultures, as cosmopolitan groups in the metropolises start to identify more completely with global consumer and elite culture while provincial and peripheral traders, workers, and peasants turn to their own new *bricolages* of whatever suits them best. Similarly, the anthropologist Arjun Appadurai (1996) maintains that the new forms of global communication, in particular audiovisual productions, strongly speak to the imagination and the needs of peripheral and diaspora populations. In his work, more than in Hannerz's, this leads not so much to any global ecumene, but rather to an upsurge of potentially inflammatory ethnic identity politics.

While the consumption paradigm is primarily market-based and emphasizes the erosion of national cultures or regional civilizations from within, the "hard cultures" paradigm bases itself in state institutions and makes a claim for the continued or even deepened interest in ethnic cultural boundaries in the global era. Anthony Smith, for example, in his work on nationalism (1995), maintains that increased economic integration does not forestall increased demands for national autonomy on the part of dominated ethnic minorities, certainly not since nation-states have become ever more active on more deeply culturally suffused terrains like educational, family, and health policies. Peter Kloos in his contribution to this book works out an important point of the logic of the process by which repressed minorities can start to articulate their need for cultural recognition, claims for autonomy, or outright territorial independence, and he connects this more systematically and instructively with globalization than Smith does. Globalization is not only about markets, he shows, but also about a global political, juridical, and institutional network, mainly centering on the United Nations and regional political alliances like the European Union, which impinge on sovereign states in ways that help minorities to claim more independent space. He shows how this transnational regime is facilitating the continued struggle by the Tamil population of Sri Lanka against the dominant Sinhalese.

The "hard cultures paradigm" can also come in more bellicose versions, such as those of the political scientist Samuel Huntington (1996). He is much less focused on world-market forces or UN regimes, than on the geopolitics of globalization that accompany the world market. He foresees a veritable clash of civilizations now that the ideological divides of the Cold War have ended and U.S.-based global capitalism is trying to create a new international order. This clash, however, will not so much unfold between the hard nations of Anthony Smith, which in the end are supposed to softly cooperate within the international division of labor, as between the mainly religion-based world civilizations, each centered in a coalition of states around one powerful core state, such as China, India, the United States, and Russia.

In strong opposition to both the creative consumption paradigm and the various hard cultures theories stands the "Americanization paradigm," and it is here that the voices expecting or fearing a far-reaching homogenization of world culture can be found. Americanization theories are built on the experience of successful large-scale, technology-based, capitalist production. A good example is George Ritzer's McDonaldization thesis (1993), which claims that rationalized capital intensive forms of production, distribution, marketing, and consumption are conquering older or alternative forms of provision everywhere in the world. The same specter is evoked by Benjamin Barber (1996), who fears that there might be little public choice between this sort of 'McWorld' and its territorialist and parochial opposite, symbolized by the Jihad and ethnic cleansing.

The contributions of both Alan Warde and Orvar Löfgren sound an important skeptical note here. While both are engaged with the consequences of the export of American capital, know-how, and technology, they show that such flows are not all of a piece (see also Miller 1997). In fact, they warn against a totalizing notion of capitalism and technology that has its roots as much in Weber as in Marx.

Warde demonstrates that the British restaurant scene has certainly been affected by McDonaldization, but much more so by the spread of ethnic cuisine, based on networks of migrants and family labor. Food is an important signifier for one's identity, he rightly contends, and eating habits seem more shaped by labor mobility and migration than by the mobility of capital. Certainly so since a substantial part of global capital works by providing ever better access to a whole cornucopia of different diets through supermarkets and special niche brands. He also indicates, paradoxically, that elite and cosmopolitan classes prefer such cuisines over the rationalized Americanist alternatives, and suggests that social classes that fail to carve a niche in the global economy feel more at home with traditional British cuisines and the traditional pub than with McDonalds or equivalent suppliers. Similarly, his article shows that receiving societies also have quite a substantial impact on what is received. Ethnic cuisine in England has regularly reshaped original recipes along the preferred tastes of the Britons.

Löfgren's is an even more complicated case. He shows that all over the twentieth century new technological inventions that were supposed to connect people transnationally, such as the telephone and the wireless, in the end helped to strengthen the nation-making project. Technological determinism helps us little, he suggests, and we have not much ground to assume that any one actor can envision the ultimate practical use to which new technological possibilities will be geared. His argument that the uses of "technologies of communication and togetherness" ultimately depend on the timing of their introduction vis-à-vis other large-scale social processes is an important one. It leads to the suggestion that whether Internet and telecom technologies will on the whole have a culturally globalizing, nationalizing, or perhaps even an urbanizing and localizing effect is still open. It also proposes that such outcomes need not be mutually exclusive (see also Geertz 1998).

NOTES

1. The example comes from Gerald Sider (1981).
2. This suggestion has been made by Wallerstein (1997).
3. We are thinking of various strands of work in anthropology, such as Katherine Newman (1994) on the "fear for falling" among American middle classes; Christopher Hann's collection on property and identity (1998); interdisciplinary work in the humanities such as Lowe and Lloyd (1997); and of course intensive area studies that concentrate on the specific paths, conditions, and parameters of globalization-induced social change, such as Katherine Verdery's work on Romania (1995).

REFERENCES

Appadurai, Arjun. (1996). *Modernity at Large; Cultural Dimensions of Globalization*. Minneapolis: University of Minnesota Press.
Barber, Benjamin, and Andrea Schulz, eds. (1996). *Jihad Versus McWorld*. New York: Ballantine.
Geertz, Clifford. (1998). The World in Pieces: Culture and Politics at the End of the Century. *Focaal, Tijdschrift voor Antropologie* [Focaal, Journal for Anthropology] 32: 91–117.
Hann, Christopher. (1998). *Property Relations: Renewing the Anthropological Tradition*. Cambridge: Cambridge University Press.
Hannerz, Ulf. (1992). *Cultural Complexity*. New York: Columbia University Press.
———. (1996). *Transnational Connections: Culture, People, Places*. London: Routledge.
Huntington, Samuel. (1996). *The Clash of Civilizations and the Remaking of World Order*. New York: Simon and Schuster.
Lowe, Lisa, and David Lloyd, eds. (1997). *The Politics of Culture in the Shadow of Capital*. Durham, NC: Duke University Press.
McNeill, William. (1991). *The Rise of the West*. Chicago: University of Chicago Press.
———. (1993). *The Global Condition*. Princeton, N.J.: Princeton University Press.
Miller, Daniel. (1997). *Capitalism: An Ethnographic Approach*. Oxford: Berg.

Newman, Katherine. (1994). *Declining Fortunes: The Withering of the American Dream*. New York: Basic Books.

Ritzer, G. (1993). *The McDonaldization of Society*. Thousand Oaks, Calif.: Pine Forge.

Robertson, Roland. (1992). *Globalization*. London: Sage.

Sider, Gerald. (1981). The Ties That Bind. *Social History* 5, no. 1: 1–39.

Smith, Anthony. (1995). *Nations and Nationalism in a Global Era*. Oxford: Polity Press.

Staring, Richard, et al., eds. (1997). Globalization/Localization: Paradoxes of Cultural Identity. *Focaal, Tijdschrift voor Antropologie* [Focaal, Journal for Anthropology] special issue: 30–31.

Verdery, Katherine. (1995). *What Was Socialism and What Comes Next?* Princeton, N.J.: Princeton University Press.

Wallerstein, Immanuel. (1974). *The Modern World-System*. New York: Academic Press.

———. (1980). *The Modern World-System II*. New York: Academic Press.

———. (1997). The National and the Universal: Can There Be Such a Thing as World Culture? In Anthony King, ed. *Culture, Globalization, and the World-System: Contemporary Conditions for the Representation of Identity*. Minneapolis: Minnesota University Press.

Waters, Malcolm. (1995). *Globalization*. London: Routledge.

Wolf, Eric. (1982). *Europe and the People without History*. Berkeley: California University Press.

17

The Dialectics of Globalization and Localization

Peter Kloos

The topic of this chapter is the apparent contradiction between two contemporary social processes both occurring on a worldwide scale: globalization and localization. Globalization stands for the emergence of a world economy, a world polity, and perhaps a world culture, in short, for the emergence of a world society in the widest sense of the term (Giddens 1991). Localization stands for the rise of localized, culturally defined identities, sometimes within, sometimes transcending, the boundaries of a state. While globalization represents ever-wider horizons of universalistic sociocultural networks until they encompass the whole world, localization stresses sociocultural specificity, in a limited space.

Globalization and localization are not static conditions: both are processes—albeit unfinished—in a certain direction. As processes they seem to point in an opposite direction and thus on first sight appear to be contradictory. This contradiction is tangibly present in the realms of politics and of language. In the realm of politics the national state is rapidly loosing its glorified sovereignty in favor of transnational, continental, and even global regimes, while at the same time a number of substate minorities are clamoring for more autonomy and political independence. For instance, in an era in which a number of countries unite to form a European Community, secession accounts for sixteen new states in the same continent since 1989: that is 40 percent of the total number of states now forming Europe (cf., Kloos 1997a). Political separatism is present even in prototypical states like the United Kingdom and France. In the United Kingdom, the Scottish National Party for many years has aimed at independence. In France, Corsican movements for decades have used violent methods to reach independence. In Bretagne and in Aquitaine there are movements aiming at more autonomy, and the ancient duchy of Savoie (since 1860 the French Departement Haute Savoie) declared itself independent in May 1996. Until now this unilateral declaration has had no civil effect, but still it betrays the existence of powerful forces of fission in France.

In the use of language one can observe the growing importance of English as a veritable panhuman language, while at the same time local languages and dialects (even dead ones) are being rekindled, and speakers are calling for their recognition. In the United Kingdom, where English became the dominant language in the nineteenth century, a language believed to be dead, namely the Celtic language of Cornwall, is being revived (see Vink 1993). Even in France, where the Parisian government for generations used stern methods to make French as spoken in Paris and the surrounding Ile de France the hegemonic language of the country, the use of regional languages is nowadays allowed.

The general opinion of scholars at the moment is that the contradiction between both processes is indeed only apparent. In a recent article Geana speaks of complementarity of globalization and ethnicity (Geana 1997). To express the inherent relationship between the two processes Rosenau introduced the term "fragmegration," a conjunction of fragmentation and integration (see Rosenau 1994). Robertson uses the term "glocalization." It is formed by telescoping globalization and localization into one word (see Robertson 1994, 1995).

Here I shall not use these neologisms. I am more interested in the connection between the apparent contradictory processes. My point of departure is the assumption that there is a complex and necessary relationship between globalization and localization. The relationship can, provisionally, be formulated as follows. (1) Processes of globalization trigger identity movements leading to the creation of localized, cultural-specific, identities. (2) Movements in search of a localized, cultural-specific identity make use of global regimes to reach their ends. The state plays a crucial role in these processes, as a loser in view of globalization, as an oppressor of identity movements, and, occasionally, as a victim, namely in a case of political separation.

What I want to develop here is a conceptual framework that may help us to better analyze the connection between globalization and localization. A major aim will be the breakdown of the unmanageable concepts of globalization and localization into concepts better amenable to empirical investigation.

For the relationship between the global and the local I use the much-abused term "dialectic" in its classical Greek meaning. For the ancient Greek thinkers *dialektikè* denoted a dialogue in which the discussants constantly adjusted their views on the basis of what the other said. A dialectical relationship, therefore, is one of continuous mutual influence between ever changing entities. In this context these entities are covered by the terms globalization and localization. These terms, however, are very clumsy container terms that hide more than they disclose. This means that we have to find a better language to talk about that Janus-faced process of globalization and localization.

CONCEPTUALIZATION

If globalization is conceived of as the formation of a kind of world society and culture in the widest sense of the terms, and if localization refers to the rise of localized identities, concentrated within the boundaries of a state, then we have to deal with at least three levels of social reality: first, the level of the state; second, the suprastate, global level; and, third, the substate, local level.

The State

With regard to the state I basically follow Max Weber's well-known conceptualization: the state is seen as a political community in which a central government claims the monopoly of the legitimate use of physical force in a certain territory (see Gerth and Mills 1958: 78).

The typical state of today is the nation-state. This is a European invention. Before its invention there were states without nations as well as nations without states. The nation-state, however, can be regarded as an amalgamation of the state as political community and the nation as a self-conscious cultural group. This amalgamation took place, historically speaking, fairly recently, mainly in the course of the nineteenth century.

In the present context I wish to make an unambiguous analytical distinction between national states (and empires) and nation-states. A national state is a state "governing multiple contiguous regions and their cities by means of centralized, differentiated, and autonomous structures" (Tilly 1992: 3). In a national state there need not be any sense of solidarity based on a common language, history, culture, etcetera. In nation-states, however, the people sharing a territorial, political organization also share a sense of linguistic, religious, and symbolic identity.

Even in Europe the nation-state is an ideal rather than a reality. Denmark, Iceland, and Ireland are probably the only examples of states that come close to the ideal. Most states are in fact national states whose governments try or have tried to reach a higher degree of homogeneity by expanding the culture of the politically dominant group and by repressing the cultures and languages of minorities. In some countries this repression often took place quite consciously. In other cases it was the consequence of the formation of the modern state, with its bureaucracy; its army based on general conscription; its unitary legislation; its system of education, dominated by the views of the political and cultural majority; etcetera. The project of the nation-state remained unfinished, however, and it is for that reason that the term "nation-state" stands for an ideal rather than for a sociopolitical reality (see also Porter 1994).

Although even in the case of European states the project of unification rarely really succeeded, the ideal of the nation-state was imported by indigenous elites in other continents in the wake of nineteenth- and twentieth-century colonialism and twentieth-century decolonization (Badie 1992; Davidson 1992). It is this nation-state from which the standards of the twentieth-century state are derived in all continents: new states all over the world have tried to establish a unitary state, which supposes a degree of homogeneity that is almost always at odds with the reality of their precolonial and colonial past and also their postcolonial present. Moreover, most non-European states are highly artificial constructs of colonial rule. Their boundaries are not the result of continental wars, as was usually the case in Europe, but of rivalry solved at Atlantic conferences tables. Culturally, non-European states are almost invariably very heterogenous. It is the dynamics of the culturally pluriform national state that pretends to be a nation-state we have to keep in mind when studying globalization— outside Europe, but also in Europe itself.

Transnational Regimes

The concept of globalization is too vague and too general to be of much practical use. Moreover, what is emerging is not so much one global order as a number of disparate transnational phenomena, variously termed organizations, institutions, networks, etcetera.

These terms are vague too, and in many cases give a wrong idea of ongoing events. Transnational phenomena are certainly not always organized in any strict sense. The term "institution" suggests a formality that not always exists. And the term "network," finally, is too weak and too noncommittal to cover the global interdependencies that may rule quite strictly the daily behavior of people all over the world.

For transnational phenomena I will use the term "regime."[1] A widely used definition of the term in political science is Krasner's. According to him a regime consists of "implicit or explicit principles, norms, rules and decision-making procedures around which actors' expectations converge in a given area of international relations" (Krasner 1982). For political scientists the concept is indeed closely tied to inter-national relations— literally so, to relationships between states or state governments. In many definitions this is explicitly stated (cf., Junne 1992). The restriction to international relations under emerging global realities is not practical: many transnational regimes came into being without much state interference and may even turn themselves against the state.

In the creation of the capitalist market and especially global monetary regimes state governments and their central banks did participate. Having created these regimes, however, governments quickly found that they lost control over them, and consequently over their own monetary situation. There is now a host of information showing how powerless state governments are vis-à-vis the transnational money market (Philips 1994; Went 1996). Furthermore, even deliberately *inter*national institutions (and here I use the term on purpose), initiated by state governments, may, because they acquire a dynamic of their own, turn against the state. A prime example is of course the Security Council of the United Nations that over the past decades many times violated accepted principles of state sovereignty (see Ratner 1995).

The important point, to repeat, is that in the context of globalization we are not dealing with inter-national regimes but with transnational ones: regimes that transcend states and do not depend on relationships between states. Departing from Krasner's just quoted definition I would define a regime as consisting of implicit and/or explicit principles, rules, and decision-making procedures enabling and constraining actors in a given area of activity. A transnational regime, then, is one that enables and constrains activities of actors on a transnational, even global level.

The disadvantage of this definition is that it emphasizes the principles, rules, procedures, and actors as mere subjects. It tends to underemphasize the creative role of the actors (in the plural) in forming regimes. Many transnational regimes (like the feminist movement, the ecological movement, and various Human Rights movements), are closely tied to networks between individual actors. Anthropologists and also sociologists tend to approach regimes from the point of view of actors, and it is obvious that we should not leave out actors from the conceptualization of regime. This means that a regime might therefore be conceived in a more balanced way, as a formalized constellation of human interdependencies in which implicit and/or explicit principles, rules, and decision-making procedures created by actors enable as well as constrain their behavior in a given area of activity. Again, such a regime becomes transnational once the constellation of human interdependencies transcends state boundaries. And this is precisely what has happened in the course of human history.

But how to study regimes? From an analytical point of view transnational regimes can be systematically studied in terms of (1) origins and development, (2) degree of organization and of centralization, (3) geographic range (how wide does a regime casts its net?), (4) scope (which activities are covered?), and (5) degree of coercion and effectiveness.

Globalization, I would argue, is simply the sum-total of the rise and extension of transnational regimes along these five dimensions.

Although the term globalization came into general use in the early 1980s, the rise of transnational, global regimes is far older (see Kloos and de Silva 1995). Some argue that Christianity was the first truly global regime—not so much in reality as in its pretention to be the panhuman religion. I prefer to let the era of globalization begin with the European expansion—to some extent globalization can even be regarded as a consequence of European expansion. It is in the wake of seafaring, for instance, that the first transnational law was formulated and defended—Grotius's idea of the *mare liberum*, the "free sea."

The big leap in the growth of transnational regimes came with the development of electronic communication. McLuhan in *Explorations in Communication* (1960) was one of the first to ask attention for the shrinking of the world as a consequence of electronic communication. In many fields the world is nowadays even smaller than a village. A top manager of a large bank has quicker access to the assets of his bank wherever in the world than a farmer to his potatoes growing a mile away from his farmhouse. The coining of the term and its quick popularity in the 1980s and later probably symbolizes the growing awareness of the increasing influence of global regimes, the capitalist market in particular.[2]

The capitalist market is the most fully fledged transnational regime. It is rather arbitrary to let this regime begin in a particular year. Markets as such are ancient phenomena. The growth of a world market, and of the total commoditization it eventually might entail, gained momentum from the fifteenth and sixteenth centuries onward. The industrial revolution added significantly to its growth. The market is not a centralized regime, and although it is more organized than liberal ideology says it is, the general idea is that it functions best when left alone by the state.

Since the demise of socialist economies (in the former Soviet Union) and the reluctant admittance of capitalism to China its geographic range is practically the whole world. Moreover, fewer and fewer things manage to escape from being turned into commodities. Even human organs run the risk of becoming commoditized. Concomitantly, the degree of coercion is increasing fast: a decreasing number of human needs can be met without money, which makes the whole world population a prisoner of the global monetary regime.

Being aware of the existence of transnational regimes, the opportunities offered by them as well as the constraints, is of strategic importance for the rise of local identity movements. It is to these movements, an operationalization of localization, that I will turn now.

Identity Movements

At first sight, localization appears to be the opposite of globalization. In contradistinction to transnational, regional and global, universal tendencies, localization stresses restricted (often, but not always, geographically restricted) cultural specificity. As far as the twin process of globalization and localization is concerned, far less theoretical attention has been paid to the second of the two, however volatile localizing tendencies often are from a political point of view. As in the case of globalization, localization as such is an analytically useless concept. I would argue that as a process, localization is embodied in identity movements, often ethnic and/or religious movements that stress or create a social and cultural identity on behalf of groups or categories of people, and in some cases inspire political autonomy. In all continents and possibly in the majority of countries one can observe such identity movements struggling for ethnic recognition and fighting for it if the effort is frustrated.

One should be weary with regard to the qualification "ethnic" in expressions like "ethnic identity' and "ethnic conflict," and even in "ethnic movement." First, a so-called ethnic conflict is rarely a conflict between ethnic categories as such. It is usually a conflict between representatives, or leaders, of movements who purportedly act on behalf of a category of people defined in ethnic terms. Second, ethnic differences are rarely the real bone of contention: ethnicity is an idiom and a principle of mobilization, used by a movement in a fight over scarce resources. According to this view ethnic categories, like ethnic groups and ethnic identities, are the result of conflict rather than the cause—but this is a view fiercely disputed by "ethnic groups" themselves, who tend to defend "ancient ethnic roots" that, if investigated, are often of doubtful validity (cf., Kloos 1995). Ancient ethnic roots may have been invented quite recently (see Hobsbawm and Ranger 1983). Having said this, I would stress, however, that ethnic feelings—feelings of belonging to an imagined ethnic group—can be strong and have to be taken very seriously. However artificial in origin, subjective feelings of ethnicity are a political factor of prime importance: people are willing to kill and die for them.

My preference for the term "movement" in the present context rests on the consideration that it conceptually links potentially large numbers of people (and their ideas, expectations, frustrations, and feelings) to often charismatic leaders. Dissatisfied masses can show a high amount of active and passive resistance without being organized. To implement alternatives, however, persons must rise who put words to what many feel and who, often via a mantle of followers, are able to mobilize even larger numbers of dissatisfied people.

One can describe ethnic movements in terms quite similar to transnational regimes (movements can profitably be regarded as regimes): namely in terms of (1) origins and development of localized movements, (2) degree of organization and of centralization of the movement, (3) geographic range (how concentrated or dispersed is a movement?), (4) scope (which activities are covered by the movement?), and (5) degree of coercion.

Like globalization, localization defined as the rise of identity movements is not a recent phenomenon. The first example I personally came across was in Surinam, in the late 1960s, where I was carrying out fieldwork among Carib fishermen *cum* shifting cultivators living along the lower reaches of the Maroni River (the border river between Surinam and French Guyana). In these villages, far away from Surinam's capital Paramaribo, I saw the Amerindians slowly loose their specific cultural characteristics. On the Surinam side of the river they became Surinamese, on the French side they became French *citoyens* (Kloos 1971; Hurault 1972). In Paramaribo, however, I met young, urbanized Indians who were trying to again speak Carib or Arowak, and who revived customs they called Amerindian. They tried to find an answer to the existential question "who am I, who are we?" in a non-Amerindian environment. By seeking the answer in their own past—or in what they believed was their past—they were recreating a new, Amerindian identity. It was as if they, becoming submerged in a large urban population, grabbed the life buoy of their almost forgotten cultural heritage to distinguish themselves from the mass of the urban population.

The activities of these Amerindians did not have political consequences. In Surinam, ethnic differences are generally accepted facts of life, and no one objected when the Amerindians stressed their ethnic specificity. In other cases, however, social, especially ethnic, movements may find a government endorsing ideals of a nation-state on their path—and when a state government frustrates a movement's efforts to reach a certain degree of cultural autonomy, it may resort to violent methods to reach its ends. In Sri Lanka, for instance, there is a Tamil movement, the Liberation Tigers of Tamil Eelam (LTTE), that attracts international attention by using extreme forms of violence to realize a separate Tamil state on the island. At independence Sri Lanka, at that time still called Ceylon, was inhabited by several ethnic groups, the Sinhala, with about 75 percent of the total population being the largest. The Tamil, with slightly more than 20 percent, formed a sizeable minority. From independence onward the Sinhala have tried to turn the island into a Sinhala–Buddhist nation-state, more and more frustrating the Tamil population, especially in the fields of economic opportunity, political participation, and education. Politicians of the Tamil establishment at first tried to defend their interests by using the means of parliamentary democracy. When in the course of the 1970s this proved to be futile, Tamil youths began to radicalize, wanting to establish a separate Tamil state, and started to use nonparliamentary means. The actions of the secessionist movements led to army operations and eventually to the civil war that broke out in 1983 and is still raging (Kloos 1997c; Senaratne 1997; Spencer 1990; Wilson 1988).

With this example of Sri Lanka we are at the heart of the problem, because at least one of its secessionist movements, the Liberation Tigers of Tamil Eelam (LTTE), makes use of transnational regimes to reach its ends: in a sense it became a transnational regime itself (see Kloos 1997b). How do transnational regimes relate to local identity movements and vice versa?

THE INTERDEPENDENCE OF GLOBAL REGIMES AND IDENTITY MOVEMENTS

I now reformulate the hypotheses, in line with the proposed concepts of transnational regime and identity movement, into empirically more tractable terms. (1) How and why does the rise and spread of transnational regimes trigger local identity movements? (2) How and why do identity movements make use of transnational regimes to reach their ends?

Consequences of the Rise of Global Regimes

If identity movements are triggered by the rise of transnational regimes, then people have to be aware of the latter. In the present context I cannot demonstrate the point but by example and general reasoning, but I believe that people the world over are more and more aware that processes and events beyond their horizon, let alone their grasp, are increasingly influencing their daily life. In 1995 I came across a beautiful example, in a letter to the editor of an South Indian newspaper, and it is worthwhile quoting from it.

GLOBALISATION

Sir,—Any reasonable intelligent person . . . would vouch for what our much-pampered globalisation of the economy has done for the common man. . . . Why have my newspaper prices almost doubled in the last three years while I sell the old papers at half the price that I was getting before. Why are my toothpaste, soap, hair oil (even pure coconut oil) costing more than double. Why are my coffee/tea, milk and sugar steadily going up in price to unaffordable levels? Why are my transportation charges, electricity and water charges, vehicle taxes, communication expenses, vegetable and fruit prices, rice and cereals, medicines and miscellaneous items steadily going up all the time? . . . True, competition has set in, more varieties of the same goods are available, but is it not perplexing that the law of demand and supply does not seem to operate? Is this what goes on by the name of 'prosperity'? . . . Am I wrong in saying that we have begun to pay global prices even for our essential locally produced requirements and in return got the unaffordable freedom to choose from an endless variety of automobiles, two-wheelers, white goods, cereals and soft drinks? Perhaps our leading economists would care to explain in the layman's language, so that we can all understand. K.V. Narayanmurti, Kochi 682 035 (Letter to the Editor, *Indian Express*, 25 January 1995)

I believe this letter-writer to be correct in ascribing his financial plight to globalization—or rather to the transnational regime of the capitalist market, the money market included, and to the final phase in the spread of capitalism as a transnational regime penetrating now even the former Soviet Union and China as well as the last pockets of tribal groups in the highlands of New Guinea and the remaining up-river sanctuaries in the Amazon basin.

Given the still accelerating growth of mass communication, especially electronic communication made possible by magnetic tape and satellite television, less and less people remain oblivious of what is going on elsewhere in the world (cf., Barnet and Cavanagh 1994; Naisbitt 1994). There is less and less "elsewhere." But Mr. Narayanmurti is in his letter not referring to spectacular events conspicuously broadcasted almost the moment they occur, or to Western (or Indian) pop music and video clips, but to more difficult to grasp economic and political processes daily affecting the value of the content of his purse. He is aware of these effects, and he is also aware of the fact that these processes are beyond his understanding, let alone his control. My understanding is that such an awareness makes people think about themselves and their prospects.

Modern communication, however, does not only bring the latest information, and, with it, awareness of transnational regimes, to every place. It also brings people from here to everywhere and vice versa. Knowledge about the possibilities of emigration has spread almost as quickly as news. Political and environmental problems caused millions of people to migrate. This brought about many large-scale diasporas.

Modern communication therefore has two faces: It potentially brings the whole world to every remote corner, but it also pushes inhabitants of those corners into the large world. As a result of both there is nowadays (1) an unprecedented contact between, as well as mixing of, people belonging to very different cultural traditions; (2) an unprecedented distance over which events influence people and people can influence events, and, consequently; (3) an increased awareness that the world is indeed the place where people live.

This awareness is a necessary condition for the rise of (ethnic) identities (cf., Eriksen 1993; Romanucci-Ross and DeVos 1995). It is a generally known fact that migrants are far more likely to ask the question who they are than those who stay behind. Yet people who do not themselves move but see their local world being integrated into a far bigger one, and see the large world moving into their local world, ask the same question.

As a result, people everywhere become more and more aware of an immense world impacting on their lives. However, for most people daily life still covers only a limited space in which their primary interest lies. It involves only a limited number of persons. The majority of people live somewhere and are therefore local as a result. Thus the problem of identity (Who are we in the face of this big world?) arises. This question, "Who am I; Who are we?" unavoidably challenges one's identity: ideas about identity are based on this very question.

The weakness of this statement is that although it may be quite true that globalization in this way triggers identity movements, it does not explain anything: it merely rephrases the problem and is therefore tautological. Still, tautologies have their use (any theory is, in the end, a tautology): in this case the statement may refer to a basic characteristic of human beings to ask the question who they are whenever they are being engulfed by a world larger than the one they knew. But then the next question arises: Why is that question answered in terms of supposedly primordial groups? I have no idea what the answer is to that question, yet that is exactly what happens: ethno-nationalism has entered the modern world with a force hardly anybody had expected forty years ago (see, however, Connor, 1973) on ethno-nationalism for an early and very insightful article). The answer might be that ethnic identity contains an element of completeness or apparent naturalness that class, gender, and other identities never have and that belonging to such a purportedly natural group offers the possibility of personal and social identification an emerging global society, due to sheer size, inherently lacks. Transnational regimes are not only beyond the control of people: people are also aware of the fact that there are powers beyond their cognitive horizon—hence Mr. Narayanmurti's cry for help, quoted above. This awareness results in feelings of insecurity and a quest for configurations people feel they can trust—and if these are not available (and as a rule they are not), they are simply created. Identity movements supply an opportunity for "we" against "them" feelings, a distinction that breaks down in a global society. After all, there are no "others" any longer in a global society.

The quest for ethnic identity in the context of globalization rests on cultural contrasts. However, cultural differences in themselves are evidently not enough to let identity movements emerge. There are many steep cultural gradients in the world without the rise of identity movements. What motivates the quest for ethnic identity, I would argue, is discrimination, either against minorities who are drawn into the vortex of state and transstate development, or against migrants who have moved to other societies and have no status there at all and feel drowned by a dominant culture.

The outcome of the question of identity therefore also depends on what the surrounding society and the state government on its behalf in particular do. Basically there are two alternatives. The state government can either welcome or at least accept cultural differences within its boundaries, or it can reject them and opt for homogenization. The latter option can result in passive or active cultural discrimination.

There are few state governments that actively pursue the line of intrastate cultural differentiation. A recent yet rare example is the Swiss government that actively supports the rescue of Rätisch, a language closely related to classic Latin. It is spoken as a first language by only 0.6 percent of the Swiss population (in the canton Graubünden). As a spoken language it is in danger of dying out. On March 10, 1996, the Swiss agreed by referendum that henceforth it would be possible to address the government in Bern in Rätisch. Answers would be framed in the same language. A case of tacit acceptance is already referred to: the rescue of Cornish in England (Vink 1993) and the acceptance of radio broadcasting in France in regional languages are also examples.

If such efforts are frustrated, however, identity movements tend to radicalize and may turn into secessionist movements. This happened in Ceylon, where the Sinhalese used their majority in parliament to make Sinhala the official language. The Sinhala Only movement started in the 1950s. The 1972 constitution institutionalized the difference in status between Sinhala and Tamil. Tamil youth, seeing their chances in higher education and in acquiring government jobs diminishing, and realizing that their representatives in parliament were powerless, began to oppose the government and to assassinate Tamil public servants who were seen as traitors. The armed forces retaliated, and from 1977 onward violence escalated quickly (see Senaratne 1997) until in 1983 it exploded into a full-scale civil war between the Liberation Tigers and the Sri Lankan government.

Secessionism is a direct attack on state integrity. State governments by their very nature cannot leave such an attack unanswered. But there is usually more than a refusal to accept ethnic identity: ethnic differences as such are rarely the issue. In Sri Lanka, for instance, there is no clash between Sinhala and Tamil culture, but there is a clash of interests between Sinhala- and Tamil-speaking populations. In the Sri Lankan case the interests are first of all job opportunities, but there may be many more, and also more material interests. Although ethnic movements occasionally seem to act against evident economic interests, economic aspects are rarely absent. In many, and perhaps the majority of, cases of so-called ethnic conflict within states, cultural differences are not the prime movers of ethnic movements at all but rather the idiom in which conflicting interests are cast.

The Use of Transnational Regimes by Identity Movements

The second question was how and why movements in search of an identity of their own make active use of transnational regimes to further their cause. Let me begin with an example I know best: the Tamil secessionist movement in Sri Lanka called Liberation Tigers of Tamil Eelam, already referred to. At the root of the conflict lies the fact that the Tamil population felt (and still feels) discriminated against by the Sinhala minority. The conflict has been a power struggle from the very beginning.

Once the struggle turned into a veritable civil war, both parties were in need of money to finance it. The governments used state income. The Liberation Tigers had to find other sources. From the very beginning they robbed banks and taxed Tamils in Sri Lanka. After the massive exodus following the 1983 anti-Tamil pogrom in Colombo, they also began— under threat of using violence—to tax Tamils in Australia, Europe, and Canada. Income is also derived from the drug trade. Ganja grown in Sri Lanka is illegally exported, mainly to Australia, but more important is the participation of the Tigers in the heroin trade from Southeast and west Asia to Europe, Canada, and Australia. Part of the money collected is spent on weapons and means of communication; part of it may go to Sri Lanka itself. This means that the Liberation Tigers have become involved in the transnational criminal regimes of laundering money and the regimes of drug and weapon traders. Not much is known in any detail, but what is known points in the direction of extensive participation in these gigantic and truly transnational regimes (Anonymous 1995). Like the Basque, Euzkadi Ta Azkatasuna (ETA), the Irish Republican Army (IRA), and the Mexican Zapatistas in Chiapas, the LTTE put itself on the Internet. After the occupation of Jaffna by the Sri Lankan army in December 1995, the LTTE used the Internet to solicit humanitarian assistance to support the Jaffna population that had been evacuated—by the LTTE. This means that a local movement makes use of a variety of global regimes in order to survive and to reach its end: an independent Tamil state on Sri Lanka. The Sri Lankan government cannot do much against this strategy.

Interesting in this respect, and openly and legally organized, is a truly transnational regime in the form of an organization that serves the interests of ethnic minorities in numerous countries: the UNrepresented Peoples Organization, or UNPO. The UNPO, founded in The Hague in 1991, provides a voice for those peoples and nations that feel themselves not represented in established international forums, the United Nations in the first place. The members are quite varied: among them are Aboriginals of Australia, people of the Chittagong Hill Tracts (Bangladesh), but also Kurds (from Iraq, Turkey, and Iran), Nagas (India), the Mapuche in Chili, and the Ogoni in Nigeria. Thirty-six members represent a total number of people of about 130 million. The main aim of UNPO is to assist those peoples in conflict with the state to which they willy-nilly belong. Understandably, a basic principle of UNPO is the right of self-determination.

The UNPO Board assists identity movements in their conflicts with a state government. In March 1992, for instance, the Tatarstan government, having called for a referendum on the future of Tatarstan, asked the UNPO president to send a mission. In May 1992 UNPO's general secretary responded to a call from the Democratic League of Kosovo to witness the elections for a Kosovar president and parliament, a step taken in contravention to orders given by Serbian authorities. It was widely felt in Kosovo that the presence of international observers and press reporters prevented the Serbian forces from using force to stop the elections (Summary of the Unrepresented Nations and Peoples Organization 1991).

Four of the founding members of UNPO have meanwhile achieved independence and are now members of the United Nations (Armenia, Estonia, Georgia, and Lithuania). But many more members are striving for independence, and some of them are fighting for it (people in Chechnia, East Timor, Kurdistan, and West Papua).

To summarize: the UNPO stands for the phenomenon that cultural minorities use a transnational, even global, regime of their own making to resist a state felt as repressive in order to survive as a localized, culturally distinct group.

A DIALECTICAL RELATIONSHIP?

Let me conclude, first of all, by putting my argument in one single statement: The rise of transnational regimes, uncontrollable by state governments as well as by substate minorities, and the awareness of their plight, makes the latter resort to their own resources; by doing so they turn in their struggle against the state to idiosyncratic cultural characteristics on the one hand, and to universalistic transnational regimes on the other.

There is a beautiful example that sums up in a nutshell the intricate relationship that nowadays exists between the state, transnational regimes, and substate minorities. In the United Kingdom, the Scottish National Party struggles for an independent Scotland. It is well known that the union between England and Scotland that forms the United Kingdom was meant to be a union of equals. The Scots feel that it has turned out otherwise: they feel that the government in London places the interests of England before Scottish interests. Nowadays, however, many decisions are no longer taken in London but in Brussels, by the European Committee. Yet there too the Scots feel ill represented by Whitehall. To be properly represented, the Scots regard a seat of their own in the European Committee as a necessity—they therefore want political autonomy, up to independence.[3] This example neatly shows the dialectics of the relationship between globalization and localization: the existence of a transnational regime (the European Commission) and the failure of the London government to satisfy the Scots strengthens the Scottish efforts to reach more autonomy. Yet, aiming at full membership, the Scots will strengthen the transnational regime that is responsible for their organized protest against the state. They will also participate in that transnational regime and be part of it: they become transnational in order to keep their localized specificity.

This means that the twin process of globalization and localization has a double face: the rise of transnational regimes and the rise of local identities go hand-in-hand. In order to survive in a big world, people have to make use of globally valid cultural standards, that is, of transnational regimes. In that sense they will share in an emerging global culture. Yet because the majority of people will, also in the foreseeable future, live in numerically restricted networks of people, they are likely to derive their identity from living together with them, which will unavoidably bring along the formation of cultural specificity. If challenged they will strengthen their identity and make use of transnational regimes to fight an oppressive state. The resulting formations are not necessarily local in the geographic sense of the term. In the end the opposition is not so much between geographic categories like global and local, but between universally valid culture and specific, socially restricted, cultures. People are more and more living in two worlds. As a consequence they will not only be bilingual but also bi-cultural.

NOTES

A first draft of this chapter was presented in the form of a discussion paper at the international workshop "Global Culture and Local Identities," held at the Department of Cultural Anthropology/Sociology of Development, Vrije Universiteit, Amsterdam, 7 June 1996. I am indebted to the participants for their comments.

1. "Regime" sometimes has a negative connotation. Needless to say this is not the way I use the term.

2. Without elaborating the point I wish to point out that global environmental problems like air pollution too have contributed to the awareness that the world in its totality is the real unit we have to deal with.

3. The establishment of a Scottish Parliament, accepted by referendum in autumn 1997, may well take the wind out of the sails of the Scottish nationalist move-

ment, even though the relations with the European Community will remain the responsibility of the UK government.

REFERENCES

Anonymous. (1995). *Funding Terror: The Liberation Tigers of Tamil Eelam and Their Criminal Activities in Canada and the Western World.* Toronto: Mackenzie Briefing Notes.

Badie, Bertrand. (1992). *L'état importée: L'occidentalisation de l'ordre politique.* Paris: Fayard.

Barnet, Richard J., and John Cavanagh. (1994). *Global Dreams: Imperial Corporations and the New World Order.* New York: Simon and Schuster.

Connor, Walker. (1973). The Politics of Ethnonationalism. *Journal of International Affairs* 27, no. 1: 1–21.

Davidson, Basil. (1992). *The Black Man's Burden—Africa and the Curse of the Nation State.* Somerset: North Wootton.

Eriksen, Thomas H. (1993). *Ethnicity & Nationalism: Anthropological Perspectives.* London: Pluto Press.

Featherstone, Mike, ed. (1990). *Global Culture: Nationalism, Globalization and Modernity.* London: Sage.

———, S. Lash, and R. Robertson, eds. (1995). *Global Modernities.* London: Sage.

Geana, Georghita. (1997). Ethnicity and Globalisation. Outline of a Complementarist Conceptualisation. *Social Anthropology* 5, no. 2: 197–210.

Gerth, H.H., and C. Wright Mills, eds. (1958). *From Max Weber: Essays in Sociology.* New York: Oxford University Press.

Giddens, Anthony. (1991). *Sociology.* Cambridge: Polity Press [1989].

Goudsblom, Johan. (1995). De worm en de klok. Over de wording van een mondiaal tijdregime. In Johan Heilbron and Nico Wilterdink, eds. *Mondialisering: De wording van de wereldsamenleving.* Groningen: Amsterdams Sociologisch Tijdschrift/Wolters-Noordhoff: 142–61.

Heilbron, Johan, and Nico Wilterdink, eds. (1995). *Mondialisering: De wording van de wereldsamenleving.* Groningen: Amsterdams Sociologisch Tijdschrift/Wolters-Noordhoff.

Hobsbawm, Eric, and Terence Ranger, eds. (1983). *The Invention of Tradition.* Cambridge: Cambridge University Press.

Hurault, Jean-Marcel. (1972). *Français et Indiens en Guyane, 1604–1972.* Paris: Union Générale D'Éditions.

Jongman, Albert J., and Alex P. Schmid. (1994). Contemporary Armed Conflicts: A Global Inventory. *Pioom Newsletter* 6, no. 1: 17–21.

Junne, Gerd. (1992). Beyond Regime Theory. *Acta Politica* 27, no. 1: 9–28.

Kloos, Peter. (1971). *The Maroni River Caribs of Surinam.* Assen: Van Gorcum.

———. (1993). Globalization and Localized Violence. *Folk* 35: 5–16.

———. (1995). Publish and Perish: Nationalism and Social Research in Sri Lanka. *Social Anthropology* 3, no. 2: 115–28.

————. (1997a). Secessionism in Europe in the Second Half of the Twentieth Century. In N.A. Tahir, ed. *Ethnicity and Nationalism in Europe and South Asia*. Karachi: Area Study Centre for Europe (in press).

————. (1997b). A Secessionist Movement in an Age of Globalization: The Liberation Tigers of Tamil Eelam of Sri Lanka. In Nancy Jetly, ed. *Ethno-Sectarian Conflicts and International Dynamics of Regional Security in South Asia*. New Delhi (in press).

————. (1997c). The Struggle between the Lion and the Tiger. In Cora Govers and Hans Vermeulen, eds. *The Politics of Ethnic Consciousness*. London: Macmillan: 223–49.

————, and Purnaka L. de Silva. (1995). *Globalization, Localization, and Violence: An Annotated Bibliography*. Amsterdam: VU University Press.

Krasner, S.D., ed. (1982). *International Regimes*. Ithaca, NY: Cornell University Press.

McLuhan, Marshall, ed. (1960). *Explorations in Communication*. Boston: Beacon Press.

Naisbitt, John. (1994). *Global Paradox*. New York: Avon Books.

Østergard, Uffe. (1992). Peasants and Danes: The Danish National Identity and Political Culture. *Comparative Studies in Society and History* 34, no. 1: 3–27.

Philips, Kevin, (1994). *Arrogant Capital: Washington, Wall Street, and the Frustration of America*. New York: Little, Brown & Co.

Porter, Bruce D. (1994). *War and the Rise of the State*. New York: Free Press.

Ratner, Steven R. (1995). *The New UN Peacekeeping*. New York: St. Martin's.

Robertson, Roland. (1994). Globalisation or Glocalisation? *The Journal of International Communication* 1, no. 1: 23–52.

————. (1995). Glocalization: Time-Space and Homogeneity-Heterogeneity. In Mike Featherstone, S. Lash, and R. Robertson, eds. (1995). *Global Modernities*. London: Sage: 25–44.

Romanucci-Ross, Lola, and George DeVos, eds. (1995). *Ethnic Identity. Creation, Conflict, and Accommodation*. London: Altamira Press.

Rosenau, James N. (1994). New Dimensions of Security: The Interaction of Globalizing and Localizing Dynamics. *Security Dialogue* 25, no. 3: 255–81.

Senaratne, Jagath. (1997). *Political Violence in Sri Lanka, 1977–1990*. Sri Lanka Studies No. 4. Amsterdam: VU University Press.

Spencer, Jonathan. (1990). *Sri Lanka. History and the Roots of Conflict*. London: Routledge.

Tilly, Charles. (1992). *Coercion, Capital, and European States AD 900–1992*. Cambridge: Blackwell.

Vink, Caroline. (1993). Be Forever Cornish: The Emergence of an Ethnoregional Movement in the Twentieth Century. Unpublished M.A. thesis, University of Amsterdam.

Went, Robert. (1996). *Grenzen aan de globalisering*. Amsterdam: Het Spinhuis.

Wilson, A. Jeyaratnam. (1988). *The Break-up of Sri Lanka: The Sinhalese–Tamil Conflict*. London: C. Hurst & Company.

18

Eating Globally: Cultural Flows and the Spread of Ethnic Restaurants

Alan Warde

I live in a small, unglamorous, provincial town in northern England, yet, according to my local telephone directory I can, by traveling less than one mile, visit restaurants specializing in French, Thai, Mexican, Indian, Italian, Cajun, and Chinese cuisine. Within five miles I also have specialist African and Spanish restaurants. In addition there are take-away and home delivery services of various types. It is probable that, thirty years ago, almost none of these options would be available to me. The difference that this makes is uncertain, but it is surely one field to examine in order to explore the process of globalization, which has introduced very rapidly a vast accumulated body of international culinary knowledge and experience, not to mention some migrants and their small enterprises, to an obscure and parochial locality. The social and symbolic significance of the spread of "ethnic" foods across the advanced industrial societies is one with the potential to clarify many issues associated with economic and cultural processes of globalization.

Globalization is a vague, if not vacuous, term, probably at its least specific with respect to cultural processes; it appears to have more purchase on economic organization and on the political processes of the hollowing out of the nation-state than on culture per se. The most promising attempts to elucidate globalization rely on breaking it down into component parts that are amenable to more precise description. This was one of the achievements of Appadurai's (1990) schematic discussion of different kinds of cultural "flows" in a global world. As a working definition we might do worse than follow his recommendation that "The new global cultural economy has to be understood as a complex, overlapping, disjunctive order" (Appadurai 1990: 296), which can be decomposed into several dimensions of global cultural flow. Thus, paraphrasing Appadurai, I will take globalization to mean that more social entities (people, money, messages, ideas, and commands) are moving more frequently, farther and faster than before, with consequences for networks of interaction and social relations in different places across the world.

Much of the discussion about cultural effects of globalization has centered on the extent to which increased cultural communication tends to produce a homogeneous global culture. The perils of the diffusion of American culture throughout the world, and its potentially destructive effect on the local cultures of the periphery, remains a major concern, though few scholars currently envisage the imminent entrenchment of a homogeneous global culture. This fear has been allayed to some degree by discovery of what is often called the global–local dialectic (see Lash and Urry 1994). One aspect of this is the emergence of conscious attempts to protect, preserve, and sometimes invent locally distinctive traditions. Another is the process that Appadurai (1990) calls indigenization, whereby differently situated audiences interpret and adapt the messages transmitted by the global communication system in different ways, thus incorporating new items into an existing pattern of practice that sustains cultural diversity.

It is fairly safe to say that a better understanding of these processes and their consequences requires many more detailed studies of particular cultural forms. This chapter concerns some preliminary observations about the transnational commercial transmission of culinary knowledge and experience. What is clear is that the popularization of alien cuisines depends upon increased, but decidedly complex, flows of certain kinds of goods, people, and ideas. My focus is the provision and reception of "ethnic" cuisines into Western societies, specifically England, where I have recently completed some empirical research on the topic. *Prima facie* this is a very complex process whereby cultural items are drawn from different regional cultures, some very peripheral in contemporary world terms, into Western societies. I consider some of the processes and some of the possible cultural meanings associated with consumer appropriation of nonlocal cuisine. The empirical research concerns customers' access to restaurants specializing in ethnic cuisine, exploring the extent to which different social groups take advantage of the options available, wherein I can identify inequalities that might be inferred to have symbolic and cultural significance.

THE SPREAD OF THE "ETHNIC" RESTAURANT

The commercial restaurant is an invention of the later nineteenth century, and the self-conscious and explicit business of specializing in a particular nonnative cuisine is yet more recent. Zelinsky (1985), in one of the very few detailed studies of the spread of ethnic restaurants, estimated that the city of Philadelphia had had twenty-three establishments purveying ethnic or regional cuisines in 1920, but 253 by 1980. His survey of the telephone directories of the 271 major metropolitan areas of the United States and Canada around 1980 identified 26,527 restaurants specializing in 270 different ethnic cuisines. Metropolitan North America sported 8,000 Chinese restaurants, in eighteen different regional variants; more than 5,500 Italian; and just under 5,000 Mexican eateries. But there were also isolated Yemeni, Nicaraguan, Lithuanian, Nepalese, Burmese, and Scottish restaurants. He demonstrated that there were regional concentrations within the United States of the more popular ethnic cuisines, but rather than their being systematically a function of the spatial concentration of migrant communities they were more a consequence of the "cultural–cum–socioeconomic character" of the area of reception. Zelinsky described the process as the transnationalization of the North American diet, though he had little to say about the social and economic preconditions for the spread of ethnic cuisine. For my purpose, Zelinsky's study indicates one way in which cultural items flow not only out of America to less powerful peripheral countries but also back from the periphery.

There is no adequate historical source on the growth of restaurants serving foreign cuisine in the United Kingdom. Perhaps the most enlightening British account is given by Driver, who maintains that in the early 1950s, "outside London, the concept of an entire restaurant devoted to a non–European, or even a European, 'ethnic' style was almost wholly unfamiliar" (Driver 1983: 74). Before then there had been longstanding admiration of French cuisine; ever since the Napoleonic Wars the British elites had enjoyed the services of French chefs and the most prestigious British restaurants offered French dishes, and often complete menus written in French. There is also some evidence of Italian provision at the beginning of the twentieth century, though mostly in cafes and through the ice cream parlor. There were also some Chinese cafes in docklands areas, in Cardiff and Liverpool as well as London, and some Jewish outlets in North London. But otherwise, catering outlets, and much more so domestic provision, was overwhelmingly British. However, a recent estimate, by Payne and Payne (1993), was that there were, in 1990, about 8,000 ethnic restaurants (the most popular being Chinese, Indian, and Italian) and rather more than 5,000 take-aways selling ethnic foods.

Driver emphasizes the rapid expansion of the restaurants offering Chinese, Indian, and Middle Eastern cuisine in the period between the mid-1950s and the mid-1970s. He attributes their expansion to patterns of immigration, the specific mixture of entrepreneurial ambition among migrant communities, and the capacity of particular cuisines to be adapted to English tastes. In-migration of Hong Kong Chinese, Bangladeshis, and Cypriots was the main source of personnel for the introduction of the new cuisines that became popular by the 1970s. Thus he explicitly rejects the idea that the spread of ethnic restaurants was a result of consumer demand, inspired for example by foreign vacations, and was instead a consequence of patterns of migration of entrepreneurs. All the available evidence suggests that restaurants and take-away shops specializing in ethnic cuisine are small, often family, businesses that provide an often precarious livelihood for often highly qualified members of ethnic minority communities. In the United Kingdom it was primarily the flow of people, with their embodied culinary knowledge, that accounted for the growth of this trade.

This section of the market continues to operate as small businesses, with very little attempt to create chains or systems of franchising. Other sections of the restaurant business, however, are dominated by industrialized systems of provision, with pizza and burger chains most prominent, roadside services and pub restaurants also being significant. The chains are essentially postwar developments, their industrial "Fordist" logic having been introduced by, or copied from, American corporations like McDonald's. While the fast-food burger outlets are not in everyday language described as ethnic, they are nevertheless evidence of the uneven transnationalization of the catering industry. The UK population is the recipient of the very different outputs of both gigantic industrial organizations and the small businesses of ethnic minority entrepreneurs, and indeed have in important degree accepted both equally.

The picture is rendered even more complex—and this is somewhat ironic—by the way in which these two different sources of innovation have been accommodated by the indigenous operators in the catering trades. One of the most striking features of contemporary commercial menus in all types of venue is precisely the impact of foreign dishes. Formerly exotic ethnic dishes now appear in the most ordinary of eating places alongside more traditional staple items; pubs and cafes will very often offer dishes like lasagna, curried meats, and stir-frys alongside roast beef and vegetables or steak and kidney pie.

Some previously strange dishes have been thoroughly domesticated as a part of a more general process of the "routinization of the exotic" (see Warde 1997). Knowledge of foreign food has been cultivated through various commercial channels, there being extensive publishing and broadcasting on such topics since at least the late 1960s when there was strong encouragement, particularly from women's magazines, to experiment with foreign foods. Acceptability has been enhanced by more extensive use in the domestic kitchen of recipes from far afield and, yet more recently, through the medium of supermarket ready-prepared meals.

The complexity of the overall effect can be examined by considering the diversity of processes associated with the gradually spreading awareness of foreign cuisines. Many more foreign cuisine restaurants are now recognized by arbiters of culinary taste like the *Good Food Guide*, an annual publication of the independent Consumers Association, which identifies approximately 1,000 restaurants in the British Isles as offering the highest standards of food. The 1997 edition lists some 129 restaurants in London serving specialized foreign cuisine and a smaller number in other provincial cities. Twenty-five years ago the situation was significantly different: Driver (1983) noted that throughout the period since the Second World War there had been few restaurants specializing in ethnic cuisine with an entry, the overwhelming majority being in London. Hence a new niche for producers has emerged as greater authenticity became valued by customers encouraging businesses to advertise themselves as specialists in the regional cuisines of China, Italy, or France. The virtues of different cuisines from around the world have come to be appreciated. But what is perhaps even more significant is the way in which the vast majority of the restaurants mentioned in such guides now serve dishes that are defined and inspired by other culinary traditions. The most innovative of British chefs, who are increasingly also becoming media stars, offer dishes and menus that draw heavily on global cuisines. For example, skimming a prizewinning fish cookery book accompanying a television series by restaurateur and chef Rick Stein (1995) reveals dishes like "white-cooked ling with spring onions, chili and Szechwan pepper," "char-grilled John Dory with coriander, saffron and kumquats," and "tandooried monkfish with tomato and coriander salad." Menus have increasingly become monuments to cultural hybridity. As a previous piece of research showed (Warde 1997: 60), recipes for foreign dishes published in women's magazines and intended for domestic use, which in the late 1960s had been almost exclusively of European derivation, had become global by 1992 with nearly half drawn from non-European cuisines.

THE RECEPTION OF FOREIGN FOOD

Interpreting the meaning of the spread of the ethnic restaurant is not easy. This is partly because the very concept itself, though used fluently and confidently enough in ordinary everyday speech, is difficult. In a country like England where there has been centuries of importing of foodstuffs, purity or authenticity of either native or alien cuisines is hard to identify. Dishes from apparently foreign cuisines, even ones with foreign language descriptions, are likely to have been modified, if not transformed out of all recognition, for local consumption. It is doubtful whether British pizzas would be accepted in Italy, or that the range of dishes sold as curries would be recognized in India. Nevertheless foreign food and its provision is increasingly a topic worthy of popular discussion. The arrival of McDonald's in new locations, recently the cities of Eastern Europe, is an event much commented upon, apparently as a symbol of modernity and the accessibility of consumer culture (my daily newspaper found it worthwhile to report that McDonalds has 21,000 branches in 101 countries; *Guardian*, 26 June 1997). Whether this means the same as the arrival of Thai cuisine in the United Kingdom is uncertain, but neither event can be dismissed as culturally meaningless. Of course such innovations are not always welcome. The expansion of fast food caused something of a moral panic in France, where images of alien invasion threatening a valued national food culture provoked defensive action by government (see Fantasia 1995). On a lesser scale, regional and national tourist boards are keen to preserve, recover, or even invent dishes that represent local tradition and thereby give visitors a sense of place otherwise diluted by global miscegeny (see Hughes 1995). The imagined generic origin of dishes is almost certainly meaningful in some ways to most people, but we know little systematically about such meanings or their distribution.

THE USE OF ETHNIC RESTAURANTS

The substantial number of commercial outlets for the sale of foreign foods implies that there is considerable demand for ethnic cuisines. It does not, however, establish who are the customers of such places. Zelinsky (1985: 69) concluded his article bemoaning lack of knowledge about the mobility careers of ethnic cuisines and their geographical dispersion across the United States by commenting that

> As productive a [research] strategy as any would be the study of the sociology and social geography of the patrons of restaurants featuring ethnic items. Who are they in terms of age, class, education, occupation, religion, ethnicity, places of origin and residence, and search and travel behavior with respect to dining out?

In fact, different cuisines, or more precisely restaurants believed to specialize in different culinary traditions, do attract different sorts of customers. This is demonstrated by the findings of my recent research project, which offers a provisional answer to that question with respect to England. On the basis primarily of a survey of 1,001 people in three cities in England—London, Bristol, and Preston—in April 1995, it was possible to estimate the social characteristics of those familiar with ethnic restaurants.

There is no space here either to describe the nature of the study or to demonstrate the basis for the generalizations derived it; details can be found elsewhere (see Warde and Martens, forthcoming). One element of the study was to give respondents a list of types of eating out places, which included Italian, Chinese/Thai, American, Indian, and other ethnic (in practice mainly French, Greek, and Turkish) restaurants, and ask whether they had eaten a main meal in such a place during the last twelve months. This can be interpreted as a measure of familiarity with the variety of ethnic cuisine. Twenty percent of those surveyed had experience of three or more different cuisines, while 48 percent had none at all.

Many social factors were shown to be associated with the propensity to eat in ethnic restaurants. Table 18.1 reports crosstabulations between the sociodemographic characteristics of respondents to our survey and whether they had visited in the last twelve months any of five different types of restaurants specializing in ethnic cuisine. Some of these factors are the same ones associated with frequency of eating out. Living in a household containing two adults in full-time employment, living alone or in a student household, being single and being young increase the likelihood of eating out regularly, which would, all other things being equal, make it more probable that any individual would visit ethnic restaurants. However, other things are not equal. Some factors are particularly strongly associated with the extension of the experience of eating in specialized ethnic restaurants. There is more pronounced involvement by those with higher income, those living in London, the better educated, and higher so-

Table 18.1   Respondents Eating a Main Meal in Particular Types of Ethnic Restaurants during the Last Twelve Months and Their Social Characteristics

	Indian	*Chinese*	*Italian*	*American*	*Other*
Respondents Visiting (%)	32.9	29.2	31.0	11.7	21.3
Frequency of Eating Out	.51***	.58***	.54***	.53***	.53***
Respondent's Income	.42***	.50***	.47***	.39***	.53***
Household Income	.41***	.46***	.44***	.34***	.59***
Father's Social Class	.32***	.38***	.35***	.29***	.47***
City of Residence	.42***	.49***	.33***	.39***	.58***
Gender	.09	−.11	—	—	—
Age	−.23***	−.14**	−.17***	−.41***	.11**
Household Type	.10*	.14**	.13**	.31***	.12*
Children under 16	−.12	−.19**	−.20**	.39***	.16*
Employment Status	.19***	.17**	.26***	.17**	.26***
Educational Qualifications	.50***	.50***	.51***	.47***	.63***
Secondary School	.23***	.35***	.28***	.33***	.42***
Retired	−.52***	−.40**	−.44***	−.59***	−.59**
Social Class	.20***	.26***	.28***	.27***	.35***

Note: Measure of association, gamma; significance z (***≤.001; **≤.01; *≤.05)

cial classes than is the case with other forms of eating out. Conversely, being poor, provincial, unqualified, and working class entails low levels of experience of ethnic restaurants. This gives ground for some speculation about the meanings attached to eating foreign food.

THE SOCIAL MEANING OF ETHNIC CUISINE

In exploring the social meanings of the spread of foreign cuisine for the English customer an appropriate context is the general trend in all consumer cultures toward the rapid expansion of variety in all things, for the range of items made available routinely on a commercial basis across the world is now prodigious. Some have argued that this is a function of the shift to a post-Fordist society, where there is a fortunate equilibrium between supply and demand: the capacity to manufacture not only a more varied range of goods but also more variations of those goods coincides with the emergence of highly specialized consumer tastes, such that individuals are increasingly able to satisfy their needs and express their identity through the use and display of differentiated products. Other commentators are skeptical about whether the proliferation of products amounts to a real increase in options and choices. They maintain that many of the differences between products are trivial; that rather than being a conscious process of self-expression consumers are guided in ways similar to those of the period of mass consumption; that what is on offer is still that which it suits the producers to manufacture rather than a sign of consumer sovereignty; and that the overall effect is not one of stylized group differentiation but more undistinguished difference resulting from the way in which people put together almost arbitrarily a mix of products. The current situation can be interpreted in three different ways, in terms of the respective roles of orientations toward omnivorousness, cosmopolitanism, and distinction.

Omnivorousness

North American sociologists of culture have recently detected a condition that they call cultural omnivorousness (Peterson and Simkus 1992; Peterson and Kern 1996; Erickson 1996). Applied to many different fields, the process is one where respondents claim to recognize, or to like, an increasingly large number of cultural genres. For example, Peterson and Kern (1996) show that all groups in the population professed to a knowledge of a greater range of types of music in 1993 than in 1983, with those with more highbrow tastes having extended their repertoires most markedly. They interpret the process as a shift away from snobbish claims to exclusivity on the basis of an appreciation of high culture. However, they fail adequately to establish the meaning of omnivorousness, a task to which their data are not amenable. Appreciation of increased varieties of cultural forms may signify the incipient universalization of a mode of experimentation and adventure. Baudrillard (1988) commented on the contemporary attractions of novelty, on the "obligation to try everything." People talk about liking things "for a change." Social psychological accounts of consumption detect a universal human liking for the "stimulation" of new experience (e.g., Scitowsky 1976; Cziksentmihalyi 1992). One possible conclusion might be that the attractions of experiencing novel ethnic cuisine, which processes of global economic development in the catering trades have made possible, are associated with novelty and variety for its own sake. Adventures with foreign cuisine might then be seen as a strategy to stave off a kind of personal boredom, which consumer culture is particularly prone to encourage.

Cosmopolitanism

An alternative set of meanings might be ascribed to the reception of foreign foods, marking them instead in terms of the appreciation of cultural difference. Connections between food, xenophobia, and cosmopolitanism have been detected. As Fischler (1993) has pointed out, people refer, usually in derogatory fashion, to other nationalities in terms of distinctive items in their culinary heritage: the French are frogs, the British rotbifs. Many a racist discussion has involved expressions of disgust at cooking smells and their apparent embodiment, whether of garlic, curry, or cabbage. The deep origins of such attitudes lie in the belief that cuisines of origin are particularly important emotional and symbolic markers. People are said to be particularly resistant to giving up the food tastes of their childhood. Migrants are usually slower to discard their food habits than many other aspects of their cultural life. Food is a potent source of group and national identity.

To that extent, sharing and appreciation across social group boundaries of ethnic cuisine, made possible by the rapid evolution of ethnic restaurants in the postwar world, might have a countereffect of promoting multiculturalism. Certainly it has been taken as a key indicator of multiculturalism celebrated by Australian authors (e.g., Symons 1993; though he cites Castles et al., 1988, for the view that such symbols are trivial and superficial). Van der Berghe (1984) concurs in offering an evolutionary account of the links between food and ethnicity based on the observation that human beings share food.

> This applies, in the first instance, to our immediate kin, as nearly all of us have been nurtured in small family groups. But it also applies to ethnicity, for

ethnicity is kinship writ large. Like ethnicity itself, ethnic cuisine only becomes a self-conscious, subjective reality when ethnic boundaries are crossed.
(van der Berghe 1984: 395)

In other words, "the consciousness that one has an ethnic cuisine can only
come from alien contact" (van der Berghe 1984: 395). In modern urban
settings awareness of ethnic cuisine, and hence of ethnic identity, is commonplace. But unlike some expressions of ethnicity, that associated with
food is potentially constructive. As van der Berghe puts it (1984: 396),

> ethnic cuisine represents ethnicity at its best, because at its most sharable. It
> does not take much effort to learn to like foods, even exotic ones. Ethnic cui-
> sine is the easiest and most pleasant way to cross ethnic boundaries. As eating
> together is perhaps the most basic expression of human sociality, ethnic cui-
> sine could well be the ultimate reconciliation between a diversity we cherish
> and a common humanity we must recognize if we are to live amicably to-
> gether.

Van der Berghe may be somewhat optimistic in postulating that learning
to share a taste for the cuisine of other ethnic groups is an effective source
of social harmony and interethnic cooperation, but it may encourage
greater tolerance of cultural difference. This function is one that the American literature on omnivorousness considers, with Peterson and Kern
(1996) and Bryson (1996), keen to stress the potential of the diffusion of
musical taste for increasing tolerance. The positive associations and negative connotations of ethnic foodstuffs, and the aversions and involvements
of different social groups in eating foreign foods, may be socially significant in such a fashion.

Distinction

Sociologists have repeatedly commented on the way that social status
is registered by means of consumption. Bourdieu (e.g., 1984), the most
influential modern sociologist of consumption, for instance argues that
styles of consumption are means of acquiring new forms of economic and
social "capital," because display of goods is part of a system of reputation,
wherein judgments about suitability, expressed as definitions of good
taste, result in members of different social classes systematically picking
some items in preference to others. Some tastes are more prestigious than
others. Bourdieu presumes that cultural and social hierarchies coincide.
Thus food tastes position people in social locations that reflect the social
hierarchy. However, it is difficult to establish empirically whether there is
a commonly acknowledged hierarchy of taste, for plurality of practices
need not necessarily imply a relationship of superiority and inferiority. It

is not entirely satisfactory to conclude that merely because privileged persons engage in particular cultural practices exclusive to them that other groups recognize any special cultural merit in those practices, even while participation is a marker of social privilege. There is, of course, a reasonable sociological presumption that this is likely to be the case.

One problem in making that presumption today with respect to ethnic cuisine is that both omnivorousness and cosmopolitanism might themselves be marks of social distinction. It is possible that having wide knowledge is itself the current way to express high social position, exert social closure, and operate effective cultural exclusion of others who lack this form of cultural capital. Omnivorousness might be an emblem of distinction in its own right. Alternatively, it might be specifically the appreciation of the exotic and culturally unfamiliar that is symbolically significant; Bourdieu (1984) hints that in France a taste for the exotic is a mark of a new petite bourgeoisie challenging the hegemony of bourgeois taste. But in both cases, the social function of a taste for ethnic cuisine could be equivalent to a claim to social rank and thus a means of expressing inequalities of power through consumption behavior.

Dominant Meanings?

It is not possible a priori, nor on the basis of existing evidence, to determine which of these three alternative meanings of the contemporary obsession with variety in food is most valid or most widely held among Western populaces. However, attention to the social differentiation of the use of ethnic restaurants gives some preliminary clues. We cannot be sure whether customers of ethnic restaurants value variety for its own sake, whether they see familiarity with foreign cuisine as a statement of cosmopolitan tolerance, or whether they believe that social prestige derives from acquaintance with multiple foreign cuisines. The motives of the population remain elusive. Nevertheless, it is clear that a significant proportion of the populations of three big English cities are not availing themselves of substantial parts of the full range of available culinary experience. Not everyone is in eager pursuit of variety. If learned acceptability of ethnic food, or its frequent consumption, is an indicator of multiculturalism, then its extent is still limited, suggesting continued and widespread conservatism in taste among sections of the English population. There is a sufficiently high level of abstention from foreign foods and, as the survey also showed, an enduring popularity of the English public house, especially in the provinces, to suggest that the ecumenical effects of learning exotic tastes, anticipated by van der Berghe (1984), are still far from thoroughly diffused among the British population. Indeed, given that some ethnic foods are both cheap and easily accessible, many seem resistant to such variety. It would thus be dangerous to generalize too far about changing popular taste on the basis of the distinctive consumer behavior of the educated, metropolitan, salaried middle classes. If any style of eating out is associated with cultural and social distinction it is the use of a wide range of foreign restaurants.

DISCUSSION

Globalization and Cultural Flows

The United Kingdom now offers ample opportunities for consuming the products of foreign culinary traditions. Schematically, it seems likely that the process was one whereby particular and specific local culinary practices, which were specialized regionally even within nation-states until the mid-twentieth century, have been systematized, publicized, documented, transformed, and adapted to suit a diverse capitalist industrial sector supplying catering services. It is interesting to ask what it is that is involved in this import–export trade of such grand proportions. What, in Appadurai's terms, is flowing?

The answer is primarily knowledge. Interestingly, the spread of knowledge has not remained exclusively specialist, a property of migrant chefs who cook in the style of their place of origin, but has fed into most other areas of food and eating. Those cookery books intended for domestic use that offer recipes from particular foreign cuisines are among the most popular. The supermarket chains sell an immense range of both fresh and partially prepared ingredients, for instance bottled sauces, which render it possible to try out most recipes in a Chinese or Italian cookery book. They also offer completely prepared dishes and meals that have been prepared in accordance with the rules of many of the world's regional culinary traditions. The most celebrated British personality chefs are very likely to be versed in the techniques, flavors, and composition of several ethnic cuisines, adapting them to create inventive dishes which may, or may not in their descriptions, specifically identify their foreign culinary origin. Indeed, having worked in other parts of the globe is increasingly an aspect of the apprenticeship of contemporary British chefs. But equally the mundane pubs and cafes of Britain are now likely to include, on their short menus of the day, items deriving from several different cuisines. Whether the lasagna offered by the local public house is homemade or purchased frozen from catering suppliers, there is a growing familiarity with the essentials of many cuisines.

There has also been some movement of skilled personnel, though often it would appear that the proprietor of the small ethnic restaurant is not formally trained but learns the trade after arrival in the country of destination. It appears that most chefs in French restaurants in Britain are not themselves French and that the Greek and Turkish outlets are primarily managed by Iranians (Harbottle 1997). By contrast, Chinese, Indian/Pakistani, and Italian restaurants are owned and staffed by migrant families (Hardyment 1995). The material circumstances of small enterprises in the ethnic food markets are often precarious, relying on long hours and the exploitation of family labor. Such people are often comparatively disadvantaged in many ways, and often suffer social exclusion. They nonetheless provide a means for the transmission of culinary knowledge and also the monitoring of the authenticity of imported cuisines.

The other modality of accelerated movement on the global plane is commodification. To a much greater extent than before unfamiliar raw ingredients are being imported in substantial quantities to supply restaurants, but also to stock supermarket shelves for those who wish to incorporate ethnic cuisine into their domestic provisioning. Britain has always imported a vast range of exotic products, but most consumption was by a small, primarily metropolitan, elite. Larger quantities entail some degree of popularization and democratization of ethnic cuisine, a consequence of mass production and retailing techniques that enhance variety for many people. The same is true of the expansion of the habit of eating out, until long after the end of the Second World War restricted to a privileged minority, which is itself just another aspect of the extended commodification of food preparation. The commodity form is a basic and prior condition of accelerating global cultural flows. In the absence of a generalized system of economic exchange for profit, flows of knowledge would be much staunched, for a great deal of the relevant information is precisely sold—as cookery book, television programs, and the restaurant experience itself. Food enthusiasts notwithstanding, circulation of such information is rarely in pursuit of knowledge for its own sake. If there is anything truly global about cultural form it is probably, as Sklair (1991) maintains, the expansion of the ambit of a consumer culture.

However, the logic of commodification is not determinant of outcomes. First it does not in itself entail homogenization of cultural items. Indeed, the case of ethnic cuisine exemplifies countertendencies to the Westernization of the world (Latouche 1993) or its Americanization (Tenbruck 1990). This is precisely not a case of unidirectional export from the West. Yet while ethnic restaurants differentiate options for Britons eating out, it appears simultaneously true that the same ethnic cuisines are invading all the countries of the Western world, such that the range of alternatives is similar in London, Amsterdam, or Paris. We should not expect an end to the debate about whether homogenization or differentiation predominates for inevitably examples of both tendencies coexist. Second, commodification could not itself be the trigger for an explosion in the circulation of ethnic cuisine restaurants that occurred primarily during one quarter of the twentieth century. Other contingent social circumstances were necessary, including the generalization of the habit of eating out as a type of entertainment and long-distance migration to affluent societies at the point of their transition economies.

Toward a Model of Diffusion

A formal model to explain the diffusion of ethnic cuisine through commercial restaurants would require a degree of comparative research that is not yet available. However, the example of England indicates some of the parameters of the complex cultural disjunctures involved. In the sphere of food, there are four basic postures towards items of alien pedigree.

The first is to reject everything lacking the stamp of tradition. This is practically difficult in the United Kingdom because its long history of empire and free trade has seen the importation of a multitude of produce and flavorings that could be cultivated locally. Determining in a modern age what is and what is not part of any tradition is contentious, and this is certainly true in the field of British food. Nevertheless, there remains a marked reluctance among Britons to consume ducks' feet and horse meat, not to mention dogs and insects. By their aversions do we, in a world of immense variety, best uncover popular taste. However, it is not only by rejections, but also through positive revalorization that local tradition is preserved. At least one up-market section of the industry trades explicitly on its proficiency in preparing high quality "traditional" British dishes.

A second process is naturalization, the adaptation of recipes to render unfamiliar tastes familiar. The extent of this naturalization of dishes for the British palate is legendary. One unforgettable example from a women's magazine of 1968 was the suggestion that mussels and squid be omitted from paella because people generally did not like them. The menus of ethnic restaurants in Britain for years included many English dishes, presumably as a way of assuaging the anxiety of customers about eating strange foods. And while the level of adaptation for local taste required of Indian dishes has been much greater than that involved in the minor concessions that McDonalds reputedly makes by accommodating French tastes in mustard and British vegetarians, the process is the same. This form of indigenization, making something foreign or alien appear local, is perhaps especially prominent in the early stages of diffusion of a new cuisine and thereby tends initially to encourage homogenization. Taste and flavor principles are compromised. Differences are minimized.

Yet this is not the whole story. A third process involves restyling something local by adding foreign elements to it. British establishments have adapted local dishes through use of herbs, spices, and combinations of flavorings that have their origins in other culinary traditions. Thus other ethnic cuisines are deployed to enrich the local repertoire of dishes. Up-market British restaurants show considerable evidence of improvisation on the themes from foreign culinary traditions, thereby establishing a certain hybridity across cuisines that has become almost the norm for professional cooking. To take a random example from the *Good Food Guide* (1997: 311), an East Anglian establishment serves "potted venison with spiced black figs, grilled fillet of cod with anchovy butter, and roast fillet of beef with tarragon and orange hollandaise"—traditional local primary produce combine with innovative flavorings in the accompaniments.

A final alternative is to seek "authentic" replication of dishes from a foreign cuisine. Partly because the market for ethnic cuisine has grown and more people have become familiar with ethnic cuisines, a space for niche production has presented itself. It is profitable for some restaurateurs to pay more attention to the distinctiveness and authenticity of their menus. It is not only the gourmet and the food enthusiast who wishes to experience finer versions of the cuisines of the world. There is now also a considerable market for ingredients and techniques that symbolize the transfer of one cultural form to another place in its entirety.

These four processes, call them preservation, naturalization, improvisation, and authentication, emanate from and reproduce the disjunctive order of global cultural flows. Potentially they offer opportunities and rewards to organizations operating on both Fordist and post-Fordist principles. For the food industries in the United Kingdom comprise enterprises of all sizes, from giant and powerful mass manufacturers and mass retailers down to family-owned and operated businesses, together representing a complexly organized combination of mass and niche producers. Commercial provision generates a complex process of diffusion of foreign cuisine within the United Kingdom (and across Western industrial societies more generally). In some instances it encourages the global homogenization of products associated with the multinational corporations. But it also indicates a process of increasing appreciation of world cuisines and borrowing, by those acclaimed as the most creative and talented chefs of the age, from many, though not all, of the culinary traditions of the world. The catering industry appears to offer us copious examples of a truly disjunctive set of practices.

The food industries offer to ordinary consumers a range of options, historically unprecedented and remarkable in its apparent extent and variety. However, the fruits of the globalized menu have not diffused evenly. For reasons not only of geography, but also because of the unequal distribution of economic resources and cultural capital, the rate of diffusion is uneven.

For the poor, the uneducated, manual workers, and the elderly, the effects of this particular episode of culinary globalization are very limited.

Omnivorousness, Cosmopolitanism, and Distinction

Increased commercial variety makes the apprehension and dissection of inequality more difficult. It becomes hard to read the signs of social and aesthetic classification when there are too many cultural items on display. This is precisely the problem posed by the three general meaning principles said to encourage the eating of ethnic foods. These cannot be very precisely distinguished on the basis of existing evidence. However, on the basis of established sociological understandings of the relationship between social power and consumption behavior we should hesitate before accepting that the process of the assimilation of ethnic cuisine is necessarily, or entirely, benevolent. By and large, the spread of unfamiliar cuisine is welcomed as an addition or supplement to existing provision. But it may just be part of the normalized approval of variety, a consumer value increasingly promoted in the language of "choice" and the legitimacy of the market. It might alternatively be seen as a harmful process of cultural trespassing; whether every country or civilization welcomes the export and reconfiguration of its culinary heritage has not been established (see Harbottle 1997, which documents reluctance among Iranians to establish restaurants selling Iranian cuisine in the United Kingdom). Moreover, the taste for ethnic cuisine may be merely a new garb for traditional systems of distinction, a means of drawing social boundaries between those with and without cultural capital. But while this final suggestion probably has some truth, it occurs in a context of increasing difficulty in reading off social position from cultural preference. In Britain, social inequality has increased markedly in recent years, but without being easily visible through patterns of cultural consumption. One explanation might be that the proliferation of variety makes aesthetic judgment and the detection of a cultural hierarchy more difficult (see Warde, Martens, and Olsen 1997).

NOTE

I am grateful to the Economic and Social Research Council for funding this study, which was conducted in association with Dr Lydia Martens of the University of Stirling. It is part of the ESRC Research Programme "The Nation's Diet: The Social Science of Food Choice."

REFERENCES

Appadurai, A. (1990). Disjuncture and Difference in the Global Cultural Economy. *Theory Culture & Society* 7, no. 23: 295–310.

Baudrillard, Jean. (1988). *Selected Writings.* Cambridge: Polity.

Berghe, P. van der. (1984). Ethnic Cuisine: Culture in Nature. *Ethnic and Racial Studies* 7, no. 3: 387–97.

Bourdieu, P. (1984). *Distinction: A Social Critique of the Judgment of Taste.* London: Routledge & Kegan Paul.

Bryson, B. (1996). Anything but Heavy Metal: Symbolic Exclusion and Musical Dislikes. *American Sociological Review* 61: 844–99.

Castles, S., B. Cope, M. Kalantzis, and M. Morrissey (1988). *Mistaken Identity: Multiculturalism and the Demise of Nationalism in Australia.* Sydney: Pluto.

Cziksentmihalyi, M. (1992). *Flow: The Psychology of Happiness.* London: Rider.

Driver, C. (1983). *The British at Table, 1940–80.* London: Chatto & Windus.

Erikson, B.H. (1996). Culture, Class and Connections. *American Journal of Sociology* 102, no. 1 (1996): 217–51.

Fantasia, R. (1995). Fast Food in France. *Theory and Society* 24: 201–43.

Fischler, C. (1993). L'*(h)omnivore: Le gout, la cuisine et la corps.* Np: Editions Odile Jacob.

Hannerz, U. (1990). Cosmopolitans and Locals in World Culture. *Theory Culture & Society* 7, no. 2–3: 237–52.

Harbottle, L. (1997). Fast Food/Spoiled Identity: Iranian Migrants in the British Catering Trade. In P. Caplan, ed. *Food, Identity and Health.* London: Routledge: 87–110.

Hardyment, C. (1995). *Slice of Life: The British Way of Eating since 1945.* London: BBC Books.

Hughes, G. (1995). Authenticity in Tourism. *Annals of Tourism Research* 22: 781–803.

Lash, S., and J. Urry. (1994). *Economies of Signs and Space.* London: Sage.

Latouche, S. (1993). *The Westernisation of the World.* Cambridge: Polity.

Payne, M., and B. Payne. (1993). Eating Out in the UK: Market Structure, Consumer Attitudes and Prospects for the 1990s. Economist Intelligence Unit Special Report No 2169. London: Economist Intelligence Unit and Business International.

Peterson, R., and R. Kern. (1996). Changing Highbrow Taste: From Snob to Omnivore. *American Sociological Review* 61: 900–7.

Peterson, R.A. and A. Simkus. (1992). How Musical Tastes Mark Occupational Status Groups. In M. Lamont and M. Fournier, eds. *Cultivating Differences: Symbolic Boundaries and the Making of Inequality.* Chicago: University of Chicago Press: 152–86.

Pillsbury, R. (1990). *From Boarding House to Bistro: The American Restaurant Then and Now.* London: Unwin Hyman.

Scitowsky, T. (1976). *The Joyless Economy: An Inquiry into Human Satisfaction and Consumer Dissatisfaction.* Oxford: Oxford University Press.

Sklair, Leslie. (1991). *Sociology of the Global System.* London: Prentice Hall.

Stein, R. (1995). *Taste of the Sea.* London: BBC Books.

Symons, M. (1993). *The Shared Table: Ideas for Australian Cuisine.* Office of Multicultural Affairs. Canberra: Australian Government Publishing Service.

Tenbruck, F. (1990). The Dream of a Secular Ecumene: The Meaning and Limits of Policies of Development. *Theory Culture & Society* 7, no. 2–3: 193–206.

Warde, A. (1997). *Consumption, Food and Taste: Culinary Antinomies and Commodity Culture.* London: Sage.

———, and L. Martens. (forthcoming). *Eating Out and Eating In: A Sociological Analysis.* Cambridge: Cambridge University Press.

———, and W. Olsen. (1997). Consumption and the Problem of Variety: Cultural Omnivorousness, Social Distinction and Dining Out. Paper to European Sociological Association Conference, Essex University, August 1997.

Wood, R. (1994). Dining Out on Sociological Neglect. *British Food Journal* 96, no. 10: 10–14.

———. (1995). *The Sociology of the Meal.* Edinburgh: Edinburgh University Press.

Zelinsky, W. (1985). The Roving Palate: North America's Ethnic Restaurant Cuisines. *Geoforum* 16, no. 1: 51–72.

19

Technologies of Togetherness: Flows, Mobility, and the Nation-State

Orvar Löfgren

IN TRANSIT

"Every improvement in the means of locomotion—tends to remove national and provincial antipathies," wrote the English historian Macaulay a century ago (Macaulay 1889, I: 182). He was thinking of the railways, this new mode of transport that seemed to annihilate both time and space, as well as producing a new cosmopolitan culture. At that time the German General Staff was already busy forging the railway system into a military tool for a two-front European war.

New technologies, from the telegraph to the Internet, have always been surrounded by a rhetoric of dismantling barriers of communication and understanding. Novel forms of mobility and exchange will erase old boundaries and create new communities, transgress the local or the national. Much of this traditional rhetoric is still bombarding us today with an almost deafening effect, which calls for historical reflection. The debate on de-territorialization and globalization in a world in flux may make us overlook the forms in which old entities like the nation-state not only are disintegrating but also reintegrated in new forms and in new arenas.

This chapter focuses on the impact of different forms of mobility and communication systems on local, national, or transnational modes of social and cultural integration. Special emphasis is placed on the ways in which the nation-state is both imagined and materialized in the seemingly trivial details of everyday life and technological infrastructures: going for a drive, making a phone call, crossing a border. Finally, these experiences are related to the pedagogics of space, mobility, and belonging, as well as to the current debate on the crisis of the nation-state.

HITTING THE ROAD

Cars don't have a homeland. Like oil stocks or like classic love, they can easily cross borders. Italian Fiats clamber up the cliffs of Norway. Ever-worried specialists in Renault taxis jolt around the bumpy streets of Moscow. Ford is ubiquitous; he's in Australia; he's also in Japan. American Chevrolet trucks carry Sumatran tobacco and Palestine oranges. A Spanish banker owns a German Mercedes. 10-H.P. Citroëns in display windows in Piccadilly or Berlin cause dreamy passers-by to halt.

The automobile has come to show even the slowest minds that the earth is truly round, that the heart is just a poetic relic, that a human being contains two standard gauges: one indicates miles, the other minutes. This is Ilya Ehrenburg (1929: 129) in *The Life of the Automobile*, written in Paris. His fascinating book represents one of the first attempts to explore the globalization of a new technology. The narrative moves between striking auto workers in Paris to the coolie labor on rubber plantations in Malaysia, enters the boardrooms of Citroën and Ford, and explores the international speculations in oil stocks and the fight for new global markets.

For most Europeans in 1929, however, the car was not without a homeland; it was found across the ocean in America. America was, as Paul Morand put it that same year, "the world's fastest country." The utopia of a "car society" materialized much earlier in the United States than in Europe, where mass driving did not develop until the 1950s and 1960s (cf., Eyerman and Löfgren 1995).

The early making of a car society during the first decades of the twentieth century was very much related to ideas of individual freedom. The steam engine had collectivized travel; now the combustion engine would set it free. Going for a drive was an individual adventure—just hitting the road, exploring new settings. In this new rhetoric freedom and speed were also coupled together.

Speed and empowerment, however, did not only have to be a feeling of individual strength. We encounter it in the early national rhetoric of freeways in the 1920s and 1930s. In the United States these projects were surrounded by the same ideas as in the railway projects in the nineteenth century. The new road systems were supposed to be "teaching patriotism, sewing up the remaining rugged edges of sectionalism, revealing and interpreting America to its people," as one promoter of the Lincoln Highway put it in 1915 (quoted in Jakle 1985: 124). The making of a car society came to symbolize America's position, not only as the fastest but also the most modern nation in the world. The craze for auto-camping, which was to become an American mass movement, was also seen as something that would pull the nation together. In the new auto-camps Americans from different walks of life and different corners of the vast continent would meet and get to know each other. A new democracy of the campfire gathering was in the making.

In Mussolini's Italy and Hitler's Germany the autostradas and autobahns were demonstrations of the power of the new fascist era. Already in 1933 Hitler declared that if the national standard of living hitherto had been measured in railway miles, it would be the length of the freeways that in the future would demonstrate the level of progress. Hitler's ambitions had limited military or economic importance; Die Reichsautobahn was above all a symbolic manifestation of Nazi aesthetics and power. It was a symbiosis between a cult of technology and landscape romantics, but above all an aggressive cult of speed and strength (see Reichel 1992: 275 ff. and Stommer 1982).

From quite early on the car was a part of the American dream in Europe (cf., O'Dell 1997). Buying a car was the quickest way, not only to get to work or get the weekend family out of town, but also to gain a share of this utopian lifestyle.

In postwar Europe the American dream of a car society also carried a message of liberation from the state, which controlled other forms of mass transportation. Car ownership became a symbol of individual freedom and capitalist spirit. Unlike the heavy nationalized train systems, roads, gas stations, and car dealer strips smelled of free enterprise. The slick car salesman, the guy down at the gas station, or the waitress in the roadside cafeteria had another kind of aura than the uniformed army of train personnel. The props of car transport, from road maps to tow services, were supplied by the market, not the state. The early aesthetic of automobile life was American. Railway stations were built as national monuments with coats of arms and imposing clocks on the front; the gas station and the car dealer's lot borrowed their architectural forms from American modernism. Their global logos gave a cosmopolitan touch to even the remotest village.

In the early stages of mass driving of the 1950s and 1960s, Swedish car owners' associations stuck to a rhetoric of freedom and noninvolvement with the state. As in the United States one of the symbols of this hands-off approach was the demand for no speed limits. Soon the paradox became evident; parallel with the cries for freedom from state regulations, new demands were made by the same organizations. The state should contribute to the making of what then was called "a car-friendly society." Children must be educated about traffic problems; cities must be planned for mass auto traffic. In reality this turned the freedom of the car society into a new nation of citizen drivers. Through the car new and tight relations between the individual and the state were created. More and more Swedes shared the experience of road-sign drills in schools, driving tests as a *rite de passage* to adulthood, nationally controlled radio programs for drivers, mandatory check-ups for driving safety, confrontations with traffic wardens and police. As a driver you first and foremost became part of a new national community of drivers, which was materialized in a jungle of rules, signs, and systems for directions, which over the world retained a strong national element, in spite of heavy attempts at internationalization. In Sweden and Norway even the elk on the warning signs moved at a different pace.

This nationalization of driving also helped to discipline citizens. The driver learned to make a halt at a stripe of white paint on a deserted road, without the state being present in the form of controlling agents. For most people driving was the first (and only) contact with the state judiciary system of fines and traffic courts. A nation of law-abiders and lip-servants, illegal parkers and speed merchants was created.

In retrospect we can see how the car, which was launched as a liberator from the state, as a global means of transportation and community, also developed into a nationalizing tool. Going for a drive could both foster the feeling of free-wheeling individualism and the experience of responsible or restraining citizenship. We find similar paradoxes in many other types of communication technologies.

MAKING A PHONE CALL IN KÄRRA, ZAGREB, AND JERUSALEM

In the 1950s I used to spend my summers in Kärra, a village on the west coast of Sweden, where most households still did not possess a phone. The telephone station was situated up on the village street, in a grand-looking modernist building, inhabited by two telephone ladies. Above the entrance was a crowned blue sign saying Rikstelefon (National Telephone). I can still remember the special solemn atmosphere that arose as one of the ladies came bicycling, summer dresses aflutter, in order to convey the message that our family could expect a *national* telephone call in half an hour. In plenty of time, we wandered up the gravel walk, full of anticipation, adjusted our apparel and stepped into the office, a place whose aesthetic appearance was characteristically "Statish" in its austerity, with a spittoon in a corner and neatly displayed luxury telegram forms on the wall, together with official notices. There was an unmistakable smell of national telephony, a whiff of the nation-state, within these walls. Similarly, the pleasant telephonists were not merely service staff but civil servants, representatives of the state, just like the postmistress in the house next door and the station-master down by the railway station. Their habitus was different from that of the local grocer or the driver from the private bus company; they carried the benevolent but serious state in their body language and style of talking.

In her memoirs *How We Survived Communism and Even Laughed*, Slavenka Drakulic remembers her visits to her local post office in Zagreb, where people paid their bills and made phone calls. She describes the feeling of being at home, "as if the post office was a living room," but also the ambivalence:

> one of the post office as an accomplice of the state in the sacred duty of protecting the famous "security of the country" from its enemies (and thus making communication more complicated, if not impossible), and the other of the post office as a service that facilitates communication. The problem with the first concept is that the history of the communist state shows that the category of "enemy" could spread to the whole nation. The problem with the second concept is that, in spite of good intentions or proclamations, we never have a chance to experience it. In some strange, twisted way, it was we who served the post office: we paid weird, unexplained bills; we never complained (and when we did, it didn't change anything); with our money we fed their arrogant clerks, and with our conversations we fed the police. The amalgam of fear and general helplessness on one side, and the need to be privileged, to be able to communicate, on the other, consecrated the post office, turning it into an impenetrable institution of power. (Drakulic 1993: 101–2)

She adds that this feeling of control is still with her in the young democracy of Croatia. Now she has learned about the little secret room next to the counter, from which the police monitored the phone calls during the Communist era; but can she be quite sure that they are gone?

From his Jerusalem childhood during the Second World War, Amos Oz remembers the highly ritualized phone calls to kin in Tel Aviv, planned a week in advance by a letter. On the designated day and hour the whole family trooped to the local pharmacy to make the call, and if the line to Tel Aviv was busy a feeling of anxiety started to grow.

> I could virtually see this one and only line connecting Jerusalem with the exchange in Tel Aviv, and through it, with the rest of the world. And here this line is busy, and as long as it is busy Jerusalem is cut off. I could envision this line winding its way over the hills and between the mountains. I thought of it as a miracle. But what if wild beasts were to attack and gnaw the line at night? Or some bad Arabs were to cut it with their knives? or there were a brushfire? God knows, a thin vulnerable line was stretched out there, roasting in the sun. Anything could happen. (Oz 1996: 51)

MAKING CONNECTIONS

The new communication systems of the nineteenth century promised to restructure time and space. They could be heralded as global forces, but the rhetoric surrounding them was often very national. There was a highly materializing pedagogy about the ways in which telegraph poles or new tracks advanced into the wilderness, uniting different parts of the nation, as well as a constant search for metaphors in order to grasp what new technologies actually did to everyday life. Sometimes visions of the new world preceded actual technological changes. Electricity would later be the most important technology in producing a national infrastructure, but already in 1833 a local Swedish newspaper used this elusive and not yet developed power to try to capture the nature of an imagined community.

> In our present times there has arisen an element, always powerful, but never more powerful than now. This is public opinion. . . . It has no voice. But it does not need this because its power is of the mind. It lies in thought. It can be likened to electricity which runs through a chain of citizens who, on account of this current, feel at the same moment an identical unpleasantness or the same healing warmth. (Johannesson 1988: 30)

A similar language would emerge with the arrival of national radio in the 1920s and 1930s. In 1934 the German Nazi party ideologist Eugen Hadamovsky put it like this in his book *Dein Rundfunk*:

> we are possessed by the magic strength of the electric sparks which open the heart and set the spirit in motion, a strength which does not stop at city limits and is not turned back from closed doors, which knows no boundaries and is able to draw the people into the spell of one mighty spirit." (quoted in Browne 1989: 183)

Most new technologies entered the world full of promises but also with rather diffuse ideas about their actual potential and future use. This was very much the case with the telephone. When Alexander Bell demonstrated his innovation in 1876, he began by reciting from *Hamlet*. The two-way communication technique had not yet been developed, and many people thought the telephone could never be more than a one-way medium for information and entertainment. The notion that the future of the telephone lay primarily as a medium for listeners underlay Emerson's reaction to the suggestion of telephone cable traffic across the Atlantic: "But will they have anything to say?" When, considerably later, Archbishop Nathan Söderblom inaugurated the Swedish two-way Atlantic connection, he did so by singing the national anthem over the line to a somewhat surprised gathering on the other end. (The same kind of improvised singing occurred at the opening program of the Swedish Broadcasting Company in 1926, when the new director general suddenly burst out in the anthem after his opening speech.)

In Sweden, as in many other settings, the state at the beginning paid scant attention to the telephone. It was first and foremost defined as a local medium, something that would integrate local communities and regions, but soon the state stepped in to control the medium in a manner similar to that of national post and telegraph services.

For a long period the technology was seen as serving the (male) public sphere, businessmen and administrators. In order for the phone to become a mass movement it had to be domesticated, made to seem part of ordinary family life before it was widely adopted (cf., Marvin 1988: 63 ff. and Fischer 1992). We find a similar process of intimization in the history of the radio (cf., Löfgren 1995).

TOUCHED BY THE STATE

The telephone thus developed both into a tool of national integration and as a way of creating and supporting networks of intimacy inside or across borders. In 1915 the Bell system proudly presented itself as "the welder of the nation" (Fischer 1992: 163). "Ma Bell," like many other American communication corporations, learned to imitate the officialness of the state.

In the United States the flag is still waving above every post office. In other settings the presence and power of the nation-state was echoed in the stern (and often fortress-like) architecture of the local post and telephone station—all over the world. The architecture could be part of a symbolic demonstration of power (an impregnable bastion as in Zagreb), an icon of modernity (as in Kärra), or as an actual bastion of defense, against enemies from within or without. In the colonies the local post office could also be the rallying point for defense. In the rituals of coups d'état we find the same focus: seizing the local post and telegraph station, securing the radio station, or cutting the wires was not only about controlling or disrupting communications, it also carried a strong symbolic statement of exposing the fragility of the state: "the vulnerability of the thin lines stretching across the nation," as Amos Oz remembers them.

My point is that the nation-state made itself visible and concrete very successfully in the everyday routines of movement and communication. In a myriad of trivial situations it kept drawing attention to itself, quietly but in an extremely tangible way. (With the phone there was always the possibility of the state actually listening in on your most private conversations, in the form of either a nosy telephone operator or the secret police.)

The telecommunications examples illustrate the ways in which technology also becomes part of the magic aura of the state, the kind of "state fetishism" that Michael Taussig (1992: 111) has discussed. The ways in which images of the state are produced and maintained—the benevolent, caring, but fussy Mother (as in Kärra); the irritating and interfering Big

Brother (as in Zagreb); or the frailty of the struggling Father in pioneer nationhood (as in Jerusalem)—can also be analyzed in the microphysics of making a call, jumping a train, posting a letter. These systems of communication, I argue, represent a more effective way of "being touched by the state" than many of the national rhetoric and rituals of flag-waving. This is why the last decade of Western debates over privatization of communication technologies are as much about ideology and sentiments as about economy.

Communication systems have thus often been seen as a battle between the local, the national, and the transnational. If some media situations produce the feeling of statehood (with positive or negative overtones), others will in given situations and given periods come to symbolize the threatening or fascinating outside world: an appetizing cosmopolitan flavor or an instrument for protecting the local from the outside world. Such transformations are, for example, very evident in the twentieth-century history of the radio.

This medium has been put to work to produce local, national, and transnational communities of listeners, at different times and in different settings (cf., Löfgren 1995.). There was a crucial timing in this process. The new technology emerged as a relatively cheap medium in a period of heavy investments in national electrification, and could thus expand very rapidly in the 1930s. In Scandinavia, the radio became a very important part of Social Democratic welfare nationalism, with its emphasis on education, the making of active citizens, and modern living. In a very effective way it synchronized the nation, as listeners all over the country tuned in for the news, the national weather or a children's program (Löfgren 1995). In a later period the radio, mainly thanks to the development of cheap transistor receivers, became a key medium for the nation-building in many emerging Third World countries (cf., Sussman and Lent 1991).

CROSSING BORDERS

Among the different ways of organizing identities and communities, the pedagogy of space is very striking: borders as markers of territories, transitions, passages. In preindustrial Europe one of the most highly developed border systems kept town and countryside apart. Here the system of walls and gates not only controlled the material flow of people or goods, it also marked the differences both in privileges and status as well as in the symbolic worlds of the two territories. It was—for a long time—a very successful way of territorializing cultural alterity. In the industrial state national borders came to play a similar, central role, and one can argue that the immense success of the national project during the last two centuries to a large extent rests on the skillful deployment of the pedagogy of space and the ritualization of border crossings. In many ways national borders have become the archetypal border, the model for materializing boundaries with props like red striped bars and warning signs.

Early states focused on the importance of strong centers and rather porous borders (cf., the discussion in Linde-Laursen 1995). Before the era of modern nationalism, border crossings were mainly controlled for economic reasons: the absolutist state defending its economy against smugglers or political pamphlets challenging the royal power. Later on the ritualization of border crossings took on other forms. Paul Fussell (1980: 24 ff.) has discussed the new dramatization of border crossings in Europe after the First World War, when the frontiers were redrawn everywhere and also charged with strong national sentiments. This was the period when crossings became linked to anxiety: the suspicious scrutiny of passports and visas, the power demonstrations of little irritated men in uniform. You cross the border like a criminal under surveillance. Who are you, is this passport photo really you? Are you quite sure you have nothing to declare? Here the powerlessness of being a noncitizen, an alien, is installed. Although some border-crossings, for some categories of travelers, have been made a lot more relaxed, many of us still experience a slight anxiety when approaching the passport or customs control, although we know our papers are in order and our baggage lacks contraband.

"Welcome home again" was the first message that I used to meet in the arrival hall when coming back to Sweden in the early 1990s. To make sure the message got across it was stated in both Swedish and English. Some of the people lining up for the passport control, however, soon realized that this message should not be taken literally. During these years the policing of borders was again heavily increased in Sweden, as immigration laws were tightened here as well as in other European countries.

This production of anxiety is also a machine for focusing on national differences. As you look into the eyes of the customs officer you start searching for traits of national character: "You know those rigid French officials hardly looked at our kids, but on the Italian side the customs man immediately tickled them under the chin and started joking!" In the history of border crossings it is evident that the nationalizing gaze increases during the nineteenth century. People start to interpret cultural differences on both sides of the bridge as national, not local, regional, or class differences.

The changing production and reproduction of the nation-state can be read in the transformations of the scenography and dramaturgy of the border crossing. When the state was defined as a coconut, a hard shell with a soft interior, rather than an avocado, the physicality of the border became important. There was a clear pedagogy of space at work, which made the homogenization of all the stuff inside the shell easier. To this era belongs the whole dramatization of frontier crossings. Later on some national borders are seen as threatened not by neighbors but by global/transnational forces. It is not the neighbors but Americanization which is seen as invading Sweden, lurking across the border, and has to be contained, controlled, checked.

As the nature of transnational flows changes, the border landscape changes. Today it is often the airports that constitute the outposts and fortifications of the nation-state. Here bodies, movements, and goods are monitored through all kinds of surveillance techniques, which many Third World travelers will experience in very direct ways, or as Okwui Enwesor has put it:

> I hate airports and their false cleanliness . . . But more especially, I detest the slumped shoulders, the frightened eyes and undisguiseable sadness of the masses who congregate in its waiting rooms, its long queues; the teeming numbers who walk the plank of the slow conveyor tracks ferrying them to god-knows-what humiliation. (Enwezor 1996: 65)

Apart from the tightened immigration control, the state must find other ways of controlling or monitoring the transnational flows. Borders are transgressed in new ways, through satellites dishes and the World Wide Web. Discussing the development of Khomeini's Iran, Ryszard Kapus'cin'-ski has put it this way:

> A nation trampled by despotism, degraded, forced into the role of an object seeks shelter, seeks a place where it can dig itself in, wall itself off, be itself. This is indispensable if it is to preserve its individuality, its identity, even its ordinariness. But a whole nation cannot emigrate, so it undertakes a migration in time rather than in space. (quoted in Price 1995: 57)

Such a "walling in" process calls for new technologies of policing and screening out transnational influences, as the media can no longer be stopped at the old borders. Even in remote areas of Iran helicopters are circling to spot illegal satellite dishes. The whole national defense has to be reorganized. How can the Internet be policed?

THE CRISIS OF THE NATION-STATE

The shifting landscapes of border controls reflect changing technoscapes (cf., Appadurai 1996: 33) and the new ways in which people, capital, ideas, and goods are moved transnationally. These technoscapes are also restructured. Telephone companies and airlines are privatized; other national prestige projects such as car factories are dismantled. Today the nation-state is increasingly described as an entity squeezed from below by ethnic conflicts and local and regional wishes for greater autonomy, from above by the transnational reorganization of power and capital. The European Union (EU) is often used to exemplify this, but such an argument misses the ways in which EU at the same time strengthens the nation-state.

The squeezing metaphor can be seductive as well as other metaphors used to describe the weakening of the nation-state, often with terms like "draining, hollowing, emptying" (see for example Peck and Timell 1994: 293 ff.), but we should be cautious in our use of too sweeping predictions and the claims of a new "post-national" era.

We need to ask when, where, how, and for whom the nation-state is in crisis or the old forms of belonging are being displaced? Rather than trying to generalize the present in terms of devolutionary or evolutionary scenarios, we should scrutinize the different and sometimes contradictory movements occurring at the same time. There are winners and losers in such transformations.

The resurgent feelings of national identity are sometimes analyzed as nostalgia, an attempt to revert to the days of clear-cut borders and contained national cultures, or as an attempt to compensate for the loss of political and economic power in the nation-state by an increased focus on its cultural politics (see for example Walsham 1994: 208 ff). EU membership has produced new forms of national flag-waving in many states, but such theories of cultural compensation run the risk of being too one-dimensional.

My argument has been that the historical experience should caution us against making too rapid predictions. I have been looking at the ways in which new communication technologies—often seen as global—were put to work in nation-building. There is a crucial element of timing in such processes. Some nation-states have been able to synchronize new technologies with specific stages in a national culture-building. My examples have mainly been taken from one such nation: Sweden, which represents a specific tradition of welfare nationalism and a strong integration between state, civic culture, and national identity. In a global perspective the strong nation-states of northwestern Europe may seem like very special cases, but the ways in which nations like Sweden very successfully created a strong civic culture during the era of welfare nationalism has also had a normative effect. What happens when young or weak states cannot live up to these expectations of what a "real" nation-state should look like or be able to do? What happens when they cannot deliver the goods, defined within a traditional framework of welfare nationalism, cannot provide for or protect their citizens?

Another important aspect has to do with the ways in which well-established nation-states can afford to lose their grip on citizens, precisely because the everyday integration has been so successful. In the 1980s many old state radio monopolies were dismantled, but one may also argue that the state-controlled radio in Europe had done most of its national work by that time. For example, the ban on local dialects lifted on Swedish radio after the 1960s was seen as a revival of regionalism, but it could also be argued that regional differences no longer threatened the national project. Local dialects were now defined as something quaint or enriching, not as a threat to the firmly established norms of Standard Swedish.

New communication technologies often open up spaces of hopes and anxieties for the rapidly approaching future. Many of the electronic media are seen as disruptive in their pioneer stage, threatening old orders and hierarchies. This dystopian outlook is matched by the utopian optimism of creating new (and better) forms of networks and alliances. One such type of argument has to do with the inherent democratic nature of the new technology, as when the Internet is presented as a return to grassroots politics, creating new communities of citizens gathering out there on the village lawn of cyberspace.

In practice technologies often move in different directions from such utopian scenarios. Many new systems of communication have strengthened national or ethnic ties. The new technologies of togetherness, for example, serve the diaspora very well. Dispersed or displaced national subjects or members of ethnic groups maintain much stronger contact with the homeland through a constant flow of telephone calls, recorded audio and video tapes, and Kodachrome snapshots, as well as by the availability of cheap jet flights.

THE PEDAGOGICS OF MOBILITY

Place and space are constituted by movement, but the experience of movement can be very different. Moving on can be a way of staying the same. Many labor migrants go abroad in order to secure a life back home. For others the skill of being cosmopolitan is a cultural capital that may give many advantages as they return home or create alternative identities (cf., Hannerz 1996: 102 ff.). Some people move all the time, but are safely anchored in their local identities; others travel business class through the world and have created their own safe and secure transit spaces. The cosmopolitan confidently handles his American Express card and his cellular phone in the business-class lounge, while the refugee is trying to flush her passport down the toilet next door in the transit lounge.

In different periods we find the notion that new forms of mass travel, mass migration, or mass tourism will change the world; turn locals into cosmopolitans; and break down artificial boundaries between nations, localities, classes, or generations. Nineteenth-century emigration, modern tourism of the twentieth century, or contemporary interrailing would produce a more international world. But this is not always the case: today most of the pioneer interrailers sit in their little houses taking care of their families. The restlessness and mobility of youth may just be a *Sturm und Drang* stage in the life cycle, and before we accept the idea that mobility equals cultural and social change or new identities we have to look much closer at what people learn or experience, or don't learn and experience, by leaving their homes, their localities, their nations.

The current debate about a world in transit sometimes gets trapped in too much "post": post-national, post-modern, post-local, and too much "de," as in de-focused, de-centered, de-territorialized, de-localized. We need to balance our use of post and de with a greater focus on pre, re, and in. In what ways can a de-territorialization be part of a re-territorialization; how does the defocused become refocused—in new forms and combinations? A longer historical perspective may help us to remember that the other side of dissolution and disintegration is remaking and reanchoring. Are we really facing a future of intense displacement, or are we not observing the new ways in which people and identities take place in new arenas and in novel ways?

We constantly need to develop new entries and exits to the debate on processes of localization, nationalization, or globalization. In this chapter the focus has been mainly on the national level, but I find it important that the contemporary debate on the purported weakening of the nation-state is grounded in an understanding of the processes through which it has gathered its strength, all those kinds of fluids which now are said to be drained or emptied out of the protective shell of the nation (cf., the discussion in Löfgren 1993 and 1997: 106 ff.).

It may well be that we are seeing a weakening of the nation-state in some arenas, but history teaches us the chameleon-like nature of the nation-building project, changing forms and focus, serving very different political interests. The nation-state is continuously being reinserted in new arenas and new forms, and in a world where fewer and fewer identities are based on the clear-cut pedagogy of space, the nation-state still tries to provide an absolute space: Sweden or the United States starts here! There is a very powerful territorialization of culture and history behind this situation. Few other identity projects have managed to stage this kind of representation and materialization of boundaries.

Finally, in much of the current debate on the global and the local I miss the ethnographic detail and the historical comparison, the focus on the ways in which media dreams and media practices are linked, or different technologies of movement interact in everyday life.

A historical perspective should not get trapped in the tired genres of "nothing new under the sun" but should seek to understand the similarities and dissimilarities in the ways in which new forms of moving people, goods, and ideas are anticipated, institutionalized, and routinized, often taking quite other routes and forms than those expected. There is an openness in new kinds of communications that may surface in a comparative perspective. In different circumstances the same technology of togetherness can become local, national, or global.

NOTE

A first version of this paper was presented at the workshop "Flows, Borders, and Hybrids: A Conference on Cultural Processes in Contemporary Society," October 25–27, 1996, in Arild, Sweden, organized by the project "National and Transnational Cultural Processes," financed by the Swedish Council for Research in the Humanities and Social Sciences. I am grateful for the many constructive comments by the participants and my discussant Robert Foster.

REFERENCES

Appadurai, Arjun. (1996). *Modernity at Large: Cultural Dimensions of Globalization.* Minneapolis: University of Minnesota Press.

Browne, Donald R. (1989). *Comparing Broadcast Systems: The Experiences of Six Industrialized Nations.* Ames: Iowa State University Press.

Drakulic, Slavenka. (1993). *How We Survived Communism and Even Laughed.* London: Vintage.

Ehrenburg, Ilya. (1929/1985). *The Life of the Automobile.* London: Pluto Press.

Enwezor, Okwui. (1996). In Transit. In Octavio Zaya and Anders Michelsen, eds. *Interzones: A Work in Progress.* Copenhagen: Kunstforeningen: 61–67.

Eyerman, Ron, and Orvar Löfgren. (1995). Romancing the Road: Roadmovies and Images of Mobility. *Theory, Culture & Society* 12, no. 1: 53–80.

Fischer, Claude S. (1992). *America Calling: A Social History of the Telephone to 1940.* Berkeley: California University Press.

Fussell, Paul. (1980). *Abroad: British Literary Travelling between the Wars.* New York: Oxford University Press.

Hannerz, Ulf. (1996). *Transnational Connections: Culture, People, Places.* London: Routledge.

Jakle, John A. (1985). *The Tourist: Travel in Twentieth-Century North America.* Lincoln: University of Nebraska Press.

Johannesson, Kurt. (1988). Opinionens makt. Om ett begrepp och dess historia. In *Litteraturens vägar. Litteratursociologiska studier tillägnade Lars Furuland.* Stockholm: Gidlunds: 30–52.

Linde-Laursen, Anders. (1995). *Det nationales natur.* Copenhagen: Nordiska ministerrådet.

Löfgren, Orvar. (1993). Materializing the Nation in Sweden and America. *Ethnos* 1993 (3–4): 161–96.

———. (1995) The Nation as Home or Motel: Metaphors of Media and Belonging. (Lecture delivered at the Society for the Anthropology of Europe, Washington, D.C., November 18, 1995).

———. (1997). Scenes from a Troubled Marriage: Swedish Ethnology and Material Culture Studies. *Journal of Material Culture* 2, no. 1: 95–113.

Macaulay, Thomas Babington. (1889). *The History of England from the Accession of James II*. London: Popular Edition.

Marvin, Carolyn. (1988). *When Old Technologies Were New: Thinking about Communications in the Late Nineteenth Century*. New York: Oxford University Press.

O'Dell, Tom. (1997). *Culture Unbound: Americanization and the Swedish Experience*. Lund: Scandinavian Academy Press, in press.

Oz, Amos. (1996). *Don't Call It Night*. New York: Harcourt Brace.

Peck, Jamie, and Adam Timell. (1994). Searching for a New Institutional Fix: The After-Fordist Crisis and the Global–Local Disorder. In Ash Amin, ed. *Post-Fordism: A Reader*. Oxford: Blackwell: 280–315.

Price, Monroe E. (1995). *Television: The Public Sphere and National Identity*. Oxford: Clarendon Press.

Reichel, Peter. (1991). *Der Schöne Schein des Dritten Reiches: Faszination und Gewalt des Faschismus*. München: Hanser.

Stommer, Rainer, ed. (1982). *Reichsautobahn: Pyramiden des Dritten Reichs*. Marburg: Jonas Verlag.

Sussman, Gerald, and John A. Lent, eds. (1991). *Transnational Communications: Wiring the Third World*. New York: Sage.

Taussig, Michael. (1992). *The Nervous System*. London: Routledge.

Walsham, Sarah van. (1994). Mixed Metaphors: The Nation and the Family. *Focaal. Journal for Anthropology* 22/23: 199-218.

Part V

Global Flows, Global Institutions

20

Flows and Institutions: Globalization in the Twenty-First Century

Bart van Steenbergen

The last part of this book is devoted to the future. What will be the effects of globalization processes in the twenty-first century? Should we look at it with fear (in the chapter by Jos de Beus referred to as "Goldsmith's fear") or will globalization be benevolent for mankind? As an ancient Chinese proverb states, Forecasting is difficult, especially when it concerns the future. The implication is that nobody can tell us what the world will look like in the near future, let alone the more distant future, but this does not leave us with empty hands. What future-oriented social scientists can do and are doing in this respect is analyzing and projecting certain trends, writing scenarios, developing so-called "early warnings," and giving indications of possible and desirable developments toward a better future, mostly in the form of alternative options. Characteristic for almost all future-oriented studies is that the classical scientific distinction (not to say separation) between empirical and normative statements is blurred.

The contributions to this final part fit into the rich tradition of the so-called global models, which started in the 1970s when the first wave of global models emerged. Global modeling can be seen as one of the first expressions of social scientific concern with globalization processes. This first wave was based upon two perils that affected the world as a whole. The first one has become known as the "ecological problematique," by which was meant the combined problems of nonrenewable resource depletion, environmental deterioration, overpopulation, and pollution, which threaten the survival of humankind. In particular the study of Meadows et al., *Limits to Growth* (1972), which became known as the first report to the Club of Rome, launched a heavy political debate on the future of our planet and also laid the foundation of a series of scenario studies on the

335

survival of mankind like *Mankind at the Turning Point* (Mesarovic and Pestel 1974), *A Blueprint for Survival* (1972), and the Organization for Economic Cooperation and Development (OECD) study *Facing the Future* (1979). The second impetus for global modeling was the debate on a new international economic order, launched in the mid 1970s in the United Nations by the representatives of the so-called Third World. Their request to the United Nations was to promote an economic order that would close or at least diminish the (income) gap between the rich and the poor nations. Global models focussing on these problems are Leontief's *The Future of the World Economy* (1976); *Catastrophe or New Society* (1976), by the Argentinean Bariloche Foundation; and *Reshaping the International Order* (1976), by a research team led by the Dutch economist Jan Tinbergen. In short, the 1970s were a rich period with bold, creative, challenging, and encompassing studies on the future of the planet. Moreover, they were based on the hope and expectation that these models could make a contribution to the solution of these problems.

After the 1970s the golden age of global modeling seemed to be over, for during the 1980s there was little action on this front. There were some exceptions like the Brandt report (1983) and the Brundtland report (1986), but as a whole that decade did not witness many new activities in this field. It has been argued that this decline was the outcome of frustration, since the influence of these models was less than expected and hoped for. Global problems proved to be more stubborn than foreseen, partly because in the 1980s the world was confronted with an economic crisis, and as we know from history, in times of a crisis there is a tendency to focus on short-term problems and solutions. Another explanation for this decline is a change in the overall "mood of the time." The 1980s were the decade of a no-nonsense mentality, pragmatism, short-term thinking, piecemeal engineering, and skepticism concerning the possibilities of changing economic structures.

Whatever the reasons were, the fact is that now in the 1990s we are witnessing a comeback of global modeling. We mention here the most influential ones: the CEPII study *World Economy 1990–2000* (1992), Attali's *Millennium: Winners and Losers in the Coming World Order* (1990), and *Scanning the Future: A Long-Term Scenario Study of the World Economy 1990–2015* by the Central Planning Bureau of the Netherlands. In the following we want to raise two questions. First, how should we evaluate this new wave? What are the main differences from the old models of the 1970s? Second, we want to investigate to what extent the contributions of Falk and de Beus fit into this picture.

The first and probably most striking difference is the relative optimism of the new models compared to those of the 1970s. The ecological scenarios gave a gloomy perspective of the future and created a doomsday atmosphere. Moreover, the need to raise the income level in the poor countries, which was at the heart of the models for a new international economic order, was seen as in contradiction with the perceived need for lower or even zero economic growth necessary to avoid an ecological catastrophe. This does not mean that in the new models everything is all roses, but the perceived problems of the future are seen as surmountable and are formulated in terms of risks that societies are willing to take and no longer in terms of contradictory goals (ecological balance versus economic growth). This relative optimism is also reflected in the contributions of Falk and de Beus. The latter argues that under certain circumstances globalization processes may promote global equality, and Falk points at the significant contribution globalization can make to the realization of his goal for the future: humane governance. He adds that the overall influence of globalization seems to be making major war into an anachronism.

A second difference between the two waves concerns the role of the actors in the global drama: Who are the heroes and who the villains? Here the UN distinction between the three systems is relevant: the first one consisting of governments and inter- or transgovernmental organizations; the second one formed by the business world (and especially the transnational corporations); and the third created by people acting collectively through social movements, voluntary institutions, and associations. In the old models most attention was devoted to the first system, as the (potentially) main shaping actor for global reform. Concerning the villain here, particularly in the ecological models, the blame was put on industrialism in general and on capitalism, with its inbuilt drive for growth, in particular. In that context it is not surprising that the transnationals were often seen as the bad guys, the most visible expression of the threat to human survival. The new models differ from this in many ways and the contributions of Falk and de Beus reflect that.

To start with, in most recent models there is less emphasis on governments and intergovernmental organizations (with the possible exception of the European Union) as the solution to the problem. We recognize this in Falk's plea for (humane global) governance, a concept that should be clearly distinguished from government. He does not seem to believe in a world government. Furthermore, what is remarkable is the positive evaluation of the role of the second system and especially of the multinationals in most recent models. They seem to have changed roles from villain to hero. Both our authors reflect that new attitude. De Beus points at the revival of what he calls "doux commerce" and adds that some enlightened multinationals (like Shell) have committed themselves to moral business codes against corruption and exploitation and to invest in "welfare capitalism." Falk adds to that the remarkable financial contributions to the satisfaction of global public goods by such capitalist superheroes as Ted Turner and George Soros. Both authors also emphasize that this new enlightened attitude of the second system is at least partly the outcome of pressure by the third system (consumer groups, environmental movements), which implies a strengthening of the role of that system. In some cases a reverse development seems to take place: from hero to villain. De Beus suggests that some modern welfare states are making that turn. They used to be looked at as the champions of benevolent internationalism, but nowadays "welfare states, far from being unambiguously globalization-friendly, tend to orientate governments towards measures of protectionism and nationalism."

A third difference between the two waves of global models is that the old ones are more normative and the new ones more scientific in the positivistic sense, i.e., they limit themselves to presenting information, ideas, models, scenarios, etcetera, but they do not come up with solutions and strategies, let alone make a plea for certain policies or visions of desirable futures. One can make that difference very visible by comparing the title of the famous study by Jan Tinbergen, *Reshaping the International Order,* as a political imperative with the one of the more recent studies of the Netherlands Bureau of Central Planning (of which Tinbergen was the founding father) *Scanning the Future,* which implies a much more limited and "pure" scientific approach to global modeling [emphasis added].

With regard to this latter difference both de Beus and Falk seem to have more affinity with the tradition of the 1970s than with the new wave. There is no doubt that both contributions are explicitly normative and that the authors develop ideas, suggestions, and pleas for a better world. De Beus has a vision of a more egalitarian planet, and he investigates the preconditions for that, whereas Falk is primarily concerned with the possibilities of a humane governance system on a global scale. It is interesting to speculate on the idea whether such a more normative approach will make a comeback in the global models of the next decade.

REFERENCES

Attali, J. (1990). *Millennium: Winners and Losers in the Coming World Order.* Paris: Artheme Fayard.
"A Blueprint for Survival." (1972). *The Ecologist.*
The Brandt Commission. (1980). *North–South: A Programme for Survival.* London: Panbooks.
———. (1983). *Common Crisis. North–South: Cooperation for World Recovery.* London: Panbooks.
Brundtland Commission. (1987). *Our Common Future.* Oxford: Oxford University Press.

Central Planning Bureau. (1992). *Scanning the Future: A Long-Term Scenario Study of the World Economy, 1990–2015*. The Hague: SDU Publishers.

CEPII. (1992). *World Economy, 1990–2000: The Growth Imperative*. Paris: Economica.

Herrera, A.O., et al. (1976). *Catastrophe or New Society? A Latin American World Model (Bariloche Model)*. Ottawa: IDSC.

Interfutures. (1979). *Facing the Future: Mastering the Probable and Managing the Unpredictable*. Paris: OECD.

Leontief, W. (1976). *The Future of the World Economy*. New York: United Nations.

Meadows, D.H., D. Meadows, J. Randers, and W. Behrens. (1972). *The Limits to Growth*. New York: Universe Books.

Mesarovic, M., and E. Pestel. (1974). *Mankind at the Turning Point*. New York: E.P. Dutton.

Tinbergen, J., et al. (1976). *Reshaping the International Order*. Amsterdam: Elsevier.

21

Does Equality Travel? A Note on the Institutional Preconditions of Global Equality

Jos de Beus

> Never before—not at the time of various democratic revolutions in Central Europe in 1848 or at the conclusion of World War I—has wealth disparity been so great as after the Cold War. And never before, because of the global communications revolution, has the disparity been so visible.
>
> —Robert Kaplan (1996: 435)

SOPHISTICATED LIBERALISM

Keynes once wrote, "Ideas, knowledge, science, hospitality, travel—these are things which should of their nature be international. But let goods be homespun whenever it is reasonably and conveniently possible, and above all, let finance be primarily national" (quoted in Kapstein 1994: 1). Now that finance has globalized, it seems only natural to examine whether "homespun equality" is liable to scale-lifting as well. Do global markets engender global equality, that is to say, will the expansion of exchange and economic interdependency lead toward decreasing differences between the economic prospects of the rich and the poor, both on the global scale and within the countries that join the globalizing economy?

In the nonliberal view of Marxists and realists the very question is utopian. It is unlikely that globalization of "anarchy," the short phrase for unconstrained rivalry between about 40,000 multinational corporations and 190 sovereign states, will bring 5.5 billion individuals to coexist as equals. In the naive liberal view the answer is unflinchingly affirmative. Together, the iron hand of world government and the invisible hand of world markets will improve the quality of life of all members of the world population alike. This chapter suggests a third answer in the spirit of sophisticated liberalism.[1] Globalization may turn into an egalitarian trend when (a) global public opinion forces multinational firms to support social policy in host countries and (b) local public opinion forces national elites in these countries to base their strategies of internationalization on democratic procedures in a wide sense (by building broad domestic coalitions, cultivating public debate and free opposition, participating in democratic international and supranational governance, and enforcing social rights and compensating vulnerable losers).

In the second section I point at "Goldsmith's fear." This is the current fear that globalization means the collapse of well-ordered egalitarian arrangements in the West through the most perverse transfers of income and wealth, namely from the poor in rich countries to the rich in poor countries. In the third section I introduce the problem of this chapter. Is there a way to understand the notion of expansion of the domain of equality in a market-driven world economy that sets Goldsmith's fear at rest without using shallow metaphor and voodoo social science? In the fourth section I argue that cosmopolitan egalitarianism is missing under the present "global circumstances of justice" (Hume's canonical term for structural limits to abundance, altruism, and common knowledge). In the fifth section I try to show that forward-looking egalitarians should not bet on the redistributive potential of the Heckscher–Ohlin model of global market ordering since it does not contain an adequate analysis of the role of institutions and organizations. The other sections are similarly yet more constructively engaged with the Enlightenment view of formation of a one-world social order. In the sixth section I try to restore the theory of "doux commerce" with respect to the softening of manners of distributive authorities, in particular of multinational firms. In the seventh section I examine the probability of convergence toward democratic capitalism within nation-states or alliances of nation-states. In the final section I try to spell out the institutional preconditions for a kind of equality in ever closer transnational relations between accountable actors that is neither organized (such as the distributive branch of world government) nor spontaneous (such as equalization of factor prices in neoclassical theory). I conclude that the world market can fulfill its liberal-egalitarian promise if, and only if, other constitutive features of global civil society than the cash-nexus emerge as well.

GOLDSMITH'S FEAR

France happens to be the cradle of "Tocqueville's dread," the fear that modernization boils down to universal democratization and equalization at the cost of personal liberty, political autonomy, and economic efficiency (Rae et al. 1981: 1–4; Dahl 1985: 8–9). But today France has become the exit route for something different I would call Goldsmith's fear. When Sir James (Jimmy) Goldsmith died in the summer of 1997, this corporate raider, multimillionaire, member of the European Parliament, and founder of the Referendum Party of British Eurosceptics was instantly commemorated as the author of a best-selling book, *The Trap* (1993), in which global free trade and European unification are held responsible for undermining community life, privileging big corporations, depriving European workers of jobs and social benefits, dislocating people in poor countries, in short for generating extreme inequality: "Le libre-échangisme mondial fait que les pauvres des pays riches enrichissent les riches des pays pauvres" [Global free trade makes that the poor of the rich countries enrich the rich of the poor countries] (*Le Monde*, Tuesday 22 July 1997: 14).[2]

Although Goldsmith's intellectual and political credentials are dubious—though not weaker than those of Berlusconi, Perot, Soros, and Turner—his worry is legitimate. In the most simple scenario of egalitarians the global distributive ranking of all members of the world population coincides with national rankings; the money is taken from Bill Gates (the world's and America's richest man) and is given to the anonymous starving child in the most miserable place on earth, somewhere in Africa. If these transfers are exhausted or politically impossible, the second-best scenario would entail transfers from the middle classes in rich countries to the lower and middle classes in poor countries. Compared to these egalitarian schemes, Goldsmith's case of poor Westerners involuntarily subsidizing rich non-Westerners amounts to a worst-case scenario.

Evidently there are many reasons to feel skeptical about the relevance of imagining globalization as the latest cunning of egalitarian reason. First, the pursuit of economic human rights by global distributive authorities, such as the World Bank, has been extremely limited, weak, and controversial. Bok (1995) and Kaplan (1996) have recently given a terrifying account of the widening gap between the universalist rhetoric of human development and the reality of spontaneous, uneven, and often barbaric globalization.

Second, while globalization will equalize the prices of factors of production, such as wages, under certain ideal conditions, in the real world global markets seem to be as fallible as national markets (Boyer 1996: 30–31). This does not imply that the force of factor price equalization will be entirely suspended but that its distributive consequences will be ambivalent from the point of view of global distributive justice. Massive migration from poor to prosperous countries—in itself a factor movement and an alternative to trade—would cause redistribution of income from capital to labor in the underdeveloped home countries and improve the migrants' prospects, but it would also cause redistribution of income from labor to capital in the developed host countries and deteriorate the prospects of lower categories of workers and social benefit recipients there (Reder 1982: 30).[3] A related point is made in the debate on the influence of international trade on earnings inequality in the West. Trade economists focus on the distribution of income between skilled and unskilled labor. Krugman argues that

> Increased trade with the Third World . . . while it may have little effect on the overall level of First World wages, should in principle lead to greater inequality in those wages, with a higher premium for skill. Equally, there should be a tendency toward " factor price equalization," with wages of low-skilled workers in the North declining toward Southern levels. (Krugman 1996: 65)

Wood concludes that " trade can hurt unskilled labor even where it does not raise import penetration . . . by depressing the prices of labor-intensive goods [and] by forcing firms to find ways of using less unskilled labor to stay competitive" (Wood 1995: 65).

Third, "free" markets in which moral rules of conduct and political regulations regarding surplus sharing are absent or weak are not terribly impressive mechanisms for equalization. Unorganized capitalism, though it is often a powerhouse for economic growth and may reinforce an egalitarian ethos (Gellner 1987),[4] seldom promotes and protects a clean path of material equalities between classes, sexes, and regions.

Fourth, globalization since the 1970s tends to go in tandem with polarization between rich and poor countries and with "ruthless growth" (growth plus rising poverty and inequalities) within both sets of countries. And if there is a positive relation between economic growth and reduction of poverty, it is not a universally numerical constant. In East Asia 1 percent growth relates to 3 percent reduction of poverty, while this elasticity is slightly more than one in sub-Saharan Africa and even less than one in Latin America (according to a recent study by Oxfam, see NRC Handelsblad, 13 September 1997). There is no such thing as global "trickle down" (growth-based improvement of the standard of living of the most vulnerable, both absolutely and relatively), except as the ideology of laissez-faire (United Nations Development Programme, UNDP, 1996: 11 cf., United Nations Development Programme, 1997: 7, 9).

Finally, many right-wing supporters of globalization are inclined to deny any positive role of egalitarian policies in their wishful thinking, while many left-wing critics of globalization are prepared to proclaim the end of the welfare state in their doomsday thinking. Globalization signifies the final proof of the emptiness of the concept of social justice as far as the impossibility of civil consensus on global redistribution is concerned (according to the right) or of its exactingness as far as global solidarity is concerned (according to the left).

FROM GOLDSMITH'S LOCAL EGALITARIANISM OF FEAR TO LIBERAL GLOBAL EGALITARIANISM OF HOPE

It is indeed tempting to stress certain contradictions between the egalitarians' cause and the darkest face of globalization, namely, the hollowing out of national democracy, the rise of transnational oligarchy, religious intolerance, ethnic conflict, violently contested boundaries and identities, laissez-faire ideology, and social exclusion. Yet such an analysis would also be one-sided (see Guéhenno 1993; Barber 1995; Offe and Schmitter 1995; and Greider 1996). The current wave of globalization is mainly a shift of scarcity and power relations within the triad Europe, East Asia, and North America, where the flows of trade and foreign direct investment are concentrated (Hirst and Thompson 1996: 67–72; cf., UNDP 1997: 84). Yet, an increasing number of non-Western governments choose the strategy of modernization by internationalization.

> This is a strategy of adopting political, economic, and cultural organization already existing elsewhere: democracy, markets, and an individualistic, consumption-oriented culture that dominates the advanced capitalist world. In this strategy, modernization becomes synonymous with internationalization: integration into the world economy, combined with an imitation of economic, political, and cultural patterns prevalent in the advanced capitalist countries. (Przeworski et al. 1995: 3)

Western governments in the "advanced capitalist countries" are not passive either. They try to prevent decline by inventing new strategies of modernization by internationalization, like the formation of an economic and monetary union in Europe. The assessment of the role of egalitarian considerations in this clash of insiders and invaders of the triad is far from easy.

First, one has to distinguish between public policies of both home countries and host countries concerning trade, migration, and transfers; strategies of multinationals with respect to investment, corporate governance, and moral business coding; strategies of nongovernmental associations (such as trade unions and new social movements) concerning international and transnational mobilization and pressure; and private behavior in the context of global markets and global politics of producers, consumers, workers, and poor persons dependent on transfers. One example with mixed egalitarian credentials is forced emigration policy: "Governments facing unemployment within the majority community and conflicts among ethnic groups over language and educational opportunities often regarded the expulsion of a prosperous, well-placed minority as a politically popular policy" (Weiner 1995: 30).

Second, one has to distinguish between forms of cooperation, conflict, and cooperative conflict between different actors, in particular between different distributive agencies. Elster developed a framework for the analysis of the role of egalitarian principles and norms in local and national bargaining settings that should be extended to supranational settings, such as development aid by coalitions of governments and social policy coordination in the European Union (Elster 1989: 248–49, 284–86; Elster 1992: 248).

Third, one has to distinguish between successes, unrealized intentions, and unintended consequences of egalitarian adaptations to the global market. There are very few examples of successful entry into the First World of rich industrial democracies. Japan is one of them, but its egalitarian arrangements do not fit well in T.H. Marshall's canonical ideal of liberal social citizenship (according to the famous critique of van Wolferen 1989). Many world government plans for redistribution, such as Tinbergen's optimal international order and Tobin's tax on international financial speculation, illustrate the multiplicity of unrealized intentions. Binding a growing population to declining earnings and welfare benefits is generally seen as one of the consequences of neoliberal plans for globalization, but the relatively egalitarian reforms of welfare states in Scandinavia and Continental Europe (compared to, say, the United Kingdom and New Zealand) also produce negative side effects, namely massive exclusion from the labor market, growing taxation, and mounting public sector deficits (Esping-Andersen 1996: 258–59).

Finally and most importantly, one must draw subtle distinctions between types of egalitarianism. There are classic egalitarian instruments (such as introducing a minimum wage) and novel instruments (such as basic income and workfare) (Bowles and Gintis 1995). There are inclusive campaigns for economic modernization, such as fair sharing of the profits of privatization, and exclusive ones, such as "nationalism by trade" in Catalonia, Flanders, and Lombardy.[5] And there is instrumental support for egalitarianism in terms of its contribution to productivity and national competitiveness, next to intrinsic valuation of equality. The former may invite broad social consensus; the latter may invite the willingness to continue making sacrifices.[6]

What could the metaphor of "traveling equality" possibly mean in this complicated interplay of risky, cross-cutting, and partly rival strategies of modernization by internationalization? It departs from determinist thinking about the equilibrium outcome of such strategies. Episodes, country-specific stories, and scenarios of (de-)equalization will replace long-term trends, world history, and numerical predictions (see Atkinson 1996: 5; Krugman and Venables 1995). Even if we could confidently predict some process of stable growth of the world product, we seem to miss sound scientific means to predict either the coming of global Egalitaria (of, say, convergence of all world regions toward a "Japanese" ratio of income of the highest 20 percent of households to lowest of four) or an overall sharp increase of inequalities within and between nations (see, respectively, Lane and Ersson 1995: 44 and Przeworski 1995: 9–10).

An intermediate scenario is the gradual increase of the share of underdeveloped countries in the world economy combined with security, that is, the removal of precarious living conditions in both the underdeveloped countries and the developed ones by the creation and maintenance of peaceful coexistence, constitutional democracy, and a decent standard of living. This standard can be attained either by a strategy of growth-mediated security (first the expansion of private incomes, then improvement of public support) or by a strategy of support-mediated security (simultaneous and mutual reinforcement of the private sector and the public sector) (Drèze and Sen 1989: 183; Rothschild 1995). Of course, I do not claim literal "traveling," in the sense that China will take over American leadership or that Brazil and the Nordic countries will change places as far as economic equality is concerned. But I do expect that continuing globalization will end the status quo in which Marshall's ideal of social democratic civilization got stuck in a small set of resilient welfare states in the West. In the long run it will "travel." Gradual integration of partially peripheral countries into the triadic system of production and distribution, say of Vietnam into the Japanese bloc, will not necessarily maximize the prospects of the global worse-off, but it will contribute to expansion of the domain of economic equality. The political upshot of Goldsmithian analysis of the world market as the new empire of evil is "red" protectionism: the nation-states in Western Europe should stick to (labor) market regulation by closing their borders, thus literally insulating the laboriously won social rights of its labor classes (Beck 1997). I do not deny the present tension between national obligations ("What about the pensioners?") and international obligations ("What about the victims of famines?"). But my intermediate scenario suggests that there are alternatives to both global laissez-faire and local "egalitarianism of fear."

The phenomenon of traveling equality is contested. One prominent researcher suggests that globalization and convergence in the late nineteenth and late twentieth centuries have a similar impact, namely rising inequality in rich countries and falling inequality in poor countries. Another one suggests that trade with developing countries will only cause minor and temporary welfare losses for unskilled workers in developed countries (see Williamson 1996 and Lawrence 1996: 15). However, this chapter is not empirical but theoretical. One of the crucial variables here concerns a moral and rational trade-off between less equality in rich countries and more equality in poor countries. Under which conditions would a transfer from poor Dutchmen (the lowest 20 percent with an average income of $9.024) to rich Indonesians (the highest 20 percent with an average income of $4.877) become feasible and justifiable in a global perspective?[7] A case in point is the relocation of multinationals. In the short run this results in rising unemployment for American low-skilled workers and rising employment for Indonesian low-skilled workers at levels of remuneration that are higher than conventional local remuneration. In the long run the relative prosperity of Western countries vis-à-vis non-Western countries will go down, even if Western governments are forced by the voice of the people to protect those vulnerable citizens who are the losers in the new free trade. Whereas progressive scholars like Fitoussi, Hirst, Jordan, van Parijs, Reich, Rosanvallon, Sen, and Thompson are quite critical in their analysis of the politics of structural adjustment and social expenditure cuts, the economics of secession by the rich and the pseudo-universalist discourse of commercialism, they all agree that there is no escape from institutional adaptation to globalization and the issue of world market-driven redistribution. Is the West prepared to give up the privileged and protectionist aspects of its egalitarian arrangements if this is the price for making room for the workers of poor countries and making the world safe for creative international competition, booming international trade, and durable international growth? (See Reich 1991; Sen 1994; van Parijs 1995b; Fitoussi and Rosanvallon 1996; Hirst and Thompson 1996; Jordan 1996; and Sen 1997).[8]

WHY COSMOPOLITAN EQUALITY IS A DREAM

Most studies of distribution, whether positive or normative, take for granted that societies are national and self-contained. Globalization is pressing social scientists to take transnational society into account, that is, to revise the assumption of distribution confined to the national level and to examine counterfactual cosmopolitan equality. This intriguing and most far-reaching counterfactual contains at least the following assumptions: (i) the coherence of the cosmopolitan principle of equality, (ii) the flourishing of world community, and (iii) the legitimacy and effectiveness of world government and its distributive branch. I will give a rough outline of cosmopolitan equality and leave out the discussion on details (see Pogge 1992; Rawls 1993; Held 1995; and McGrew 1997).

In the liberal conception of cosmopolitan equality economic differences between individuals should not be sensitive to the nationhood of these individuals insofar as nationhood is part of force and luck. The single fact that you are born and raised in country X (resourceful, powerful, technologically advanced) or country Y (resourceless, powerless, technologically backward) should not affect your position in the global distributive ranking. In the cosmopolitan view your nationality is as morally arbitrary as your family background. National differences may only reinforce economic differences when and because these differences follow from choices and efforts of free persons and peoples. The benchmark for assessing the present distributive processes and outcomes worldwide is the distribution of global product within and between nations, which matches an ideal distribution of national membership, determined by voluntary participation of adult "world citizens" who are well-informed about life chances in all territories of the planet. This benchmark is supposed to provide reliable data about the classification of persons with unearned surplus income, persons with unearned income deficits, and a grey zone of persons with economic prospects that are nearly fair from a cosmopolitan point of view. It must also be instrumental for designing a scheme for centralized redistribution.

Although the specification of a nation-insensitive distribution between all world citizens (like the correction of distributive consequences of imperialism and colonialism) runs into deep conceptual and empirical problems, its practical meaning is less elusive. There is a wide gap between the massive poverty, gross inequalities, and large disparities of political power at present and the general ideal of cosmopolitan principles and practices (see Theil and Seale Jr. 1994; Hurrell and Woods 1995; Jones 1997; Pritchett 1997; and, more generally, Bradshaw and Wallace 1996). For pragmatic reasons cosmopolitans will aim at balancing domestic and international transfers, giving priority to certain classes of vulnerable persons (see Rae et al. 1981 and Elster 1993).

The cosmopolitan principle of equality specifies what is due to any one inhabitant of the planet by reference to what is being done to all other inhabitants. It entails equal treatment to each inhabitant, such as an equal share in ecological space. It presupposes that all persons concerned (policymakers and the ultimate donors and recipients) perceive certain economic differences "beyond borders" as inequalities, that is, as public bads. Such a political community of principle between human beings on the largest scale must be solidaristic. It is imbued with mutual recognition and respect, mutual loyalty, and mutual trust and willingness to cooperate. While it does not necessarily drive out non-global ties (nation, denomination, profession), it demands fundamental and weighty allegiance to humanity as a whole (Nussbaum 1996).

Although cosmopolis is unbounded in a moral sense, its governance does acknowledge and establish formal boundaries in a legal sense. Worldwide collection and redistribution of money, goods, and services require a bill of social rights within a constitutional framework for debate, struggle, and public decision making, procedures for implementing social policies and assigning formal duties (such as taxpayers' and employers' duties), division of tasks and coordination between many distributive authorities at many administrative levels (like the principle of subsidiarity), and organizations for regulating both deviant and complying citizens. So cosmopolitan equality is not only liberal and solidaristic, it is also complex since it can only be enforced by multitiered, quasi-federal governance (see Burnheim 1985, 1986).[9]

Cosmopolitan equality does not exist today, and the present episode of globalization hardly goes in that direction. Neither world associations, such as the United Nations, the World Bank, and the International Monetary Fund, nor regional associations, like the Organization of African Unity, the Association of Southeast Asian Nations, and the European Union, were founded as distributive agencies. Nor do they function that way today (see Nickel 1987 and Murphy 1996). The only association that comes close is the European Union, with its special funds for the temporary unemployed and poor regions and its majority decisions on social rights, including equal labor market treatment of men and women (Social Charter, Social Protocol) (see Leibfried and Pierson 1995 and Walzer 1997: 48–51). But European redistribution is small, relative to both total European product and domestic transfers within the member-states. Furthermore, European social law has not been prominent in stopping social dumping, overshooting public expenditure cuts, and the gradual shift of taxation on capital to taxation on labor.

Globalization of trade, investment, and migration may, of course, provide opportunities and incentives for strong cosmopolitan movements that transform Hume's idea of the "party of mankind" into really existing egalitarianism. However, such movements are latent or weak because of structural obstacles concerning the lack of universally binding law, the limited expansion of humanitarian sensitivity and responsibility, dilemmas of collective action, asymmetric representation of different views of world citizenship, corruptibility of international politics and administration, and certain contradictions within emergent cosmopolitanism (for example, a long peace may decrease the desire to join professional-humanitarian armies). Furthermore, cosmopolitan scholars have to come to terms with the dual fact that certain properties of globalization facilitate the reinforcement of national differences and the proliferation of small nation-states and that certain plans for global redistribution beyond traditional development aid owe their workability to a determinate effort of coalitions of rich countries to protect their own niches and to block migration (see, respectively, Smith 1995 and de Swaan 1994).

The final and most problematic aspect of cosmopolitan equality concerns an old Kantian puzzle. How can the global demos prevent world government from becoming either super-tyrannical or super-inefficient? It seems almost impossible to attain a boundary-less social order that supplies mankind in an organized and rule-bound way with the long list of entitlements that left-communitarians (such as socialists) usually aspire to. The order may degenerate and turn into a despotic superstate; it may become a platform for opportunistic argument and inefficient bargaining; it may introduce administrative boundaries on a technical basis that are either artificial and ineffective or effective but inconsistent; or it may reduce its workings to the demands of minimal morality, such as world peace and world tolerance (see, for a pessimistic view and an optimistic one respectively, Hoffmann 1995 and March and Olsen 1995).

WHY GLOBAL MARKET JUSTICE IS NOT AROUND THE CORNER

If one accepts the argument of the impossibility of cosmopolitan equality, it becomes imperative to examine whether free global markets may realize the ideal of global equality as unintended consequence of profit seeking. In this perspective, the formal neoclassical theory of trade is one of the most impressive legacies of the Enlightenment, on a par with the philosophy of the cosmopolitan end of history (Anderson 1992: ch.13). It states that:

(i) Given differences between countries (endowment of factors of production, intensity of factor usage) will give rise to trade and gains from trade (indirect production, enlarged consumption).

(ii) Gains from trade between countries will be distributed according to the relative prices of the goods that nationals (persons, households, classes) are able to produce, while these prices are converging behind their back.

(iii) Convergence of relative prices of traded and tradable goods will cause equalization of factor prices (land rents, wages, profits).

(iv) Factor price equality will promote egalitarian justice if the winners (owners of scarce resources in the export sector; of abundant, cheap resources in the national territory; of mobile resources) absorb losers by expansion of their sector, if they create positive linkages within the domestic economy, or if they compensate chronic losers by redistribution.

It is ironic to notice that many contemporary economists do not accept this argument any longer (Kapstein 1996: 24). Some argue that empirical evidence is poor, others that the theoretical assumptions are wrong. The empirical debate concerns issues like the relative weight of foreign trade in rich countries compared to the distributive impact of technological change; estimation methods; and the choice of dependent variables (such as earnings inequality), countries, and periods. There is not much evidence that the gap between developed and underdeveloped countries is closing in the way that is predicted by the Heckscher–Ohlin model (Landes 1990; Burtless 1995; Freeman 1995; Lawrence 1996; and *The Economist*, "The Future of the State," September 20, 1997). One textbook author writes that "the theory cannot be proved or refuted" (Asheghian 1995: 88).

The theoretical criticism concerns certain basic assumptions, such as constant returns to scale and absence of transport and communication costs. Since the models of Heckscher–Ohlin, Samuelson–Stolper, and their followers are highly abstract and idealized, it is not surprising to learn that these models were the outcome of questioning some assumptions of Ricardo's model of comparative advantage, which were replaced by other questionable assumptions (see Krugman and Obsterfeld 1994: part one, and Asheghian 1995: part one). First, there are cases of prohibitive transaction costs. Rational agents consider the relative costs of either trade or movement of capital, labor, and technology; they may decide to stop long-distance trade with foreigners and to start living with them, setting up a company or finding tenure there. Second, there are cases of failing international markets, such as monopolistic competition, dumping, and external effects. Third, there are cases of missing international markets, caused by extreme international differences (regional underdevelopment, absolute advantages in terms of factor endowments such as energy or human capital). Sometimes the gap between two countries is so wide that economic interdependency just does not arise. Fourth, there are cases of blocked international markets (artificial barriers of trade and transfer). Governments may strive for autarky. They may protect their own producers, either defensively (tariff-walls) or aggressively (subsidies). They may, in the business of concluding commercial treaties with other governments, discriminate between domestic producers of tradables and between foreign trading partners. And they may fail to pay attention to the losers of internationalization, thus provoking resistance toward open exchange and competition.

From the viewpoint of distribution it is the neglect of the "politics of international economics" that turns the pure theory of factor price equalization into a special case with a vengeance. Recently, a team of political economists led by Keohane explored the relation between internationalization of exchange and domestic political institutions. Although Keohane did not focus on the relation between economic openness and social equality, his framework sheds light on the capacity and willingness of distribution-sensitive democratic governments to support integration of their economies in the world market as a crucial variable (Keohane and Milner 1996).[10] There are three pathways for institutional reform driven by shocks or waves of internationalization. First, a change of relative prices of tradables affects the incentives of groups of asset holders to support or reject liberalization. It also affects political power relations and political coalitions. In particular, the owners of mobile factors of production (financial capital, multinational producers) gain bargaining advantages over immobile factors (blue-collar workers, domestic producers). Second, an expansion of the tradables sector increases sensitivity to world price trends; promotes domestic debate about the international economy; and, most importantly, forces all affected actors (including public officials and political representatives) to face possible crises, like currency crises and balance of payments crises. Third, an integration of trade and financial markets undermines the efficacy of macroeconomic policies and trade and capital controls. Unilateral manipulation of interest rates, capital taxes and regulations, governmental spending, and public transfers becomes more difficult, costly, and risky. Keohane predicts that internationalization will lead to institutional reform, but this prediction is a qualified one since the political power of mobile capital is not unconstrained. Furthermore, institutions are not fully flexible. They can block external price signals, freeze domestic coalitions and policies in place, and channel political responses to changes in relative prices. Although these qualifications make Keohane's framework somewhat inconclusive, his analysis of the politics of international economics clearly shows that there is nothing automatic or self-evident about political leaders who accept or pursue Pareto-optimal factor price equalization, that is, forms of trade in which nobody on both sides loses and international inequalities decrease.

DOUX COMMERCE REVISITED

According to the classical Enlightenment view global markets soften manners: "greater control of the passions in general and more predictability of the actions of the sovereign and restraints on *grands coups d'autorité* in particular, thanks to increased stability and *douceur* in the management of human affairs" (Hirschman 1995: 24, see Hirschman 1977 and 1986). There are many mechanisms at work here:

- the transition from aggressive power seeking to relatively innocent and benign forms of moneymaking and accumulation of private wealth;

- the reorientation of social leadership by managers of private firms and state managers toward the welfare of citizens as consumers;
- the recognition of the human standing of business partners beyond borders (respect, understanding, trust, reciprocity, tolerance); and
- the articulation of interdependence and the build-up of common organizations, rules, and practices for regular exchange and guaranteed prosperity.

Such mechanisms turn noncooperative problems of interdependence between actors from different nations into cooperative problems that are liable to mutually accepted and justifiable solutions. The prominent thinkers of the Enlightenment did not foresee that global markets would bring global distributive justice. Montesquieu proposed policies for assistance of the poor and public employment in order to restore the balance of commercial democracy. Rousseau pictured a republic of needs that combined the advantage of foreign trade with protectionism, proportional direct taxation, and the repression of luxury. Hume and Smith contended that both civil liberties under the rule of law and continuous economic growth would preempt the need for social and redistributive measures by the liberal state. And Paine suggested that civil nations should settle for peaceful coexistence in order to set up just republican constitutions: The advanced nations should pursue equality among their citizens first (*inter alia* by funding a citizen's income via inheritance taxes), while underdeveloped nations would follow later. Yet all these thinkers argued that globalization of the economy would reinforce the spirit of secular and universal individualism both by eliminating unfair (extreme, feudal) inequalities of income and wealth and by bringing about fair (balanced, bourgeois) assignments of natural and man-made goods.

The classical view of globalization has many flaws, as Marx pointed out in his famous indictment of Dutch colonialism in Java (Marx 1973: 779–80). Empirically, it is simply wrong, since it failed to predict the destruction of aboriginal peoples, the rise of capitalist empires, the globalization of wars between bourgeois nation-states, and other less disastrous cases of dominance in pseudo-global markets. Theoretically, it lacks an explanation of the existence of structurally violent moneymaking (Why criminal markets alias mafia capitalism?) and of nation-states (Why these inefficient barriers of maximal planetary production?). Still, the classical view rightly suggests that global markets contribute to internationalization and globalization of legal private conflict solution, news and information, and moral obligations (see Sassen 1996; Rothschild 1995: 76; and Sen 1997: 18). It contains a ladder of three important and topical ideas.

First, full-scale insulation from the emerging market order will not lead to more equality among the members of the excluded community but to less equality. The UNDP notices that the share of the poorest 20 percent of the world population—living in the poorest countries—in global trade decreased from 2.3 percent in 1960–70 to 1.3 percent in 1990. The shares in global investment, savings, and commercial credit reveal a similar trend (UNDP 1993: 27). Furthermore, the UNDP calculates that in 1993 forty-two countries were immersed in major conflicts, and thirty-seven others experienced lesser forms of political violence: sixty-five of these seventy-nine countries were in the developing world. Kaplan made an unsentimental journey through these areas, from Liberia via Kazakhstan to Laos and Cambodia. His title *The Ends of the Earth* implies that none of these countries did fulfill the minimal requirements of decency and justice. None of them belong to the world market system. Many of them, in particular countries where people suffered invisibly without any power to mobilize domestic, regional, and global authorities, are also marginalized with respect to transnational political and cultural systems. The empirical connections are obviously complex, but Kaplan's observations roughly corroborate the old idea of globalization of markets as a civilizing force (Kaplan 1996).[11]

Second, economic openness is located somewhere between insulation and open borders since it is embedded in nation-states. To the extent that the state combines openness with the promotion of domestic equality it will cover some collective external risks (such as terms-of-trade uncertainty). Rodrik's statistical analysis confirms that there is a robust association between the extent to which an economy is exposed to trade and the size of its government sector (Rodrik 1996).[12] At the same time, equality requires some closure of external boundaries since the legitimacy of formal redistributive schemes and policies depends on some distinction between beneficiaries and nonmembers (Walzer 1981). The social democratic and Christian democratic welfare states in continental Europe are still the best examples of well-ordered egalitarian regimes. Their relative equality is based on constitutional or consensual rights and understandings, on broad universalist arrangements and clear restrictive rules of the game against parasitism. All these countries have "a managed but market-oriented economy exposed with a degree of cushioning to world trade and monetary arrangements" (Dahrendorf 1988: 116). And they also have some prominent features of a closed community. The community features concern the common memory of the Depression and the Second World War, the trust in good government, and the loyalty to public systems of social protection. The closure features concern insulation from Eastern European goods and services and the introduction of restrictive immigration policies. So the elimination of internal boundaries between members of national egalitarian regimes was combined with the establishment of external boundaries between nationals and foreigners. As Jordan puts it: "Welfare states, far from being unambiguously globalization-friendly, tend to orientate governments toward measures of protectionism and nationalism, even when other factors (such as the need for labor immigration, JdB) might indicate the opposite orientation" (Jordan 1996: 231; cf., Klaussen 1995; and van Parijs 1996).

Finally, the stability of any emerging public and authoritative plan for global equalization beyond the current schemes for humanitarian intervention in cases of natural catastrophes, famines, and crimes against mankind depends not only on the access of all communities-polities to the world market, but also upon the balance within these units between openness and closure, which goes with formal redistributive schemes. It also depends on the balance between unity and plurality in global governance. Look at the most successful cases of global civilization to date, like the multinational corporation, the United Nations, and the Olympic Games. Such global schemes are effective when and because their basis of unity is not detailed, closed, and hierarchical but incomplete, that is, vague, open-ended, and loosely structured. Encompassing global communitarianism seems impossible because such an extended union needs the reference to some other union (say inhuman or extrahuman entities: angry gods, tyrants, UFOs). But its best operational components will only stand a chance if they require a commitment to unity that does not destroy human diversity and practical pluralism.

These lessons from classical Enlightenment are quite general. They do not explain why today's globalization is accompanied by equalization in Malaysia, new social inequalities in China and Mexico, and marginalization of many countries in sub-Sahara Africa. But they do show that both strategic public choices between growth-led security and support-led security and strategic private choices by multinational firms are crucial. Since the former choices are thoroughly discussed in recent development economics, I will only discuss the latter ones (see Drèze and Sen 1989; Dasgupta 1993; and Drèze and Sen 1995). A multinational firm investing abroad has many options. It may lobby for monopolistic privileges, passively abide by the law of the land, finance its own social policies and local public goods, or join a corporatist mode of labor relations and economic policy making in the host country. The last two alternatives may illustrate the possible egalitarian consequences of today's "doux commerce." Under the pressure of consumers' boycotts and nongovernmental organizations in the West, some enlightened multinationals (such as Shell) have decided to commit themselves to moral business codes against corruption and exploitation and to invest in what American sociologists used to call "welfare capitalism" (Skocpol 1992: 26–30). In this case the struggle for profits and power in new world markets seems to be compatible with social business responsibility and moderate egalitarianism (see Baumol 1991 and van Parijs 1995: 62–65).[13]

THE PROBABILITY OF DEMOCRATIC CAPITALISM

Democratic capitalism is a mixed social order in which constitutional law and public policy facilitate the lively and creative interplay between civil political society (freedom of participation, public choice, consent of the sovereign people, and political pluralism) and civil economic society (freedom of exchange, competition, private property rights, and economic polycentrism). In table 21.1 I distinguish between old and new democratic capitalism, autocratic capitalism (legal markets within hierarchical society, imposed or permitted by absolute state leadership), and anarchical capitalism (market practices within fragmented society but without centralized political authority). A modern Enlightenment view would suggest that globalization will promote global equality partly unintendedly—since there is no global distributive agency—when and because (a) anarchies and autocracies transform themselves into new democratic capitalism (following the democratic wave in Southern Europe, Latin America, and Eastern Europe) and (b) both the old and the new liberal democracies are stable. It does not claim that democratic capitalism will universally engender equalization of income and wealth. But it does contend that strong democracy (with regular fair elections, free contestation by opposition parties

Table 21.1   Models of Capitalism in a Globalizing Economy

Old Democratic Capitalism (ODC)
  United States
  Japan
  France
New Democratic Capitalism (NDC)
  Russia
  Poland
  Czech Republic
Authoritarian Capitalism (AUC)
  China
  Indonesia
  Singapore
Anarchical Capitalism (ANC)
  Zaire
  Nigeria
  Rwanda

and social movements, and open forums for public debate and criticism of
political and social powers) is conceptually impossible without social
rights and the correction of the distributive failure of the price mechanism
(the twin idea of political and economic equality in civil society), that it is
instrumental to legitimate redistributive policies, and that it gives many
opportunities for quick rectifying responses to injustices. As two prominent comparative political scientists observe,

> If a democracy never produced policies that generated government mandated
> public goods in the areas of education, health, and transportation, some safety
> net for its citizens hurt by major market swings and some alleviation of gross
> inequality, democracy would not be sustainable. (Linz and Stepan 1996:
> 12–13)

It is not hard to detect flaws in this second Enlightenment view. First, there
is a lot of variation in the policy performance and distributive outcome of
countries that share the same model (compare the United States and the
United Kingdom with Germany and Sweden). Many comparativists criti-
cize the hard determinism in neo-Hobbesian, neo-Smithean, neo-Marxian,
and neo-Ricardian theories of globalization. But they tend to neglect the
lack of determinacy of their own theories about institutional legacies, in-
herited system characteristics, and vested interests.[14]

Second, there is no solid knowledge about the linkages between political
and economic institutions, as Hirschman has demonstrated. Some autocracies, like Indonesia, are more equal in some respects than some democracies, like Chile. It is wrong to believe that all good institutional things go
together, say world peace, civic nationalism, republican constitutionalism,
dynamic capitalism, cultural pluralism, and humanistic egalitarianism.
The only truth here is the Hobbesian one about the overall inferiority of
anarchy (Hirschman 1995: 221–30). So there is no plausible institutional
account of the statistical fact that the poor are more marginal in Brazil
(NDC), Guatemala (AUC), Guinea-Bissau (ANC), and the United States
(ODC) than in Bangladesh (NDC), Hungary (NDC), Indonesia (AUC),
Japan (ODC), and Nepal (AUC) (UNDP 1996: 13, see also UNDP 1997:
87–89).

Finally, new public policies may matter more than old institutions. The
new inequality in the Americas and the two Europes seems to be caused
by the specific neoliberal transition to globalizing capitalism since the late
1970s. This objection, however, needs further interpretation. As Wilson,
Galbraith, Dahrendorf, and other political analysts have noticed, the retreat
of the Western welfare state under the ideological legitimation of globalization was and is related to the exclusion of large minorities of voters
and the reduction of political participation by the less well-off. The new

inequality between the wealthy, the workers, and the unemployed is related to a domestic democratic deficit (see Dahl 1996 and Lijphart 1997).

Therefore I would like to derive a minimal claim from the neo-Kantian argument about "eternal social democracy." The claim is that in the long run the imperative of popular legitimacy (no public policy without representation) will force democratic governments to counterweight the imperative of accumulation (no public policy without response to the demands of mobile financial and productive capital). It seems outlandish to deny that the imperative of accumulation in an era of globalization will press left-wing politicians to take the mobile production factor into account, to cherish firms and rich nationals at the expense of families and poor nationals, and to strengthen national competitiveness by undermining the standard of living and the rights of workers and trade unions. A global capital market compels governments to favor foreign investors and to abandon expansive fiscal and monetary policies. A global market for goods compels governments to lower taxes and to allow deterioration of labor conditions in both the open and the sheltered sector. A global labor market (transnational companies, massive migration) compels governments to deregulate domestic industrial relations and to follow the wage rate of Beijing. Yet, the accumulation imperative will be compromised by the legitimacy imperative. Political elites at the national level are called to account, even in minimal democracies in Schumpeter's. Therefore, they must use their policy space in ways that are identifiable and inspiring in the eyes of the voters and public opinion leaders. In this perspective, it becomes necessary for governments, in particular for left-wing governments such as the social democratic leadership in Western Europe, to control the institutional preconditions for correcting the global market for egalitarian reasons. This is the topic of the last section.

SMOOTHENING THE TRADE-OFF BETWEEN INEQUALITY HERE AND EQUALITY THERE

I argued that globalization may promote global equality if it leads to diffusion of a framework of democratic capitalism that promotes the softening of manners of distributive authorities at both the supranational level (multinational corporations) and the national level (governments with their policies of internationalization). Unintended global equality presupposes a specific evolution of both market culture and the structure of democratic politics. I did not predict what will happen. In the rosy scenario of traveling equality multinational managers will follow decent business codes in both host and home countries, national politicians in the former First World will confine themselves to the elimination of egalitarian waste in social policy (reform of the welfare state instead of abolition), and national politicians in the former Third World will boldly wage wars against poverty and extreme inequality.[15] But this chapter did not discuss the list of different intermediate scenarios. Its point is that global equalization trends in the real world will stop the present trend of global polarization (since even the powerful members of the world system learn that polarization is destructive and that global trickle down is not a credible alternative) but will also fall short of cosmopolitan justice (since members of nation-states will continue to pursue special distributive advantages of national citizenship).

I emphasized that global equality will be the unintended consequence of many strategies of internationalization of many players with diverging resources of power. This does not exclude a practical role of makers of public policy. As van Parijs has put it, moral players will "steer clear of Penguins Island," where the prevailing norm is that "little should be asked from those who possess a lot; for otherwise the rich would be less rich and the poor would be poorer" (van Parijs 1995: 227). Van Parijs proposes the principles of universalist social protection, solidaristic patriotism, and supranational democratic engineering. The conclusion of my argument is similar. Egalitarian policymakers must control the introduction, maintenance, or restoration of institutional preconditions for markets within global civil society (cf., Elster, Offe and Preuss 1998). The most urgent of these preconditions are:

- the rule of law in all states (Adam Smith's "peace, easy taxes, and tolerable administration of justice");
- the sense of solidarity in all states (universalist social policy);
- the sense of human dignity beyond national difference (minimal global morality);
- the open access to legal markets (national and supranational gate-keeping);
- the national and supranational scales of civil society (civic responsibility of firms, trade unions, political parties, and nongovernmental organizations, in particular their willingness to join public deliberation and action); and
- the national and supranational scales of democracy (imaginative representation, confederalism).

The condition of the rule of law is self-evident. Much more challenging is John Rawls's conviction that the rule of law and autocracy (or "hierarchical society" as he calls it) are compatible in the real world today. Autocracies may not accept the liberal terms of a global social contract, but some of them do accept (a) peaceful diplomacy and trade within international relations; (b) general rights and obligations, a common good conception of justice, the integrity of judges, and a reasonable consultation hierarchy within their legal order; and (c) respect for basic human rights in both domestic and international affairs (the right to life, the right to liberty, the right to property, the right to procedural justice) (Rawls 1993: 60–63).

The condition of solidarity implies that the circle of solidaristic sentiments and opinions should be expanded (new nation building, for example by the European Union) without diluting the most important circle today, which is national solidarity. In order to reinforce national solidarity, one needs revitalization of both the solidaristic ethos (between workers and unemployed, natives and migrants) and universalist social policies (child benefits, health care, and old age provisions for all social classes, and so on). The main task of supranational authorities is to enable strong national governments to enforce legitimate redistribution (minimal social rights, prohibition of social dumping, prevention of cutthroat fiscal competition).

The condition of minimal global morality concerns the arrangement of humanitarian intervention and partial global redistribution. There seems to be common substantive ground in the rival conceptions of minimal global morality: basic human rights (Rawls), minimization of "murder and the destruction of life, imprisonment, enslavement, starvation, poverty, physical pain and torture, homelessness, friendlessness" (Hampshire), and "the positive duties of mutual care and reciprocity; the negative injunctions concerning violence, deceit, and betrayal; and the norms for certain rudimentary procedures and standards for what is just" (Bok) (see Rawls 1993; Hampshire 1989: 90; and Bok 1995:16; cf., Walzer 1994). It seems clear that any plausible view of humanitarian obligations today would include public and corporative obligations with respect to minimal economic equality between all human beings. The real issue concerns the democratic institutionalization of international and supranational principles concerning the transfer of economic means.

The condition of open access to global markets may be seen as correlative to the condition of the rule of law. What is needed here is the foundation and creative interplay of strong and multitiered antitrust authorities (like the World Trade Organization and Directory General 4 on European competition law). For example, the European Union should fight (non-)tariff barriers to entry within member-states. This implies the elimination of the protection of European farmers, fishermen, and steel industrialists.

The condition of civil society boils down to the simple idea that all civil associations are jointly responsible for the public interest, *casu quo* for economic equality among nationals and foreigners. If globalization is leading to extreme inequalities, then these associations should be prepared to join public deliberation and action (in which the appropriate response is at stake). This condition does not require a general stop of capital export. It simply forces the holders of global economic power to give good public reasons for their plans and strategies, to abandon parasitism (evasion of the fiscal costs of redistributive policies), and to follow national and supranational rules of distributive justice.

The condition of democracy should block the hollowing out of democratic institutions and practices by the rise of transnational "networks." First, globalization should not be an excuse to national politicians for not representing their constituencies (goodbye to political determinism about the inevitability of the North American Free Trade Agreement, NAFTA; EMU, European Monetary Union; and so on). Second, national parliaments and referendums should be strengthened. Third, no centralization of economic and social policy should take place without proper constitutional guarantees for strong supranational democracy. Fourth, the choice between cosmopolitan governance and confederal governance is easy. Since there is no solid practical theory about multitiered governance that solves Kant's old problem (How do you design a world government without realizing the greatest despotism or inefficiency?), it is better to build globally organized capitalism on the basis of confederal experience (see the closing chapter of Hirst and Thompson 1996; Newman 1996; and Pogge 1997).

NOTES

I am grateful for comments from Steven Hartkamp, Michiel Jenniskens, Lolle Nauta, and Robert van der Veen.

1. See, about this classification of views of international relations, Robert Keohane (1996) and Hall (1996).

2. See about the strange birth of egalitarianism of fear in the case of Goldsmith and France in general Buruma (1996) and Hoffmann (1997).

3. Other negative effects concern irresponsible demographic policy, destruction of local community and resistance against universalist social policy. See Van Parijs (1995a: 296–7).

4. Gellner's remarks about the tendency to equality in industrial society are an echo of Tocqueville's account of the social democratic state of equal access to political power, absence of legal privileges, and high rates of mobility.

5. Privatization is discussed in Przeworski (1995: 95–106) and Eatwell et al. (1995). Nationalism by trade is discussed by Hall (1995: 24–25) and Judt (1996: 110–14).

6. "To the extent the institutions in question are not adopted for the intrinsic *values and principles embodied in them*, but just for the *outcomes expected from them*, they enjoy much less of a counterfactual validity and will hence more easily fall victim to some empirical evidence of failure. This in turn will tend to shorten the lifespan credited to them, and it may even lead to their abolition at the point before their desired side-effects have had a chance to unfold. Institutions adopted

for instrumental reasons are disappointment-sensitive," says Claus Offe (1995:132).

7. I owe this example to Steven Hartkamp, who points out that the clearest case of traveling equality (decreasing prosperity and growing inequality in the West plus increasing prosperity and decreasing inequality in the East, both with reference to a global pattern, and not to Western and Southern local patterns) is also the hardest one from a moral point of view.

8. Sen notes that the increasing Asian and African share of the world population (63.7 percent in 1950, 71.2 percent in 1990, 78.5 percent by 2050) would imply that Asians and Africans will be almost as numerous as they were before 1650–1750, that is, before the demographic shift caused by the European industrial revolution.

9. This conclusion also applies for nonhierarchical cosmopolitan schemes, such as Burnheim's functional democracy.

10. The authors stress the point that "internationalization of exchange" is exogenous in their framework (it is not seen as an instrumental variable of state elites) and that it should not be confused with democratization (the impact of the world market on autocratic states is not set aside).

11. The optimistic point about the distributive advantages of future entry in the global market is completely missed by Kennedy (1996).

12. The modern reformulation of this classical insight is Ruggie (1982).

13. These authors reduce welfare capitalism to the self-interest of managers and the invisible hand. Philip Pettit has recently developed a different view, which focuses on the social regard of managers and the "intangible hand." Pettit's view is rather plausible when local public opinion in host countries begins to influence multinationals that settle down and face shrinking exit options.

14. See Berger and Dore (1996) and Esping-Andersen (1996).

15. Part of this scenario is already spelled out by Haveman 1985. More specific is UNDP 1997: 89–93.

REFERENCES

Anderson, Perry. (1992). *A Zone of Engagement*. London: Verso.

Asheghian, Parviz. (1995). *International Economics*. St. Paul, MN: West.

Atkinson, Anthony. (1996). The Distribution of Income. *De Economist* 144: 1–21.

Barber, Benjamin. (1995). *Jihad vs. McWorld*. New York: Random House.

Baumol, William. (1991). *Perfect Markets and Easy Virtue*. Oxford: Basil Blackwell.

Beck, Ulrich. (1997). *Was ist Globalisierung?* Frankfurt: Suhrkamp.

Bok, Sissela. (1995). *Common Values*. Columbia: University of Missouri Press.

Bowles, Samuel, and Herbert Gintis. (1995). Productivity-Enhancing Egalitarian Policies. *International Labour Review* 134: 559–85.

Boyer, Robert. (1996). The Convergence Hypothesis Revisited. In Suzanne Berger and Ronald Dore, eds. *National Diversity and Global Capitalism*. Ithaca, NY: Cornell University Press.

Bradshaw, York, and Michael Wallace. (1996). *Global Inequalities*. London: Pine Forge Press.

Burnheim, John. (1985). *Is Democracy Possible?* Cambridge: Polity Press.

———. (1986). Democracy, Nation States and the World System. In David Held and Christopher Pollitt, eds. *New Forms of Democracy*. London: Sage/Open University.

Burtless, Gary. (1995). International Trade and the Rise of Earnings Inequality. *Journal of Economic Literature* 33: 800–16.

Buruma, Ian. (1996). Fear and Loathing in Europe. *New York Review of Books*, 17 October 1996.

Dahl, Robert. (1985). *A Preface to Economic Democracy*. Berkeley: University of California Press.

———. (1996). Equality versus Inequality. *Political Science and Politics* 29: 639–48.

Dahrendorf, Ralf. (1988). *The Modern Social Conflict*. Berkeley: University of California Press.

Dasgupta, Partha. (1993). *An Inquiry into Well-Being and Destitution*. Oxford: Clarendon Press.

Drèze, Jean, and Amartya Sen. (1989). *Hunger and Public Action*. Oxford: Clarendon Press.

———. (1995). *India*. Oxford: Clarendon Press.

Eatwell, John, et al. (1995). *Transformation and Integration*. London: IPPR.

Elster, Jon. (1989). *The Cement of Society*. Cambridge: Cambridge University Press.

Elster, Jon (1992). *Local Justice*. New York: Russell Sage Foundation.

———. (1993). Ethical Individualism and Presentism. *The Monist* 76: 333–48.

———, Claus Offe, and Ulrich K. Preuss. (1998). *Institutional Design in Post-Communist Societies*. Cambridge: Cambridge University Press.

Esping-Andersen, Gøsta, ed. (1996). *Welfare States in Transition*. London: Sage.

Fitoussi, Jean-Paul, and Pierre Rosanvallon. (1996). *Le nouvel age des inègalités*. Paris: Seuil.

Freeman, Richard. (1995). Are Your Wages Set in Beijing? *Journal of Economic Perspectives* 9: 15–32.

Gellner, Ernest. (1987). The Social Roots of Egalitarianism. In Ernest Gellner, ed. *Culture, Identity, and Politics*. Cambridge: Cambridge University Press.

Greider, William. (1996). *One World, Ready or Not*. New York: Simon and Schuster.

Guéhenno, Jean-Marie. (1993). *La fin de la démocratie*. Paris: Flammarion.

Hall, John. (1995). Nationalisms, Classified and Explained. In Sukumar Periwal, ed. *Notions of Nationalism*. Budapest: Central European University Press.

———. (1996). *International Orders*. Cambridge: Polity Press.

Hampshire, Stuart. (1989). *Innocence and Experience*. Cambridge, Mass.: Harvard University Press.

Haveman, Robert. (1985). *Does the Welfare State Increase Welfare?* (Inaugural Lecture). Leiden: Stenfert Kroese.

Held, David. (1995). *Democracy and Global Order*. Cambridge: Polity Press.

Hirschman, Albert. (1977). *The Passions and the Interests*. Princeton, N.J.: Princeton University Press.

———. (1986). *Rival Views of Market Society*. New York: Viking.

———. (1995). *A Propensity to Self-Subversion*. Cambridge, Mass.: Harvard University Press.

Hirst, Paul, and Grahame Thompson. (1996). *Globalization in Question*. Cambridge: Polity Press.

Hoffmann, Stanley. (1995). Dreams of a Just World. *New York Review of Books*, 2 November 1995.

———. (1997). Look Back in Anger. *New York Review of Books*, 17 July 1997.

Hurrell, Andrew, and Ngaire Woods. (1995). Globalization and Inequality. *Millennium* 24: 447–70.

Jones, Charles I. (1997). On the Evolution of the World Income Distribution. *Journal of Economic Perspectives* 11: 19–36.

Jordan, Bill. (1996). *A Theory of Poverty and Social Exclusion*. Cambridge: Polity Press.

Judt, Tony. (1996). *A Grand Illusion?* London: Penguin.

Kaplan, Robert. (1996). *The Ends of the Earth*. New York: Random House.

Kapstein, Ethan. (1994). *Governing the Global Economy*. Cambridge, Mass.: Harvard University Press.

———. (1996). Workers and the World Economy. *Foreign Affairs* 75, no. 3 (1996): 16–37.

Kennedy, Paul. (1996). Doomsterism. *New York Review of Books*, 19 September 1996.

Keohane, Robert. (1996). International Liberalism Reconsidered. In John Dunn, ed. *The Economic Limits to Modern Politics*. Cambridge: Cambridge University Press.

———, and Helen Milner, eds. (1996). *Internationalization and Domestic Politics*. Cambridge: Cambridge University Press.

Klaussen, Jytte. (1995). Social Rights Advocacy and State Building. *World Politics* 47: 244–67.

Krugman, Paul. (1996). *Pop Internationalism*. Cambridge, Mass.: MIT Press.

———, and Maurice Obsterfeld. (1994). *International Economics*. 3rd ed. New York: HarperCollins.

Krugman, Paul, and Anthony Venables. (1995). Globalization and the Inequality of Nations. NBER Working Paper 5098. Cambridge, Mass.: National Bureau of Economic Research.

Landes, David. (1990). Why Are We So Rich and They So Poor? *American Economic Review*, Papers and Proceedings, 80: 1–13.

Lane, Jan-Erik, and Svante Ersson. (1995). *European Politics*. London: Sage.

Lawrence, Robert. (1996). *Single World, Divided Nations?* Washington, D.C.: Brookings Institution Press.

Leibfried, Stephan, and Paul Pierson, eds. (1995). *European Social Policy*. Washington, D.C.: Brookings Institution Press.

Lijphart, Arend. (1997). Unequal Participation. *American Political Science Review* 91 (1997): 1–14.

Linz, Juan, and Alfred Stepan. (1996). *Problems of Democratic Transition and Consolidation*. Baltimore: Johns Hopkins University Press.

McGrew, Anthony, ed. (1997). *The Transformation of Democracy?* Cambridge: Polity Press.

March, James, and Johan Olsen. (1995). *Democratic Governance*. New York: Free Press.

Marx, Karl. (1973). *Das Kapital, vol. I*. Berlin: Dietz Verlag.

Murphy, Sean. (1996). *Humanitarian Intervention*. Philadelphia: University of Pennsylvania Press.

Newman, Michael. (1996). *Democracy, Sovereignty and the European Union*. London: Hurst.

Nickel, James. (1987). *Making Sense of Human Rights*. Berkeley: University of California Press.

Nussbaum, Martha, with Respondents. (1996). *For Love of Country*. Boston: Beacon Press.

Offe, Claus. (1995). Some Skeptical Considerations on the Malleability of Representative Institutions. In Joshua Cohen and Joel Rogers, eds. *Associations and Democracy*. London: Verso.

———, and Philippe Schmitter. (1995). Future of Democracy. In Seymour Lipset, ed. *The Encyclopedia of Democracy. Vol. III*. London: Routledge.

van Parijs, Philippe. (1995a). *Real Freedom for All*. Oxford: Oxford University Press.

———. (1995b). *Sauver la solidarité*. Paris: Cerf.

———. (1996). Justice and Democracy: Are They Compatible? *Journal of Political Philosophy* 4: 101–17.

Pogge, Thomas. (1992). Cosmopolitanism and Sovereignty. *Ethics* 103: 48–75.

———. (1997). Creating Supra-National Institutions Democratically. *Journal of Political Philosophy* 5: 163–182.

Pritchett, Lant. (1997). Divergence, Big Time. *Journal of Economic Perspectives* 11: 3–18.

Przeworski, Adam, et al. (1995). *Sustainable Democracy*. Cambridge: Cambridge University Press.

Rae, Douglas, et al. (1981). *Equalities*. Cambridge, Mass.: Harvard University Press.

Rawls, John. (1993). The Law of Peoples. In Stephen Shute and Susan Hurley, eds. *On Human Rights*. New York: Basic Books.

Reder, Melvin. (1982). Chicago Economics. *Journal of Economic Literature* 20: 1–38.

Reich, Robert. (1991). *The Work of Nations*. New York: Vintage.

Rodrik, Dani. (1996). Why Do More Open Economies Have Bigger Governments? NBER Working Paper 5537. Cambridge, Mass.

Rothschild, Emma. (1995). What Is Security? *Daedalus* 124: 53–98.

Ruggie, John. (1982). International Regimes, Transactions and Change. *International Organization* 36: 195–231.

Sassen, Saskia. (1996). *Losing Control?* New York: Columbia University Press.

Sen, Amartya. (1994). Population: Delusion and Reality. *New York Review of Books*, 22 September 1995.

——. (1997). Social Commitment and Democracy. In Paul Barker, ed. *Living as Equals*. Oxford: Oxford University Press.

Skocpol, Theda. (1992). *Protecting Mothers and Soldiers*. Cambridge, Mass.: Harvard University Press.

Smith, Anthony. (1995). *Nations and Nationalism in a Global Era*. Cambridge: Polity Press.

Swaan, Abram de, ed. (1994). *Social Policy beyond Borders*. Amsterdam: Amsterdam University Press.

Theil, Henry, and James Seale Jr. (1994). The Geographic Distribution of World Income, 1950–1990. *De Economist* 142: 387–420.

United Nations Development Programme. (1993). *Human Development Report 1993*. Oxford: Oxford University Press.

——. (1996). *Human Development Report 1996*. Oxford: Oxford University Press.

——. (1997). *Human Development Report 1997*. Oxford: Oxford University Press.

Walzer, Michael. (1981). The Distribution of Membership. In Peter Brown and Henry Shue, eds. *Boundaries*. Totowa, N.J.: Rowman and Littlefield.

——. (1994). *Thick and Thin*. Notre Dame: University of Notre Dame Press, 1994.

——. (1997). *On Toleration*. New Haven, Conn.: Yale University Press.

Weiner, Myron. (1995). *The Global Migration Crisis*. New York: HarperCollins.

Williamson, Jeffrey. (1996). Globalization and Inequality Then and Now. NBER Working Paper 5491. Cambridge, Mass.: National Bureau of Economic Research.

Wolferen, Karel van. (1989). *The Enigma of Japanese Power*. New York: Knopf.

Wood, Adrian. (1995). How Trade Hurt Unskilled Workers. *Journal of Economic Perspectives* 9 (1995): 57–80.

22

The Quest for Humane Governance in an Era of Globalization

Richard Falk

TAKING ACCOUNT OF GLOBALIZATION: POSITIVE AND NEGATIVE EFFECTS

The quest for global governance during the long period of the Cold War focused on peace and security issues, especially the avoidance of general war between the two nuclear superpowers. Other important developments were of course occurring, including the collapse of colonialism and the regional integration of Western Europe. But the dominant world picture consisted of two asymmetrically arranged hierarchical blocs of countries repeatedly confronting one another, generating varying degrees of tension. This encounter established the pattern of geopolitics for the interval between 1945 and 1989.

The idea of humane governance in such a setting emphasized the virtues of nonalignment and generally supported the efforts of countries in the South to proceed with development along the lines dictated by the dynamics of self-determination. From these perspectives, intervention from the North, by either side in the Cold War, was perceived as highly destructive of prospects for humane governance on the level of the state. Such perceptions were epitomized by the worldwide reactions against the U.S. interventionary war in Vietnam and the later Soviet invasion of Afghanistan.

In a fundamental ordering sense, an initial objective of progressive world order thinking during the Cold War was to curtail the impact of geopolitics on the development of societies within recognized international boundaries to the extent possible. In this sense, the Westphalian model of autonomous sovereign states became both a defining feature of the postcolonial system and a remote aspiration; the fiction of "nation-state" was unanimously endorsed in decolonizing settings, including Africa, to avoid divisive ethnically based conflict that would arise in the event colonial boundaries, however artificial, were opened for discussion. Yet at the same time, the suppression of "nations" within such states, as well as the division of Europe—including even the prior (and subsequently) unified state of Germany—into hegemonic zones, placed a heavy burden on substantive sovereignty that was reinforced by the retention in Europe of Soviet and U.S. troops from World War II. In a different sense, the imposition of a state upon the postcolonial reality of Africa has often resulted in nonviable entities in various forms (Jackson 1991). Such arrangements both conformed to Westphalian expectations by respecting the formal independence of existing states and deformed these expectations by its geopolitical denial of the substantive reality of sovereignty for many states and the entrapment of many nations in hostile state environments (as, for instance, within the borders of the Soviet Union).

The idea of humane governance responded to these realities additionally by reference to the authority and normative claims of the United Nations Charter, which had the dual advantage of treaty status and active participation by both blocs in the Cold War. But this participation was again asymmetrically in favor of the West, yet it still provided a semblance of common normative ground by affirming the same constitutional document, along with a welcome framing of the world order agenda in the nonrealist political language of peace, justice, development, and human rights. The Charter was important in this respect as it imposed major legal restrictions on the rights of states to use force as an instrument of policy, thereby openly challenging earlier Westphalian ideas that had left recourse to force in international law essentially at the discretion of states, being treated as an element of sovereignty. The Charter also seemed to provide an alternative to the self-help character of the pre–World War II phase of the Westphalian system by offering the prospect of collective action in support of states under attack. Much of the thinking about humane governance during this period, in effect, if not literally, sought to convert these Charter expectations into real norms of behavior by invoking the authority of international law and by encouraging governments to engage in serious disarming and demilitarizing negotiations.

It is also true that more ambitious conceptions of humane governance, such as advanced by the World Order Models Project, were insisting during this period upon a more encompassing view of the adjustments that would be beneficial and necessary from the perspective of a set of world order values (Mendlovitz 1975; Falk 1975). These values were specified as follows: minimizing violence, promoting economic well-being, realizing social justice, and maximizing environmental protection. Such a normative agenda encouraged a critical posture toward mainstream reformist thinking that favored incremental adjustments and managerial approaches to international conflict, typified by an emphasis on arms control (and rejection of disarmament) and support for functional expansion of UN activities by way of the specialized agencies. This more radical stream of thought was rooted in utopian traditions of reflections about human potentiality, as well as on integrative interpretations of history that regarded the unification of humanity as a natural fulfillment of an animating ethos of solidarity, exhibiting a human identity that supplemented and transcended specific identities based on race, ethnicity, gender, class, nationality, and ideology with an overarching identity to humanity as a whole.

The end of the Cold War has shifted the debate on humane governance in rather profound ways. The role of the United States as sole superpower in a global setting without a credible strategic conflict creates an ambiguous geopolitical climate, especially given the prominence of global market forces. Associating this prominence with a preoccupation about "globalization" generates a tension between what might be described as the old geopolitics related to such doctrines as the balance of power, deterrence, and containment and the new geopolitics related to currently dominating ideas about market share, free trade, and competitiveness and, to a lesser extent, issues of human rights, international crime, and environmental protection. The United States has confusingly positioned itself at the interface between the new and the old, sometimes associated with the interpretation of modernist and postmodernist attitudes and arrangements (Tehranian 1992; Borgmann 1992), thereby helping to spread a sense of uncertainty about the character of world order in this early phase of the era of globalization.

The old geopolitics continues to be expressed by efforts to contain "rogue states" by a reliance on coercive diplomacy, including sanctions, and through pressure on third countries to withhold critical technology and even resources. In contrast, the subordination of ideological differences, normative objections, and balance of power considerations in favor of trade and investment opportunities, as in relation to China, is expressive of the new geopolitics. The realities of globalization, together with this unresolved tension between the old and new geopolitics, underscores the importance of rethinking humane governance and extending its relevance to current world order challenges.

To interpret this interplay from the perspective of promoting humane governance requires some initial specification of the impact of globalization upon world order. To do this a summary is presented, organized by reference to detrimental and beneficial impacts. First, the detrimental impacts.

(1) A widening gap between winners and losers; according to the *Human Development Report 1997*,

[t]he share of the poorest 20 percent of the world's people in global income now stands at a miserable 1.1 percent, down from 1.4 percent in 1991 and 2.3 percent in 1960. It continues to shrink. And the ratio of the income of the top 20 percent to that of the poorest 20 percent rose from 30 to 1 in 1960, to 61 to 1 in 1991—and to a startling new high of 78 to 1 in 1994. (UNDP 1997: 7)

These widening gaps are also evident in the relations among regions and in the internal relations between rich and poor segments of society and seems to be undermining the sense of political community, upon which societal cohesion depends, at the level of the state, as well as having an alienating effect upon individuals. These developments give rise to various chauvinistic and xenophobic outlooks and movements; for a full-fledged rationale for such a posture on the part of the West, see the book-length, somewhat modified, formulation of Huntington's famous "clash thesis" (Huntington 1996).

(2) A new orthodoxy and harshness that constrains the role of government in relation to the losers, by emphasizing considerations of competitiveness and fiscal austerity as necessary priorities, given the logic of global markets. Such a pattern of thinking and acting is left largely unchallenged, partly reflecting the decline of organized labor as a relatively coherent social force that could be counted on to advance a people-oriented perspective on the role of the state. The effect is to diminish the disposition and capacity of the state to take initiatives, thereby tolerating widespread long-term homelessness and acute urban decay that persists in the midst of glittery affluence or, alternatively, regarding chronically high unemployment as the necessary price that must be paid if wage levels are to be kept high and inflation low, as in most of Europe. Such "principled indifference" has also undercut support for economic assistance to sub-Saharan Africa where the political outcomes that mattered during the Cold War are no longer of strategic consequence, and hence not worth an investment that had been previously justified according to the rules of the old geopolitics.

(3) The ideology associated with contemporary globalization has encouraged comprehensive privatization. This tendency has been reinforced by the current widespread societal dislike of government and bureaucracy, and further emboldened by the glorification of supposedly self-organizing systems, especially the market and Internet, and by the abject failures in economic and social performance of centrally planned economies of the Soviet type. The policy effect of such a shift in attitude about collective social responsibilities has been to exert strong downward pressures on support for most public goods, and especially for global public goods, such as the funding of the United Nations and action taken to sustain the

global commons in the face of disturbing trends in ocean pollution and climate change. This diminished support for public goods is especially pronounced in the United States, which has given the strongest neoliberal spin to the economic imperatives of globalization, choosing in late 1997 to approach even the reduction of the emission of greenhouse gasses by way of market devices such as tax incentives and pollution vouchers. Europe and Japan have so far exhibited a stronger capacity to strike compromises between pressures associated with the discipline of global capital and the ethos of social democracy. Despite this diversity of adaptations to pressures associated with the global market, the American leadership role has interfered with efforts in the 1990s to achieve needed levels of global governance. For instance, mainly as a result of governmental action by the United States it was possible to nullify widespread world citizen support of major proposals to strengthen the United Nations that had been mounted in relation to the fiftieth anniversary of the organization a few years ago. Instead, the organization has been treated like a sick corporation that needed restructuring by way of downsizing to make it again seem viable.

(4) A demobilization of progressive alternatives combined with a tendency of the political agenda to be established by the imperatives of the externally situated global (and regional) marketplace, thereby diminishing the effectiveness of traditional modes of political participation through such means as parties, elections, and legislative institutions. The synergistic effects of these trends is to raise serious doubts about whether the virtues of "democracy" can be any longer adequately achieved within the conventional frameworks of constitutional democracy. One important dimension of the disillusionment of the young in much of the world seems related to this subtle and inconclusive type of disempowerment of the citizenry to achieve change. An opposite effect is to revitalize right-wing fringe politics that seek to conserve a purist sense of "the nation" in the face of Westernizing consumerism and ethnic challenges of greater human mobility. Religious extremism has also emerged, in part, to protect traditionalist identities that seemed at risk in a globalized world that seemed in the process of being thoroughly secularized.

Set against these problematic impacts of globalization are some significant contributions to the realization of humane governance.

(1) The economistic focus associated with globalization diminishes traditional incentives to wage war associated with the acquisition of resources and territory; oil is a partial, and probably temporary, exception to this trend, playing, as it does, such a vital role in the world economy, and the Gulf War is illustrative of the type of warfare that can be generated despite and in some senses, because of globalization. Similarly, it is possible, although unlikely, that the energy riches of the South China Seas could generate warfare in a future struggle among claimant countries for control of

these possibly major resources. Despite these examples, the overall influence of globalization seems to be making major war, at least, into an anachronism. This tendency, which is far from a certainty, is reinforced by the growing reluctance of the United States, and other countries in the North, to pursue interventionary diplomacy in view of its often inconclusive and long-deferred results, its unpredictably high costs in human life and resources, and the difficulty of mobilizing and sustaining citizen support. The risks for political leaders associated with intervention have been increasing over the course of the last several decades, commencing in the reactions to the Vietnam War, but growing over the years, reflecting, also, the reluctance to engage in high-risk commitments unless national security was credibly threatened. Especially in the individualist atmosphere of neoliberalism, altruistic and humanistic grounds of intervention are difficult to sell to the public.

(2) The mobility of capital, the global application of the principles of comparative advantage and economies of scale, as well as the accompanying spread of technological innovation have enabled some of the poorest and most populous countries to achieve high rates of economic growth over significant periods of time. The effect has been to rescue hundreds of millions from acute poverty, especially in the Asia/Pacific region, and to make non-Western countries more important global participants, bringing other considerations to bear on global issues.

(3) Perhaps most encouraging of all is the extent to which it now appears feasible and generally beneficial to address problems of acute poverty of the sort that continues to afflict between 1.2 and 1.3 billion people. The basic cost of eradicating poverty for the countries in the South is estimated to be about $40 billion per year for ten years, or less than one percent of global income, and only two to three percent of national income in all but the very poorest countries (UNDP 1997: 97, 112). Furthermore, it can be argued that unless poverty is substantially reduced, it is likely that the richer countries will experience the effects, both by environmental disaster and through the spread of infectious disease, as well as by an intensification of destabilizing backlash politics that include the formation of cults composed of "successful" citizens (for instance, Aum, Heaven's Gate) and militias with paranoid conspiracy images. Already, it is reported that tainted foods sent from South to North are spreading disease resulting from reliance on polluted water in the exporting country. Globalization is itself implicated in this instance, to the extent, by way of the World Trade Organization, that it disallows stricter inspection of imported food than domestic food. What is also true is that the awareness of the interrelation creates a self-interest in the richer countries to facilitate pro-poor styles of economic growth in the South.

(4) The activation of civil society, both in relation to the deepening of

democracy in response to the perceived and actual reduction in the extent of political space available to government and mainstream opposition and in relation to a transnational agenda involving human rights, environmental protection, nuclear testing and disarmament, feminism, and social and economic justice. This latter phenomenon, which I have described elsewhere as globalization-from-below, is motivated by a people-oriented sense of politics and is thus opposed to the detrimental social and environmental impacts attributed to globalization-from-above, that is, driven by market forces in coalition with most governments (Falk 1993; Wapner 1996; Lipschutz and Conca 1993). The related effort of these civic initiatives, often inarticulate, is to find more meaningful forms of political participation than are provided by the familiar constitutional forms of representative democracy. Such democratizing projects involve expanding the idea of what qualifies as a political arena to include workplace, neighborhood, family, shopping mall, and corporate facilities. It also has involved the launching of a project to establish democracy on a global scale, also called transnational democracy and cosmopolitan democracy (Archibugi and Held 1995; Falk 1997; Falk 1998).

(5) The power of global market forces has led many political elites to seek new institutional forms that would reconcile the logic of capital with the retention of cultural and social autonomy. The main expression of this development has been the emergence of various forms of regionalism, most dramatically evolved in Europe. Undoubtedly, the European initiative was originally mainly based on creating a security community strong enough to avoid any further intra-European wars, as well as united enough to protect Europe against the perceived Soviet threat. But as time passed, the economic dimensions of European regionalism, as typified by the bureaucracy in Brussels, became the focus of attention. Since the Maastricht Treaty of 1992, European regionalism has been increasingly interpreted as a means for Europe to cope with the competitive challenges emanating from Asia/Pacific and North America, as well as a way to retain discretion at the level of the state to deal with internal social demands. In this respect, regionalism becomes a response to globalization-from-above. Similar considerations seem to apply to non-European regionalism, including the slogan "the Asianization of Asia," as well as developments in Africa and Latin America. Whether regionalism should be understood as a means to carry forward the project of humane governance is a complicated and unresolved matter. It is necessary to ask the following question: Is regionalism serving primarily as an instrument for globalization-from-above or does it represent a potentially and actually liberating compromise that is able to preserve the gains from globalization while reducing or overcoming some of its highest costs?

This effort to identify the positive and negative world order effects of globalization is intended only to set the stage for an inquiry about humane governance within the historical setting of an emergent future. It is a setting that disclosed a recent capacity to generate surprises, both those that build hope and those that dash expectations. The great liberating experience of the end of the Cold War and the collapse of Soviet imperialism came about as a welcome surprise, startling the experts who had built their scenarios of the future without even contemplating the sequence of events that occurred as one of several possibilities. Similarly, the modern march of secularism was utterly unprepared for the religious resurgence that erupted initially in the Iranian revolution and then spread in a variety of cultural spaces to the far corners of the globe. Also, few would have thought that the end of the Cold War would result in the weakening of the United Nations, especially as its weakness earlier had been so largely explained as a result of the gridlock produced by East–West tensions.

This lack of insight into the unfolding dynamics of history carries both a message of humility to those who would instruct us about the future and an invitation to all those who dream of a better world to extend the political imagination with boldness far beyond the horizons of possibility as depicted by mainstream realism. It is this latter invitation, especially as we approach the threshold of the twenty-first century and embark upon a new millennium, that suggests the importance of reviving the project of humane governance despite the formidable obstacles that particularly seem at the end of the twentieth century to preclude success for such an undertaking: disillusionment with big visions, an economistic sense of the role of institutions, a passion for privatization, an autonomy for financial markets that is accentuated by secrecy and remoteness from regulatory authority, and a hegemonic reading of recent history that discredits any but the most inconsequential approach to social change.

REFORMULATING HUMANE GOVERNANCE TO MEET THE CHALLENGES OF GLOBALIZATION

On the basis of the contrasting assessments in the prior section, it becomes possible to contextualize the quest for humane governance in this era of globalization. Instead of the emphasis on the attainment of discrete world order values as seemed appropriate in the Cold War era, there are now three more generic tasks that appear to link academic inquiry and world order activism: (1) theorizing the various issue-oriented struggles against globalization-from-above in a coherent manner that is sensitive to the unevenness of circumstances existing in various parts of the world; (2) giving ideological unity to the quest for humane governance by stressing its commitment to democracy as process and as outcome, but democracy reconceived and extended in light of the decline of electoral politics; and (3) stressing the importance of democratically accountable innovations in governance, both at micro levels to take account of pressures for self-determination within the state and at macro levels to address the problems of the global commons and to offer the peoples of the world procedures and arenas that are capable of regulating global market forces.

Globalization-from-Below

The activation of civil society on a transnational basis has challenged both states and market forces in substantive areas in which global market forces and states were perceived to be endangering human well-being. These civic pressures were often focused on reshaping the outlook of governments to be more protective of a range of public goods, including economic and social rights, public health, and the environment. In this regard, the ideological outlook of those closely linked to market forces tended to restrict most expenditures on public goods, leaving unattended societal suffering to the largesse of the private sector.

In this regard, it is notable to take account of the large, financial contributions to the satisfaction of global public goods made by such capitalist superheroes as Ted Turner and George Soros. These initiatives have as their objective the facilitating of the humanitarian activities of the United Nations with a gift of $1 billion spread across a ten-year period in the former instance and the encouragement of the democratization of Russia through a gift of $500 million over a shorter period in the latter. What is striking and problematic here is that the private resources possessed by the winners in the globalization sweepstakes seem often more readily available for these purposes than are the resources of rich states. Also relevant is the degree to which the sainted posthumous portrayal of Princess Diana was associated with her acts of compassion directed at those outside her own country, especially the victims of antipersonnel landmines. These developments reflect innovative aspects of the response by elements of global civil society to the extent to which the state is losing its capacity and will to address the social and humanitarian agenda of the world.

Another type of response is connected with resistance activity, as when consumer power is brought to bear on behalf of the global commons. When Shell Oil proposed the sinking of its oil rig in the North Sea a few years ago, an oppositional effort that mobilized users of gas to boycott Shell service stations was effectively orchestrated by Greenpeace. The entire story is complicated, and the environmental argument not entirely resolved, but the political message was clear: if corporate action in the global commons is not regulated by the Westphalian institutions of government and intergovernmental character, then the civil sector can make trouble transnationally by mobilizing resistance efforts through the dissemination of information that harm will result unless the challenged activity is halted.

There are several related conclusions to be drawn. First of all, individuals are now commanding resources on a scale that permits them to provide support to global public goods that is comparable to what might be provided by enlightened state actors. This process weakens the position of the state in relation to the promotion of public goods, and it also means that society as a whole is not represented in the priorities chosen from among the various possible undertakings within the domain of public goods. It also creates a very real danger that affluent individuals will contribute significant assets to "negative global public goods," ranging from giving support to terrorist activity and regressive political causes across a wide range, including the financing of antidemocratic political movements in various parts of the world. Even the provision of peacekeeping capabilities, a task that was previously seen as essentially falling within the domain of global public goods, particularly being regarded as the core assignment of the United Nations, seems to be in the process of being monetized and marketized. Former security officials associated with South Africa's apartheid regime have formed an organization called Executive Outcomes that sells its services to African governments confronted with internal unrest or external threats, often receiving large shares of corporate and mining investments.

Whether the cumulative impact of this activation of civil society, and its transnational projections of influence by way of information, ideas, money, and organizational initiatives, can be considered as lending credibility and support to the project for humane governance is problematic at this point. There is no doubt that the rise of transnational social forces involves, to a significant degree, a reaction to globalization, but the multifaceted nature of this reaction makes it difficult to assess its overall normative impact. There was some earlier tendency to romanticize these transnational activities, but there is now a more nuanced realization that their roles are diverse and contradictory. Nevertheless, globalization-from-below is mounting an array of challenges to globalization-from-above and confronting political elites in control of states with some hard political choices.

Normative Democracy

The collapse of progressive politics in the 1990s is closely connected with the discrediting of traditional Left perspectives in the last stages of the Cold War and the impact of globalization as ideologized by neoliberalism. The two serious consequences of these developments are to weaken support for vulnerable peoples and segments of society and to make it more difficult to mobilize resources on behalf of global public goods. It seems evident, as well, that a progressive politics capable of meeting these two minimal challenges cannot expect to be successful by reviving progressive politics by relying on Marxist categories of analysis and socialist political language. There is an irony present here, as one consequence of globalization is to make economistic approaches to political explanation much more prevalent than ever before.

Globalization-from-below has been responsible for a variety of local and transnational initiatives based on democratic ideas of participation and direct action, and often animated by such world order values as human rights, environmental protection, and social justice. These initiatives have generated voluntary associations of citizens, as well as potent transnational networks focused on particular issues, and make use of a range of arenas for promoting goals. The UN conferences on global issues held during the first half of the 1990s illustrated this new political energy as focused on environment, women, human rights, and development. But what was lacking was a cross-issue orientation that would be necessary to sustain a coherent politics from below that could in some ways balance the coherence of neoliberalism in its differing, yet mutually reinforcing, forms. It remains the case that the politics arising from transnational social forces has so far been of an ad hoc and issue-oriented character, and thus neither effectively institutionalized nor ideologized. Without such steps, the capacity to challenge the excesses of globalization-from-above are likely to be transitory, and in the end, unsuccessful.

The possibilities of a new coherent progressive politics seems dependent upon the creative energies of globalization-from-below, as mainstream parties and perspectives seem generally subject to the discipline of global capital, or to be generating various reactionary forms of backlash politics, which embody narrowly protectionist ideas that are often combined with a chauvinistic ethos inducing the most dangerous of nationalist sentiments. In the 1980s the green movement, especially in Europe, came forth with a new progressive politics that was both compassionate and committed to the realization of public goals, especially environmental protection. The greens had an impact, especially in relation to environmental policy, influencing the entire political spectrum, but their capacity to provide a progressive alternative seems limited. Their agenda was perceived as being too narrowly green, and although their actual concerns were far broader, generally extending to human rights and security policy, it has proved impossible for greens to mobilize sufficient support to take command of government. Besides, in most countries their bases of support included a coalition of former leftists and conservative libertarians, placing limits on their capacity to develop a comprehensive, coherent program. Further, especially in the crucial setting of West Germany, green ranks were badly split between reformist and radical orientations toward industrial civilization. But the green parties, acting mainly within traditional state/society frameworks, although active on a European level, suggested the possibility of a post-Marxist progressivism that was responsive to the particular challenges and opportunities associated with globalization, including tactical moves to reengage civil society in active, meaningful politics that relied on imaginative ways of gaining support.

At present, various political groupings toward a new outlook and language are becoming evident in various settings, especially relying on the widely endorsed normative frameworks associated with human rights and democracy. The striking feature here is a realization that democratic politics needs to be introduced into all political arenas, and can no longer be understood primarily as a type of politics at the level of the sovereign state. Various terminologies have been used to express this double movement in the direction of both the globalization and localization of democratic forms of participation, accountability, and legality, including references to "cosmopolitan democracy" and "substantive democracy" (Archibugi and Held 1995; Falk 1997; Falk 1998). A comparable deepening and expanding of human rights is also occurring, especially extending the reach of human rights to the social and economic agenda, as well as a variety of efforts to take account of cultural differences. These still embryonic efforts to shape a progressive outlook are also by their very transnational nature building political support for a coherent program of reform at all levels of social organization, which would in effect amount to a movement for humane governance. That is, the prospects of the project of humane governance, aside from its intellectual expression, depends on the potential political agency provided by the consensus and conception of democracy that is being evolved in different circumstances around the world. It is this orientation toward values and action that I am identifying with the term "normative democracy."

Governance

Globalization alters the substantive approach to humane governance, particularly with reference to the role of the state. In most earlier work, the sovereign territorial state was perceived as the obstacle, resisting efforts to achieve a disarmed world and opposing efforts to establish degrees of supranational authority to protect the global commons and to provide an effective alternative to geopolitics as the foundation of security (Mendlovitz 1975; Falk 1975). The onset of globalization has disclosed political elites far more disposed than their citizens to transfer sovereignty over economic activities to international institutions, as in relation to the establishment of the World Trade Organization or such regional initiatives as North

American Free Trade Association. This pattern is evident, as well, in the European moves toward monetary union, as prescribed in the Maastricht Treaty process.

With the rise of market forces and the acceptance of neoliberal ideas, the state has lost a portion of its autonomy and is no longer oriented, as fully, to the well-being of people, including its own citizens. Given this reality, from the perspective of humane governance it would be beneficial to reorient the state so as to enhance its willingness to be more people-oriented, including a renewed disposition to invest in global public goods such as an effective United Nations, an ambitious approach to climate change, and a willingness to create institutions for environmental governance comparable to those that have been established for the sake of economic governance (Falk 1997b). In these regards, given the continuing capacity of the state to act and to mobilize resources, the only plausible means to respond to the harmful aspects of globalization is by reliance on the state to recover its role as guardian of people. Such a result can only be brought about by an active, organized civil society that is motivated by a reconceived, less territorial, understanding of democracy and is focused on challenging the neoliberal ideas that shape economic policy, substituting a stronger sense of responsibility at the level of the state.

A CONCLUDING NOTE

Globalization is not inherently opposed to the struggle to achieve equitable and effective governance structures for the planet, ranging from local to global settings, but there are tensions associated with the ideological and historical climate that prevails at the present time. Also, the structures of globalization are embedded so deeply in the dynamics of technological innovation and the efficient use of resources as to amount to an unchallengeable presence for the foreseeable future. In this respect, then, the political agenda for global reform involves two central undertakings: offering the perspectives of normative democracy as an alternative to the outlook of neoliberalism and creating the local, national, and transnational pressures, by way of the further activation of social forces associated with globalization-from-below, to resituate the state so as to make it more responsive to people-oriented priorities, including the financing of global public goods. Against this background, it will be possible to revive the project of humane governance as a coherent conception of world order for the twentieth century.

REFERENCES

Archibugi, D., and Held, D., eds. (1995). *Cosmopolitan Democracy: An Agenda for a New World Order*. Cambridge: Polity Press.

Borgmann, A. (1992). *Crossing the Postmodern Divide*. Chicago: University of Chicago Press.

Falk, R. (1975). *A Study of Future Worlds*. New York: Free Press.

———. (1993). The Making of Global Citizenship. In J. Brecher, J.B. Childs, and J. Cutler, eds. *Global Visions: Beyond the New World Order*. Boston: South End Press: 39–50.

———. (1997). The Quest for Normative Democracy in an Era of Neo-Liberal Globalization. Unpublished Hesburgh Lectures, University of Notre Dame, South Bend, Indiana (February 19– 20, 1997).

———. (1997b). State of Siege: Will Globalization Win Out? *International Affairs* 73 (January): 123–36.

———. (1998). Global Civil Society: Perspectives, Initiatives, Movements. *Oxford Development Studies* 26: 99–110.

Huntington, S.P. (1996). *The Clash of Civilizations and the Remaking of World Order*. New York: Simon & Schuster.

Jackson, R.H. (1991). *Quasi-States: Sovereignty, International Relations, and the Third World*. Cambridge: Cambridge University Press.

Lipschutz, R.D., and Conca, K., eds. (1993) *The State and Social Power in Global Environmental Politics*. New York: Columbia University Press.

Mendlovitz, S.H., ed. (1975). *On the Creation of a Just World Order*. New York: Free Press.

Tehranian, K., and M. Tehranian, eds. (1992). *Restructuring for World Peace: On the Threshold of the Twentieth Century*. Cresskill, N.J.: Hampton Press.

UNDP. (1997). *Human Development Report 1997*. Oxford: Oxford University Press.

Wapner, P. (1996) *Environmental Activism and World Civic Politics*. Albany: State University of New York Press.

Index

About the Contributors

Giovanni Arrighi is professor of sociology at Johns Hopkins University, Baltimore. He is the author or coauthor of many books, including *The Geometry of Imperialism: Dynamics of Global Crisis* (with S. Amin, A. G. Frank, and I. Wallerstein); *antisystemic Movements* (with T. K. Hopkins and I. Wallerstein); and *The Long Twentieth Century* (winner of the Distinguished Scholarship Award of the Political Economy of the World System section of the American Sociological Association). His latest book is *Chaos and Governance in the Modern World System* (with B. J. Silver et al.).

Jos de Beus is presently dean of the department of philosophy of the University of Groningen. In 1999 he moved to the University of Amsterdam to hold the chair of political theory in the department of political, social, and cultural sciences. His current research interests are the relation between democracy and globalization and the political theory of European unification. Recent publications are *Eeuwige Democratie* (1997) and "Modernized Social Democracy and the Fundamental Democratization of Europe" in Cuperus and Kandel eds., *European Social Democracy* (1998).

Jack Burgers is associate professor of sociology at the Erasmus University of Rotterdam. He has published on local consequences of economic restructuring, migration, and the use and meaning of public space.

Richard Falk is Albert G. Milbank professor of international law and practice at Princeton University, where he has been a member of the faculty since 1961. His latest books are *On Humane Governance: Toward a New Global Politics* (1995); *Law in an Emerging Global Village: A Post-Westphalian View* (1998); and *Predatory Globalization: Critique and Response* (1999).

Michael Hanagan teaches comparative and social history at the New School for Social Research in New York City. He has published on historical collective action and European social history and is coeditor of *Challenging Authority: The Historical Study of Collective Action* (1998) and *Extending Citizenship: Reconfiguring States* (forthcoming). He is currently involved in a comparative study of the origins and development of the welfare state in Europe and the United States.

Paul Hirst is professor of social theory at Birkbeck College, University of London, and academic director of the London consortium graduate programme in humanities and cultural studies. Among his books are: *Reversing Industrial Decline* (1988) with Jonathan Zeitlin, *After Thatcher* (1989), *Representative Democracy and Its Limits* (1990), *Associative Democracy* (1994), *Globalisation in Question* (1996) with Grahame Thompson, and *From Statism to Pluralism* (1997).

Connie Hum is an undergraduate student at the University of California, Los Angeles.

Don Kalb is an anthropologist and associate professor of general social sciences at Utrecht University, the Netherlands. He leads the Social Consequences of Economic Transformation in East Central Europe Program (SOCO) at the Institute for Human Sciences (IWM), Vienna. His publications include *Expanding Class: Power and Everyday Politics in Industrial Communities, The Netherlands, 1850–1950* (Durham, NC: Duke University Press), 1997; as well as various articles on globalization, industrial class formation, class theory, and social theory, including the conjunction of anthropology and history. His current research, apart from globalization, focuses on problems of economic restructuring, culture, class, and citizenship in Eastern Europe.

Rebecca Kim is a graduate student at the University of California, Los Angeles.

Peter Kloos studied social geography and cultural anthropology at the University of Amsterdam, where he graduated in 1962. He received his Ph.D. from the same university for his study *The Maroni River Caribs of Surinam.* He taught at the Universities of Amsterdam, Brussels, and Leiden and is now professor of sociology of non-Western societies at the Vrije Universiteit Amsterdam. He has carried out field research in the Netherlands (Drente, Flevoland), in Suriname (among Caribs and among Akuriyo), and in Sri Lanka.

Marco van der Land is a sociologist and consultant for urban issues in The Netherlands. His research topics include the new middle class, urban revitalization, and globalization. He is currently writing his dissertation on urban ties of the Rotterdam new middle class.

Ivan Light is professor of sociology at the University of California, Los Angeles. He is the author of several articles and of six books on immigration, entrepreneurs, and urban sociology. His earliest book is *Ethnic Enterprise in America* (University of California, 1972). *Cities in World Perspective* (Macmillan, 1983) is a comparative and historical treatment of urban society. His next two books were *Immigrant Entrepreneurs: Koreans in Los Angeles* (University of California, 1988; in collaboration with Edna Bonacich) and *Immigration and Entrepreneurship* (Transactions Publishers, 1993; in collaboration with Parminder Bhachu). There followed *Race, Ethnicity and Entrepreneurship in Urban America* (Aldine de Gruyter, 1995; in collaboration with Carolyn Rosenstein). His latest book, coedited with Richard Israelowitz, is *Immigrant Entrepreneurs and Immigrant Absorption in the United States and Israel* (Avebury, 1997).

Orvar Löfgren has held the post of professor of European ethnology at the University of Lund since 1993. His research interests have been class and culture in nineteenth-century Sweden; comparative studies of national identity; and, more lately, identity politics, media, and consumption between the local and the global. Among his publications in English is *Culture Builders: A Historical Anthropology of Middle-Class Culture* together with Jonas Frykman (1987). Together they also coedited *Force of Habit* (1995). His latest book is *On Holiday: A Transnational History of Tourism* (forthcoming).

Jan Luiten van Zanden studied economics and history at the Free University of Amsterdam. He is currently professor of economic and social history at Utrecht University and general secretary of the International Economic History Association. Among his books are *The Rise and Decline of Holland's Economy: Merchant Capitalism and the Labour Market; The Economic History of the Netherlands 1914–1995;* and, with Lee Soltow, *Income and Wealth Inequality in the Netherlands Sixteenth–Twentieth Century.*

Erik Olin Wright is Vilas professor at the department of sociology of the University of Wisconsin. Recent books include *Class Counts: Comparative Studies in Class Analysis, Interrogating Inequality,* and *Reconstructing Marxism.*

Alejandro Portes has held faculty positions at the universities of Illinois at Urbana-Champaign, Texas at Austin, Duke, and Johns Hopkins. Since

1987 and until he joined Princeton, he was John Dewey professor in the school of arts and sciences at Johns Hopkins. He is also president of the American Sociological Association. He has published extensively on national development, economics, sociology, immigration, and urbanization. His most recent books are *City on the Edge: The Transformation of Miami* (with A. Stepick; winner of the Robert E. Park Award), *Immigrant America: A Portrait* (with Ruben G. Rumbaut), and *The Economic Sociology of Immigration.*

Jan Reijnders is associate professor of economics at Utrecht University, The Netherlands. His main research topics are long-term economic dynamics, economic policy, and history of economic thought. Among his publications are *Foundations of Long Wave Analysis: Theory and Methodology, Economics and Evolution, Socio-economic Policy in a European Perspective* (in Dutch), *Long Waves in Economic Development,* and *The Theory of Income and Wealth Distribution.*

Saskia Sassen is professor of sociology at the University of Chicago and Centennial visiting professor at the London School of Economics. Her most recent books are *Guests and Aliens* (New York: New Press, 1999), *Globalization and Its Discontents* (New York: New Press, 1998), and *Losing Control? Sovereignty in an Age of Globalization* (New York: Columbia University Press, 1996). Her books have been translated into ten languages. *The Global City* has recently appeared in French (Paris: Descartes, 1996), Italian (Milano: UTET, 1998), and Spanish (Buenos Aires: EUDEBA, 1999). She continues work on two projects, "Cities and Their Crossborder Networks," sponsored by the United Nations University, and "Governance and Accountability in a Global Economy." She is a member of the Council on Foreign Relations and a fellow of the American Bar Foundation.

John Schmitt is a labor economist with the Economic Policy Institute. He is a coauthor of *The State of Working Ameria 1998–99* and has written for general and academic publications on wage inequality, the minimum wage, unemployment, and comparative economic development. He has a Ph.D. in economics from the London School of Economics.

Richard Staring is an anthropologist with the Rotterdam Institute for Social Policy Research at the Erasmus University of Rotterdam, The Netherlands. He conducted ethnographic research on undocumented Turkish immigrants in The Netherlands, which will also be the subject of his forthcoming dissertation. Recent research focuses on immigrants and poverty in The Netherlands. He is coeditor of *Focaal, Journal for Anthropology.*

Bart van Steenbergen studied sociology at the University of Utrecht in The Netherlands and at Temple University in Philadelphia. He received his Ph.D. in 1983. He is presently associate professor in the department of general social sciences at the University of Utrecht. He has previously been secretary of studies of the foundation "Working Group 2000," John Parker Compton fellow at Princeton University, visiting fellow at the University of California at Berkeley, and secretary-general of the European Sociological Association. Recent publications are *The Condition of Citizenship* (Sage 1994), editor and coauthor; and *European Societies: Fusion or Fission* (Routledge 1999), coeditor and coauthor.

Göran Therborn is director of the Swedish Collegium of advanced study in the social sciences at Uppsala and professor of sociology at Göteborg University. From 1981 until 1987 he was professor of political science at the Catholic University, Nijmegen, in the Netherlands. His latest book is *European Modernity and Beyond—The Trajectory of European Societies 1950–2000.*

Alan Warde is professor of sociology at Lancaster University, UK. He has worked in the past on industrial, political, and urban sociology but most recently has researched the sociology of consumption with special reference to food. Recent publications are *Consumption, Food and Taste: Culinary Antinomies and Commodity Culture* and *Eating Out: A Sociological Analysis* (with Lydia Martens).

Nico Wilterdink is professor of sociology at the University of Amsterdam and holds the Norbert Elias chair in the study of long-term social processes at Utrecht University.

.